History, Memory, and the Law

The Amherst Series in Law, Jurisprudence, and Social Thought

Each work included in The Amherst Series in Law, Jurisprudence, and Social Thought explores a theme crucial to an understanding of law as it confronts the changing social and intellectual currents of the late twentieth century.

The Fate of Law, edited by Austin Sarat and Thomas R. Kearns

Law's Violence, edited by Austin Sarat and Thomas R. Kearns

Law in Everyday Life, edited by Austin Sarat and Thomas R. Kearns

The Rhetoric of Law, edited by Austin Sarat and Thomas R. Kearns

Identities, Politics, and Rights, edited by Austin Sarat and Thomas R. Kearns

Legal Rights: Historical and Philosophical Perspectives, edited by Austin Sarat and Thomas R. Kearns

Justice and Injustice in Law and Legal Theory, edited by Austin Sarat and Thomas R. Kearns

Law in the Domains of Culture, edited by Austin Sarat and Thomas R. Kearns

Cultural Pluralism, Identity, Politics, and the Law edited by Austin Sarat and Thomas R. Kearns

History, Memory, and the Law, edited by Austin Sarat and Thomas R. Kearns

History, Memory, and the Law

Edited by
AUSTIN SARAT
and
THOMAS R. KEARNS

Ann Arbor

THE UNIVERSITY OF MICHIGAN PRESS

2002   2001   2000   1999   4   3   2   1

A CIP catalog record for this book is available from the British Library.

Library of Congress Cataloging-in-Publication Data

History, memory, and the law / edited by Austin Sarat and Thomas R.
    Kearns.
       p.   cm. — (Amherst series in law, jurisprudence, and social
    thought)
    Includes bibliographical references and index.
    ISBN 0-472-11045-4 (acid-free paper)
    1. Law—United States—History.   2. Law—Methodology.   3. Law and
    literature.   I. Sarat, Austin.   II. Kearns, Thomas R.   III. Series.
    KF389   .H54   1999
    349.73—dc21   99-6462
                                                                  CIP

Acknowledgments

We are grateful to our colleagues Lawrence Douglas and Martha Umphrey, both of whom are doing important work on law's history and memory, for their help in shaping the ideas that inform this book. "Law's History" is the subject of a course taught by Professor Umphrey. We thank our students in Amherst College's Department of Law, Jurisprudence and Social Thought for their interest in the issues addressed in *History, Memory, and the Law*. Finally, we would like to express special appreciation to the Keck Foundation for its generous financial support.

Contents

Writing History and Registering Memory in
Legal Decisions and Legal Practices: An Introduction   1
    Austin Sarat and Thomas R. Kearns

Forms of Judicial Blindness: Traumatic Narratives
and Legal Repetitions   25
    Shoshana Felman

Memory, Law, and Literature:
The Cases of Flaubert and Baudelaire   95
    Dominick LaCapra

Collective Memory and the Nineteenth Amendment:
Reasoning about "The Woman Question" in the
Discourse of Sex Discrimination   131
    Reva B. Siegel

Held in the Body of the State: Prisons and the Law   183
    Joan Dayan

Stigmas, Badges, and Brands: Discriminating Marks
in Legal History   249
    Brook Thomas

Analogical Reasoning and Historical Change in Law:
The Regulation of Film and Radio Speech   283
    G. Edward White

Contributors   319

Index   321

Writing History and Registering Memory in Legal Decisions and Legal Practices: An Introduction

Austin Sarat and Thomas R. Kearns

> There can be no one historical narrative that renders perfect justice (just as perhaps there is no judicial outcome that can capture the complexity of history). . . . [T]he historian would like to do justice; the judge must establish some version of history. . . . If good judges and historians shun these tasks, they will be taken on by prejudiced or triumphalist ones.
>
> Charles Maier

> The struggle of man against power is the struggle of memory against forgetting.
>
> Milan Kundera

> We must know the right time to forget as well as the right time to remember, and instinctively see when it is necessary to feel historically and when unhistorically.
>
> Friedrich Nietzsche

Generally when scholars talk about the relationship between history, memory, and law, the latter is thought of solely as a passive object of historical change.[1] Legal history is regarded as the study of the forces that have shaped law. It is the history of the evolution of law with law

---

1. Lawrence Friedman, *The History of American Law* (New York: Simon and Schuster, 1973), 18. Friedman remarks that "law moves with its times and is eternally new."

perpetually lagging behind society and being pushed and pulled from the outside.[2] This view, as rich and productive as it is, ignores what might be called an "internal" perspective, one that would examine law for the way it uses and writes history as well as for the ways in which it also becomes a site of memory and commemoration.[3]

History, Memory, and the Law focuses on this internal perspective. It examines law as an active participant in the process through which history is written and memory constructed. In so doing, the essays presented in this book reverse the usual presentation of law as a "victim" of historical forces external to itself. They interrogate the particular hermeneutics through which history and memory are represented in law.[4] They open up the question whether history and memory operate to constrain law, or whether their presence in law provides simply another field for improvisation.

When the essays in this book talk about law's history, and the hermeneutics to which it gives rise, they do so with no intent to compare law's history to the "facts" of history itself or the disciplinary practices of academic history.[5] By refusing the temptation to engage in this comparison they privilege no particular way of doing history, and they display an interest in law's history as an interpretive practice the understanding of which is essential to an understanding of law itself. Here law is treated as the author of history, not just in the instrumental

---

2. This is what Robert Gordon labels "functionalist history." "Critical Legal Histories," *Stanford Law Review* 36 (1984): 64.

3. When scholars have turned their attention to the internal perspective, it has often been to evaluate the way the courts use history against some standard of historical accuracy or in comparison to the way professional historians do history. Typical is the view expressed by William Nelson, who has differentiated between "lawyers' legal history, written to generate data and interpretations that are of use in resolving modern legal controversies, . . . [and] historians' legal history, written to provide and support new and interesting interpretations and bodies of data to advance exploration of the past." Quoted in Richard Bernstein, "Charting the Bicentennial," *Columbia Law Review* 87 (1987): 1578. See also Charles Miller, *The Supreme Court and the Uses of History* (Cambridge: Harvard University Press, 1969); Alfred Kelly, "Clio and the Court: An Illicit Love Affair," *Supreme Court Review* (1965): 122; and Laura Kalman, *The Strange Career of Legal Liberalism* (New Haven: Yale University Press, 1996), chap. 6.

4. For other examples of this approach see Aviam Soifer, "Objects in the Mirror Are Closer Than They Appear," *Georgia Law Review* 28 (1994): 533. See also Christopher Eisgruber, "The Living Hand of the Past: History and Constitutional Justice," *Fordham Law Review* 65 (1997): 1611.

5. Miller, *Uses of History*; Kalman, *Strange Career*, 180. As Kalman puts it, "For all their excursions into other disciplines, historians still favor context, change, and explanation. . . . [A]uthors of lawyers' legal history value text, continuity, and prescription."

sense in which law can be said to make a difference in society, but in the ways that law constructs and uses history to authorize itself and to justify its decisions.[6] As John Philip Reid puts it, "The forensic historian . . . searches the past for material applicable to a current issue. The purpose of the advocate . . . is to use the past for the elucidation of the present, to solve some contemporary problem or, most often, to carry an argument. It is the past put in the service of winning the case at bar."[7]

This book is based on the assumption that while law lives in history, it has a history all its own. While law responds to historical change, it also makes history.[8] Law writes the past, not just its own past, but the past for those over whom law seeks to exercise its dominion.[9] Law constructs a history that it wants to present as authoritative, when, as Laura Kalman argues, no historian "considers the past authoritative."[10] And law uses history to tell us who we are.

Law looks to the past as it speaks to present needs. In the adjudication of every dispute, law traffics in the slippery terrain of memory, as different versions of past events are presented for authoritative judgment. Moreover, in the production of supposedly definitive statements of what the law is in the form of judicial opinions, law reconstructs its own past, tracing out lines of precedent to their "compelling" conclusion.[11] The relationship of law to history is thus complex and multidi-

---

6. Jack Rakove suggests that we should regard judicial appeals to history "not as reasons driving decisions but as an attractive rhetorical method of reassuring citizens that courts are acting consistently with deeply held values." "Fidelity through History," *Fordham Law Review* 65 (1997): 1591.

7. John Philip Reid, "The Jurisprudence of Liberty: The Ancient Constitution in the Legal Historiography of the Seventeenth and Eighteenth Centuries," in *the Roots of Liberty: Magna Carta, Ancient Constitutions, and the Anglo-American Tradition of Rule of Law*, ed. Ellis Sandoz (Columbia: University of Missouri Press, 1993), 167. Some suggest that the doing of history is itself lawlike in its orientation. "Historians . . . proceed inferentially. They investigate evidence much as lawyers cross-question witnesses in a court of law, extracting from that evidence information which it does not explicitly contain." Paul Connerton, *How Societies Remember* (Cambridge: Cambridge University Press, 1989), 13.

8. Guyora Binder and Robert Weisberg suggest that "law neither reflects nor distorts a social world of subjects that exists independent of it. Instead, law helps compose the social world." "Cultural Criticism of Law," *Stanford Law Review* 49 (1997): 1152.

9. On the relationship between the production of memory and power see Richard Terdiman, "Deconstructing Memory: On Representing the Past and Theorizing Culture in France since the Revolution," *Diacritics* 15 (1985): 13.

10. Kalman, *Strange Career*, 180.

11. Here too the reconstruction of the past is contested. Different judges produce different readings of precedent. See Lawrence Douglas, "Constitutional Discourse and Its Discontents: An Essay on the Rhetoric of Judicial Review," in *The Rhetoric of Law*, ed. Austin Sarat and Thomas R. Kearns (Ann Arbor: University of Michigan Press, 1994).

rectional. Rather than asking only about the history of law, *History, Memory, and the Law* considers how law treats history, how history appears in legal decisions, and how the authority of history is used to authorize legal decisions. This book examines history as it appears on the inside of law as a constituent element of law's rhetoric, of its justificatory structure, and of its place as a social institution.[12]

The most obvious example of the way law constructs and uses history is found in the doctrine of stare decisis and the practice of justifying present decisions in light of precedent.[13] In the common-law tradition the past is supposed to govern the present. Like cases are to be treated alike.[14] Precedent tells a judge to adhere to the decision in a previous *similar* case. As Shauer notes, an argument "from precedent . . . urges that a decision maker give weight to a particular result regardless of whether that decision maker believes it to be correct and regardless of whether that decision maker believes it valuable in any way to rely on that previous result."[15] In this understanding, adherence to precedent is a rule, according judges no judgmental discretion. There is, of course, another way of understanding how precedent works that accords judges greater interpretive possibility. Past decisions create standards or expectations whose gravitational force is not ironclad, but is instead a matter of judgment. Precedent creates a presumption, but a presumption that can be, and sometimes is, rebutted.[16] Yet both of these conceptions treat the past as discoverable and potentially constraining or authoritative. The judge researching precedent constructs a doctrinal history in the service of elucidating a present problem.[17]

These two different ways of thinking about precedent imply two

---

12. As Eisgruber puts it, "History serves a specific and indispensable rhetorical role" ("Living Hand," 1622).

13. Kelly, "Clio and the Court," 122; also Frederick Shauer, "Precedent," *Stanford Law Review* 39 (1987): 571. Peter Burke asks, "What is the function of social memory?" He speculates that if a lawyer were asked, "[H]e or she might well discuss the importance of custom and precedent, the justification or legitimation of actions in the present with reference to the past." "History as Social Memory," in *Memory: History, Culture, and the Mind,* ed. Thomas Butler (Oxford: Blackwell, 1989), 105.

14. Earl Maltz, "The Nature of Precedent," *North Carolina Law Review* 66 (1988): 367; Michael Gerhardt, "The Role of Precedent in Constitutional Decision Making and Theory," *Georgia Washington Law Review* 60 (1991): 68; Larry Alexander, "Constrained by Precedent," *Southern California Law Review* 63 (1989): 1.

15. Shauer, "Precedent," 576.

16. Henry Monahan, "Stare Decisis and Constitutional Adjudication," *Columbia Law Review* 88 (1988): 723.

17. Id., 725.

different attitudes toward the past, as commander of the present and barrier to change, or as guide, suggesting paths, but mandating no particular way of being in the present.[18] And beyond these different attitudes toward the past there are the difficulties of determining what counts as an applicable precedent as well as what a precedent stands for in the way of its legal meaning. Neither is self-generating.[19] Analogies proliferate almost without limit. Judges read the relevance of past cases differently, and there are no metarules that govern such determinations of relevance.[20] This is not to say that the search for relevance is a free-for-all. Conventions, habits, intuitions, reasons all guide the judgment of what is relevant. Yet judges with different conceptions of their role adopt different standards of relevance as well as entirely different orientations toward the way the past should be used in law.[21]

Even when judges agree on the relevance of a past case to a present one, they may, and frequently do, disagree about how the applicable precedent should be read. Thus judges construct law's own history in the process of deciding present cases.[22] They do so through a complex genealogical operation that accords them enormous discretion, and yet allows them to claim that they are fully and completely bound by the past. In law "the past is primarily a source of authority—if we interpret it correctly, it will tell us how to conduct ourselves now. History is not only a source of authority but of legitimacy."[23] Reading and decoding the past, arguing about its meaning, and shaping decisions as if they were the inexorable product of an uncontested history is the very stuff of law. Judges make history anew with each opinion, all the while proclaiming that they are simply discovering a past whose significance is, or should be, self-evident.[24]

Indeed the authority or legitimacy of a judicial decision is to some

18. Frank Easterbrook, "Stability and Reliability in Judicial Decisions," *Cornell Law Review* 73 (1988): 422.

19. As Cass Sunstein puts it, "Different factual situations are inarticulate; they do not impose order on themselves." *Legal Reasoning and Political Conflict* (New York: Oxford University Press, 1996), 73.

20. Roger Shiner, "Precedent, Discretion, and Fairness," in *Law, Morality, and Rights*, ed. M. A. Stewart (New York: Columbia University Press, 1983).

21. William Nelson, "The Uses of History by Judges," typescript, 1978.

22. Kalman, *Strange Career.*

23. Robert Gordon, "Foreword: The Arrival of Critical Historicism," *Stanford Law Review* (1997), 49:1023.

24. For one particularly vivid example of this phenomenon see *Trident Center v. Connecticut General Life*, 87–6085, D.C. No. CV-87–2712-JMI (1987), 8145.

extent a product of its ability to cloth itself in the history of law, to plausibly claim that there is nothing innovative or new being done or said even while new departures are being undertaken.[25] Alternatively, when judges make a radical departure from the past, the gravitational force of law's history "compels" them to find a loophole, a gap in the seamless web of history, or to say that there are no applicable precedents, or that the applicable precedents are somehow less relevant than they might otherwise seem. In this sense law is always facing backward, engaged with the past, constructing majestic narratives of continuity with occasional flaws in the tapestry.

Let us note but two examples of the use of precedent in the construction of a historical narrative that, in turn, works to supply authority and legitimacy. The first is found in *Planned Parenthood v. Casey*, the 1992 Supreme Court decision upholding, while limiting, abortion rights under the Fourteenth Amendment.[26] In the now famous opinion by Justices O'Connor, Kennedy, and Souter, those justices took pains to explain their own reservations about *Roe v. Wade*, whose "essential holding" their opinion in *Casey* was intended to reaffirm. "Some of us," the justices noted, "find abortion offensive to our most basic principles of morality, but that cannot control our decision."[27] It could not do so if they were to uphold their duty to protect the "liberty of all"[28] and to respect their obligation to "follow precedent."[29] This obligation flows from "the very concept of the rule of law," which, in their view, "requires such continuity over time that a respect for precedent is, by definition, indispensable."[30]

---

25. See Stanley Fish, "Law Wishes to Have a Formal Existence," in *The Fate of Law*, ed. Austin Sarat and Thomas R. Kearns (Ann Arbor: University of Michigan Press, 1991), 193. Fish calls this "the amazing trick."

26. *Planned Parenthood v. Casey* 60 LW 4795 (1992). For an important essay on the significance of *Casey* see David Garrow "From *Brown* to *Casey*: The U.S. Supreme Court and the Burdens of History," in *Race, Law, and Culture: Reflections of Brown v. Board of Education*, ed. Austin Sarat (New York: Oxford University Press, 1997). "[T]he *Casey* majority presented perhaps the Court's most extended discussion of the concept of precedent in this century" (81).

27. *Casey*, 4800.

28. Id.

29. Id., 4801.

30. Id. As Morton Horwitz put it, *Casey* was "unique in American constitutional history for its highly self-conscious discussion of the question of constitutional legitimacy" and for constructing a historical narrative to "provide a standard for determining when overruling precedent is appropriate." "Foreword: The Constitution of Change; Legal Fundamentality without Fundamentalism," *Harvard Law Review* 107 (1993): 36–37.

Yet in spite of this rather striking defense of the role of precedent in our legal system, O'Connor, Kennedy, and Souter went on, almost as if to take back what they had just said, to note that adherence to precedent was not "an inexorable command."[31] The decision whether to adhere to precedent was, in their view, always one that had to be guided by "prudential and pragmatic considerations,"[32] including whether the rule developed by a prior case has proven to be unworkable, whether people have come justifiably to rely on it, and whether subsequently developed principles of law have rendered the prior rule a nullity. By taking this pragmatic and prudential approach to precedent the three justices constructed an historical narrative that made room for the possibility of change, of evolution.[33] They wrote a history of constraint, yet also of possibility, rather than of an iron hand of the past inexorably determining present policy. They allowed themselves to be seen as *judging* a past that they themselves first had to interpret. Yet they acknowledged that the past created a presumption in favor of continuity and that in no case should a decision to overrule precedent, and in so doing to rewrite history, rest simply on a "belief that a prior case was wrongly decided."[34]

The history constructed in *Casey* was a history of turning points, of great moments, in the life of the Supreme Court, of which, in a rather magisterial moment, this case was imagined to be one.[35] Thus O'Connor, Kennedy, and Souter compared the case for overruling *Roe* with the case made in *West Coast Hotel* for repudiating *Adkins v. Children Hospital* and in *Brown v. Board of Education* for departing from *Plessy v. Ferguson*. As Horwitz explains,

> [T]he joint opinion in *Casey* struggled to articulate a persuasive account of constitutional change that would justify its refusal to overturn *Roe*. Its own theory merges from its characterization of the overruling of *Lochner* by the New Deal Court and the overruling of *Plessy* by *Brown*—truly the twin peaks of modern constitu-

---

31. *Casey*, 4801.

32. Id.

33. Sunstein, *Legal Reasoning*, 72. See also David Koehler, "Justice Souter's 'Keep What You Want and Throw Away the Rest' Interpretation of Stare Decisis," *Buffalo Law Review* 42 (1994): 859.

34. *Casey*, 4804.

35. On the idea of a "monumental history" see Friedrich Nietzsche, *The Use and Abuse of History*, trans. Adrian Collins, 2d ed. (New York: Macmillan, 1985).

tional law. The joint opinion's theory echoes the "changed circumstances" formulation advanced by Justice Brandeis, but it is a premodern version infused with the static originalism that gave birth to it.[36]

At each turning point, the justices argued, the Court had to resolve an "intensely divisive controversy" in such a way as to call "the contending sides of a national controversy to end their national division."[37] Again constructing a monumental history,[38] the justices announced, "The court is not asked to do this very often."[39] In these rare moments the Court has to stand firm; it has to defend a previously made "watershed decision" lest the Court's own legitimacy be jeopardized.

Here the Court writes a history that goes beyond a history of legal doctrine; it is a history that takes into account the social and political world in which it is portrayed as playing a decisive role. Adhering to precedent in such circumstances gives testimony to the power of principles to guide the nation. By imagining the possibility of departing from precedent, by treating precedent as a standard, not a rule, the justices are able rhetorically both to elevate the stakes in its present decision and marshal a narrative of the past to serve as a springboard for an explanation of why it is both wise and prudent to adhere to a decision about whose substantive judgment they had earlier expressed doubt. In the history that *Casey* tells, the Court faced a severe challenge; adhering to precedent presented the best, though not the only, answer.

Yet there is another image of precedent, of law's history, in which the force of precedent *compels* judgment, in which precedent is treated as a rule foreclosing the possibility of any other legitimate considerations. This image is perhaps best exemplified in Justice Marshall's dissent in *Payne v. Tennessee*.[40] In *Payne* the Supreme Court overruled its earlier decision in *Booth v. Maryland* in order to hold that the use of so-called victim impact statements in the sentencing phase of capital trials was not a violation of the Eighth Amendment.[41] The majority opinion written by Justice Rehnquist explained its overruling of *Booth* by invok-

---

36. Horwitz, "Foreword," 71.
37. *Casey*, 4804.
38. Nietzsche, *Use and Abuse of History*.
39. *Casey*, 4804.
40. *Payne v. Tennessee*, 111 S.Ct. 2597, 2619 (1991).
41. David Paul, "*Payne v. Tennessee*: A Case of Precedent Forgotten," *University of Pittsburgh Law Review* 54 (1993): 893.

ing the attitude toward precedent that would later emerge in *Casey* to justify adhering to precedent. As Rehnquist put it, "Adherence to precedent is 'usually the wise policy.'"[42] It is not, Rehnquist warned, a "mechanical formula" of adherence to the latest decision no matter how misguided.[43]

Marshall responded by conjuring a different relationship of law's present to its past. He called for "fidelity" to precedent and claimed such fidelity was essential if courts were not to subject the People to the rule of "an arbitrary discretion."[44] In his view the Court has a "duty to stand by its own precedents."[45] Discharging that duty, against the tides of changing personnel on the Court or a changing political climate in the country, was, Marshall claimed, necessary to a judiciary that sought to be a "source of impersonal and reasoned judgments."[46] The history that Marshall constructed is a history in which the past should rule the present, in which authority could and should be excavated from a continuous process of reading and rereading of the judiciary's own products. It is a history of "fidelity," of "duty" in the face of temptation. Failing to follow precedent would mean that "power, not reason," would be the currency of judicial decision making.[47]

These two different attitudes toward precedent reveal an important part of the terrain of inquiry into law's use and construction of history. They remind us of the complex and contingent interpretive possibilities of a legal order dedicated to a faithful respect for its past. Reasoning by analogy, distinguishing cases, identifying rules and their exceptions provide, in one sense, the very substance of legal reasoning. But in another they provide the resources with which law can live within the prison of history and yet escape it as needed. They provide but one indication of the fact that law's history is almost always the subject of contest and interpretive dispute, that its is a purposive and politicized attitude toward history. They also suggest that the interpretive touchstone for such contestation is the question of legitimacy.

While there is contest about the meaning of the past, of the precise

---

42. *Payne,* 2609.

43. Id., 2610. See Amy Padden, "Overruling Decisions in the Supreme Court: The Role of a Decision's Vote, Age, and Subject Matter in the Application of Stare Decisis after *Payne v. Tennessee,*" *Georgetown Law Journal* 82 (1994): 1684.

44. *Payne,* 2621. On the fidelity problem see Eisgruber, "Living Hand," 1612.

45. *Payne,* 2623.

46. Id.

47. Id., 2619.

relevance law's history, to its present, there is little dispute about the place of an historical sensibility in legal decision making. Yet as we turn from history to memory, this consensus disappears.[48] To turn from history to memory is to move from the disciplined effort to marshal evidence about the "truth" of the past to the slippery terrain on which individuals and groups invent traditions[49] and record partisan versions of the past on the basis of which they seek to construct particular conditions in the present.[50] "Memory," Pierre Nora writes,

> is life, borne by living societies founded in its name. It remains in permanent evolution, open to the dialectic of remembering and forgetting, unconscious of its successive deformations, vulnerable to manipulation and appropriation. . . . [H]istory, on the other hand, is the reconstruction . . . of what is no longer. . . . History, because it is an intellectual and secular production, calls for analysis and criticism. . . . At the heart of history is a critical discourse that is antithetical to . . . memory.[51]

Acts of commemoration are the very stuff of politics;[52] in and through our political processes we decide who or what should be

---

48. As James Fentress and Chris Wickham note, "In Western society, the history of memory is one of its steady devaluation as a source of knowledge." *Social Memory: New Perspectives on the Past* (Oxford: Blackwell, 1992), 8.

49. Eric Hobsbawm and Terence Ranger, eds., *The Invention of Tradition* (Cambridge: Cambridge University Press, 1983).

50. On the distinction between history and memory see Jacques LeGoff, *History and Memory*, trans. Steven Rendall and Elizabeth Claman (New York: Columbia University Press, 1992).

51. Pierre Nora, "Between Memory and History: *Les Lieux de Memoire*," *Representations* 26 (1989): 8–9. But see Natalie Zemon Davis and Randolph Starn: "Rather than insisting on the opposition between memory and history . . . we want to emphasize their interdependence" ("Introduction," *Representations* 26 [1989]: 5). Or, as Burke argues, "Both history and memory are coming to appear increasingly problematic. Remembering the past and writing about it no longer seem like the innocent activities they were once taken to be. Neither memories nor histories seem objective any longer. . . . In both cases . . . selection, interpretation and distortion is socially conditioned" ("History as Social Memory," 97–98).

52. See John Gillis, ed., *Commemorations: The Politics of National Identity* (Princeton: Princeton University Press, 1994). See also Nathan Wachtel, "Introduction: Memory and History," *History and Anthropology* 2 (1986): 218; Barry Schwartz, "The Social Control of Commemoration: A Study in Collective Memory," *Social Forces* 61 (1982): 15; and Michael Kammen, *Mystic Chords of Memory: The Transformation of Tradition in American Culture* (New York: Knopf, 1991).

remembered or memorialized and in what ways.[53] As David Thelen argues, "[M]emory, private and individual, as much as collective and cultural is constructed, not reproduced. . . . [T]his construction is not made in isolation but in conversations with others that occur in the contexts of community, broader politics, and social dynamics."[54] Should law and legal processes lend themselves to these processes? Can they do so without compromising values central to law's integrity?[55] These normative questions have so far driven scholarship on law and memory.[56]

To talk about law and collective memory is almost immediately to conjure images of the show trial where individual rights and truth were sacrificed in the service of political goals. Mark Osiel notes that

> acts asserting legal rights or officially stigmatizing their violation have often become a focal point for the collective memory of whole nations. These acts often become secular rites of commemoration. As such, they consolidate shared memories with increasing deliberateness and sophistication. These events are both "real" and "staged." In this regard, they seem to problematize the very distinction between true and false representations of reality.[57]

In the classic, liberal conception, justice requires impartial adjudication of claims and accusations. The sole question with which law should concern itself is whether, according to the evidence presented and the rules of proof, someone "did" what they were accused of doing or some event did or did not happen. How the result serves particular collective memories is an illegitimate consideration, the introduction of which may distort those values. Playing out larger issues in culture and

---

53. Connerton, *How Societies Remember*, 21.

54. David Thelen, "Memory and American History," *Journal of American History* 75 (1989): 1119.

55. See Gerry J. Simpson, "Didactic and Dissident Histories in War Crimes Trials," *Albany Law Review* 60 (1997): 801.

56. See Mark Osiel, *Mass Atrocity, Collective Memory, and the Law* (New Brunswick, N.J.: Transaction Books, 1997): "The orchestration of criminal trials for pedagogical purposes . . . is not inherently misguided or morally indefensible. The defensibility of the practice depends on the defensibility of the lessons being taught" (65). See also Carlos Nino, *Radical Evil on Trial* (New Haven: Yale University Press, 1996); and Nancy Wood, "Crimes or Misdemeanors: Memory on Trial in Contemporary France," *French Cultural Studies* 5 (1994): 1.

57. Osiel, *Mass Atrocity*, 6.

politics through the trial seems, if we take the liberal view seriously, a misuse of the judicial process.

But the relationship of law and collective memory need not simply be discussed in terms of these normative concerns, namely whether it is right intentionally to use legal processes in the effort to create or vindicate collective memory. We might also approach the relationship between law and collective memory in a more descriptive vein and ask how and where law remembers as well as how and where it helps us remember.[58] This question is one that engages the authors whose essays are collected in *History, Memory, and the Law*.

In the present moment, as Nora reminds us, memory is "above all archival. It relies on the materiality of the trace, the immediacy of the recording, the visibility of the image. . . . Even as traditional memory disappears, we feel obliged assiduously to collect remains, testimonies, documents, images, speeches, any visible signs of what has been."[59] Museums, monuments, and so on are today, Nora argues, the locations of memory, the sites to which collective memory is attached. If that is indeed the case, one might ask whether law itself might be one of what Nora calls "les lieux de mémoire."

Here our interest is directed to the temporal dimension of legality, the way law stands in relation to the past, the present, and the future. Law in the modern era is, we believe, one of the most important of our society's technologies for preserving memory. Just as the use of precedent to legitimate legal decisions fixes law in a particular relation to the past, memory may be attached, or attach itself, to law and be preserved in and through law. Where this is the case, it serves as one way of orienting ourselves to the future. As Drucilla Cornell puts it: "Legal interpretation demands that we remember the future."[60] In that phrase, Cornell reminds us that there are, in fact, two audiences for every legal act, the audience of the present and the audience of the future. Law materializes memory in documents, transcripts, written opinions;[61] it reenacts

---

58. "The historical study of memory would be the study of how families, larger gatherings of people, and formal organizations selected and interpreted identifying memories to serve changing needs" (Thelen, "Memory and American History," 1123).

59. Nora, "Between History and Memory," 13.

60. "From the Lighthouse: The Promise of Redemption and the Possibility of Legal Interpretation," *Cardozo Law Review* 11 (1990): 1690.

61. "Legal documents . . . are written to be preserved and consulted. . . . The form and syntax of a legal document, whether from the twelfth century or the twentieth, reflect the form and syntax of other written documents" (Fentress and Wickham, *Social Memory*, 9).

the past, both intentionally and unconsciously, and it is one place where the present speaks to the future through acts of commemoration.[62]

Because the litigated case creates a record, courts can become archives in which that record serves as the materialization of memory.[63] Due process guarantees an opportunity to be heard by, and an opportunity to speak to, the future. It is the guarantee that legal institutions can be turned into museums of unnecessary, unjust, undeserved pain and death.[64] The legal hearing provides lawyers and litigants an opportunity to write and record history by creating narratives of present injustices, and to insist on memory in the face of denial. By recording such history and constructing such narratives lawyers and litigants call on an imagined future to choose Justice over the "jurispathic" tendencies of the moment.[65]

This is not to say that the litigated case, the celebrated trial, the judicial opinion, or the rites of execution are first and foremost memorial. It is, however, to attend to the temporality of legal acts and to their relentless insistence on record keeping and remembrance. Law memorializes not just in its archival activities, but in acts that give particular meanings to our past. In every legal act there is an invitation to remember; in the testimony of the witnesses at a trial, in the instructions a judge gives to a jury, in particular interpretive theories, and in the monumental buildings that house our courts as well as our prisons,[66] there is an insistent call to remember.

Law is one site to both "remember the future" and to insure that the future remembers. Perhaps by paying attention to how law serves memory we can gain new understandings of law's crucial role in knit-

---

62. Gillis, *Commemorations.*

63. Nora, "Between Memory and History," 15.

64. Martha Minow suggests that "legal rights matter not just because they provide dignity to law's victims, or because they help to mobilize them to undertake political action, but because they provide an opportunity to tell a story that might not otherwise get to be told." "Interpreting Rights: An Essay for Robert Cover," *Yale Law Journal* 96 (1987): 1860.

65. See Robert Cover, "Foreword: Nomos and Narrative," *Harvard Law Review* 97 (1983): 16.

66. For a fascinating discussion of the semiotics of legal architecture see John Brigham, "From Temple to Technology: The Construction of Courts in Everyday Practice," in Austin Sarat et. al., *Everyday Practices and Trouble Cases* (Evanston, Ill.: Northwestern University Press, 1998).

ting together our past, present, and future. Perhaps by attending to the contestation that inevitably accompanies efforts to materialize memory in law we can gain a better understanding of the ways that social conflict plays itself out on the terrain of remembrance.[67]

The essays in *History, Memory, and the Law* address this subject, each in its own distinctive voice. They present grounded examinations of particular problems, places, and practices rather than grand theories. In so doing they address the ways in which memory works in and through law, the sites of remembrance that law provides, the battles against forgetting that are fought in and around those sites. Here we attend to what Lucie White has labeled both the "epic" style of remembering the past, the "grand, monumental, Manichean style . . . that splits the world, morally, along temporal lines,"[68] as well as to what she calls the "tragic" style of remembering. This style, White claims, "teases out the multiple, tangled, always partial threads that comprise the space where 'civility' has been enacted and resisted and reshaped." This kind of remembering spurns "grand gestures." It remembers in "grounded, gradual ways."[69] It makes the accomplishments of the past more hard fought, more tentative, more elusive, and more deeply intertwined with the moral horrors to which it insists we attend.

The essays in this book also inquire about the way history is mobilized in legal decision making, the rhetorical techniques for marshaling and for overcoming precedent, and the different histories that are written in and through the legal process. Among the questions that they address are, How are the histories and memories created by law different by virtue of the site of their creation? Through what representational practices are the seeming continuities between past and present that are necessary to legitimize legal decisions constructed and preserved? Whose histories and memories "count" in law? What does history do to, and for, law, and what does law do to history? Under what conditions do legal institutions, such as courts or prisons, become sites of memory?

The first two essays—by Shoshana Felman and Dominick LaCapra—focus on the criminal trial as a site of commemoration and

---

67. Thelen, "Memory and American History," 1127.
68. Lucie White, "'Why Do You Treat Us So Badly?' On Loss, Remembrance, and Responsibility," *Cumberland Law Review* 26 (1996): 812.
69. Id., 813.

remembrance. The particular trial on which Felman focuses is the criminal trial of O. J. Simpson. She deploys psychoanalytic theory as well as Nora's understanding of history and memory to inquire about what made this a "landmark" trial and what are the constituent elements of any such trial. One of the key elements that Felman claims marks a landmark trial is the way it repeats elements of other trials. The landmark trial is a site of memory, a moment of legal intertextuality in which key elements of the drama of law are reenacted.

The Simpson trial memorialized, in Felman's view, two earlier moments in law, one being the first trial arising from the beating of Rodney King, the other found in Tolstoy's famous short story, *The Kreutzer Sonata*. In relation to the former, the Simpson case reenacted what Felman labels the "trauma" of interracial violence. But it also recalled, almost perfectly, the trauma of gendered violence that Tolstoy's story so compellingly told. Both *The Kreutzer Sonata* and the Simpson case were composed of an almost identical chain of events consisting of the murder of a woman followed by the trial and acquittal of her husband. In both the husband points an accusing finger at the social order; in the Tolstoy story to indict it for its corrupting modernization, in the Simpson case to indict it for its institutional racism. And what is memorialized in both is precisely what could not, in Felman's view, be seen, namely the deep and problematic relationship of marriage and violence. This failure of vision also recapitulates the trauma of the first Rodney King trial, in which what could not be seen, for example society's racism, overcame what seemed inescapably visual.

For Felman the criminal trial always recapitulates law's troubled relation to trauma. The structure of trauma, she argues, controls the trial, not the reverse. Trials revisit our inability to reason in the face of trauma, our inability to produce an adequate historical record of its workings. As a result, we turn to literature to remember precisely what cannot be made available in the law. Thus the verdict in the Simpson case is at once about what law's history remembers and what it forgets. As Felman puts it, the verdict in a landmark trial is a decision about "what to admit into, and what to transmit of, collective memory." She notes that a legal case can be, and Simpson was, a "locus of embodied history, a 'site of memory'" in Nora's terms. That case, like other landmark trials, "triggers inadvertently the movement of a repetition or the dynamics of a *legal recall*. . . . [It] repeats . . . all these repetitions—legal, literary, psychoanalytical, historical—by which the trial tries, and retries, to resolve the trauma, and by which the trauma inadvertently repeats itself as an unconscious legal memory under the conscious legal process."

The second essay, by Dominick LaCapra, also takes up the theme of repetition as it asks what makes a legal trial worth remembering. Focusing on the nineteenth-century trials of Flaubert and Baudelaire for "outrage to public and religious morality and to good morals," LaCapra demonstrates that the aesthetic standard used to judge these writers demanded that a work of art provide "purely symbolic and 'spiritual' resolution of the problems it explored." Flaubert and Baude-laire were, in essence, subject to criminal prosecution for their commit-ment to a literary realism that led them to flout some of the representa-tional taboos of their time.

Yet in LaCapra's view their trials were not, in a strict sense, show trials whose purpose was to instill a broad, collective memory. They were not designed to recall from the past events that "insistently made demands on collective and individual remembrance and thus necessi-tated entry into the public sphere." They were instead intended to cre-ate a memory of the consequences that would attach to writers who transgressed public norms and whose "deviant" work might have a broad public impact. LaCapra worries about the use of law for such memorial purposes, and he notes the continuing controversy over whether historiography has the function of transmitting memory. In his own view history has two related objectives, namely the adjudica-tion of truth claims about the past and the transmission of memory.

It is, however, the memory of the criminal trial, especially those in which literature is put on trial, to which LaCapra calls our attention. Such trials raise questions about how literary texts can be read in par-ticular contexts, and they call on us to remember the situatedness and contingency of all readings. When faced with literary texts that are in some sense transgressive, law, LaCapra suggests, will read through the lens of its own reconstructions of the past—through precedent—and, as a result, will read in a regulative, normalizing way. Law will seek to protect the literary canon and repress the more disconcerting features of literature in order to make it a vehicle for the promotion of conven-tional social values. Yet this kind of reading, a reading that serves to commemorate convention, defeats literature. LaCapra calls for a kind of literary privilege in which what the law may justifiably prohibit in social life should not be prohibited in art or literature. Art could thus serve society as a safe haven for exploration and experimentation.

LaCapra notes that in the trials of Flaubert and Baudelaire, while both the prosecution and the defense insisted on a view of the role of literature in society that was "conventionalizing, normalizing, and domesticating," this was especially true of the defense. In each trial the defense of literature denied its experimental or transgressive character and insisted on its role in commemorating conventional values. Although Flaubert and Baudelaire put into practice immanent critique of the social and literary conditions of their time, this critique could find no voice in a court of law.

This essay calls on us to remember the trials of these two great writers for what they reveal about the "variable historical manner in which 'literary' experimentation . . . is bound up with broader political, legal, and sociocultural issues in the production, reception, and critical reading of texts." With respect to the place of memory, LaCapra suggests that law, at least the law of crime, resists the transmission of particular understandings of literature, for example, of its transgressive, experimental value. Those seeking to use law to memorialize such understandings are regularly defeated. Unlike Felman, who sees law instantiating memory in uncanny ways, LaCapra finds no such subversive potential in the trials of literature. He insists that law constrains memory and remembrance in a relatively predictable manner and points to the limits to which law as archive can be put.

The next two essays—by Reva Siegel and Joan Dayan—turn from the criminal trial as a site of memory to two other sites in law, appellate court decisions and prisons. Siegel is interested in understanding how it is that sex discrimination has not taken on the same significance in American society as has race discrimination. She finds a basis for answering this question in the case law, in particular in the Supreme Court's reading of the Fourteenth and Nineteenth Amendments. Supreme Court treatments of sex discrimination differ from its treatment of racial discrimination at least in part in the memories the Court invokes and in the history it conjures. In her view, interpretation of the Constitution reflects and "produces the narrative structures that organize our intuitions about questions of gender justice." When judges interpret the Constitution, they engage the task as "carriers of social memory." Their decisions help to constitute and reaffirm the nation's understanding of its past and how that past shapes our present and future.

But not every decision engages memory in the same way or engages the same type of memory. With regard to race discrimination the Court relies on what Lucie White calls "epic" memory. "Claims about race discrimination . . . are located," Siegel argues, "in national and constitutional history; they refer, whether explicitly or tacitly, to past wrongful acts of the American polity." They are always linked to memories of slavery and segregation. Whatever their view about the appropriate way to respond to racial discrimination, all sides share a common historical understanding that "in matters of race, the nation has a legacy of wrongdoing that it has constitutionally committed itself to transcend."

Claims about sex discrimination memorialize no such epic structure. They are, in fact, generally cut off from any historical story whatsoever. Instead they focus on the question of how men and women differ and whether that difference makes a difference. Where a historical story is told, it is a history of social attitudes rather than a history of national or constitutional dimensions. The memory of national wrong and rectification is largely absent from the Court's understanding of sex discrimination.

Siegel tries to evoke a different memory by claiming that gendered restrictions on the franchise were tied to fundamental principles organizing our government. This remembrance is effaced in the Court's treatment of sex discrimination under either the Fourteenth or Nineteenth Amendment. With respect to the latter, the Court has construed the prohibition on the abridgement of the right to vote on the basis of sex as a "rule governing voting," the meaning of which need not be linked to memory of the nation's founding or its enduring normative commitments. Moreover, the Court, Siegel argues, has failed to link the Fourteenth and Nineteenth Amendments in developing a body of constitutional protections for women's rights. Recently, however, Justice Ginsburg has insisted on the relevance of epic memory to the resolution of sex discrimination claims. For her, according to Siegel, heightened scrutiny of such claims "performs a kind of commemorative act, tacitly invoking a regrettable past the nation is aspiring to transcend."

Siegel concludes by asking, "What difference would a memory of constitutional wrongs make to the adjudication of women's constitutional rights?" She answers by suggesting that memorialization in and through law is itself a form of rectification. Such memorialization provides a collective acknowledgment of collective wrongdoing and allows a community to redefine itself in opposition to its own past practices. Moreover, were the Court to recount a narrative of constitutional wrong and rectification of the kind that it has done in the area of race, the social memory of the next generation might well differ from the memory of those who inaugurated modern sex discrimination jurisprudence.

Whereas Siegel holds out the hope that new narratives can create new memories that, in turn, can have progressive political potential, Joan Dayan tells a story of a very different kind of memory, what White calls "tragic" memory, encoded in a very different legal practice, and with very different political results. The practice to which Dayan calls our attention is the use of chain gangs in American prisons. Her work reminds us that the commemorative sites of law are not simply textual, but may also involve particular kinds of materialization of legal power. The memory that is encoded in the materializations of law's power found in chain gangs is the memory of slavery, and the politics of memorialization with which they are associated is, in her view, anything but progressive. She points out that "the current spectacle of chain gangs, control units, and execution . . . preserves the memory of slavery. . . . As a set of legal acts that has its own history, the law defines how material considerations and a concern for order and discipline can produce the judicial nonexistence of the person through degrees of deprivation."

Dayan argues that the practices of contemporary imprisonment provide a "semantic genealogy of slavery and involuntary servitude." The courts condone these practices, all the while being committed to the eradication of the vestiges of slavery. How can the law live with this dual rejection and embrace of the worst of our past? The answer, she suggests, is found in an absolute separation between the formal existence of law and the "day-to-day records that underpin the law's authority." Judicial decisions on prisoners' rights construct their own history, "founded on precedent, repeated, and gaining in force with each repetition." Precedent, she argues, operates like ritual in that it gains authority the more it is tried and used. The law, in the histories it constructs and the memories cited there, "is a tomb of dead ideas."

Changing circumstances become "immobilized" in the face of law's own commitment to respect its past; they are "the lifeblood for the constancy, the deathlessness of legal inquiry."

Burying itself in its own history and thereby blinding itself to the memories encoded in its material practices, the law considers it reasonable to force inmates to labor in chains and to live without human contact in the special-management units of maximum-security prisons. While the attachment of chain to a person claims that person as part of a history of degradation and abuse that the law formally disavows, Dayan's essay shows that the construction of a particular kind of history—the precedents through which inmates have historically come to be seen as civilly dead or as "slaves of the state"—insulates the law from confronting the horrifying memory of what it condones. This insulation reminds us that memorialization is no guarantee of memory, that one structure of history may work to suppress another, that the commitment to remember needs to be cultivated alongside memory itself.

Law's forgetfulness, or its refusal to find remembrance beyond the narrow confines of its own doctrinal structure, sanctions a public policy in which imprisonment is about hardship, not help, degradation, not rehabilitation. Dayan demonstrates that forgetfulness is, in this context, the key to a legal regime that espouses the protection of rights and human dignity and yet refuses really to see what is done in its name to an entire class of persons. In this refusal to see, work done in chains gets called labor, not punishment; classification is labeled the rational administration of prisons, not an excuse for dehumanization. In spite of this linguistic transformation, Dayan insists that through the practices of chain and classification "the indigent, the criminal, and the slave are joined in, and delimited by, the law."

Concern for the memory of slavery and its place in law also animates the next essay, by Brook Thomas. His concern, however, is less with memory than with the way law both lives in, and finds resources to escape, the precedential world it creates. Thomas wants to illuminate what might be called the indeterminacy of historical argument in legal decision making as well as the way judges can both appeal to history and yet evade the history to which they appeal. He argues that, at least in the context of decisions on racial discrimination, judges deploy metaphors to produce novel interpretations of legal doctrine while continuing to honor the doctrinal history that they are changing.

"Metaphor . . . allows for innovative interpretations that paradoxically claim to stay true to the meaning of the text at hand."

The particular metaphors in which Thomas is interested are metaphors of racial marking. Thomas's essay examines some of these metaphors—stigmas, badges, brands—for what they can tell us about the history of law's response to racial discrimination. But he also shows that the Supreme Court uses those metaphors to change the course of legal history without explicitly invoking history. The history of attempts to "get out from under the history of racial discrimination," Thomas contends, "is marked by metaphors from the history that it would escape."

Thomas starts his consideration of the relationship of history and metaphor with Justice Taney's use of the idea of stigma in *Dred Scott*. In that case Taney claimed that persons of African descent had been, and would always be, stigmatized by "deep and enduring marks of inferiority." His metaphor, used in its time for pernicious purposes, has been, in Thomas's view, a touchstone to which all subsequent efforts to deal with the legacy of racism have had to return. While *stigma* suggested a mark permanently embedded on the body, others, seeking to develop a different way of understanding slavery and racism, compared stigmas to "badges" that were affixed to blacks. Unlike stigmas, a badge is "worn rather than incorporated into the body." This metaphor thus suggests that the evil of slavery could be removed through legal and political acts.

The move from stigmas to badges as metaphors moves legal doctrine to the view that "once slavery had been eliminated, the Court's job was to guarantee complete emancipation by removing the lingering effects of the institution's 'shadows.'" Justices seeking to bring law to the service of racial justice could, by using the metaphor of badges of slavery, agree with Taney that even free blacks were marked as inferior "without agreeing that those marks permanently stigmatized them." In so doing, they could, through a creative use of metaphor, turn Taney's history to a purpose other than the one he intended.

Thomas notes that the Supreme Court in *Brown* did not directly confront either Taney's metaphor or the precedent of *Plessy*. Instead it spoke of racial segregation as having "generated" a sense of inferiority among black schoolchildren. The metaphor of generation allowed the Court to avoid ruling on the motive behind Jim Crow laws, just as it avoided ruling on the original intention of the Fourteenth Amendment.

Thomas claims that the genius of *Brown* was that it used metaphor to adhere to precedent while, at the same time, altering the course of history. Opposing a static view of history, the *Brown* Court treated temporality as a component of reality. If reality changes, a truly historical approach requires that law update itself as well.

Finally, Thomas notes the continuing relevance of metaphors like stigmas and badges in contemporary judicial decisions concerning affirmative action. There too he claims that "strategic uses of metaphor have allowed the Court to make history more effectively than explicit uses of history itself." Metaphors have given the Court a way to honor the history of legal doctrine on race while providing it the space to fashion new responses.

While metaphor provides a space for innovation, the last essay— by G. Edward White—shows how reasoning by analogy is used to stitch together the threads of precedent that comprise law's own history. Analogical reasoning, White argues, "is in fact the standard technique of reasoning in the Anglo-American legal system. It consists of establishing previously decided cases as 'authoritative' because they embody certain rules that the system has internalized." It allows judges to construct a history of doctrine with little overt reference to the world outside law and, as a result, provides a crucial component of the argument that legal decision making is autonomous. And, White notes, while analogical reasoning may seem to the nonlawyer to impose few constraints on judges, in practice the legal system places a "high value on following precedent and thus treats most previous decisions whose rules appear arguably apposite as being so." When lawyers and judges seek to be creative, the vehicle for their creativity is the marshaling of rich and persuasive analogies. Yet since those analogies "invariably summon up existing cases, rules, and principles, the discourse of American law is inherently time-bound and conservative."

White examines the hold of analogical reasoning on the legal imagination by assessing the way courts responded to innovations in the social world. The two examples that are the subject of this essay are the treatment of radio and motion pictures in the early part of the twentieth century. He looks at how law responded to these innovations and, in particular, how courts responded to challenges to efforts to impose a regulatory regime on them. The drive to regulate emerged from a particular awareness of the media's mass quality and the immediacy of the effects they created; in addition, it was fueled by the Progressive Era's tendency to approve regulation by experts as a way of addressing social concerns. Yet these regulations, at least from the perspective of today, raise serious First Amendment issues. White examines cases challenging regulation to show that analogical reasoning was used to construct a legal history in such a way as to justify regulation in spite of the First Amendment.

In the case of film, courts constructed such a history by categorizing it as a form of property. Like property, film might be used to do "evil." Courts then conjured the history of the "police powers" by which states could invoke their powers to protect the morals of the public. In addition, they brought the regulation of film within the history of administrative law and, as a result, focused only on the nature of the legislative delegation involved. Having established a framework of analogies, courts then were able to bring to bear the relevant precedents. In their treatment of those cases they tended to anticipate the position of Marshall in *Payne*, insisting on the value of consistency and continuity in law's doctrinal structure.

White finds "striking parallels" as he explores the way law's history was brought to bear on the question of the regulation of radio. Faced with an evolving and developing First Amendment jurisprudence, courts nonetheless had little trouble, White argues, upholding the Radio Act of 1927, through which the Congress asserted government ownership of the airwaves. They focused on radio's potential to reach vast audiences as well as the scarcity of radio frequencies. They drew an analogy to film and claimed that, like the former, radio was intrusive and pervasive in its reach. Yet today, somewhat paradoxically, the latter is subject to a far more restrictive regulatory regime than the former, though today new analogies and new precedents prevail. Film and radio are now regarded not simply as property; the new analogical structure provides greater First Amendment protection by treating them as like the print media.

In the end, White claims that analogical reasoning in itself, though powerful in explaining the way innovations are accommodated in the construction of a doctrinal history, is insufficient to explain this process. He suggests that we can understand how law's history gets created by focusing on both the concerns that are vital in the larger culture in which decisions are being made, and the available analogies through which legal discourse can respond to those concerns. Precedent constrains yet leaves room for adaptation. The internal history that law constructs to legitimate itself is not, and cannot be, completely insulated from the external history that gives rise to problems, cases, and calls for legal resolution

The essays in *History, Memory, and the Law* deploy a wide range of theories in diverse contexts to show law's role in commemoration and the ways it constructs its own history. Yet each illuminates the limits of law as a site of memory and as a reader and interpreter of history. Each also highlights its flexibility, responsiveness, and adaptability. No memory, no matter how important or powerful it would seem to be, reliably can be preserved in and through legal decisions and institutions. No memory, no matter how powerful or important it would seem to be, reliably can make its presence felt to open up, to correct, or to control law. And similarly, the history that law constructs, as well as the techniques used to construct that history, cannot ensure a certain outcome. Law's history and its hermeneutics are neither linear nor immune to improvisations, inventions, and ingeniously artful readings. To study history and memory in law, then, is to be reminded of law's almost inexhaustible capacity to be, and do, many complex and contradictory things, all the while denying the contradictions and plausibly proclaiming its "formal existence."[70]

---

70. See Fish, "Law Wishes to Have."

Forms of Judicial Blindness: Traumatic Narratives and Legal Repetitions

Shoshana Felman

This essay will propose a theory of legal repetition, based on a comparative structural interpretation of a legal case and of a fictional, imaginary story written by one of the great writers of all times. I will attempt to integrate a literary vision with a legal vision, with the intention of confronting evidence in law and evidence in art. The case in the equation will be one that has impacted on our times—the notorious O. J. Simpson criminal trial, apparently an all-too-familiar legal case that will, however, be somewhat estranged by the analysis and sound less familiar through its unpredictable illumination by the literary case, equally a case of crime and trial. The literary text in the equation is a famous story by Tolstoy entitled *The Kreutzer Sonata*.

In both the legal drama of the case and the literary drama of the

The present essay is an excerpt from a book entitled *Dilemmas of Justice (Literature/Psychoanalysis/Law)* (to be published). An earlier version of this text was published in *Critical Inquiry* 23 (1997): 738–88.

This text could not have been written without the ongoing critical feedback of two people whose proficiency and expertise in two specific areas (here conjoined and thought together) is greater than mine: Michal Shaked for jurisprudence (and legal thinking); Cathy Caruth for trauma theory (and its conceptual implications). I thank both for their rigor, which was for me a guiding inspiration, and for their help in sharpening the concepts here developed. Pnina Lahav read an early version of the manuscript and offered supportive comments that encouraged me to pursue it further. Finally, I wish to thank Dalia Tsuk for her highly discriminating expert assistance in legal and historical research.

text, what is at issue is a marriage that ends up in murder. In both, a jealous husband is arrested and put on trial for the murder of his wife—and is acquitted. A difference is, however, striking from the start: the husband in Tolstoy's work acknowledges his guilt, and is precisely telling us the story to explain not only why, but *how* he killed his wife.

A trial and a literary text do not aim at the same kind of conclusion, nor do they strive toward the same kind of effect. A trial is presumed to be a search for truth, but, technically, it is a search for a decision, and thus, in essence, it seeks not simply truth but a finality: a force of resolution. A literary text is, on the other hand, a search for meaning, for expression, for heightened significance, and for symbolic understanding. I propose to make use of this difference in literary and legal goals, by reading them *across* each other and against each other. I propose, in other words, to draw the questions of what was entitled at the time "the trial of the century" into Tolstoy's text, but even more importantly, to *draw out Tolstoy's insight,* so to speak, *into* the O. J. Simpson case in order to illuminate legal obscurities with literary insights and to reflect on ambiguities the trial has left by using textual issues that will turn out (surprisingly) to be quite relevant to them.

I

On the Separate Jurisdictions of Law and Literature

The dialogue between the disciplines of law and literature[1] has so far been primarily thematic (that is, essentially conservative of the integrity and of the stable epistemological boundaries of the two fields): when not borrowing the tools of literature to analyze (rhetori-

---

1. For recent overviews and general discussions of the field of "law and literature," see (in chronological order) Brook Thomas, "Reflections on the Law and Literature Revival," *Critical Inquiry* 17 (1991): 510–37; C. R. B. Dunlop, "Literature Studies in Law Schools," *Cardozo Studies in Law and Literature* 3 (1991): 63–110; Richard H. Weisberg, *Poethics: And Other Strategies of Law and Literature* (New York: Columbia University Press, 1992), and "Three Lessons from Law and Literature," *Loyola of Los Angeles Law Review* 27 (1993): 285–303; John Fischer, "Reading Literature/Reading Law: Is There a Literary Jurisprudence?" *Texas Law Review* 72 (1993): 135–60; Gary Minda, *Postmodern Legal Movements: Law and Jurisprudence at Century's End* (New York: New York University Press, 1995), 149–66; Ian Ward, *Law and Literature: Possibilities and Perspectives* (New York: Cambridge University Press, 1995); Bruce Rockwood, ed., *Law and Literature: Perspectives* (New York: Peter Lang, 1996); and Theodore Ziolkowski, *The Mirror of Justice: Literary Reflections of Legal Crises* (Princeton: Princeton University Press, 1997).

cally) legal opinions, scholars in the field of law and literature most often deal with the explicit, thematized reflection (or "representation") of the institutions of the law in works of the imagination, focusing on the analysis of fictional trials in a literary plot and/or on the psychology or the sociology of literary characters whose fate or whose profession ties them to the law (lawyers, judges, or accused). My approach here will be different. I will compare a trial to a text. My starting point will be their comparably real and comparably astounding *impact*, the striking similarity of their historical reception. I will proceed, then, to compare the trial's and the text's narratives of crime and trial. This juxtaposition between legal facts and literary facts is, admittedly, quite

---

For problematizations of the field, see Richard Posner, *Law and Literature: A Misunderstood Relation* (Cambridge: Harvard University Press, 1988); Richard Rorty, *Contingency, Irony, and Solidarity* (New York: Cambridge University Press, 1989); and Stanley Fish, *Doing What Comes Naturally: Change, Rhetoric, and the Practice of Theory in Literary and Legal Studies* (Durham, N.C.: Duke University Press, 1989).

For thematic studies and for rhetorical and philosophical interpretations of representations of the law in works of art, see, among others, Robert M. Cover, *Justice Accused: Antislavery and the Judicial Process* (New Haven: Yale University Press, 1975), 1–7; Barbara E. Johnson, "Melville's Fist: The Execution of *Billy Budd*," in *The Critical Difference: Essays in the Contemporary Rhetoric of Reading* (Baltimore: Johns Hopkins University Press, 1980); Richard H. Weisberg, *The Failure of the Word: The Lawyer as Protagonist in Modern Fiction* (New Haven: Yale University Press, 1984); and Shoshana Felman, "Crisis of Witnessing: Albert Camus's Postwar Writings," *Cardozo Studies in Law and Literature* 3 (1991): 197–242, reprinted in Shoshana Felman and Dori Laub, *Testimony: Crises of Witnessing in Literature, Psychoanalysis, and History* (New York: Routledge, 1992).

For legal "hermeneutics" and for rhetorical interpretations of legal opinions, statutes, and legal texts, see, among others, James Boyd White, *The Legal Imagination: Studies in the Nature of Legal Thought and Expression* (Boston: Little, Brown, 1973), *Heracles' Bow: Essays on the Rhetoric and Poetics of the Law* (Madison: University of Wisconsin Press, 1985), and *Justice as Translation: An Essay in Cultural and Legal Criticism* (Chicago: University of Chicago Press, 1990); Sanford Levinson, "Law as Literature," *Texas Law Review* 60 (1982): 373–403; Owen M. Fiss, "Objectivity and Interpretation," *Stanford Law Review* 34 (1982): 739–63; Ronald Dworkin, "How Is Law Like Literature," in *A Matter of Principle* (Cambridge: Harvard University Press, 1985); Jack M. Balkin, "Deconstructive Practices and Legal Theory," *Yale Law Journal* 96 (1987): 743–86; John Leubsdorf, "Deconstructing the Constitution," *Stanford Law Review* 40 (1987): 181–201; Sanford Levinson and Steven Mailloux, eds., *Interpreting Law and Literature: A Hermeneutic Reader* (Evanston, Ill.: Northwestern University Press, 1988); Robert A. Ferguson, "The Judicial Opinion as Literary Genre," *Yale Journal of Law and Humanities* 2 (1990): 201–19; Deconstruction and the Possibility of Justice," special issue of *Cardozo Law Review* 11 (1990); Richard H. Weisberg, "Legal Rhetoric under Stress: The Example of Vichy," *Cardozo Law Review* 12 (1991): 1371–415; Barbara E. Johnson, "Double Mourning and the Public Sphere," in *The Wake of Deconstruction* (Cambridge, Mass.: Blackwell, 1994), and "Anthropomorphism in Lyric and Law," *Yale Journal of Law and the Humanities* 10 (summer 1998) 549–74; and Judith Butler, *Excitable Speech: A Politics of the Performative* (New York: Routledge, 1997).

bold. Its rewards will be assessed by the surprises it reserves.[2] The ground for juxtaposition will be, therefore, not just an analogy of theme (of meaning) but an analogy of impact. I read the impact (of the trial, of the text) as itself a *symptom* of the (unarticulated) meaning, or as itself part of the evidence presented by the case.

The Structural Unconscious of the Law: A Theory of Legal Repetitions

I will thus compare a work of fiction whose impact has in turn generated passionate polemical reactions and a great deal of obsessional dis-

---

For narratological interpretations of legal storytelling and for general discussions of the relation between law and narrative, see, among others, James R. Elkins, "On the Emergence of Narrative Jurisprudence: The Humanistic Perspective Finds a New Path," *Legal Studies Forum* 9 (1985): 123–56, and "The Quest for Meaning: Narrative Accounts of Legal Education," *Journal of Legal Education* 38 (1988): 577–98; Derrick Bell, *And We Are Not Saved: The Elusive Quest for Racial Justice* (New York: Basic Books, 1987); Mari Matsuda, "Looking to the Bottom: Critical Legal Studies and Reparations," *Harvard Civil Rights–Civil Liberties Law Review* 22 (1987): 323–99; Richard Delgado, "Storytelling for Oppositionists and Others: A Plea for Narrative," *Michigan Law Review* 87 (1989): 2411–41, and Delgado, ed., *Critical Race Theory: The Cutting Edge* (Philadelphia: Temple University Press, 1995); Kathryn Abrams, "Hearing the Call of Stories," *California Law Review*, 79 (1991): 971–1052; David Ray Papke, ed., *Narrative and the Legal Discourse: A Reader in Storytelling and the Law* (Liverpool: Deborah Charles, 1991); Patricia Williams, *The Alchemy of Race and Rights: Diary of a Law Professor* (Cambridge: Harvard University Press, 1991); Robin West, *Narrative, Authority, and Law* (Ann Arbor: University of Michigan Press, 1993); Daniel A. Farber and Suzanna Sherry, "Telling Stories Out of School: An Essay on Legal Narratives," *Stanford Law Review* 45 (1993): 807–55; Richard Sherwin, "Law Frames: Historical Truth and Narrative Necessity in a Criminal Case," *Stanford Law Review* 47 (1994): 39–83; Martha Minow, Michael Ryan, and Austin Sarat, eds., *Narrative, Violence, and the Law: The Essays of Robert Cover* (Ann Arbor: University of Michigan Press, 1995); Kimberlé Crenshaw et al., eds., *Critical Race Theory: The Key Writings That Formed the Movement* (New York: New Press, 1995); Peter Brooks and Paul Gewirtz, eds., *Law's Stories: Narrative and Rhetoric in the Law* (New Haven: Yale University Press, 1996); and Austin Sarat, "Narrative Strategy and Death Penalty Advocacy," *Harvard Civil Rights–Civil Liberties Law Review* 31 (1996): 353–81.

For the relation between law and poetry, see Barbara E. Johnson, "Apostrophe, Animation, and Abortion," in *A World of Difference* (Baltimore: Johns Hopkins University Press, 1987); Thomas C. Grey, *The Wallace Stevens Case: Law and the Practice of Poetry* (Cambridge: Harvard University Press, 1991); and Barbara Johnson, "Anthropomorphism in Lyric and Law," in *Yale Journal of Law and the Humanities* 10 (1998): 549–74.

2. I will use "law in literature" to analyze not only "law as literature" but also "literature as jurisprudence." The analysis that follows does not merely "cross the boundaries" between the disciplines; it shifts those boundaries, it challenges both disciplines' epistemological and legal definition. I do not assume that authority (truth, knowledge, facts, reality) is a prerogative of law. I do not assume that literature, however disempowered, does not act in the real world and does not have power.

cussion with an actual criminal affair that has made legal history, and yet whose legal haunting has not stopped, a real case that had been legally decided and yet continued to translate itself obsessively into new legal and nonlegal channels. The case (the trial and the text) is, quite significantly, *one in which the legal scene repeats itself*. My theoretical analysis will focus on the primal legal scene of the criminal trial. Simpson's civil trial was act 2: it powerfully drew us *back* into the story's literary and dramatic spell and officially *authorized a legal repetition*—a reactivation of the judicial process. But the outcome of the civil trial was in turn incapable of truly closing this affair, which kept reclaiming our interest and our historical attention and thus presented itself, quite strictly (technically) as an interminable trial.[3]

This essay will propose a theory of the phenomenality of structural juridical repetitions as internal to the logic of specific legal cases, or as a legal outcome of the (literary/psychoanalytic principle of the) traumatic narratives that constitute (as I will show) at once the literary story and the actual criminal case.

The dramatic mirroring between the hard facts of the law and the imaginary facts of literature will thus result in a far-reaching lesson consisting, among other things, in a new model of perception of legal events and in the conceptual articulation of a new analytic tool (focused on the relation between the traumatic nature of a case and its compulsive legal repetition), an analytic tool that will here help us not just to rethink the meaning of a legal case but to displace the very terms and the very questions through which we interpret cases,[4] both in fiction and in the reality of legal life. This lesson, based on the contaminating interpenetration of the story and the case, will in effect become com-

---

3. The unanimous verdict of the criminal trial ("not guilty," October 1995) did not close the case because it gave rise to the civil trial. But the following conclusion of the civil trial by a unanimous verdict of liability (January 1997) did not, in its turn, bring an ending to the case: the defense immediately filed a request for a new trial. More profoundly, the civil verdict did not close the case because it could not cancel out its contradiction by the criminal acquittal, whose historical impact cannot be undone and whose outcome is, thus, irreversible, not merely legally but epistemologically. Society now knows it cannot produce, on Simpson's guilt, an *undivided* justice (a legal truth not subject to a systematic—and systemic—legal crisis). Indeed, the force of the unanimous decision of the civil verdict has immediately been challenged and interpreted (explained away) as a "white verdict." It is likely that there will be other, as yet unanticipated, legal sequels. "The case is far from over," Simpson prophetically announced in response to the conclusion of the second Simpson trial.

4. Such an analytical tool is not limited to murder cases or to criminal law. More broadly, it constructs a psychoanalytical approach to jurisprudence.

pellingly informative and dramatically, surprisingly instructive only through a destabilization of the boundaries that epistemologically define and separate the territory of the Law from that of Literature. In actual life, the living entities of law and literature—trial and story—relate to one another not as reality to fiction or as empiricism to aestheticism but as two narratives of trauma, two enigmas of emotional and physical destruction, two human responses to the shock of an unbearable reality of death and pain, and two linguistic acts of cultural and of social intervention.

In reading law through literature, and in deciphering the meaning and the impact of the literary speech act through the meaning and the impact of "the trial of the century"; in asking how Tolstoy illuminates the O. J. Simpson case and how the real case speaks from inside Tolstoy's novella, my interest is not simply—not primarily—to add yet another commentary to a much debated and much commented on case, but to articulate—through the example of the case—an innovative theoretical perspective on the highly problematic and yet, in my view, absolutely fundamental relation of the law to the larger phenomenon of cultural or collective trauma. Through a philosophical analysis of the notorious criminal trial, I will demonstrate the ways in which the law remains professionally blind to this phenomenon with which it is nevertheless quite crucially and indissociably tied up. I argue that it is because of what the law cannot and does not see that a judicial case becomes a legal trauma in its own right and is therefore bound to repeat itself through a traumatic legal repetition. This compulsion to a legal repetition (like the one that is demonstrated through the O. J. Simpson case) is accounted for by narratives of trauma (Tolstoy's story will in turn address this issue and highlight it in its own specific literary way).

Legal memory is constituted, in effect, not just by the "chain of law" and by the conscious repetition of precedents, but by a forgotten chain of cultural wounds and by compulsive or unconscious legal repetitions of traumatic, wounding legal cases. My analysis will show how historically unconscious legal repetitions inadvertently play out in the historical arena the political unconscious of the law (the unconscious of past legal cases). These traumatic repetitions illustrate, therefore, in legal history, the Freudian notion of "a return of the repressed"; in the ghost of the return of a traumatizing legal case, what compulsively, historically returns from the forgotten legal past is the repressed of the judicial institution.

The relevance and the significance of this comprehensive theoretical perspective extend far beyond the limits of the O. J. Simpson case and its particular parameters. As a singularly eloquent example, the trial of the century becomes itself not just a vehicle, a leverage for this larger understanding, but an allegory of its need and of its urgency.

II

A Trial for Our Times

How does a trial come to claim the status of "the trial of the century"?[5] What was it in the O. J. Simpson case that has been grasped as so revealing, momentous, and uniquely symptomatic of the very nature of our times?

---

5. The O. J. Simpson trial is not the only trial that has been called "the trial of the century." "A number of high-profile 20th-century courtroom events . . . have each in turn been dubbed the trial of the century," writes Marjorie B. Garber (who analyzes the Scopes trial and the Rosenberg trial) in *Symptoms of Culture* (New York: Routledge, 1998), 107. Gerald F. Uelman caustically notes that his research "has uncovered at least thirty-two trials since 1900 that have been called 'the trial of the century'" (*Lessons from the Trial: The People v. O. J. Simpson* [Kansas City: Andrews and McMeel, 1996], 204. I would suggest, nonetheless, that the redundancy of the title does not undermine the accuracy of its expressive historical significance. In referring to a trial as "the trial of the century," the media names a visceral public perception that the trial is a mirror of something larger than itself, and that the courtroom drama marks the ways in which a larger cultural crisis has come to a head. This perception is fundamentally correct. The O. J. Simpson criminal trial is nevertheless unique in that, as Erwin Chemerinsky has noted, "it received more media attention than any other legal proceeding in American or world history" ("Lawyers Have Free Speech Rights, Too: Why Gag Orders on Trial Participants Are Almost Always Unconstitutional," *Loyola of Los Angeles Entertainment Law Journal* 17 [1997]: 311–31). Other trials that have been called "the trial of the century" include the 1921 trial of Italian-born anarchists Nicola Sacco and Bartolomeo Vanzetti; the 1925 Scopes ("Monkey") Trial; the 1945–46 Nuremberg War Crimes Tribunal; and the 1951 treason (espionage) trial of Julius and Ethel Rosenberg. It is interesting to note that, in addition to major political and international crimes, several of these notorious trials of the (twentieth) century deal with private atrocities and in particular, with the murder and abuse of women and children: the 1924 trial of Nathan Leopold and Richard Loeb for the murder of a fourteen-year-old boy; the 1932 trial of Richard Bruno Hauptmann for the kidnapping and killing of Charles Lindbergh's baby; and the 1954 trial of Sam Sheppard, a prominent physician, for the beating to death of his wife Marilyn (thirty-one years old and four months pregnant). The O. J. Simpson criminal case is the last "trial of the century." In 1906, the first trial of the century evokes a similar triangular criminal scene, in which Harry K. Thaw, the madly jealous (millionaire) husband of Evelyn Nesbit, a chorus girl, is prosecuted for the murder of his wife's lover, the famous architect Stanford White (killed while dining atop Madison Square Garden, designed by him).

In a cover story that presented the case under the heading, "A Trial for Our Times," *Time* magazine suggested two definitions of the concept of legal event: "(1) what really happened, the facts, and (2) what people believe happened, the immense tapestry of folklore and conviction and myth that surrounds an event like the Simpson-Goldman murders. Category No. 1 addresses the needs of justice and history. But category No. 2 is important . . . in its own way." The purpose of a trial is, presumably, to transmute events from category number 2 to category number 1. But even if the legal process in this case has not achieved the transformation of the striking mythic images and witnessing beliefs into undoubted facts, the event behind the trial nonetheless remains sufficiently significant and sufficiently defined to *define the era* as a master-narrative, the key plot of "an unbeatably lurid end-of-the-millennium American" mixture of "race . . . , sex, celebrity, media hype, justice and injustice." "Sometimes," *Time* goes on to reflect, "a trial plays out like a culture's collective dream," acting out "society's deepest passions: its fears, prejudices and desires."[6]

The dream, of course, is not just fantasy but is composed—like any dream—of fragments of reality. To render even more acute this reading of the O. J. Simpson trial as a cultural dream, I would add that a *collective* dream is, paradoxically enough, an unconscious and yet *public secret:* a secret that, while remaining unconscious, translates itself into a public spectacle—that of the courtroom ritual—which then becomes the ritual of an *obsession,* an obsessional dream. It was, then, as an acting out of society's unconscious and of the culture's open or collective secrets that the brutal murders of Simpson's ex-wife, Nicole Brown,

---

It is interesting to note that, even in a symposium on international law and its legal "conceptualization" of contemporary ("crimes against humanity") violence, Michael P. Scharf (in a discussion of the Tadic case) moves quite naturally (in passing) to the O. J. Simpson case, which he mentions in the same category with "other renowned trials" (to differentiate them from the Tadic trial): "the treason trial of Ethel and Julius Rosenberg, the Chicago Seven trial, the Watergate trials, the Rodney King case and the O. J. Simpson trial" ("The Prosecutor v. Dusko Tadic: An Appraisal of the First International War Crimes Trial since Nuremberg," in "Symposium: Conceptualizing Violence: Present and Future Developments in International Law: Panel II: Adjudicating Violence: Problems Confronting International Law and Policy on War Crimes and Crimes against Humanity," *Albany Law Review* 60 [1997]: 863).

6. Lance Morrow, "A Trial for Our Times," *Time,* October 9, 1995, 28.

and of her companion Ronald Goldman, set the stage for "the defining trial of the 1990s" (28).

An editorial in *the Boston Globe* entitled "Sad, but True: Titillating Case Defines Our Times," agreed emphatically, if with a different emphasis; it described the way in which the impact of the O. J. Simpson case overshadowed the more consequential impact of major political events. "History textbooks of the future will make much of the Republican re-alignment. . . . They will talk about the lightning victory in the Gulf War. . . . They may even linger on the travails of Bill Clinton. But we will tell our children that, more than any of those things, our world . . . was shaped by the O. J. Simpson trial. Like it or not, it is the defining event of our time." "Many commentators are arguing that America, not simply Simpson, was on trial. . . . That's too big a thought," the article concludes. "We know one thing, though: America, even if not on trial, was at the trial. And we will be there for a long time."[7]

In the *Los Angeles Times,* the trial as the event that marks the century was read not through the fascination of the crowd of its spectators, nor through the crime that the proceedings put on trial (Simpson's or America's), but through the very legal execution or performance of the trial: the way in which the diversity of race and sex defined not just the secret crime scene but the spectacular scene of the trial. Only in the twentieth century, indeed, could a trial take place with a woman at the head of the prosecution and a black attorney at the head of the defense.[8] The trial's definition of the century, in this view, proceeded not from its statements but from its utterance; what was distinctive in the trial was its *voice:* "*We heard the American voice* in so many registers and using so many different kinds of diction, sounding itself in so many accents. . . . These days, both sexes and an astonishing cross-section of this country's ethnic resources are right in the middle of major events as significant players."[9]

<hr>

7. David Shribman, "Sad but True: Titillating Case Defines Our Times," *Boston Globe,* October 8, 1995, A32.

8. Not to speak of a presiding judge who is neither black nor white. See also Cynthia Kwei Yung Lee, "Beyond Black and White: Racializing Asian Americans in a Society Obsessed with O. J.," *Hastings Women's Law Journal* 6 (1995): 167–207.

9. Stanley Crouch, "The Agonizing Whine Down," *Los Angeles Times,* October 8, 1995, M1.

Law and Trauma[10]

I would suggest, for my part, that what gives "the trial of the century" its philosophical dimension (beyond its social meaning) and its historic

10. The word *trauma* means wound, especially one produced by sudden physical injury. The original use of the term derives from medicine; it has later been borrowed by psychoanalysis and by psychiatry to designate a blow to the self (and to the tissues of the mind), a shock that creates a psychological split or rupture, an emotional injury that leaves a lasting damage in the psyche. Psychological trauma occurs as a result of an over-whelming, uncontrollable, and terrifying experience, usually a violent event or events or the prolonged exposure to such events. The emotional damage often remains hidden, as though the person were unharmed. The full scope of the symptoms manifests itself only belatedly, sometimes years and years later. The trigger of the symptoms is often an event that unconsciously reminds the subject of the original traumatic scene, and is thus lived as a repetition of the trauma. Trauma thus results in lifelong psychological liabilities, and continues to have delayed after-effects throughout one's existence. Classic examples of traumatic catalysts include wars, concentration camp experiences, prison experiences, terrorism incidents, auto and industrial accidents, and childhood traumas such as incest or sexual and physical abuse. Classic examples of traumatic symptoms include anxiety (for signs of danger), or, conversely, numbness and depression, addictions, compulsive repetition—in thought, speech or fantasy—of the traumatic situation or conversely, amnesia, and repetitive nightmares in which the traumatic event is reproduced.

It is understood today that trauma can be collective as well as individual and that traumatized communities are something distinct from assemblies of traumatized persons (see Kai Erikson, "Notes on Trauma and Community," in *Trauma: Explorations in Memory*, ed. Cathy Caruth [Baltimore: Johns Hopkins University Press, 1995], 183–99). Oppressed groups that have been persistently subject to abuse, injustice, or violence suffer collective trauma, much like soldiers who have been exposed to war atrocities. The twentieth century can be defined as a century of trauma.

In recent years, trauma has received a renewed attention both in the humanities and in the social sciences—from psychiatrists, physicians, therapists, brain researchers, sociologists, political thinkers, philosophers, historians, and literary critics. Following in the footsteps of postwar Europe, post-Vietnam America has brought to the fore of contemporary research groundbreaking neurobiological, biochemical, and psychological studies of what is known as PTSD, or post-traumatic stress disorder. PTSD "reflects the imposition" and "engraving" on the mind and on memory of "the unavoidable reality of horrific events, the taking over of the mind, psychically and neurobiologically, by an event that it cannot control" and that it therefore suffers repeatedly beyond the shock of the first moment and beyond the terror of the original occurrence (Cathy Caruth, *Unclaimed Experience: Trauma, Narrative, and History* [Baltimore: Johns Hopkins University Press, 1996], 57). But PTSD, Caruth writes, is not merely an effect of destruction; it is also "an enigma of survival" (57–58). Indeed, "trauma theory often divides itself into two basic trends: the focus on trauma as the 'shattering' of a previously whole self and the focus on the survival function of trauma as allowing one to get through an overwhelming experience" (131). "It is only by recognizing traumatic experience as a paradoxical relation between destructiveness and survival that we can . . . recognize the legacy of . . . catastrophic experience" (58). See also Caruth's introductions to the interdisciplinary collection *Trauma*, 3–12, 151–57. For a discussion of the history of the notion of trauma and for recent attempts to define it, see Charles R. Figley, ed., *Trauma and Its Wake*, 2 vols. (New York: Brunner-Mazel, 1985–86).

depth (beyond the moment's fascination), what makes it a landmark trial of historical significance, are three profound features:

1. Its complex traumatic structure;
2. Its cross-legal nature, or the repetition it enacts of another trial; and
3. Its attempt to define legally something that is not reducible to legal concepts.

Despite its topicality in modern thought, trauma theory has not yet penetrated jurisprudential studies. Since the consequence of every criminal offense (as well as of its legal remedy) is literally a trauma (death, loss of property, loss of freedom, fear, shock, physical and emotional destruction), I advance the claim that trauma—individual as well as social—is the basic underlying reality of the law. Through the O. J. Simpson case, I illustrate this claim and analyze its implications (for law, for literature, for history, for culture).

For trauma theories generally and for discussions of trauma in specific settings, see, among others, Bessel A. van der Kolk, Alexander C. McFarlane, and Lars Weisaeth, eds., *Traumatic Stress: The Effects of Overwhelming Experience on Mind, Body, and Society* (New York: Guilford Press, 1996); Yael Danieli, Nigel S. Rodley, and Lars Weisaeth, eds., *International Responses to Traumatic Stress: Humanitarian, Human Rights, Justice, Peace and Development Contributions, Collaborative Actions, and Future Initiatives*, foreword by Boutros Boutros-Ghali (Amityville, N.Y.: Baywood, 1996); Bessel A. van der Kolk, ed., *Post-Traumatic Stress Disorder: Psychological and Biological Sequelae* (Washington, D.C.: American Psychiatric Press, 1984); Bessel A. van der Kolk, ed., *Psychological Trauma* (Washington, D.C.: American Psychiatric Press, 1987); Arnold Rothstein, ed. *The Reconstruction of Trauma: Its Significance in Clinical Work* (Madison, Conn.: International Universities Press, 1986); Robert Jay Lifton, *The Broken Connection: On Death and the Continuity of Life* (New York: Basic Books, 1979); Henry Krystal, ed., *Massive Psychic Trauma* (New York: International Universities Press, 1968); H. W. Chalsma, *The Chambers of Memory: PTSD in the Life Stories of U.S. Vietnam Veterans* (Northvale, N.J.: Jason Aronson, 1998); Joy D. Osofsky, ed., *Children in Violent Society* (New York: Guilford Press, 1997); Alice Miller, *Thou Shalt Not Be Aware: Society's Betrayal of the Child,* trans. Hildegarde Nannum and Hunter Nannum (New York: New American Library, 1984); Judith Lewis Herman, *Trauma and Recovery: The Aftermath of Violence from Domestic abuse to Political Terror* (New York: Basic Books, 1997); Inger Agger and Soren Buus Jensen, *Trauma and Healing under State Terrorism* (London and Atlantic Highlands, N.J.: Zed Books, 1996); Inger Agger, *The Blue Room: Trauma and Testimony among Refugee Women: A Psycho-Social Exploration,* trans. Mary Bille (London and Atlantic Highlands, N.J.: Zed Books, 1994); Dori Laub and Nanette Auerhahn, "Knowing and Not Knowing Massive Psychic Trauma: Forms of Traumatic Memory," *International Journal of Psychoanalysis* 74 (1993): 287–302; Nadine Fresco, "Remembering the Unknown," *International Review of Psychoanalysis* vol. 11 (1984): 417–27; Robert Jay Lifton, *The Nazi Doctors: Medical Killing and the Psychology of Genocide* (New York: Basic Books, 1986), *Thought Reform and the Psychology of Totalism: A Study of "Brainwashing" in China* (New York: Norton, 1969), and *Death in Life: Survivors of Hiroshima* (New York: Basic Books, 1967); D. W. Winnicott, "The Concept of Trauma in Relation to the Development of the Individual within the Family," and "Fear of Breakdown," in *Psychoanalytic Explorations,* ed. Clare Winnicott, Ray Sheperd, and Madeleine Davis (Cambridge: Harvard University Press, 1989); and Bruno Bettelheim, "Trauma and Reintegration," in *Surviving and Other Essays* (New York: Vintage Books, 1952).

I would suggest, moreover, that these three features are perhaps in general characteristic of every major trial with historical significance and certainly of major controversial trials that immediately grow into public or political "affairs" and whose symbolic impact is immediately perceived in the intensity with which they tend at once to *focus* public discourse and to *polarize* public opinion.

1. The Complex Traumatic Structure of the Trial (Race and Gender)

Every trial is related to an injury, a trauma for which it compensates and that it attempts to remedy and overcome. The three features I have mentioned (by which I define the archetypal theoretical significance of the trial of the century) are all related to the ostentatious way in which the structure of the trial, in this case, revealed itself to be supported by the structure of a trauma. The trial attempted to *articulate* the trauma so as to *control* its damage. But it is the structure of the trauma, I submit, that in the end controlled the trial. The trial has become itself a *vehicle of trauma:* a vehicle of aggravation of traumatic consequences rather than a means of their containment and of their legal resolution. I argue, therefore, that the case encapsulates the drama and the mystery, not simply of a link, but of a real *parallel between traumatic structures and legal proceedings:* a parallel whose consequences are momentous, and yet which neither legal theory nor psychoanalytic theory has recognized, because they do not work together (and are, for the most part, completely unaware of one another). Trauma theory, I argue, can become a powerful tool for the analysis of law.[11] This is what this essay will attempt to demonstrate.

---

11. In much the same way, trauma theory has become a powerful tool for the analysis of literature. See the remarkable philosophical and literary analyses in Caruth, *Unclaimed Experience*. See also Geoffrey H. Hartman, "On Traumatic Knowledge and Literary Studies," *New Literary History* 26 (1995): 537; Maurice Blanchot, *The Writing of the Disaster*, trans. Ann Smock (Lincoln: University of Nebraska Press, 1986); essays by Bataille, Bloom, Felman, Lanzmann, and Newmark in Caruth, *Trauma*; Jacques Derrida, "Passages: From Traumatisms to Promise," interview by Elisabeth Weber, in Weber, *Points . . . Interviews, 1974–1994* (Stanford, Calif.: Stanford University Press, 1995); Jean-François Lyotard, "Critical Reflections," in *Artforum* 29 (1991): 92, and "Ticket to a New Decor (Millennium)," *Harper's* 276 (1988): 26; Michael Holquist, "A New Tour of Babel: Recent Trends Linking Comparative Literature Departments, Foreign Language Departments, and Area Studies Programs," in *ADFL* 27 (1995): 6–12; Thomas Keenan, *Fables of Responsibility: Aberrations and Predicaments in Ethics and Politics* (Stanford, Calif.: Stanford University Press, 1997); Thomas Pepper, *Singularities: Extremes of Theory in the Twentieth Century* (Cambridge: Cambridge University Press, 1997); Geoffrey H. Hartman, ed., *Holo-*

What makes the Simpson trial unforgettable, indeed, is the way in which the legal process followed a traumatic process and the proceedings paralleled traumatic structures. What makes the trial unforgettably complex, however, is the way in which *two* traumas—that of race

caust Remembrance: The Shapes of Memory (Oxford: Blackwell, 1994); Elaine Scarry, *The Body in Pain: The Making and Unmaking of the World* (New York: Oxford University Press, 1985); Jacqueline Rose, *States of Fantasy* (Oxford: Clarendon Press, 1995); Laura E. Tanner, *Intimate Violence: Reading Rape and Torture in Twentieth-Century Literature* (Bloomington: Indiana University Press, 1994); Jacqueline Rose, *Why War?—Psychoanalysis, Politics, and the Return to Melanie Klein* (Oxford: Blackwell, 1993); Felman and Laub, *Testimony*; Ernest van Alphen, *Caught by History: Holocaust Effects in Contemporary Art, Literature, and Theory* (Stanford, Calif.: Stanford University Press, 1997); Dori Laub and Daniel Podel, "Art and Trauma," *International Journal of Psychoanalysis* 67 (1995): 991–1005.

Related works implicating trauma in philosophy and in the conjunction of philosophy, psychoanalysis, and literary theory include (among others) Emmanuel Levinas, *Ethique et infini* (Paris: Fayard, 1982), *Le Temps et l'autre* (Paris: Quadrige/PUF, 1994), "As If Consenting to Horror," *Critical Inquiry* 15 (1989): 485, "Reflections on the Philosophy of Hitlerism," *Critical Inquiry* 17 (1990): 62, *Totality and Infinity: An Essay on Exteriority*, trans. Alphonso Lingis (Pittsburgh: Duquesne University Press, 1969), and "The Face of a Stranger," *UNESCO Courier*, July–August 1992, 66; Michel de Certeau, *Heterologies*, trans. Brian Massumi (Minneapolis: University of Minnesota Press, 1986), and *The Writing of History*, trans. Tom Conley (New York: Columbia University Press, 1988); Jacques Derrida, *Adieu (à Emmanuel Levinas)* (Paris: Galilée, 1997), *Resistances: De la psychanalyse* (Paris: Galilée, 1996), *Passions* (Paris: Galilée, 1993), *Limited, Inc.*, trans. Samuel Weber (Evanston, Ill.: Northwestern University Press, 1988), *Memoires: For Paul de Man* (New York: Columbia University Press, 1986), and *Writing and Difference*, trans. Alan Bass (Chicago: University of Chicago Press, 1978); Vladimir Jankélévitch, *L'Imprescriptible* (Paris: Seuil, 1986); Jean-François Lyotard, "A Postmodern Fable," *Yale Journal of Criticism* 6 (1993) 237, *The Differend: Phrases in Dispute*, trans. Georges Van Den Abbeele (Minneapolis: University of Minnesota Press, 1988), *Heidegger and "the Jews,"* trans. Andreas Michel and Mark Roberts (Minneapolis: University of Minnesota Press, 1990), *La Condition postmoderne* (Paris: Minuit, 1979), and *Political Writings*, trans. Bill Readings and Kevin Paul Geiman (Minneapolis: University of Minnesota Press, 1993); Pierre Vidal-Naquet, *Les Assassins de la mémoire* (Paris: La Découverte, 1987); Gillian Rose, *Mourning Becomes the Law* (Cambridge: Cambridge University Press, 1996); Barbara E. Johnson, *A World of Difference, The Critical Difference*, and *Défigurations. Du langage poétique* (Paris: Flammarion, 1979); Michael Levine, *Writing through Repression: Literature, Censorship, Psychoanalysis* (Baltimore: Johns Hopkins University Press, 1994); Paul de Man, *Allegories of Reading* (New Haven: Yale University Press, 1979), *The Rhetoric of Romanticism* (New York: Columbia University Press, 1984), *Blindness and Insight* (Minneapolis: University of Minnesota Press, 1983), and *The Resistance to Theory* (Minneapolis: University of Minnesota Press, 1986); Cathy Caruth and Deborah Esch, eds., *Critical Encounters: Reference and Responsibility in Deconstructive Writing* (New Brunswick, N.J.: Rutgers University Press, 1995); Slavoj Žižek, *For They Know Not What They Do* (New York: Verso, 1991); Ned Lukacher, *Primal Scenes: Literature, Philosophy, Psychoanalysis* (Ithaca: Cornell University Press, 1986); Cathy Caruth, *Empirical Truths and Critical Fictions* (Baltimore: Johns Hopkins University Press, 1991); Christopher Miller, *Blank Darkness* (Chicago: University of Chicago Press, 1985); James Baldwin, *The Evidence of Things Not Seen* (New York: Holt, Rinehart and Winston, 1985); Anna Deveare Smith, *Fires in the Mirror: Crown Heights, Brooklyn, and Other Identities* (New York: Anchor Books, 1993), and *Twilight: Los Angeles, 1992* (New York: Anchor Books, 1994).

and that of gender—have been set *in competition* with each other in the adversarial structure of the lawyers' arguments in such a way as to confuse and radically complicate both the *perception of the trauma* that the trial strove to remedy and the very question of *who was the victim* of the case: the abused and murdered wife or the wrongfully or hastily accused black husband? At the focus of the trial, therefore, *two* forms of victimization and abuse (race abuse and sex abuse) paradoxically enter into competition and mobilize their anger and their pain to dispute each other's claim for justice: *two traumas* paradoxically attempt to overpower one another and to silence each other's outcry.

But in these two competing narratives of trauma—in the conflicting stories of the prosecution (which blames an abusive husband for the murder of his wife) and of the defense (which blames the justice system for its racial bias and an abusive law enforcement body for a rush to an arrest and an unfounded inculpation of the husband)—there is an ironic symmetry: both the husband and the agents of the law are supposed to give protection but end up inflicting harm (confusingly, deceptively) precisely under their protective guise.

Civilization and Domesticated Violence, or History and Repetition at the End of the Millennium

It is perhaps not a coincidence if such a trial takes place at the close of the twentieth century, a century whose history of wars and violence has taught us how to recognize traumatic symptoms and events of trauma (that once seemed extraordinary) as part of *normal*, ordinary life; a century of civil rights but also of unprecedented *civilized abuses*. It is, thus, not by chance perhaps if the trial of the century comes up, in parallel, with two (contradictory) interpretations of *deceptive* violence and with two legal demystifications of the confusing, intimate, domestic, *civilized* kind of abuse that masks itself as closeness or protection.

What stands at the center of the trial, therefore, is not only the trauma but the blindness it induces, the radical confusion with which the trauma is tied up because of the deceptive package of the violence (marriage, love, police protection, justice). The trial strives to cancel out this blindness, to give the hidden trauma legal visibility. Yet, in the adversarial structure of the litigation, the two "domestic" traumas (gender, race) also dispute, deny each other's claim to visibility. Each trauma, in competing for exclusive visibility, at the same time *blinds* us to the other. The result is that the trial can by no means *totalize*, or *give to see* in its totality, the trauma underlying it. The complexity of the traumatic structure of the trial thus effectively prevented the trauma from becoming fully visible, in creating a specific form of judicial *blindness* that, paradoxically, was part of the legal achievement of the trial.[12]

2. The Cross-Legal Nature of the Trial

I forge the concept of "cross-legal" (on the model of "cross-cultural") to designate a trial's reference to another trial, of which it recapitulates the memory, the themes, the legal questions, or the arguments, and whose legal structure it repeats or reenacts—unwittingly or by deliberate design.

Indeed, in everyone's perception, black or white (although in different manners and with different readings), the Simpson trial looked like a return of the ghost of the Rodney King trial. For the defense, which underscored the repetition for its own strategic purpose through Mark Fuhrman's racist monologues, the O. J. Simpson trial was a confirmation of the same police corruption and brutality and of the same racist complicity (or white conspiracy) that King was the victim of. In spite of his assimilation with the white community, Simpson became a double of black motorist Rodney King, similarly chased or hunted on the highway and (presumably) equally indicted and scapegoated merely for the color of his skin. From the defense's point of view, the outline of this repetition gave to see or put in evidence the real subject of the trial, which was not so much the murder of the wife as the bitter conflict between so-called white justice and a persecuted black community. For the prosecution, on the other hand, and for those who found the evidence of Simpson's guilt incontrovertible, the trial was a repetition in a different sense: what was ironically here reenacted was the *first* King trial—the Simi Valley trial—*in reverse*, since the legal process,

---

12. For writers who struggle against this fragmentation of our legal fields of vision and who work to counteract these shadows of invisibility and of judicial blindness cast by the race trauma and the gender trauma on each other, see, among others, Angela P. Harris, "Race and Essentialism in Feminist Legal Theory," *Stanford Law Review* 42 (1990): 581–616; and Kimberlé Crenshaw, "Mapping the Margins: Intersectionality, Identity Politics, and Violence against Women of Color," *Stanford Law Review* 93 (1991): 1241–99. See also Cheryl I. Harris, "Myths of Race and Gender in the Trials of O. J. Simpson and Susan Smith: Spectacles of Our Times," *Washburn Law Journal* 35 (1996): 225–53 (Harris examines how the O. J. Simpson and the Susan Smith trials reinscribed prevailing ideologies of race and gender).

here as there, resulted similarly (though inversely) in a verdict influenced by a race bias and which similarly chose to disregard or nullify the overwhelming evidence. Whatever is the case, the Simpson trial claimed its status as the trial of the century—a trial that, in other words, can represent or sum up the significance of an entire history—because its structure was indeed susceptible to such a repetition.

I would suggest, moreover, that what distinguishes historic trials is, perhaps, in general, this tendency or this propensity to repetition or to legal duplication. In much the same way as Freud theorizes that great historical events (especially events related to a murder) tend to repeat themselves and are inherently *dual* in nature, because their impact—as a consequence of trauma—takes effect and truly registers in history only through the gap of their traumatic repetition (or through their posttraumatic reenactment),[13] great trials equally make history, I would suggest, in being not merely *about* a trauma but in constituting traumas in their own right; as such, they too are open to traumatic repetition; they too are often structured by *historical dualities,* in which a trial (or a major courtroom drama) unexpectedly reveals itself to be the posttraumatic legal reenactment, or the deliberate historical reopening, of a previous case or of a different, finished, previous trial.[14]

---

13. Sigmund Freud, *Moses and Monotheism,* trans. Katherine Jones (New York: Vintage Books, 1967).

14. Compare, for instance, the way in which the criminal trial of Emile Zola in France (in 1898, following the publication of his pamphlet *J'accuse*—criminal proceedings instituted as the French government's response to this pamphlet's printed trial of the army and the state) reopened the closed case of the Dreyfus affair (reopened, that is, the first trial and conviction of Dreyfus, 1894; the second trial and acquittal of Esterhazy, 1898, for an additional hearing, and for a redeliberation and a reexamination of the evidence), and eventually enabled a rejudgment and a rehabilitation of Dreyfus (1906). In a similar way, I would view the Eichmann trial in Israel (1961) not just as a simple repetition or continuation of the international Nuremberg trials (1945–46) but more specifically as a traumatic reenactment of the (legal trauma of) the previous Kastner trial in Israel (1956). (For an intellectual history of the Dreyfus affair see Jean-Denis Bredin, *The Affair: The Case of Alfred Dreyfus,* trans. Jeffrey Mehlman [New York: G. Braziller, 1986]). For an intellectual history of the Eichmann and Kastner cases, see Pnina Lahav, *Judgment in Jerusalem: Chief Justice Simon Agranat and the Zionist Century* (Berkeley and Los Angeles: University of California Press, 1997), 121–62.

In these series of historic repetitions (or of historical dualities), my point is to underscore and to explore something that is legally specific, or that is specific to the legal structure. Because the social function of the legal institutions is to close disputes and not to open them, the legal system cannot, in principle, accept the reopening of a case (as distinguished from the reconsideration of a precedent) except as a scandal and a shock. A case therefore requires another trial to repeat itself in order either to reverse its verdict or

The O. J. Simpson trial, then, is structured like a trauma not simply in itself (in its own failure to provide a healing to the trauma it was meant to remedy) but *in its historical relation to other trials (and to other traumas)* on whose legal pathos it picks up and whose different claims to justice it repeats and, as it were, accumulates. What is traumatically conjured by the trial is, therefore, a (mostly unconscious) legal memory, the covered but unhealed wounds of a legal history. The trial inadvertently partakes of a trauma that is now not simply individual but is inscribed in the history of trials and whose individual complaint or grievance has now gained historical, collective, *cumulative legal meaning*. Hence, the enigmatic force, the impact of the trial; hence, the enigmatic historical momentum gained by a relatively simple (or reductive) legal argument.

The legal system, in such cases, is *cross-legally* traumatic, or is traumatic across different periods, across different legal situations, sometimes even across different legal cultures. I would suggest that the tremendous impact of the trial of the century comes not just from its immediate, conscious evocation of the Rodney King case (and of its relatively recent legal trauma) but, even more profoundly, from the way in which both Rodney King and O. J. Simpson, in their similar dramatic circumstances, may have conjured up a still less conscious echo of the Dred Scott case (1857), a case whose legal trauma, from a more remote past, still haunts American history and its history of trials, or its (changing) legal culture. As a possible unconscious echo of the Dred Scott case in its hauntingly inflammatory memory, the Simpson-King historical duality (or dual road hunt) may have unconsciously played out, replayed, issues belonging to a different period and to a slightly different legal culture, reopening old wounds of forced recaptures of alleged fugitives by a biased and committedly proslavery legal order. What the trial does, is, therefore, to repeat and to awaken, to *reopen* a traumatic history of trials.

3. The Trial's Excess of Its Legal Definitions

The last feature, which accounts for the privileged historical position of the trial of the century, and which defines its philosophical dimension,

---

to change the understanding or the reading of its evidence. Judicial re-vision must take place through another trial. I believe that such an analytical perspective on historical dualities and on traumatic legal repetition can be illuminating for an understanding of some critical, strategic moments in the history of trials.

is related to the way in which the trial situates itself precisely at the junc-ture—at the very critical convergence—of the legal and of the political.

Can the political as such be analyzed, defined, or circumscribed in legal terms? The German philosopher Karl Jaspers thought that it could not because the two domains (legal, political) are qualitatively hetero-geneous to each other and can by no means overlap with one another.[15] Jaspers argued this opinion in a letter that he wrote in 1960 to his ex-student Hannah Arendt, on the occasion of her undertaking to review for the *New Yorker* the forthcoming Eichmann trial in Jerusalem:

> The political realm [Jaspers insisted] is of an importance that can-not be captured in legal terms (*the attempt to do so is Anglo-Saxon* and a self-deception that masks a basic fact in the functionings of political existence). . . . *A dimension that in being "political" has, as it were, dignity, is larger than law, and is woven into the fabric of fate.*[16]

Larger Than Law

It could certainly be claimed that this argument could equally apply to the O. J. Simpson case: both the fight of race (against racial prejudice) and the fight of gender (against domestic violence) involve, each in its turn, a political dimension that has "dignity." This double political dimension is, indeed, inherently "larger than law" and "is woven into the fabric of fate." This is where the trial's pathos comes from. But could the realm of the struggle for this dignity—this larger political dimension—be addressed in legal terms?

On this question, Arendt takes a different stand than Jaspers. In her answer to his letter, Arendt, who was to become herself a leading political theorist and thinker in America, takes issue with her former teacher's criticism of the "Anglo-Saxon" inclination and redefines in

---

15. The relationship between law and politics has been discussed in a variety of con-texts. Throughout the early decades of this century, for example, legal realists radically challenged the very distinction between politics and law. The legal realists' attack on the autonomy (and pseudoneutrality) of law consequently lay the foundations for many con-temporary movements, including the law and society movement, law and economics, critical legal studies, legal feminism and critical race theory. Jaspers's counterchallenge, his European skepticism and his philosophical question is, however, not about the polit-ical (nonautonomous) nature of the law but about the capacity of the law (of legal con-cepts) to accurately articulate (exhaust, truly define) the political.

16. Karl Jaspers, letter to Hannah Arendt, December 16, 1960, in *Hannah Arendt/Karl Jaspers: Correspondence, 1926–1969*, ed. Lotte Kohler and Hans Saner, trans. Robert Kimber and Rita Kimber (New York: Harcourt Brace Jovanovich, 1992), 413.

her own terms the way in which the Eichmann trial illustrates, indeed, the gap, the difference and the tension, but also, paradoxically, the juncture, the indispensable critical convergence, between the realm of the legal and the realm of the political:

> All this may strike you as though I too was attempting to circumscribe the political with legal concepts. And I even admit that as far as the role of the law is concerned, I have been infected by the Anglo-Saxon influence. But quite apart from that, it seems to me to be *in the nature of this case* that *we have no tools to hand except the legal ones* with which we have to judge and pass sentence on *something that cannot even be adequately represented either in legal terms or in political terms.* That is precisely what makes the process itself, namely, the trial, so exciting.[17] (emphasis added)

This reflection holds and could equally account for the trial of the century: the O. J. Simpson case has gained both its unique position and its paradoxical symbolic representativity because it deals, profoundly and obscurely, with "something that cannot even be adequately represented either in legal terms or in political terms." It is, in other words, precisely the trial's irreducibility to the legal concepts that define it that has made it the trial of the century.

This final philosophical and analytic feature of the O. J. Simpson case could in its turn illustrate, perhaps, a general characteristic of important trials. It would be safe to say that every major trial essentially involves "something larger than law." In every major trial, and certainly in every trial of political or of historical significance, something other than law is addressed in legal terms and is submitted to the narrowness of legal definitions. And "that is precisely what makes the process itself, namely, the trial, so exciting."

III

The Murders of the Century (Which Century? or,
from America to Russia)

What can be, therefore, the relevance of literature to such an archetypal legal drama? Could a work of art offer a valid commentary on the real

---

17. Hannah Arendt, letter to Karl Jaspers, December 23, 1960, ibid., 417.

intricacies of a criminal hard case and on the real (philosophical and referential) understanding of the legal controversy of the century?

Since the O. J. Simpson case has been, indeed, collectively discussed and collectively experienced (lived) as a defining trial of our times, is it not surprising, in effect, to find the same case—or its duplicate (a wife's murder followed by the husband's trial)—in a literary text entitled *The Kreutzer Sonata* and written not by an American contemporary but by a Russian writer of the *nineteenth century?* If Tolstoy, the author of this text, seems to know so much about the O. J. Simpson case, could the trial of the century, after all, also paradoxically belong to the nineteenth century?[18]

Indeed, not only does Tolstoy, a century before us, write the story of the trial of the century; then as now, the writing and the publication of the story—(way before the media could be held responsible for its inflation)—wins publicity that seems to be out of proportion to the value or to the importance of the case. Then as now, the drama of the case provokes the same excitement and the same heated division of opinions, the same intensity of controversy and of passionate debate.

The link between the trial and the times, moreover, is also at the center of Tolstoy's text. Having read the manuscript to one of his friends (Prince Urusov), Tolstoy records, in March 1889, the friend's responsiveness as proof of the subject's topicality: "He liked it very much. It is true that it is something new and powerful."[19] Tolstoy is interested, indeed, not just in the contemporary sensitivity of his new topic, but in its impact, in its practical effect: he knows that writing, in this case, writing *this* case, is making an effective *intervention* in the world—committing a didactically political act. "I almost finished *The Kreutzer Sonata* or *How a Husband Killed His Wife*," he writes to his disciple and prospective publisher, Chertkov, in September 1889: "I am glad I wrote it. *I know that people need to be told what is written there.*"[20]

---

18. Would this coincidence of cases mean, then, that Tolstoy is *our contemporary* (implicitly *ahead of his own time*)? Or could it rather mean that we ourselves, in some major respects, are still quite retrograde, that we *have not yet truly come out of the nineteenth century?*

19. Quoted in Henri Troyat, *Tolstoy,* trans. Nancy Amphoux (New York: Penguin Literary Biographies, 1987), 660.

20. Quoted in David Magarshack, afterword to Leo Tolstoy, *The Death of Ivan Ilych and Other Stories* (New York: New American Library, 1960), 301.

Censorship and Fame

Like the O. J. Simpson case, the story of *The Kreutzer Sonata* distinguishes itself, in its own century, by a particular relation to the law. In spite of the fictional character of this innovative literary case of murder of a wife, the publication of the text immediately provokes a scandal and becomes itself a legal case: the censor bans the text, the Russian church decries its immorality, the minister of the interior outlaws it and officially forbids its publication both as a separate volume and in Tolstoy's complete works. Ironically, it is only thanks to Tolstoy's wife, who, in a personal interview with the czar, obtains permission partially to lift the ban (exclusively from the edition of Tolstoy's complete works), that the text can be published at all.

But even before its publication, the case of *The Kreutzer Sonata* becomes a compulsive topic of discussion in Russia's living rooms and in the streets—very like the O. J. Simpson trial in America. "As soon as it had been copied, the book was taken to Moscow . . . ; during the night, unpaid scribes made copies of the text and in less than a week nearly eight hundred lithographed copies were circulating in Saint Petersburg; their numbers doubled, tripled, invaded the provinces. According to Strakhov, people no longer greeted each other in the street with 'How are you?' but with 'Have you read *The Kreutzer Sonata*?' Before the book was even printed, before the censor had given its decision, the case was being hotly debated all over Russia."[21] Tolstoy' daughter, Alexandra, writes in her memoirs:

> It is hard to convey now what took place when, for example, *The Kreutzer Sonata* . . . first appeared. Before [it] had been even passed for the press, hundreds, even thousands of copies were made, which went from hand to hand, were translated into every language and were read everywhere with incredible passion; it sometimes seemed that the public had forgotten all its personal concerns and was living exclusively for the sake of the works of Count Tolstoy. . . . The most important political events were seldom the object of such overwhelming and universal attention.[22]

---

21. Troyat, *Tolstoy*, 664.

22. Quoted in David Mcduff, translator's introduction to Leo Tolstoy, *The Kreutzer Sonata and Other Stories* (New York: Penguin Classics, 1985), 16. Unless otherwise indicated, page numbers in parenthesis refer to this edition.

As in the O. J. Simpson case, what is particularly striking in the case of *The Kreutzer Sonata* is the outstanding contradiction between the seeming triviality of the private story and the impressive magnitude and scope of the community's emotional (and economical) investment in it, the utter political importance that the audience's response confirms to the drama of the crime and of the judgment, unaccountably magnified into a symbol of the times, and into a collective trial of the century.

What, then, does Tolstoy have to tell us, not merely about *The Kreutzer Sonata*, but about the O. J. Simpson case? What can the literary text teach us that can shed light on the trial of the century?

IV

Marriage and Violence

The Kreutzer Sonata is the story of a husband who killed his wife, was tried for murder, and was legally acquitted and set free. The story—about jealousy, hostility, sex, quarrels, murder, trial, and acquittal—is narrated to a stranger on a train by the now converted husband-murderer, as an unsolicited autobiographical confession.[23]

The confession, or the husband's retrospective testimony, is at the same time an *avowal* of his guilt and a *lesson* that he feels compelled to share about a retrospective insight he has gained—too late—into his tragedy: an insight into what he now believes to be a constitutional *relation between marriage and (domestic) violence*. Having thought about his case, he has come to be convinced that his outrageous, monstrous drama is in fact banal, ubiquitous; that violence, in other words, inhabits marriage as a rule and not as an exception or an accident (although everyone denies it). It is this unseen point about marriage, this blind

---

23. For interpretations of Tolstoy's text see, among others, Robert Jackson, "In the Darkness of the Night: Tolstoy's *Kreutzer Sonata* and Dostoyevsky's *Notes from the Underground*," in *Dialogues with Dostoevsky: The Overwhelming Questions* (Stanford, Calif.: Stanford University Press, 1993), 208–27; Dorothy Green, "*The Kreutzer Sonata*: Tolstoy and Beethoven," in *Tolstoy's Short Fiction*, ed. Michael R. Katz (New York: Norton, 1991); Stephen Baehr, "Art and *The Kreutzer Sonata*: A Tolstoyan Approach," ibid., 448–55; all these readings are mainstream, "orthodox" readings of Tolstoy. For a heretic's reading, see the provocatively insightful chapter on Tolstoy in Andrea Dworkin, *Intercourse* (New York: Free Press, 1987), 3–20.

spot of society, of men and women and of culture, that his confession—
his example—at the same time illustrates and puts on trial.[24]

> They asked me in court how I killed her, what I used to do it with.
> Imbeciles! They thought I killed her that day, the fifth of October,
> with a knife. It wasn't that day I killed her, it was much earlier.
> *Exactly in the same way as they're killing their wives now, all of them.*
> (60; emphasis added)[25]

Addictions

The speaker and the story's hero, an aristocrat named Pozdnyshev, had
led a promiscuous sexual life until his marriage at age thirty. This
promiscuity—characteristic of most men in his social circle—evolved
into what he himself now diagnoses as a genuine sexual addiction:[26]

> I had become what is known as a fornicator. Being a fornicator is a
> physical condition similar to that of a morphine addict, an alco-
> holic or a smoker of opium. Just as a morphine addict, an alcoholic
> or a smoker of opium is no longer a normal individual, so a man
> who has had several women for the sake of his pleasure is no
> longer a normal person but one who has been spoiled for all time—
> a fornicator. And just as an alcoholic or a morphine addict can

---

24. It is the universalizing, threateningly generalizing nature of this proposition, I
would argue (and not the public's simple prurience about Tolstoy's private life and about
what might be, presumably, his own unique confession), that accounts for the scandal,
for the heat and for the controversy caused by *The Kreutzer Sonata* (by the daring literary
treatment of the legal case). It is, in other words, not the singularity or the exceptional
nature of the case of the murder of the wife but, on the contrary, its general and unexceptional validity that Tolstoy precisely emphasizes in *his* trial of the century: the general
and unexceptional (though generally invisible) relation between marriage and abuse
(marriage and violence), which the case merely reveals in bringing it to its concretely visible extremes.

This unsettling emphasis is central to my reading and is in any case constitutive of
my own understanding of the story; it accounts for the scandalous boldness of the text
and in particular, for its provocative and paradoxical "didacticism," that is, its *collective*
lesson.

25. Tolstoy, *The Kreutzer Sonata.*

26. On sexual addiction as a clinical symptom of trauma defined by "a life of self-
destruction" see Patrick Carnes, *Don't Call It Love: Recovery from Sexual Addiction* (New
York: Bentham Books, 1991).

immediately be recognized by his features and physical manner-
isms, so can a fornicator. A fornicator may restrain himself, struggle for self-control, but never again will his relation to women be
simple, clear . . . I, too, became a fornicator and remained one, and
that was my undoing. (41)

Looking back at his own life before the marriage, he thus sees himself,
along with all his male friends, as "debauchees in our thirties with hundreds of the most varied and abominable crimes against women on our
consciences" (41). These crimes against women do not derive from the
physical act or from the sexual addiction in itself, but from the *moral
attitude* that goes along with it:

> Debauchery isn't something physical. Not even the most outra-
> geous physicality can be equated with debauchery. Debauchery—
> real debauchery—takes place when you free yourself from any
> moral regard for the woman you enter into physical relations with.
> But you see, I made the acquisition of that freedom into a matter of
> personal honor. (37)

This attitude, however, coexists in Pozdnyshev with the "intention
of getting married and building for myself the most elevated and
purest of family lives," and with this plan in mind, he looks out for "a
girl who might fill the bill" (42). He finds her, falls in love with her, gets
married.

But from the start the marital intimacy turns into an abyss of
estrangement, quarrels, jealousy, hostility, followed each time by a loving reconciliation. The sole common ground of the husband and the
wife is sex—sex, pregnancies, breast-feeding, and five children in eight
years, who, themselves, are a source of further disagreements, further
worries, quarrels, and disgust.

Between Love and Rage

At first, Pozdnyshev believes that the quarrels are pure accidents and
that his misery is an exception:

> I was tortured . . . by the fact that I was alone in having such a
> wretched relationship with my wife, and that everything was quite

different in other people's marriages. At that stage I was still unaware that this is the common experience, that everyone believes, as I did, that theirs is an exceptional misfortune, and that everyone hides their shameful and exceptional misfortune not only from the eyes of others but also from themselves, and that they refuse to admit its existence. (58)

But later, he perceives a real pattern in the alternation of his married life between love and hate:

I didn't notice it then, but I was regularly affected by bouts of animosity that used to correspond to the bouts of what we called "love." A bout of "love" would be followed by one of animosity; a vigorous bout of "love" would be followed by a long bout of animosity, while a less intense bout of "love" would be followed by a correspondingly shorter bout of animosity. We didn't realize it then, but this "love" and animosity were just two sides of the same coin. (74)

(Whose portrait, in effect, does Tolstoy describe? Could not O. J. Simpson's life equally be understood, accounted for, by this analysis?[27] Would not the O. J. Simpson case in turn answer to, and quite precisely fit into, such *Portrait of a Marriage*?)

We were two convicts serving life sentences of hard labor welded to the same chain, we hated each other, we were making each other's lives hell, and trying all the time not to see it. At that time I had not yet learnt that this hell is the fate of ninety-nine per cent of all couples. (75)[28]

After the birth of the couple's fifth child, the doctors, for health reasons, advise the wife not to get pregnant any more, and she obeys them. Pozdnyshev, who was a jealous husband from the start, becomes even more jealous now, since his thirty-year-old wife—relieved from preg-

---

27. Compare Simpson's statement to an interviewer: "Let's say I committed this crime . . . ; even if I did do this, it would have to have been because I loved her very much." "Whistling in the Dark," interview by Celia Farber, *Esquire*, February 1998, 120.

28. This last paragraph is from Henri Troyat's translation; see Troyat, *Tolstoy*, 667.

nancies and from childbearing—becomes more beautiful and more "coquettish."

"Yes, and then that man appeared," says Pozdnyshev (79).

The Triangle

One day, a violinist by the name of Trukhachevsky visits the couple, and the wife plays music with him at the piano. Pozdnyshev is immediately convinced that this common playing is the expression of a mutual attraction and a mutual seduction between the players. Yet instead of dismissing his guest, he extends an invitation to him to come again, to bring along his violin and give a true concert with his wife. The concert, in which Trukhachevsky and the wife—violin and piano— play together Beethoven's Kreutzer Sonata, takes place. In his obsessive jealousy, Pozdnyshev listens to the music like a voyeur: listening in on the musical harmony and the dramatic tension between the instruments, he furtively spies on the excitement of this common musical performance, as one would have spied on an actual intercourse or sexual performance between the two musicians.

But Trukhachevsky soon leaves with the declared intention of not coming back, and Pozdnyshev himself goes away on a business trip, apparently calmed down. Yet on the train his jealousy, no longer a response to a real situation but only to potential ones, becomes a truly maddening obsession:

> As soon as I got into the railway coach [Pozdnyshev narrates] I lost all control over my imagination: I began to paint for me, in the most lurid fashion, a rapid sequence of pictures which inflamed my jealousy . . . They were all the same thing—of what was happening there, in my absence, of her being unfaithful to me. I was consumed with rage, indignation and a kind of strange, drunken enjoyment of my own hurt pride as I contemplated these pictures, and I couldn't tear myself away from them. I couldn't help looking at them, I couldn't erase them from my mind, and I couldn't stop myself dreaming them up. But that wasn't all: the more I contemplated these imaginary pictures, the more I believed they were real. The luridness with which they appeared before me seemed proof that what I was imagining was in fact reality. (103)

The Murder

Literally intoxicated with his own projected visual hallucinations of his wife's sexual betrayal, Pozdnyshev breaks off his trip and goes back home, unexpected, to surprise his wife and spy on her, with frenzied thoughts of punishing her guilt—which he no longer doubts—on the slightest (so-called) evidence. His fears are not dispelled upon arrival, since he finds the violinist, once again, at his own home.

> For an instant I froze there in the doorway, clutching the poniard behind my back. At the same moment he smiled and started to say, ... "Oh, we were just playing a little music together ..."
> "Goodness, I wasn't expecting ... " she began simultaneously ...
> But neither of them managed to get to the end of their sentences. The same rabid frenzy I had experienced a week previously once more took possession of me. Once again I felt that compulsion to destroy, to subjugate by force, to rejoice in the ecstasy of my furious rage, and I abandoned myself to it.
> Neither of them managed to finish what they were saying ... I rushed at her, still keeping the poniard hidden in case he tried to stop me plunging it into her side, under the breast. That was the spot I'd chosen right from the outset. In the very moment I attacked her, he saw what I was doing, and seized my arm—something I'd never expected he'd do ...
> I wrenched my arm free and went for him without a word ... — he ducked under the piano and was out of the room in a flash. ... I was in a rabid frenzy, and I knew I must be a fearful sight, and was glad of it. I swung my left arm round as hard as I could, and my elbow struck her full in the face. She screamed and let go of my arm. Then, without letting go of the poniard, I gripped her throat in my left hand, threw her back and started to strangle her. How hard her neck was ... She seized my hands in hers, trying to tear them free of her throat, and as if this was the signal for which I'd been waiting, I struck her with the poniard as hard as I could in her left side, beneath the ribs. (111–13)

The wife lies butchered in her blood. She agonizes. As the husband contemplates this bloody sight and absorbs the image of his wife, he is

stunned and shocked by her bruised face; the swollen and unrecogniz-
ably disfigured face confronts him, as though from a picture.

> The first thing that leapt to my gaze was her light gray dress . . . ;
> the dress was stained black all over with blood. . . . What struck me
> most forcibly was her face: it was swollen, and along part of her
> nose and under one eye it was blue with bruises. This was the
> result of the blow I'd given her with my elbow when she'd been
> trying to hold me back. She had no beauty at all now, and I felt
> there was something repulsive about her. (116)

The Battered Face

It is here, when the intensity of the whole narrative translates itself into
one striking visual image; here, when the story reaches its dramatic
(visual) peak through this horrifying, graphic, cinematographic image
of the battered face, that the narrative becomes dramatically evoca-
tive—feature by feature reminiscent—of the similarly horrifying picture of the battered face of Nicole Brown-Simpson: an equally bruised,
swollen, and distorted face whose photographic image was projected,
during the proceedings of the trial of the century, both on the courtroom monitor and on our television screens. Let me, thus, go back for a
brief moment from the dying wife of Pozdnyshev to the murdered wife
of O. J. Simpson, whose swollen and disfigured face we have all seen,
eternalized precisely in those photographs kept in her safe and that
have reached us, through the courtroom monitor, like an uncanny
visual *communication* from beyond the grave, like an unsettling, voice-
less testimony of a battered, murdered woman—the wordless and suppressed appeal of a mute body—now forever silenced. Like Pozdnyshev, we have eyewitnessed this disfigured face. Like Pozdnyshev, we
can bear witness to its horrifying, haunting visual legacy.

But such a face is always seen (and recognized) too late. "We know
now," wrote John Gregory Dunne in *The New York Review of Books*,

> as we always do in the aftermath of bloodshed, that the marriage
> of Nicole and O. J. Simpson prior to their 1992 divorce had been
> volatile, and occasionally violent. There were frequent 911 calls to
> settle domestic disputes, and in 1989 the Los Angeles city attorney

filed a spousal battery complaint against Simpson after a fight on New Year's eve. "He's going to kill me, he's going to kill me," she wept to the officers who answered her 911 call early that New Year's morning. They had found her hiding in the bushes outside her . . . house . . . wearing only sweatpants and a bra; her eye was blackened, her lips cut and swollen, there were scratches on her neck, and bruises on her cheek and forehead. Simpson shouted angrily at the police that it was a "family matter . . . why do you want to make a big deal out of it," and sped away in his Bentley. Cooling down, . . . Nicole refused to press charges. . . . O. J. Simpson pleaded no contest to spousal battery and received the same light sentence that most first-time wife-beaters receive—a small fine, community service and mandatory counseling. After sentence was imposed, the couple issued a joint statement: "Our marriage is as strong today as the day we were married."[29]

Let me return, now, to Pozdnyshev's own wife, and to the husband's final contemplation of the image of her battered face.

What struck me most forcibly was her face: it was swollen, and along part of her nose and under one eye it was blue with bruises. This was the result of the blow I'd given her with my elbow when she'd been trying to hold me back. She had no beauty at all now, and I felt there was something repulsive about her. (116)

She looked up at me with difficulty—she had a black eye—and she said, haltingly: "You've got what you wanted, you've killed me . . ." (117)

I looked at the children, at her battered face with its bruises, and for the first time I forgot about myself, about my marital rights and my injured pride; for the first time I saw her as a human being. And so insignificant did all that had hurt me and made me jealous appear, and so significant what I'd done, that I wanted to press my face to her hand and say: "Forgive me!"—but I didn't dare to. (117)

---

29. John Gregory Dunne, "The Simpsons," *New York Review of Books*, September 22, 1994: 36.

The Trial

The wife dies a few hours later. Pozdnyshev is arrested and is put on trial. He is acquitted, since his crime is deemed to be a crime of passion caused by the betrayal of his wife. His attempt to explain to the court that his wife may not have been unfaithful after all, that the murder was not truly motivated by the wife's betrayal, fails. He thinks the court has not truly understood his case.

> At my trial the whole thing was made to look as though it had been caused by jealousy. Nothing could have been further from the truth. I'm not saying jealousy didn't play any part at all, mind you—it did, but it wasn't the most important thing. At my trial they decided I was a wronged husband who'd killed his wife in order to defend his outraged honour (that's the way they put it in their language). So I was acquitted. During the court hearings I tried to explain what was really at the bottom of it all, but they just thought I was trying to rehabilitate my wife's honour. (80–81)

In prison, while awaiting trial, Pozdnyshev has grasped a truth that has revolutionized his world. "My eyes," he tells us, "have been opened, and I've seen everything in a completely new light. Everything's been turned inside out. It's all inside out!" (38).

It is this obscure truth that he could not articulate during the trial (this truth he could not bring to the knowledge of the court) that he is now trying to communicate in his confession.

V

Portrait of a Case, or the Profile of a Murderer

Let me, now, sum up and analyze the common points between this story and the O. J. Simpson case. We know already that both cases become vehicles for an enlarged political debate and for a broader cultural trial of the times—or of the century (although the times have changed and the century moves up toward us with the O. J. Simpson case). Both cases are composed of an identical chain of events consisting in two basic and defining episodes: (1) the murder of the wife; (2) the trial of the husband. I will distinguish, now, the analytical perspective of the murder from the analytical perspective of the trial and will examine separately the areas of overlap and intersection of the cases, first, in the story of the murder, then, in the story of the trial.

1. The Story of the Murder

Both murders are of an "unfaithful" wife. Both stories, therefore, are about a wife's unfaithfulness—and punishment. Whether the punishment should be attributed to a divine or human justice, to mere coincidence or to a marital revenge, the punishment is death. Both stories are stories of jealousy, and their main character is a possessive husband. Both husbands practice stalking as a means of ascertaining the behavior of their wife. Both cases implicate a triangle, in that the crime scene implicates the unexpected presence or intrusion of a third participant— another man. Both stories dramatize a beating of the wife. Both are, thus, stories of domestic violence. Both cases sketch out the same "portrait of a marriage," in their repeated and compulsive switches between love and hate, desire and enraged hostility. The psychological makeup of the case is, thus, essentially the same. The husband in both cases is a sexual addict. Indeed, domestic violence could be itself another form of addiction—of sex addiction, since in both cases, violence is sexual. After her 911 call, Nicole is found dressed only with a bra; and the stabbing is explicitly described in *The Kreutzer Sonata* as a destructive sexual act, a forced erotic penetration with a knife. The penetration of the knife is common to both stories; both murders are accomplished through a stabbing.

2. The Story of the Trial

If we consider, now, the functions and procedures of the trial, as distinct from the mere logic of the crime, the analogies between Tolstoy's case and the legal case are even more surprising and quite significantly systematic.

Indictments and Acquittals

(a) In both cases, the husband points an accusing finger towards the social order and the social institutions; the husband's case is argued, in both stories, not so much as a defense against the murder but as a prosecution (and indictment) of society.

(b) The *verdict*, in both cases, is the same: *acquittal*. This verdict is, however, rather enigmatic in the context of the literary text, since it stands in explicit contradiction to the husband's own confession that he did in fact commit the murder and is therefore unambiguously guilty. The question thus arises, Why does the literary text need to include at all a legal trial that acquits the husband in contradistinction to the facts? How is the acquittal necessary to the story? How does it partake of the writer's *literary* understanding (or interpretation) of the case? It seems to me that Tolstoy wants to suggest, precisely, by the introduction of the verdict a certain *complicity between the murder and the trial*, between the law and the transgression of the law—a secret but significant complicity between the crime and the society that judges it and puts the criminal on trial. Criminal proceedings are always instituted, in effect, not in the victim's name but in the name of the community whose law is broken. But the community, here, through the symbolism of a verdict that will not convict as its representative communal utterance, speaks in a voice that gives the husband's criminal offense a certain sanction of quasi legitimacy. The murderer, in Tolstoy's text, implicitly acquires (or is legally granted by the court) a certain sort of communal amnesty, in resonance, indeed, with the communal absolution O. J. Simpson has received from his own community and with the communal sanction of legitimacy he has been granted, as a man and as a husband, by the court's pronouncement in the trial of the century.

Messages

(c) A third common denominator between Tolstoy's case and the O. J. Simpson case is that both cases illustrate what I would be call *a pedagogical use of the trial*. By his own explicit definition and avowed intention, Tolstoy is, at this point in life, a didactic writer and his art is a didactic art. *The Kreutzer Sonata* is thus, paradoxically and quite provocatively, a *didactic* story about murder (the murder of a wife). A didactic story is, indeed, a narrative that is subordinated to a lesson, to a message it purports to illustrate or to exemplify.

Now, in the O. J. Simpson case the story of the trial has been equally transformed into the medium of a message. In his closing argument, defense attorney Johnny Cochran thematized explicitly this function or didactic purpose of the trial, in conjuring the jurors to acquit so as to (in his terms) "send a message" to society—about its racism, its corruption, and the fundamental unreliability both of its justice system and of its police department. Since the jury indeed acquitted Simpson, the trial *has* been used to register and to convey this message.

But, in the literary case as in the legal one, I wish to underscore the fact that it is not only the trial but the very murder of the wife that has become *a tool* for the transmission of the message. Cochran's proposition—or his message—in effect ignores, actively forgets that the trial is not simply about Simpson, but about a murder. What does it mean, however, that a message about racism *must be given through this trial* rather than through other channels? To the extent that the verdict in effect *erases* Simpson's murdered wife, or makes the murder—and the murdered woman—totally *irrelevant*, precisely, to the message, the trial in effect *repeats* the murder. The decision inadvertently reenacts the crime in killing once again the victims.

The lesson that the trial in the end incorporates, the pedagogical use of the proceedings, raises, therefore, serious questions about the moral value (the ethical significance) of murder as ideological tool. Since the body of the message is a corpse; since the message must use a dead body to promote and to legitimate itself, to what extent is such a usage—such abstraction of the body—in itself legitimate? This question can be asked both of Tolstoy's text and of the O. J. Simpson trial. Should the wife's corpse be the vehicle, moreover, of someone else's message?

The Failure of the Trial

(d) A fourth and final point of resemblance between Tolstoy's case and the O. J. Simpson case is that what is at the center of both stories is not just a trial but a *failure of the trial*. This failure of the legal framework, of the process, is what I take to be the most significant and most important common point. In Tolstoy's text, the confessing hero talks about this failure, this misfire of the trial, when he says to the narrator (his interlocutor on board the train) that the court has not really understood his case. He was acquitted on the understanding that the murder was a crime of passion, a case of jealousy and "outraged honour." But he himself has understood about the case something altogether different.[30] What it is precisely he has figured out remains obscure and is subject to

---

30. "If jealousy hadn't been the pretext, some other one would have been found" (81).

the reader's own interpretation. But whatever it might be, the court has failed to understand it, in concluding—wrongly—that his protestations at the trial (his insistence that his wife may *not* have been unfaithful after all), his stuttering testimony or his failed attempts at testifying to a different truth, were mere words of courtesy to his wife's memory, a charitable cover-up or a rhetorical attempt to rehabilitate her name: "During the court hearings I *tried to explain what was really at the bottom of it all*, but they just thought I was trying to rehabilitate my wife's honour" (81). The court has failed, thus, both to understand and to translate into a legal language the hero's stuttering search for the truth.

I will argue that the O. J. Simpson case is similarly marked by a *failure of the trial* and that this failure is, in turn, equally essential to an understanding of the case. Indeed, the verdict that set free O. J. Simpson (like the one that has acquitted Pozdnyshev) similarly did not *close* the case, or did not give the *sense of closure* that a verdict is designed precisely to provide. The verdict's effect was not that of an intellectual or an emotional catharsis, but that of an anticlimax that left large portions of the audience of the trial with a sort of emptiness.

I would suggest that, as in Tolstoy's case, this failure of the trial had to do with something that, within the legal framework, could not be seen. *Something that could not be seen and that in fact was not seen by the court was at the center of the trial;* something that the trial could not see was at the story's heart. What is it, therefore, that was not seen or could not be seen in the trial of the century?

"Critical Episodes of Married Life"

I would suggest that part of what could not be seen in Simpson's trial has to do with what Tolstoy precisely points to as culture's *blind spot*, namely, the invisible relation between marriage and domestic violence. In a television interview given a day after the verdict, Brenda Moran, one of the jurors in the O. J. Simpson trial, referred to her juridical experience of looking at the evidence of the domestic violence as a sheer "waste of time." As a key witness to the trial, she therefore testified to the recalcitrant *invisibility of the domestic violence*, as well as to the jury's legal and judicial act of *looking through the beaten body* (of looking through and past the pictures of the battered face), in spite of the lawyers' endeavor to expose the evidence—the visual traces of the husband's blows—precisely to the jurors' *eyes* and thus to give the battered face a legal visibility. But in their verdict and, especially, in the absence of deliberation that preceded it, the jury did not so much "nullify the evidence" as it *nullified its visibility*, and, in so doing, nullified the visibility of the face. The jury used, in other words, the court's authority to ratify, indeed, the inherent cultural *invisibility* of the battered face.

The jury, therefore, *did not see the domestic violence*. And, in line with Cochran's claim that Simpson had a normal marriage subject to "domestic discord," which merely proved that his client was "not perfect," juror Moran even insisted, in that interview, that Simpson was not even an abusive husband; all the trial proved, she said, was *one episode* of violence (or maybe two). One or two "episodes" of violence do not make out of someone an abuser.

Curiously enough, *The Kreutzer Sonata*, in its turn, opens with a conversation with a *lawyer*, who (like Cochran, like Moran) talks about "the critical episodes" of "married life" in defending marriage against Pozdnyshev's denunciations of it. This polemical debate on the benign or nonbenign significance of marriage (which spontaneously evolves among passengers aboard a train) precedes (and frames) the story proper (the narrative of the confession). To Pozdnyshev's argument that "marriage nowadays is just a deception" that "usually ends either in infidelity, or violence," the lawyer replies:

> "Yes, there's no doubt that married life has its critical episodes," said the lawyer, endeavouring to bring to an end a conversation that had grown more heated than was seemly. (35)

But rather than bringing an end to the conversation, this reference to "critical episodes" gives Pozdnyshev the opportunity to introduce himself by name (and introduce his story of the murder of the wife) both to the lawyer and to us. He introduces, thus, the fact or the reality of murder *into its cultural invisibility* and *into its legal denial*.

> "Yes, there's no doubt that married life has its critical episodes," said the lawyer . . .
> "I can see you've recognized me," said the gray-haired man quietly, trying to appear unruffled.
> "No, I don't think I have the pleasure . . ."
> "It's not much of a pleasure. Pozdnyshev's the name. I'm the fellow who had one of those critical episodes you were talking about.

So critical was it, in fact, that I ended up murdering my wife."
(35–36)

To go back now to O. J. Simpson in his relation to Tolstoy's text, it
is quite interesting that in both cases the "critical episodes"—the story
of the violence and the event of murder—are linked to something that
essentially (in culture and in discourse) cannot be seen and that indeed
fails to be seen within the framework of the trial.

Blind Justice (Seeing and Judging)

Could justice in effect be blind—in ways other than the ones in which it
is normally expected to be?[31] Is not seeing crucial to the very practice
and the very execution of the law,[32] because, as the saying has it, "justice must not only be done, but must be *seen* to be done"? A trial is,
indeed, in its origin and in its essence, a theatrical event in that, by definition, it takes place upon a stage before an audience. The trial of the
century was only more exemplary in that respect, since it had been
from the beginning a *show trial,* a spectacularized case whose evolving
courtroom drama was being reproduced throughout the world, magnified and multiplied by millions of television screens. But any criminal
proceedings implicate "the people" in whose name they are initiated as
a community of viewers, a communal circle of social observers or of
political (historical) spectators. Any court decision, in a way, is a his-

---

31. Justice, as is well known, is customarily represented as a blindfolded goddess
(see Raphael's fresco *Justice*). In this concrete image, the blindness stands of course for
impartiality. The metaphor of the blindness of justice has been underscored by the vocabulary of legal liberalism: an impartial constitution is often presumed to be color-blind as
well as gender-blind.

32. Seeing as a metaphor of judgment has a rather concrete history in the jury box.
For years, federal and state courts upheld juror qualification statutes that precluded
"individuals with immutable characteristics such as blindness, deafness, and paralysis"
from jury service. In 1993 the Supreme Court of the District of Columbia declared categorical exclusions a violation of the Rehabilitation Act, the American with Disabilities
Act, and the Civil Rights Act of 1871 (*Galloway v. Superior Court of the District of Columbia,*
816 F.Supp. 12 [D.D.C. 1993]). See Andrew Weis, "Peremptory Challenges: The Last Barrier to Jury Service for People with Disabilities," *Willamette Law Review* 33 (1997): 18. The
court allowed, however, for exclusion in particular cases, that is, cases "*with a great deal of
visual and physical evidence* or if the right to a fair trial is threatened." See similarly Robert
J. Brookes, "Symposium: Municipal Liability: Recent ADA and Rehabilitation Act
Cases," *Syracuse Law Review* 44 (1993): 871. Still, nothing protects an abused victim from
the possibility of *cultural* blindness (or from the unwritten prescription not to see).

torical decision about the significance, the meaning the community derives from its spectatorial stance with respect to various happenings and, more generally, from its spectatorship of history.[33] The rules of evidence, moreover, are in turn based on seeing. The strongest proof admitted by the court is proof corroborated by the eye: the most authoritative testimony in the courtroom is that of an eyewitness. Every trial, therefore, by its very nature as a trial, is contingent on the act of seeing.

Yet, in the case of the people v. O. J. Simpson, the jurors look but do not see. They do not see the beaten body. They look at pictures of Nicole's bruised countenance, but declare they cannot see either the husband's blows or the wife's (the victim's) battered face. The jurors, in the O. J. Simpson case, are thus themselves *the trial's failed eyewitnesses*. This failure of the court to see evokes, indeed, once more, Pozdnyshev's frustration with the court's shortsightedness or blindness and the parallel philosophical and legal failure of the trial in Tolstoy's case.

But in this sense, precisely, of the failure of the court to see (or of the *failure of the trial* to *eyewitness* its own evidence), the O. J. Simpson case repeats, indeed, with an ironic symmetry, the history, the trauma, and the structure of the Rodney King case or of the Simi Valley trial, which, in its turn, was precisely about *beating*—and about an *unseen* beating, about an inexplicable, recalcitrant relation between beating and blindness, beating and invisibility, an invisibility that cannot be dispelled in spite of the most probatory visual evidence. Indeed, quite similarly to the way in which Simpson's domestic violence was visually corroborated by the photos of Nicole's bruised face, Rodney King's beating by police was documented by a videotape. And yet, the jurors in the Simi Valley trial (all white) *did not see the beating* (of the black). The jury watched the film but claimed it *did not see* police abuse and acquitted the four white policemen. Both decisions hinge, thus, on a failure to see beating. In both cases, what the jury *cannot see*, in other words, is (paradoxically) *the very blows that inflict trauma*. Both verdicts are in turn traumatic in that they *deny, in fact, the very trauma that the*

---

33. Compare Charles Nesson's argument that evidentiary rules and the rules governing the conduct of judges and juries help the legal system to project substantive legal rules and behavioral messages by facilitating public acceptance of the verdicts as statements about events (rather than about evidence presented at trial). "The Evidence or the Event? On Judicial Proof and the Acceptability of Verdicts," *Harvard Law Review* 98 (1985): 1357–92.

trial was supposed to remedy. It is by virtue of this legal and historical resemblance of their basic structure in relation to the trauma (and the consequent trauma of the trial) that the Rodney King case and the O. J. Simpson case narrate together the story—and the trial—of the century.

Beating and Invisibility, or Hatred's Prohibited Sight

If the decision, in both cases, registers a legal failure to see trauma, this inherent failure is in turn reinforced, compounded, by an equal cultural failure to acknowledge hate.[34] It is significant, indeed, that, in both cases, what the jury fails to see—what cannot be seen precisely by the law—is *hate* (hate for women, hate for blacks) and that this secret, mute, insidious hate—this hate prohibited to sight—finds its expression, in both cases, in the graphic image—and in the physical translation—of a beating.

Beating is, indeed, a quintessential figure of *abuse of power* (physical and moral). As an emblem of oppression and humiliation, as a symbol of transgression of the other's property and of invasion of the other's body, beating is not just physiological, but is inherently political. A radically offensive act, it is, I would suggest, the most rudimentary political offense and has the impact (physical and moral) of a political act par excellence.

But seeing—as the essence of the cognitive activity and as the foundation of both consciousness and memory—is in turn an act that is not simply physiological; it can in turn be inherently, unwittingly political. The French philosopher Louis Althusser[35] explains how seeing and not seeing are contingent on the limits (the ideological exclusions)

---

34. Compare Martha Minow, "Speaking and Writing against Hate," *Cardozo Law Review* 11 (1990): 1393; and Judith Butler, "Implicit Censorship and Discursive Agency," in *Excitable Speech,* 127–63.

35. I take it as a pure coincidence that Louis Althusser, the famous, brilliant French philosopher who combined Marxism with Lacanian psychoanalysis and became an authority on ideology, ethics, and political philosophy, also ended up murdering his wife, in one of the most notorious French crimes of the century (1980). Declared "unfit to plead," Althusser was spared a trial. However, he later felt that "the absence of a trial" deprived him of the possibility of a public debate he would have desired. This is why he later wrote a confession, an "autobiography" that was published after his death under the title *The Future Lasts Forever.* "The fact is I strangled my wife, who meant everything to me, during an intense and unforeseeable state of mental confusion, in November 1980," wrote Althusser when he was released from his first period of confinement following the murder. "In the case of someone held responsible, a straightforward procedure is set in motion. . . . The person is brought before a court and there is a debate in public. On the other hand, if someone is held not to be responsible in *juridico-legal terms,* he is

of a frame of reference. "It is the whole field of a problematic," writes Althusser, "which defines and structures the invisible as its definite outside—*excluded* from the domain of visibility and *defined* as excluded by the existence and the structure of the problematic field itself":

> The invisible is defined by the visible as *its* invisible, its prohibited sight. . . . To see this invisible . . . requires something quite different from a sharp or attentive eye; it takes an *educated eye*, a revised, renewed way of looking, itself produced by the effect of a "change of terrain" reflected back upon the act of seeing.[36]

I would argue, in my turn, that the limitations of the possibilities of seeing, the structural exclusions from our factual frames of reference, are determined not only by (conscious or unconscious) *ideology* but by a built-in cultural *failure to see trauma*. As is evident from both the Rodney King case and the O. J. Simpson case, *the abuse of power* (beating) is *inscribed in culture as a trauma*. But, as we know from psychoanalytic studies[37] and as both cases demonstrate, trauma is precisely what can-

---

denied the whole procedure of a public, confrontational court appearance. . . . If the murderer is acquitted after a public trial, he can return home with his head held high (in principle at least, since the public may be indignant at his acquittal and make its feelings known . . .). . . . I want to free myself from the murder and above all from the dubious effects of having been declared unfit to plead, which I could not challenge in law. . . . But I can also help others to reflect upon a concrete case. No one before me has made such a critical confession. . . . I lived through an experience of the most acute and horrifying nature which I cannot fully comprehend, since it raises a number of legal, penal, medical, analytical, institutional, and intimately ideological and social questions. . . .When I speak of that trying experience, I refer not just to the period of confinement but to my life since then and what I clearly see I shall be condemned to for the rest of my days, if I do not intervene *personally* and *publicly*, to offer my own testimony." Louis Althusser, *The Future Lasts Forever: A Memoir*, ed. Olivier Corpet and Yann Moulier Bountang, trans. Richard Veasey (New York: New Press, 1992), 3, 18–29; Althusser's emphasis.

36. Louis Althusser, *Lire le Capital* (Paris: F. Maspero, 1968), 1:26–28 (Althusser's emphasis; all translations not otherwise attributed are my own). Compare Judith Butler's analysis of the way in which the Simi Valley jurors failed to see the beating of Rodney King: "This is not a simple seeing, an act of direct perception, but the racial production of the visible, the workings of racial constraints on what it means to 'see.'" Judith Butler, "Endangered/Endangering: Schematic Racism and White Paranoia," in *Reading Rodney King/Reading Urban Uprising*, ed. Robert Gooding-Williams (New York: Routledge, 1993), 15–22.

37. See Caruth, *Trauma*. See also Caruth, *Unclaimed Experience*. (See, in addition, further bibliography on trauma theory and its particular relation to perception and to knowledge in note 10, above.) It is Caruth's illuminating *philosophical synthesization* of the psychoanalytic/psychiatric/scientific lessons of contemporary trauma theory, and her *pioneer interdisciplinary insight* into the conceptual ungraspability of trauma, that have most pointedly informed and enabled the reflection here engaged.

not be seen; it is something that inherently, politically and psychoana-
lytically, defeats sight, even when it comes in contact with the rules of
evidence and with the trial's legal search for visibility. The political is
thus essentially tied up with the structure of the trauma. It is to the
structure of the trauma, therefore (and not simply to a different ideology), that our "eyes" should be precisely *educated*.

To return, now, to the beatings that remain persistently unseen in
both the Rodney King case and the O. J. Simpson case, to return, thus,
to both juries' failure to eyewitness the (physical and moral) violence
whose literal invisibility cannot be dispelled in court, in spite of the
most probatory visual evidence, in both cases, in effect, the photographic image (photos or videotape) turns out to be incapable of lifting
out or of canceling the cultural blind spot, or the political prescription
not to see.[38] The century might well be, in Walter Benjamin's acute
terms, "the age of mechanical reproduction" or the legal century of
videotapes. But in spite of the advances in the technological methods of
recording or of memorizing visual evidence, the trial of the century
remains *a story of the century's blind spots*.

As Tolstoy's text shows, however, concerning gender, the legal
story of the century is essentially the same as that of the preceding one.
As regards marriage and violence, it seems we have made little
progress and have not truly come out of the nineteenth century.[39] In

---

38. Andrea Dworkin, writing in the *Los Angeles Times*, cites another stupefying case
concerning the recalcitrant invisibility of beating (a case, however, whose political invisibility seems to relate to gender, rather than to race):

> On the same day the police who beat Rodney King were acquitted in Simi Valley, a
> white husband who had raped, beaten and tortured his wife, also white, was
> acquitted of marital rape in South Carolina. He had kept her tied to a bed for hours,
> her mouth gagged with adhesive tape. He videotaped a half-hour of her ordeal,
> during which he cut her breasts with a knife. The jury, which saw the videotape,
> had eight women on it. Asked why they acquitted, they said, he needed help. *They
> looked right through the victim.*

Andrea Dworkin, "Trying to Flee," *Los Angeles Times*, October 8, 1995, M6.
39. "The English law of legalized wife beating was transplanted to America through
Blackstone's reference to the doctrine of moderate chastisement. 'For, as [the husband] is
to answer for her misbehaviour, the law thought it reasonable to intrust him with this
power of restraining her, by domestic chastisement, in the same moderation that a man is
allowed to correct his apprentices or children.'" William Blackstone, *Commentaries on the
Laws of England* (Chicago: University of Chicago Press, 1979), 1:444, quoted in Marina
Angel, "Susan Glaspell's Trifles and a Jury of Her Peers: Woman Abuse in a Literary and
Legal Context," *Buffalo Law Review* 45 (1997): 792.

any case, we have not yet entirely emerged from a traumatic story (or from a trauma) whose very pattern is characteristic of the previous century. As the coincidence between the literary text and the contemporary trial shows, as far as women are concerned as targets of abusive or appropriative violence, we seem to have inherited, quite strictly and specifically, the nineteenth century's blind spots. The murders and acquittals of the nineteenth century are still with us as our tragically intact inheritance.[40]

"During the nineteenth century, an era of feminist agitation for reform of marriage law," writes Reva B. Siegel, "authorities in England and the United States declared that a husband no longer had the right to chastise his wife. Yet, for a century after courts repudiated the right of chastisement, the American legal system continued to treat wife beating differently from other cases of assault and battery. While authorities denied that a husband had the right to beat his wife, they intervened only intermittently in cases of marital violence: men who assaulted their wives were often granted formal and informal immunities from prosecution, in order to protect the privacy of the family and to promote 'domestic harmony'" ("'The Rule of Love': Wife Beating as Prerogative and Privacy," *Yale Law Journal* 105 [1996]: 2117–207). It was the feminist movement of the 1970s that began the process of fighting against such social malpractices by promoting both conceptual and legal changes of perception (see, for example, Catharine A. MacKinnon, *Toward a Feminist Theory of the State* [Cambridge: Harvard University Press, 1989]). But, as Senator Joseph Biden, author of the Violence Against Women Act, acknowledges in an address to the Senate: "this common law principle has left *a legacy of legal blindness* toward violence against women" (Joseph R. Biden, "Domestic Violence a Crime, Not a Quarrel," *Trial*, June 1993, 56).

See also Linda Gordon, *Heroes of Their Own Lives: The Politics and History of Family Violence, Boston, 1880–1960* (New York: Viking, 1988); Bernadette Dunn Sewell, "History of Abuse: Societal, Judicial, and Legislative Responses to the Problem of Wife Beating," *Suffolk University Law Review* 23 (1989): 983–1017; and Martha Albertson Fineman and Roxanne Mykitiuk, eds., *The Public Nature of Private Violence: The Discovery of Domestic Abuse* (New York: Routledge, 1994).

40. Estimates are that "[i]n the United States, a woman falls victim to domestic abuse at the hands of her husband or boyfriend once every nine seconds"; it has also been estimated that "more than half of the women murdered in America are killed by their male partners." Jill Lebowitz, "Pursuit of Tort Claims for Domestic Violence in New Jersey and the Creation of a New Tort Cause of Action for 'Battered Woman's Syndrome' (Case Comment: *Giovine v. Giovine*)," *Women's Rights Law Reporter* 17 (1996): 259. Estimates are also that domestic violence is the most underreported crime in America, with only one in ten victims making a report (*Chattanooga Free Press*, September 30, 1997, C2). Catharine MacKinnon notes that "sexual violation is a sexual practice." She adds, "Because the inequality of the sexes is socially defined as the enjoyment of sexuality itself, gender inequality appears consensual." "Women are systematically beaten in our homes by men with whom we are close. It is estimated that between one quarter and one third of married women experience serious violence in their homes—some studies find as many as 70 percent. Four out of five murdered women are killed by men; between one third and one half are married to their murderers. When you add the boyfriends and former spouses, the figures rise" (Catharine A. MacKinnon, *Feminism Unmodified: Discourses on Life and Law* [Cambridge: Harvard University Press, 1987], 6–7, 24).

Law and History: Inheritance of Trauma

What have we done, thus, in a hundred years? Has history not taken place to register at least a legal difference? Or is it law itself that is responsible not just for the recording but for the censorship of history? Could the voluminous *legal recording* of the O. J. Simpson trial be itself merely the witness of the way in which history is paradoxically deprived of memory? How do verdicts (the acquittal, in the O. J. Simpson case) mark at once what history *remembers* and what history *forgets*, at once what is pragmatically included in, and what is programmatically excluded from, collective memory?

In their arbitrating function between contradictory facts and between conflicting versions of the truth, verdicts are decisions about what to admit into and what to transmit of collective memory. Law is, in this way, an organizing force of the significance of history.[41] But law relates to history through trauma.[42] What should have been historically remembered, in effect, is not only the trial but the trauma that has made the trial necessary, the individual and social trauma that the trial was supposed to remedy, to solve or to resolve. Yet a trauma cannot simply be remembered when, in the first place, it cannot be grasped, when, as

---

41. Law takes up, thus, indirectly and unwittingly (implicitly), the traditional tasks of historiography. Historiography, however, is inherently a cognitive or constative endeavor, whereas law is, and remains, inherently performative: it inadvertently competes with historiography (or duplicates its organizing or interpretive functions) only through the radical difference of its performative endeavor, in its essence as performativity.

42. Law relates to trauma through the social function of the trial as a structural (procedural and institutional) remedy to trauma. In a different, larger philosophical sense, Walter Benjamin has inaugurated (in the wake of Marx, but with a different kind of insight and of emphasis) an innovative tradition of historiography, whose goal is to articulate the past historically (always against the version of official or established "history"), not from the perspective of "the victors" but from the perspective of "the tradition of the oppressed," in which Benjamin underscores precisely the centrality of the experience of trauma. "To articulate the past historically," writes Benjamin, "does not mean to recognize [the past] 'the way it really was.' . . . It means to seize hold of a memory as it flashes up at a moment of danger. . . . The tradition of the oppressed teaches us that the 'state of emergency' in which we live is not the exception but the rule. We must attain to a conception of history which is in keeping with this insight. Then we shall clearly realize that it is our task to bring about a real state of emergency. . . . Where we perceive a chain of events, [the angel of history] sees one single catastrophe which keeps piling wreckage upon wreckage." Walter Benjamin, "Theses on the Philosophy of History," in *Illuminations*, ed. Hannah Arendt, trans. Harry Zohn (New York: Schocken, 1968), 255–57.

these trials show, it cannot even be seen. Rather than memory, it compels a traumatic reenactment.[43]

I would argue, therefore, that a legal case truly becomes a locus of embodied history, a "site of memory" or a material, literal "lieu de mémoire" in Pierre Nora's sense,[44] only when it is spontaneously endowed with what Freud calls a "historical duality,"[45] when it reverberates, in other words, with what I have defined as a *cross-legal* resonance, or triggers inadvertently the movement of a repetition or the dynamics of a *legal recall*. In its simultaneous gesture of commemoration and of forgetfulness of what it in effect repeats, the O. J. Simpson trial constitutes precisely such a "site of memory" *(lieu de mémoire)* because it constitutes a "site" (a locus, a location, an abyss) of traumatic repetition.[46]

---

43. "The forgotten recalls itself in acts," says Jacques Lacan ("L'oublié se rappelle dans les actes"). "Fonction et Champ de la parole et du langage," in *Ecrits* (Paris: Seuil, 1966), 262.

44. Cf. Pierre Nora, "Entre Mémoire et Histoire," introductory essay to *Les Lieux de mémoire*, Pierre Nora (director), vol. 1, *La République* (Paris: Gallimard, 1984). An English version of excerpts of this introduction ("Between Memory and History: Les Lieux de mémoire," trans. Mark Roudebush) was published in "Memory and Counter-Memory," a special issue of *Representations* 26 (1989).

45. See Freud, *Moses and Monotheism*, 64, and chap. 7 of part 2.

46. What acquitted Simpson is, thus, history: a repetitive historical pattern of abuse of African Americans by agents of the law. Those who voted or who would have voted for acquittal (and they are not limited to blacks) wanted to exonerate black trauma, to vindicate, to exculpate, and to empower the historical defenselessness of African-Americans before the law. It is an entire history of trauma that here weighed on the decision. What acquitted Simpson was the way in which his confrontation with the law allowed him (irrespective of his guilt or innocence) to play an inadvertent role he did not seek and did not in effect desire: that of a physical custodian— a keeper in his very body—of black collective memory. This legal and symbolic mythic role begins unwittingly when Simpson chooses to attempt to earn freedom by a physical escape or by a run in the face of the law. The dramatic televised pursuit—the mute scenario of the slow-speed chase and Simpson's ultimate surrender and return as state property—enacts or reenacts in the collective memory at once the recent drama of the high-speed chase of Rodney King (ironically pursued for speeding), and a more ancient primal scene of running slaves pursued so as to be returned to their proper, *legal* owners. Not only in the case of gender, therefore, but in the case of race as well, the traumatic legal story of the twentieth century has not entirely emerged from a traumatic story of the nineteenth century (Dred Scott, 1857).

In his embodied posture as a captured runaway and in the need to be or to become now *a survivor of the law* (or of the legal system), Simpson symbolically recovers a collective cultural past he had been trying to forget and to deny, and a shared history he had been trying, his life long, to run away from. In running from the law, he runs back toward the past. In Simpson's very body (and in his bodily presence in the court), "blackness"

The O. J. Simpson case unwittingly repeats, thus, both the twentieth-century traumatic legal narrative of Rodney King and the nineteenth-century traumatic legal story of Tolstoy. But Tolstoy's own literary, legal case consists already in a repetition, since its very starting point is the hero's *reenactment of the legal trial* (his reopening of the criminal proceedings' failed search for the truth) through the narrative of *the confession* that, in turn, undertakes to repeat or to narrate again (to recapitulate, once more) the story that could not be heard in the proceedings and that failed to be communicated, or transmitted, to the court. The trial of the century repeats, then, all these repetitions—legal, literary, psychoanalytical, historical—by which the trial tries, and retries, to resolve the trauma and by which the trauma inadvertently repeats itself as an unconscious legal memory under the conscious legal process. The O. J. Simpson case, in summary, is the defining trial of our times because it recapitulates, precisely, all these repetitions. It is the trial of the century because it reenacts the Rodney King case; but this defining trial of the twentieth century turns out to be itself a repetition of the trial (of the trauma) of the nineteenth century.

I would suggest, indeed, that the main difference in this century's trials and acquittals is that history enables us, today, at least to catch up with Tolstoy—at least *to see that we do not see*—and thus, historically to raise these questions: to ask about *the meaning of the repetition*. If history, indeed, repeats itself, and if events must happen at least twice to be perceived, might the repetition in itself, some day, help bring about (help train) "an educated eye"?

Eyes and Education, or Beating and Seeing

All three cases, therefore—Pozdnyshev's or Tolstoy's case, the Rodney King case, and the O. J. Simpson case—resonate with one another in similarly dramatizing, in the courtroom, a striking and misunderstood

---

historically returns as erased (forgotten) memory; it *returns* therefore *as unconscious or repressed:* repressed, erased by Simpson's own assimilation. This (in part at least) accounts for the emotional explosion at the verdict. The intensity of the triumphant identification of the black community with Simpson's *survival of the law* derived precisely from the force of this *historical return of the repressed,* all the more forceful for symbolically returning an *erased* collective and traumatic memory.

From this perspective, the legal drama of the century became a *legal narrative of black survival,* and of the survival and resuscitation of black memory. (Ironically, this narrative of recall doomed to forgetfulness the story of the murder.)

relation between seeing and beating, between *a violence that harms* or that seeks to hurt or kill and *a violence that blinds* or seeks to prohibit sight. In the literary scene as in the legal one, in their fictions and in their realities, all three cases (Simpson, Rodney King, Tolstoy) similarly concretize a failure of the trial through the story of the legal implications, on the one hand, of hatred as prohibited to sight and, on the other hand, of suffering or of trauma as *the structure of a blow* (or of an injury) *that cannot be seen.* All the trial can prove, therefore, is the trauma's *unlocatability,* the injury's constitutive invisibility, the blow's traumatic *nonjusticiability.* All the trial does is, therefore, to *repeat the trauma* in enacting, once more, its recalcitrant invisibility and in showing how *the trauma's power to defeat sight* infiltrates the very workings of the legal process and insidiously takes over the very structure of the trial. It is precisely this complex political and epistemological *relation of the beating to the seeing,* and this profound human and political enigma of a trauma that cannot be seen and cannot be located, or translated into seeing (into seeability) even at the level of the trial, that seems to be at the center of Tolstoy's text and at the center of the story Pozdnyshev *cannot quite bring to the knowledge of the court.* But this is what, for him and for Tolstoy, the trial—and the story—are really all about.

VI

The Abyss

What is it, then, that Pozdnyshev has failed to articulate and to transmit about his story (or about the real nature of his case) during the trial? What is this insight he tries desperately to articulate, but which remains deprived of legal language, this speechless, inarticulate, unheard, excessive truth that remains outside the hearing of the court, that exceeds both what is said and what is heard in the proceedings, and that is defined, in Tolstoy's text, precisely—only—as *an excess of the narrative (of literature) over the trial?* What legal event is it that is defined— or that can only be accounted for—by an excessive literary truth?

This question can be asked from two opposed perspectives: (1) What sort of paradoxical event creates a crisis that exceeds what can be legally articulated, but that nonetheless *necessitates a trial for its very definition?* (2) What is, on the other hand, this crisis or this paradoxical event that cannot do without a legal process, but that, literarily and philosophically, can only be transmitted *through a failure of the trial—through an explosion of the legal framework?* Such is the murder of the wife in Tolstoy's text (in its relation to the trial). And such, I would propose, is, similarly, the paradoxical relation of the murder of Nicole Brown-Simpson to the O. J. Simpson trial, into which Tolstoy might be, indeed, a literary *key*. Philosophically, Tolstoy seems to be asking, not by chance, perhaps, a question that applies both to his fiction and to the intricate legal reality of the contemporary trial: What is the story that can be told only through an *unpaid debt* of the *decision* to the *truth,* or of the verdict to the facts? *What is this* (literary, psychological, political, historical) *debt* that the decision, the acquittal, still holds with respect to the full legal truth, but which a conviction (as the mixed reactions to the civil verdict proved) could not in its turn possibly reduce, resolve, or fully pay?

What is it we can therefore understand, with Tolstoy's help, about the real nature of the (fictional and real) murder case? What can we ultimately understand or learn from the text—from the *confession*—of *The Kreutzer Sonata?* And how can *what* we understand illuminate the riddle of the legal case? How can the perspective of the literary text (and of a literary understanding) shed light on the overall historical performance of "the trial of the century"? What is it that Tolstoy is struggling, in conclusion, to communicate?

Let us listen, one last time, to Pozdnyshev's testimony, in its effort to convey the story that the court has missed:

> At my trial the whole thing was made to look as though it had been caused by jealousy. Nothing could have been further from the truth. I'm not saying jealousy didn't play any part—mind you—it did, but it wasn't the most important thing. At my trial they decided I was a wronged husband who'd killed his wife in order to defend his outraged honour (that's the way they put it in their language). So I was acquitted. During the court hearings I tried to explain what was really at the bottom of it all, but they just thought I was trying to rehabilitate my wife's honour. (80–81)

Jealousy was just a pretext, Pozdnyshev insists, almost an indifferent pretext: "If it hadn't been him, it would have been some other man. If jealousy wasn't the *pretext,* some other one would have been found."

Whatever her relationship with that musician was, it wasn't important to me, any more than it was to her. What was important was what I've been telling you about—my pigsty existence. *It all happened because of that terrible abyss there was between us,* the one I've been talking about, the terrible stress of our mutual hatred for each other, that made the first *pretext* that came along sufficient to cause a *crisis.* (81)

Chasm

The case, then, is about the relation of the (private, sexual, trivial) *pretext* to the (social, legal) *crisis* of the violence and of the murder: "It all happened because of that terrible *abyss* there was between us." The real motivation of the story derives, thus, neither from the wife's (real or fantasized) unfaithfulness nor from the jealousy that this presumed unfaithfulness provokes, but from the very existence of "that terrible abyss." The story, then, is not the story that we thought; it is not the banal case of adultery (of jealousy) we had at first believed that we were reading. What is it, then? I would argue that what we discover in Tolstoy's text is, far less predictably, the narrative of an abyss, a case, precisely, of the unexpected revelation of a hidden and profound chasm.

The metaphor of the abyss repeats itself throughout the text of *The Kreutzer Sonata.* Although Tolstoy's Russian uses several different words to concretize and to nuance this image of a precipice *(propast, puchina, bezdnia),* all these words depict the same experience of a break (a loss) of contact and of ground; all these figures point to the same insistent image of a fissure, a dividing gulf, a bottomless ocean, or a terrifying, gaping wound within the ground:

> It all happened because of that terrible abyss there was between us, the one I've been talking about, the terrible stress of our mutual hatred for each other, that made the first pretext that came along sufficient to cause a crisis. (81)

> It's horrible, horrible, horrible . . . the *abyss of error* [*misunderstanding*] we live in regarding women and our relations with them. (38)

And so we continued to live, in a perpetual fog, without ever being aware of the situation we were in. If what finally happened hadn't happened, and I'd go on living like that until my old age, I think that even when I was dying I'd have thought I had a good life . . . ; *I would never have come to perceive the abyss of unhappiness,* the loathsome falsehood in which I was wallowing. (75)

The first quarrel had a terrible effect on me. I call it a quarrel, but it wasn't really a quarrel, it was just the *revelation of the abyss that actually separated us.* (57)

An Abyss of Sexuality: An Abyss of Difference

What is this precipice that Tolstoy so insistently returns to?

In its most obvious significance, the metaphor of the abyss in *The Kreutzer Sonata* seems to be linked to the space of sexuality as a frightening enigma. But what is sexuality, precisely? Sexuality is, first and foremost, in this story (as it is, indeed, in O. J. Simpson's story) an *abyss between the sexes.* And this gulf between the sexes, this ill-understood abyss that so radically and so incurably separates the woman from the man and estranges the husband from the wife, refers in turn not just to the unfathomable abyss of sexuality and sexual desire (as the story's obscure origin) but, more specifically, to a fissure or a split *within* sexuality itself, to an inner schism or a chasm not just *between the narrator and his wife* but *within the narrator's own sexual desire;* there is an abyss, precisely, that inhabits human sexuality, like an internal hollowness at the bottom of a whirling chaos of attractions and repulsions, of rivalries and of conflicting, secret sexual ambiguities. This abyss of difference (internal and external) cannot but become an abyss of conflict. The relative positions in the story of the jealousy—in the triangle of the sexual competition—can change dynamically and secretly: desire for the wife and jealousy toward the male rival; attraction for (or fascination with) the rival and a secret sexual competition with the wife;[47] love-hate for the wife; love-hate for the would-be lover; jealousy, respectively, of both; a maze of attractions and repulsions; an abyss that inhabits sexu-

---

47. Cf. *The Kreutzer Sonata,* 80: "Yes, he was a musician, a violinist. . . . He had moist eyes, like almonds, smiling red lips, and a little moustache. . . . He was slight of physique . . . and he had a particularly well-developed posterior, as women have. . . . He and his music were the real cause of it all. At my trial the whole thing was made to look as though it had been caused by jealousy. Nothing could have been further from the truth."

ality like a chaotic whirlpool or an internal hollowness that constantly sucks it, splits it from inside itself; an abyss that fatally and radically divides sexuality from itself, makes it different from itself.

But what is even more important than the sexual significance of the abyss, what is even more significant than its (split) sexual nature, is the relation of the split—the precipice—to its *obscure depth* or to its *abyssal, enigmatic core of darkness*. This concrete obscurity (of the abyss) is recapitulated by a metaphor of darkness that runs throughout the text[48] and that, in resonance with that of the abyss, dramatizes (concretizes) *a resistance from inside the story to what can be seen* (or to what can pierce into awareness).[49] "It all happened because of that terrible abyss there was between us." Resisting awareness,[50] the radical darkness inside the abyss, the (literal and metaphorical) obscurity inside the story, functions, therefore, like a literal *black hole* that is the story's center. This narrative black hole (the dark abyss inside the story) dynamically resists the trial's search for legal visibility and undercuts the story's constant effort to obtain both light and sight.

---

48. Like the crime scene in the O. J. Simpson case, the scene of *The Kreutzer Sonata* (the confession) takes place in a literal obscurity outlined only by shadows and by shades (see Jackson, "Darkness of the Night," 208–27). It is nighttime, dark both outside and inside the train; the story is surrounded (governed) by a darkness, in which (metaphorically and literally) nothing is entirely or simply readable: "It was too dark to read, so I closed my eyes and pretended I wanted to go to sleep" (36), says the narrator. Pozdnyshev confesses in this total darkness, which protects him; his voice is heard, but his face, symbolically and literally, is never clearly seen. Like O. J. Simpson, he remains "a shadowy figure." The story never entirely emerges from the darkness in which it is plunged:

It was *so dark* that I *could not see his face*, only hear his forceful, pleasant voice. (38)

His face kept altering strangely in the *semi-darkness* where he sat. (42)

"The light is getting in my eyes—do you mind if we pull the shade over it?" he said, pointing to the lamp. (53)

I started to get a sinister feeling, lying there in the dark, and I struck a match. . . . He continued his story . . . and all that could be heard in the *semi-darkness* was the rattling of the windows. . . . In the half-light of the dawn, *I could no longer make out Pozdnyshev's features*. All I could hear was his voice. (101–2)

49. "'And so we continued to live, in a perpetual fog, without ever being aware of the situation we were in. If what finally happened hadn't happened . . . I would never have come to perceive the abyss of unhappiness, the loathsome falsehood in which I was wallowing" (75).

50. On the way in which trauma resists awareness, see Miller, *Thou Shalt Not Be Aware*.

The Trial's Central Darkness, or the Narrative
Black Hole

Like the trauma, like the narrative black hole that is the story's center,
the abyss, indeed, is something normally hidden from sight, something
whose obscure depth (or whose end) cannot be fathomed and whose
bottom (or whose starting point) *cannot be seen.* But when the bottom is
touched through the murder, when the abyss can suddenly and unexpectedly be glimpsed, what can be seen is nothing but an emptiness
and an obscurity. At the story's end (at the conclusion of the trial, and
at the horizon of the text), what is dramatically revealed is not depth,
but the unsuspected bottomlessness of a terrifying chasm.

And so it was, I would propose, precisely in the O. J. Simpson case.
The performance of the trial of the century was nothing if not a historical encounter with the unexpected bottomlessness of a chasm. What
was finally revealed at the trial's end was, similarly, not the curtain's
fall, not the closure of the case or a catharsis finally obtained by a legal
resolution, but here again only the terrifying opening, only the emptiness[51] of an ungraspable abyss: an *abyss between the sexes;* an *abyss
between the races;* an abyss between legality and justice; a gap in perception between blacks and whites; an abyss between contradictory experiences of the significance of law enforcement and between conflicting
views of the use or the abuse of the power yielded to the justice system
and to the agents of the law; an abyss between conflicting views of the
significance or of the insignificance of domestic violence; an abyss
between the rich who can buy justice and the poor who cannot afford to
pay its price; an abyss between conflicting views or contradictory emotional perceptions of the verdict as a victory or as an absolute defeat.
"Yet there was no real victory, no real defeat," wrote Robert A. Jordan,
"for blacks and whites who are on opposite sides of this verdict. Rather,
there is the fresh realization that . . . the divide between blacks and
whites, is still *very deep* in this country."[52] But the impact of the trial,

---

51. Cf. Lisa Kennedy: "The karmic payback of this verdict [O. J. Simpson] for that
injustice [Rodney King] has an *empty* quality" (*Village Voice*, October 17, 1995, 25) and
Henry Louis Gates Jr.: "It is a discourse . . . in which everyone speaks of payback and
nobody is paid. . . . And so an *empty* vessel like O. J. Simpson becomes filled with meaning, and more meaning—more meaning than any of us can bear" ("Thirteen Ways of
Looking at a Black Man," *New Yorker*, October 23, 1995, 65; reprinted in Gates, *Thirteen
Ways of Looking at a Black Man* [New York: Random House, 1997], 121–22).

52. Robert A. Jordan, "No Victory, No Defeat, Only an Angry Divide," *Boston Globe*,
October 8, 1995, "Focus" section.

and the schism suddenly uncovered by the shock of the verdict of the century, had to do with something *deeper* still and not quite so definable, something that escaped definition at the very heart of the abyss revealed by the conclusion of the trial. As in Tolstoy, the sudden opening of the abyss was linked to the emergence of a split in the very integrity of legal justice.

An Abyss of Trauma

"But will Americans even bother to wonder how racially cleft . . . the criminal justice system must have been long before this case?" asked Francis X. Clines. "Will whites—so shocked at the television scenes of some blacks triumphant at the verdict announcement—now be ready to believe blacks' first-hand tales of negative contacts with police?"[53] "The verdict," wrote Isabel Wilkerson, "exposed a chasm in place for generations."[54] I would argue that this broken integrity (the schism in society, the split in the integrity of justice) was tied up with a splitting that, itself, was (and *repeated*) the effect of a traumatic shock. The chasm between blacks and whites becomes, ironically, a dialogue of shocks. The shock was related to an "accidented" space through which culture as a whole suddenly revealed itself as nothing other than a *cultural gap,* an "accidented" and inherently dissociated space of cultural trauma, insofar as trauma (individual as well as social) is precisely constituted by a gap in consciousness.

What should have been perceived, at the conclusion of the O. J. Simpson trial, is, thus, the concrete reality of the traumatic gap—or the concreteness of the trauma. What was perceived, instead, was the abyss—the gap—between two traumas: that of race and that of gender. But race and gender differed, mainly, in this trial, in their relation to a third trauma: that of law itself.

In its prosecution of a husband's murderous abuse, the law has been appealed to, here, by gender as a guardian of the victims' rights and thus as a necessary ally and, possibly, as the only *vehicle of correction of the abuse.* But in the argument of the defense (and in the collective memory of race), law is invoked as part and parcel of the trauma, and its *enforcement* is remembered and historically commemorated (liti-

---

53. Francis X. Clines, "And Now, the Audience Rests," *New York Times,* October 8, 1995, 4.

54. Isabel Wilkerson, "Whose Side to Take: Women, Outrage, and the Verdict on O. J. Simpson," *New York Times,* October 8, 1995, 4.

gated) as *the very source, the very vehicle of the abuse.*[55] Race and gender differ, thus, in their thematized relation to the law and in their consequent legal perception of the trial as itself part of the problem (part of the abuse), or as its possible redress, its cure.

But it was for gender that the criminal trial was ironically destined to become a *legal trauma;* it was for gender that the verdict of the century turned out to be, precisely, *legally traumatic.*[56] And this pronounce-

---

55. In his famous essay "Violence and the Word," Robert Cover underscores the systematic way in which the violent, traumatizing side of the law is always underplayed, denied, or altogether ignored. As a result, we emphasize law as (legal) meaning. But "pain and death" are limits on the possibility of totalizing this meaning. Pain and death (which the law inflicts) are by definition what cannot be understood, what cannot be transformed into meaning by those who suffer them. Legal meaning, therefore, is not shared by those whom the law overwhelms. See "Violence and the Word," in *Narrative, Violence,* 203–38, and *Justice Accused.* See also Walter Benjamin, "Critique of Violence," in *Reflections: Essays, Aphorisms, Autobiographical Writings,* ed. Peter Demetz, trans. Edmund Jephcott (New York: Schocken, 1978), 277–300; and Jacques Derrida, "Force of Law: The 'Mystical Foundation of Authority,'" *Cardozo Law Review* 11 (1990): 921–1045.

56. While the injuries of race and sex abuse are comparable—and have indeed been compared throughout history—the legal remedy of one has been sometimes achieved (as in this case) at the expense of the other. During Reconstruction, for example (when marital "chastisement" was no longer recognized as a husband's right), southern judges responded to the abolition of slavery by closing the law's eye to domestic abuse. (See Laura F. Edwards, "'The Marriage Covenant Is at the Foundation of All Our Rights': The Politics of Slave Marriages in North Carolina after Emancipation," *Law and History Review* 14 [1996]: 81–89.) To the extent that this (willed) form of judicial blindness was triggered by the reawakened need to protect the integrity of the domestic sphere, it may be viewed as a posttraumatic legal and jurisprudential response to the political subversion/loss of "the domestic institution" (as slavery was called). One "domestic institution" (beaten wives) substituted for another (slavery). One trauma compensated for another, through the legal medium of a symptomatic (and symptomatically prescribed) judicial blindness. "If no permanent injury has been inflicted," argued a 1874 legal opinion, "nor malice, cruelty nor dangerous violence shown by the husband, it is better to *draw the curtain, shut out the public gaze,* and leave the parties to forget and forgive" (North Carolina; quoted in Siegel, "The Rule of Love," 2158). Even in the North, it seems, the destabilization of the boundaries of "domesticity" may have had posttraumatic legal compensations concerning women: in several cases northern juries acquitted husbands who had murdered their wives' lovers. For a discussion of such cases in a different framework, see Hendrik Hartog, "Lawyering, Husbands' Rights, and 'the Unwritten Law' in Nineteenth-Century America," *Journal of American History* 84, no. 1 (1997): 67–96.

Conversely, race was made to compensate for the trauma of gender. Lynching, masquerading as justice (and sometimes complicitly applied through the judicial institution), was meant to be a pseudo-"legal" remedy for the underlying *gender trauma* of the failed white male attempt to control the (white) woman's sexuality. Lynching was thus also (among other things) meant to remedy the uncontrollability (the uncontainability) of female sexuality as such. Race subordination and gender subordination acted in concert. Even the black activist Ida B. Wells, who crusaded against lynching during the late nineteenth century and spoke on behalf of its black (male *and* female) victims, wrote that

ment of the law, this tacit, indirect, seeming legitimation of gender abuse that aggravated, ratified the trauma through the channels of a vehicle of law in turn entailed further traumatic, splitting consequences. "The verdict exposed a chasm in place for generations. . . . And nowhere was the divide more stark than it was between black women and white women," writes Isabel Wilkerson: "Pressed to choose between men with whom they share race experience . . . and white women with whom they share the experience of sexism," black women jurors had no choice but to "break ranks." In choosing race sol-

---

"white men used their ownership of the body of white females as a terrain on which to lynch the black male" (quoted in Dorothy E. Roberts, "Rape, Violence, and Women's Autonomy," *Chicago-Kent Law Review* 69 [1993]: 359, 366). Almost a century later Catharine MacKinnon notes that the definition of rape as a crime committed by black men against white women has obscured and legitimated the more common incidents of sexual abuse by acquaintances (*Feminism Unmodified*, 81–82; see, in this conjunction, Nancy S. Ehrenreich, "Perceptions and Decision Making: Gender Perspectives, O. J. Simpson, and the Myth of Gender/Race Conflict," *University of Colorado Law Review* 67 [1996]: 931, 939–40; see similarly Jacquelyn Dowd Hall, " 'The Mind That Burns in Each Body': Women, Rape, and Racial Violence," in *Powers of Desire: The Politics of Sexuality*, ed. Ann Snitow, Christine Stansell, and Sharon Thompson [New York: Monthly Review Press, 1983]; and Roberts, "Rape, Violence").

Unlike these authors (with whom I am in basic agreement), my own emphasis is not on the mutual reinforcement of the ideological *stereotypes* of race and gender, but on the mutual reinforcement of the two *traumas* (histories of suffering subject to a specific psychoanalytic logic), and on the traumatizing impact of the trial (meant to be a remedy) as a result. The black women jurors in the O. J. Simpson trial identified so deeply with the suffering of the defendant (with the terror of his flight and with the desperation of his struggle with the law) that they were blinded to the gender trauma. They relived, through the spectacular dramatization of the trial, (what they took to be) an all-too-familiar *reenactment* of *a primal lynching scene*. In this view, O. J. Simpson was implicitly accused of having had sex with a white woman; the prosecution's argument (and visual evidence) concerning Simpson's regular behavior of sexual abuse was lived (and screened) precisely as a déjà vu, an *already seen* (an all-too-seen) charge of an interracial sexual crime, for which O. J. Simpson was now going to be lynched, according to the archetypal script of history. It was for this primal scene and for its wounding repetition that the black women jurors sought a *legal remedy*. They *acquitted trauma* (and vindicated black males' innocence). Marcia Clark, on the other hand, identified so deeply with the trauma of the battered woman (which she in turn relived) that she was blinded (not ideologically, I submit, but traumatically) to the race trauma. Ideologically, on the contrary, she was "color-blind." Despite the advice of her jury consultant, she could not believe that women jurors would not listen to her, and would not *see* the evidence—and the battered face. She did not know that she was talking to them across an abyss of trauma. She did not believe in judicial blindness. For her and for all those who, like her, felt the suffering of Nicole (and did not or could not believe in blindness), the verdict was an added injury inflicted on the battered face. (On violent misuses of "the lynching metaphor," see Kendall Thomas, "Strange Fruit," in *Race-ing Justice, En-gendering Power*, ed. Toni Morrison [New York: Pantheon Books, 1992], 364–89.)

idarity with men over (and against) gender solidarity with female victims of abuse, the women jurors could not but create a cleavage within
the integrity (the unity) of gender itself and have in effect revealed an
abyss inside the community of women—a schism concretized in the
televised images, after the acquittal, of "black women smiling to the
heavens, thanking Jesus," and of "white women sobbing, unable to
speak."[57]

Philosophically, indeed, the abyss revealed by the trial of the century has compromised not only the integrity of gender, and not only
the integrity of the legal process, but the integrity of truth itself. Or,
rather, the conclusion of the trial has shown truth as an abyss between
incommensurate realities, a schism between different ways of seeing,
between incommensurable ways of looking at the very same facts.
"Nothing that happened in the O. J. Simpson trial was as awful as the
way it ended," the *Economist* commented:

> Was the Jury wrong? One cannot know. . . . The distressing part
> was not the verdict itself; it was the proof thus confirmed that
> black and white America have been watching different trials. . . .
> This verdict makes plain what so many Americans—and so many
> of their friends abroad—had not wanted to believe. Thirty-odd
> years after the civil-rights revolution, America is two countries,
> not one. And they are growing apart, not together.[58]

"It all happened," says Tolstoy, "because of that terrible abyss
there was between us." "It wasn't really a quarrel, it was just a revelation of the abyss that actually separated us." "It's horrible, horrible,
horrible . . . the abyss of misunderstanding we live in regarding women
and our relations to them."

To live like that would have been insufferable if we'd understood
the situation we were in, but we didn't understand it—we weren't

---

57. Wilkerson, "Whose Side to Take," 1, 4.
58. "Two Nations, Divisible: The Intolerable Lesson of the O. J. Simpson Trial,"
Economist, October 7, 1995. The depth of the amazement at the depth of the race cleavage
was itself, however, yet another symptom of how history is inherently deprived of memory: forgetful of the still not so remote legal enforcement of "two countries"—two Americas—through racist segregation laws.

even aware of it. It's the salvation as well as the punishment of human beings that when they're living irregular lives, they're able to wrap themselves in a blanket of fog so that they can't see the wretchedness of their situation . . .

And so we continued to live, in a perpetual fog, without ever being aware of the situation we were in. If what finally happened hadn't happened, and I'd go on living like that until my old age, I think that even when I was dying I'd have thought I had a good life . . . ; *I would never have come to perceive the abyss of unhappiness*, the *loathsome falsehood* in which I was wallowing. (74–75)

Seeing the Gap

Could *The Kreutzer Sonata* be the narrative of what it takes (in tragedy and in destruction) to make one *see* precisely the abyss? Is the O. J. Simpson case the story of the price to pay, in turn, for the revelation of this chasm that had been there all along but that, like the protagonists of *The Kreutzer Sonata*, we in turn *could not see* or *did not want to see?* Could the trial of the century be, in other words, the legal drama or the case of law that historically sums up the century as a century that, blindly, has lived on the brink of an ungrasped historical abyss, an amnesiac century that needed, paradoxically, a defining trial to *discover* (suddenly to see) *its own history (its memory) as an abyss*—an essentially ungraspable, and still essentially *invisible*, "abyss of unhappiness and loathsome falsehood"? And if the trial of the century is indeed the cultural story of our blindness, could this legal story of our blindness turn, like Tolstoy's, into the story of a revolutionary seeing?

It's no good, I just can't talk calmly about it. It's not merely because of that episode, as that gentleman called it, but because ever since I went through it *my eyes have been opened* and I've seen everything in a completely new light. Everything's been turned inside out, *it's all inside out!* (38)

Suddenly, thus, the abyss was *inside out.*

! ! !

I will argue, to conclude, that the O. J. Simpson trial *was* the trial of the century *because* it has revealed precisely an abyss, or told the legal story of the century's severance in consciousness. The abyss might well be "inside out": insofar as it is not just an abyss of cultural hypocrisy, but an abyss of cultural trauma, it remains the trial's secret. I argue that the case, in other words, has claimed its unique status as the trial of the century *because we still cannot decide*—and do not completely understand— *what the trial was about,* because we still do not know or cannot decide where exactly to locate the trauma, or what was really at the bottom of this (legal, cultural, and historical) abyss.

Between Law and Literature:
Comparative Epistemologies

Thus it is that the comparison between the O. J. Simpson case and Tolstoy's text has helped us to review and to rethink the implications— and the impact—of the contemporary trial.

I have examined factual and interpretive legal uncertainties in the instructively imaginative and dramatically suggestive light of literary facts whose narrative logic (whose own dramatic legal tale of murder and of trial) decisively resembled the contemporary case and whose intuitive, imaginative insight into criminal (human) behavior and into the enigma of the structure of the case and of the structure of the murder (as well as of the murder's paradoxical relation to the trial) turned out to be at once compelling and inspiring.

Thus it is that the comparison between the trial and the literary text, between the intricate legal reality and the imaginative literary vision of the case of the murder of the wife (and of the trial of the husband) has cued us into the significance—and into the suggestive literary resonance—of the abyss.

I have proposed that the abyss was at the center—at the heart— both of the literary story and of the contemporary trial; and that both the trial and the text consisted in the unexpected revelation of the image—and of the ungraspable significance—of the abyss, both as an obscure original causality ("It all happened because of that terrible abyss there was between us") and as the fatal repetition, the unexpected and yet unavoidable return of a form of radical dispute ("I call it a quarrel, but it wasn't really a quarrel. It was just a revelation of the abyss that actually separated us").

Between Law and Literature (an Abyss)

But the comparison between the legal drama and the literary drama has also shown that law and literature have radically different philosophies (different approaches) with respect to the abyss. Governed by their different goals, the legal practice and the literary practice embody, in effect, two different ways of *addressing* the abyss and two ways of *relating the significance of the abyss*, specifically, *to the significance and to the functions of the trial.*

As we have seen, in both the trial and the literary text, the abyss— an abyss of difference, hatred, racism, sexuality, "unhappiness," and trauma—a "quarrel" that "is not really a quarrel" but the "revelation" of a radically divisive inner breakdown, is above all something terrifying. But it is also what we cannot grasp and do not understand. It is something we can see only from outside. It is therefore what, essentially, *cannot be totalized,* what a *closing argument* will of necessity fail to contain, to *close* or to *enclose. By definition, an abyss is what escapes legal summation, what eludes reflective or conceptual totalization.*

What, then, can a trial do with an abyss? The trial of the century sought (as the law always attempts to do) *to throw a bridge over the abyss,*[59] to stand in, or to step into, the breach by precisely *filling in the gap,* by closing the abyss or by enclosing it within the rationality of its legal categorizations (gender, race) in an attempt to cover or to *cover up its bottomlessness,* to integrate or to assimilate the gap within known categories of the social or political or legal order. In its pragmatic role as guardian of society against irregularity, derangement, disorganization, unpredictability, or any form of irrational or uncontrollable disorder, the law, indeed, has no choice but to guard against equivocations, ambiguities, obscurities, confusions, and loose ends. All these the abyss embodies, in the image of a danger the law fears above all: that of a failure of accountability (or of a breakdown in foundation and in founda-

---

59. Compare Robert Cover's definition of law as bridge: "Law is neither to be wholly identified with the understanding of the present state of affairs nor with the imagined alternatives. *It is the bridge*—the committed social behaviour which constitutes the way a group of people will attempt to get from here to there." Each community, Cover emphasizes, builds its bridges in its own way. "Thus, visions of the future are more or less strongly determinative of *the bridge which is 'law'* depending upon the commitment and social organization of the people who hold them" ("The Folktales of Justice: Tales of Jurisdiction," in *Narrative, Violence,* 176–77, 201). On law as bridge, see also Sarat, "Narrative Strategy," 366.

tional stability); that of a *loss*, of a *collapse* (absence) *of grounds*. Under the practical constraints of having to insure accountability and to bring justice, the law tries to *make sense of the abyss* or to reduce its threat (its senselessness, its unintelligible chaos) by giving it a name, by codifying it or by subsuming its reality (which is inherently nameless and unclassifiable) into the classifying logic and into the technical, procedural coherence of the trial. But in so doing, the law (the trial or the litigation) inadvertently denies the abyssal nature of the abyss in pretending, or in misguidedly assuming the abyss is something else, something that can be assimilated to known rules or precedents, something that can be enclosed, contained within the recognizability of known (stereotypical) legal agendas.

But the purpose of the literary text is, on the contrary, to show or to expose again the severance and the schism, to reveal once more the opening, the hollowness of the abyss, *to wrench apart what was precisely covered over, closed, or covered up by the legal trial*. The literary text casts open the abyss so as to let us look, once more, into its depth, and see its botttomlessness.[60]

And in so doing, in *reopening the case* and in revealing, once more, the obscurity, the empty opening of the abyss, the literary text enacts

---

60. The legal thinker who comes closest to this view is Robert Cover. Cover has proposed, indeed, a uniquely sophisticated reflection on the connection and on the difference between law and literature. To know law, Cover insists, one must understand a literature and a tradition. To understand law one must also recognize its connection (and commitment) to reality. Judges often exercise caution, as they should do, but in so doing they "risk losing law to the overpowering force of what is and what is dominant. Integrity . . . is the act of maintaining the vision that it is only that which redeems which is law." Literature and tradition, according to Cover, teach commitments that we then use to build "bridges to the future." In stories one may find an insight to a legal ideal that real judges are cautious not to provoke (Cover, "The Folktales of Justice," 176–77, 201). However, Cover adds, there is a crucial element that radically differentiates between literature and law: the very real violence of the judicial institution, its performative injurious power. This is all too often forgotten in the treatment of "law as literature." "I fully agree [says Cover] that the dominant form of legal thought ought to be interpretive. However, the emergence of interpretation as a central motif does not, by itself, reflect upon the way in which the interpretive acts of judges are simultaneously performative utterances in an institutional setting for violent behavior" (Cover, "Violence and the Word," 216 n. 24). "We begin, then, not with what the judges say but with what they do. The judges deal pain and death. . . . In this they are different from poets, from artists. It will not do to insist on the violence of strong poetry, of strong poets. Even the violence of weak judges is utterly real. . . . Whether or not the violence of judges is justified is not now the point—only that it exists in fact and differs from the violence that exists in literature or in the metaphoric characterizations of literary critics and philosophers" (213–14).

(or carries out through its own narrative, through its confession) a *repetition of the story* that the court has missed or has misunderstood, and that the trial could not tell. Literature enacts, thus, an artistic recapitulation of the dynamics of the trial and of the trial's search (and research) for the truth. By its own specific means, by its literary power or by the acuteness of its own search (struggle) for expression, the artistic trial strives to *transmit the force of the story that could not be told* (or that failed to be transmitted or articulated) in the legal trial.

What Tolstoy's text, in this way, inquires into is not just the meaning of the case, nor even simply the enigma of the case's force, but *the general significance of failed attempts (in law, in history) to close abysses,* the meaning of repeated yet impossible historical attempts to use the vehicles of law to cover over great collective traumas by the rationality and by the technicality of legal trials, by accounts of the law and by the settlements of courts.

In repeating, thus, both the story of the trauma and the dynamics of the trial, literature explains why and how the trial (like the trauma) is not closed, but partakes of a traumatic memory and of an unfinished business that is bound to receive a future legal sequence. Literature explains, in other words, why the trial, like the trauma, will (historically, traumatically) repeat itself.

The most important question of the trial of the century is the question of the final opening of the abyss as a future destiny of repetition of the trial that was supposed to close or to enclose it. But what, precisely, is the meaning of this *legal, social gap* and of the *gap in understanding* that confronts it and that is bewildered, puzzled, taken by surprise by it? What lies hidden from the eye inside the gap, what is *at the bottom* of this legal, cultural, or historical abyss, or what was *left in abeyance* by the trial and what, precisely, will repeat itself again is, I would suggest, a question whose significance we should have to reflect upon, to ponder, for the next few hundred years. It encapsulates already the historical significance, the ungrasped legal meaning of the trial of the twenty-first century.

To add to this remarkable analysis, my study insists on the way in which the law as such is inhabited not simply by a (very real) violence, but also more precisely (as I show) by *an abyss.* The abyss exists *inside the law* as well as inside literature. Unlike Cover, I insist upon the fact that the difference between law and literature resides not simply in the difference between *literal violence* (the judge's, the criminal's) and *metaphorical violence* (Tolstoy's), but in the fact that *literature opens the trial that the law closes.* The law exhibits (and gives to see) the violence of the criminal, but hides its own. Literature lays open and exposes the violence that is hidden in culture (including the violence of law).

VII

Postscript: The Authority of Literature

"Literature," writes Paul Celan, "often shoots ahead of us."[61] Literature is ahead of us. I have suggested elsewhere[62] that literature can be defined (accounted for, and understood) as a specific mode of testimony; and that writers often feel compelled to testify through literary or artistic channels precisely when they know, or feel intuitively that, in the court of history (and, I will now add, in a court of law) *evidence will fail* or will *fall short;* when they know that other sorts of testimonies will, for different reasons, not come through or that events have taken place that will, for different reasons, not be evidenced. Writers testify not simply when they know that knowledge cannot be obtained through other channels but, more profoundly, when they know or feel that knowledge, though available, cannot become eloquent, that *information cannot become consequential.*[63] I have argued that such writers can be understood (defined) as *precocious witnesses*[64] ("literature often shoots ahead of us") and that their art, their narrative, their literary style, or their artistic rhetoric is a precocious mode of bearing witness and of accessing reality when all other modes of knowledge are precluded or are rendered ineffectual. I am suggesting here that Tolstoy's literary text is, in effect, such a *precocious testimony* in (and to) the O. J. Simpson trial.

"I almost finished *The Kreutzer Sonata* or *How a Husband Killed His Wife*," Tolstoy announced in September 1889; "I am glad I wrote it: I

---

61. Paul Celan, "The Meridian," speech given in 1960, on the occasion of Celan's receipt of the Georg Buchner Prize from the German Academy for Language and Literature, trans. Jerry Glenn, *Chicago Review* 29 (1978): 34.

62. See Felman and Laub, *Testimony.*

63. Compare, for instance, the way in which, during World War II, messengers (such as the underground Polish courier Ian Karski) or escapees from Nazi concentration camps failed to inform the world about the Nazis' final aims. Information was forthcoming, but it could not reach its destination; knowledge existed, but it could not be effectively *transmitted* either to the Allied governments or to the endangered victims. Most Jews in Europe had at least heard rumors about some horrible events in Western Europe. But they were either not believed or it was assumed that "it cannot happen here." The bearers of the rumors were stigmatized as unreliable or mad. See Felman and Laub, *Testimony,* chaps. 3, 4, 6, 7, esp. 103–5, and 231–39.

64. Ibid., xx, and chap. 1, "Education and Crisis," 12–40, 52.

know that people need to be told what is written there."[65] A century later, they still do (as the obsession with the murder story of the century has once more shown). "I've only got one thing," says Pozdnyshev: "It's *what I know. Yes, I know something it will take other people quite a while to find out about* . . . No, people aren't going to find out what I know for quite a while to come" (68). What knowledge (what secret knowledge about murder, what secret knowledge about death, what secret knowledge about life) does the confessant feel he has and that, unless he shares it, people are not likely to find out about? What does the husband-murderer know? And what does Tolstoy know? How does he know, why does he know? *For whom has Tolstoy confessed?*

And why was this confession of the husband—a confession that the O. J. Simpson trial could not get—in turn censored by the law? Why was there a conflict, in Tolstoy's day, between the confession and the law? Why did the Russian law try to reduce to silence the confession? What does Tolstoy know, that can be confessed only *outside the law?* And why did the confessant, even in the fiction, in the literary story of *The Kreutzer Sonata,* feel that his confession could not be transformed into evidence in court, inside a trial? What sort of knowledge guided both Tolstoy and Pozdnyshev precisely as excluded from the trial? What sort of confession was it that had to be confessed not *to* the law, but *despite* the law? And why does the master writer treat the law itself as yet another subterfuge, another misrepresentation with respect to the truth of the confession?

The Confession and the Law (between Violence and Speech)

While Simpson goes to Oxford, England, to complain about the prejudices of the legal system and about the inequities of American justice,[66] Tolstoy writes a confession that declares the law incompetent to truly comprehend the crime or to address the real nature of the case. But the legal flaws do not become his alibi. He speaks not to evade responsibility but to testify: he speaks to *plead responsible.* While Simpson feels accomplished for the fact that he has been "convicted," as he says, "of

---

65. Quoted in Magarshack, afterword, 301.
66. Cf. Joanna Coles, "My Dinner with OJ," *Guardian,* May 16, 1996, 1–3.

nothing,"[67] and, within the trial, denies guilt and denies his presence at the crime scene irrespective of the evidence, Tolstoy pleads guilty irrespective of the verdict. Outside the trial, inside the confession, inside literature, he assumes the burden of a crime that is not literally his own but that he nonetheless profoundly acknowledges as his, and for which he assumes an exemplary personal (and cultural) responsibility. The confession does not ask, How can the law prevail? The confession asks, *What does speech mean in relation to an act of violence?* How can we recognize, how can we *expiate* a violence that is inscribed in culture as invisible, and that cannot be rendered visible in court? How can speech *make visible* a violence whose very nature is to blind? How can we *see* this blinding violence? How can we use speech to *see hate*, to look at our own hatred, when hatred (and especially our own) is normally prohibited to sight?

The confession wishes to confer on speech the highest moral value and the highest epistemological responsibility: that of *accessing the truth;* that of truly *looking* at what has been accessed, no matter how unbearable or how incriminating; that of sacrificing alibis and of *acknowledging reality,* for whatever price.

The discourse of the alibi speaks, on the other hand, precisely *not to know* and especially *not to acknowledge.* "On the night of the murder, I was asleep." You will understand that, asleep, I was not a witness to myself. How can I know where I was? Even were I to be a somnambulist, I wouldn't know. Has there been a murder? Who was murdered? I cannot be cross-examined, since I have no answers. But I can be interviewed—I love to be interviewed—since I do have lots and lots of replies. "At the night of the murder, I was playing golf; I was playing games with myself." The discourse of the alibi speaks to continue to play games with itself, to maintain both consciousness and conscience in a state of numbness, to remain asleep. The confession speaks to wake up.

Inside literature, outside the trial and despite the law, the confession speaks to turn away from subterfuge. Ordinary people—like Simpson, like ourselves—do not speak to turn away from subterfuge. We speak to avoid guilt. We speak to avoid pain. We use speech to protect ourselves. Profoundly, we speak to hope. "White America is still with me,"[68] insists Simpson to his British hosts. "I'm more popular with

---

67. Ibid., 2.
68. Simpson quoted (from a British television interview) by Stuart Jeffries, in "OJ Survives 10-Minute Trial by Television," *International Guardian,* May 14, 1996, 2.

women now than I was before."[69] "Our marriage," said Nicole and
O. J. Simpson after the police had intervened on the issue of domestic
violence, "our marriage is as strong today as it was on the day we married."[70] Only master writers are prepared to say, like Kafka, "there is
hope, but not for us." Only a Camus can write, "hope is not our business. Our business is to turn away from subterfuge."[71] Only a Tolstoy
can have, indeed, the strength, the courage, the integrity, the moral
readiness to pay the price of this confession (a price of guilt, of cruelty,
of suffering, of loneliness, of death; a legal price: a price of censorship,
of legal prohibition, of exclusion from the law), to dispossess himself
(and us) of all emotional illusions, to sacrifice all self-deceptions so as to
unmask lies at all costs and, at all costs, to destroy—to take apart—all
social, all emotional, all cultural alibis. What does Tolstoy know, to feel
so compelled to give life to this brutal legal case and publicly to bare the
husband's guilt? What moves the master writer, in assuming thus
responsibility for a crime he did not in fact commit, to shock the world,
to shake up his readership, to challenge and to tease the public's
incredulity and scandalized amazement, to provoke the censor's ban,
to defy the rage, the outrage, of the church and of the state (not to speak
of that, more private, of his own wife); all the while declaring (implying
by the story) that no court of law can bring this case to justice, that the
law is not equipped to understand the nature of the crime or to address
the nature of the case. Could Tolstoy be right?

In the twentieth century, the law attempts, but fails, to solve or to
resolve the case—to bring truth to the light or bring the murderer to a
confession. In the nineteenth century, the law attempts, but fails, to
silence the confession's truth. It tries to outlaw the confession's publication, but it cannot arrest the case. Even censored, the text spreads.
The handwritten manuscript is secretly read and, swiftly copied by
thousands of hands, is reproduced, handwritten, by the thousands and,
despite the censor, is made public and immediately distributed
throughout the world, translated into many languages. "According to
Strakhov, people no longer greeted each other in the street with 'How
are you?' but with 'Have you read *The Kreutzer Sonata*?'"[72] A century

---

69. Quoted in Coles, "My Dinner with OJ," 3.

70. Quoted in Dunne, "The Simpsons."

71. Camus, "L'Espoir et l'absurde dans l'oeuvre de Franz Kafka," appendix to *Le
Mythe de Sisyphe* (Paris: Collection Folio, Gallimard, 1942), 187.

72. Troyat, *Tolstoy*, 664.

later, it is the same kind of obsession that propels the eager public toward the murder story of the O. J. Simpson case. "This has been a walking Rorschach test," says Medria Williams, a Los Angeles psychologist, of the fascination with the O. J. Simpson trial: "People are reacting as if it's O. J. when it's really about themselves."[73] To whom, then, has Tolstoy confessed? Why have people been so *interested* at once in the *confession* and in the *absence of confession* that has marked the trial of the century? Why have people been so drawn both to the fiction and to the reality of this case? For whom has Tolstoy confessed?

> I'd been taken to the local police station and from there to prison. And there I remained for eleven months awaiting trial. During that time I thought a great deal about myself and my past life, and I grasped what it had all been about.

The Secrets of the Case

> "I only began to grasp it when I saw her in her coffin . . ." He gave a sob, but continued hastily, at once: "It was only when I saw her dead face that I realized what I'd done. I realized that I'd killed her, that it was all my doing and that from a warm, moving, living creature she'd been transformed into a cold, immobile, waxen one, and that there was no way of setting this to rights, not ever, not anywhere, not by any means. If you've never experienced that, you can't possibly understand." (117–18).

"There was no way of setting this to rights, not ever, not anywhere, not by any means." Does Pozdnyshev narrate the out-of-court truth of the O. J. Simpson trial? Can literature be viewed precisely as the *record* of what has remained *out of the legal records?* What does Tolstoy know? And, having read Tolstoy, having watched the trial of the century, what do we in our turn know?

Of course, we cannot say we know—we do not know—whether Simpson did or did not in effect murder his wife. We *do* know that, like Pozdnyshev, he treated her with cruelty and brutal violence. We *do* know, therefore, that the nature of his love was murderous. And this he probably in turn did not grasp and did not realize until it had become

---

73. Medria Williams, quoted in Wilkerson, "Whose Side to Take," 4.

too late. Whether or not he killed Nicole, the overwhelming terror of his own brutality Simpson must have faced only when, like Pozdnyshev, he suddenly saw his ex-wife dead.

We also do know that, whereas Tolstoy confesses to a murder he did not empirically commit, the brutal double murderer, whoever he might be, walks free and has not confessed to a crime he did most certainly commit.

Pozdnyshev was tried and acquitted, but the acquittal has not managed to redeem, to fix, or to restore his shattered life. The havoc that the murder has caused in his soul does not cease with the execution of the crime, nor do its repercussions in his life stop with the resolution of the trial. Having been pronounced "not guilty," freed, he nonetheless remains chained to the bloody murder that no washing will erase, eradicate, or cleanse out of his life. He thus becomes the haunted captive of the bloody saga of which he has become the bearer and whose guilty secrets he will try, but will remain inherently unable, to divulge.

His destiny henceforth is to remain a hostage to the story of his violence: a (willing or unwilling) medium to the transformation of his case into a legend.

Pozdnyshev is willing. But he cannot acquit himself from this Sisyphean, endless task that goes against the grain of culture. He convicts himself. Culture acquits him. He cannot, in confessing, completely overcome the cultural taboos. But this is also his Sisyphean punishment—the testimonial or discursive punishment he takes upon himself. A haunted captive of a guilt that culture will not recognize, he will remain forever the life-prisoner of a confession that he still (as in the trial) feels he cannot quite *transmit* (pass to the other's comprehension, *transform into evidence* on which a consensus can be reached), and that he therefore cannot quite unload and cannot fully *terminate*.

A Confession without End

He can only close the narrative of the confession with the outside interruption of the train's (interminal) arrest. The narrator quits confessing since he has to get off, go outside the train. Tolstoy himself will die in a train station, in the middle of the route and of a life itinerary that was not as yet exhausted, terminated.

But Pozdnyshev has not quite finished. He will certainly repeat again the story to some other passenger aboard some other train, on his way to a final destination that has not yet been—perhaps cannot be— reached. In the meantime, as the writer takes a (temporary) leave by bringing the last sentence to a close and by repeating (with a difference, with a double meaning) a last word that signals a departure and an ending (*proschayte,* "goodbye"), the confessant punctuates his exit from the train—and the story's open-endedness—only with the stated knowledge that his confession has not reached (or will not reach) its end, that it is bound to remain misunderstood:

> There was no way of setting that to rights, not ever, not anywhere, not by any means. *If you've never experienced that, you can't possibly understand.* (118)

(In Tolstoy's own terms, Simpson might be the one reader who will understand Tolstoy; but of course, if only for this very reason, he wouldn't read.) The confession thus remains, despite all the publicity that the confessant gives it and despite himself, his secret, a secret he cannot communicate. And this guilty secret that the court will never understand remains, at the same time, the case's and the trial's secret.

> They asked me in court how I killed her, what I used to do it with. Imbeciles! They thought I killed her that day, the fifth of October, with a knife. It wasn't that day I killed her, it was much earlier. Exactly in the same way as they're killing their wives now, all of them. (60)

Recapitulations

It is because what "they have asked in court" cannot receive a simple answer—cannot be answered in effect except by *recapitulating* the whole story from the start; because the knife (the murder weapon or the signifier of the trauma) is unlocatable (unfindable) except in the life story as a whole, and in the marriage story as a whole—that the confession has to renarrate not just the murder but the failure of the marriage of which it reiterates again the violence, in showing how this unseen violence, of which the unseen knife was just the final signifier, inhabited the marriage from the start: a figure in the carpet.

Trying to make visible this figure in the carpet, trying to narrate again the story that could not be told in court, the confession in its turn cannot but *repeat* the trial and once more *relive* (retell) the horror of the crime. But it cannot divulge the trial's secret. It cannot *locate* the starting point of the trauma or fully translate the trauma's origin into articulateness, into evidence or into seeability. And it cannot convert the blindness of the court and the misunderstanding of the trial into a transparent meaning or into a fully formulated and exhausted intelligibility. The confession, therefore, cannot end. It is a discourse and a speech act that go on and that will continue to go on, for as long as Pozdnyshev lives, for as long as Tolstoy lives; a speech performance— a confession—whose assumed responsibility of renunciation of all alibis, whose cultural insight into the ungraspability of gender traumas, and whose burden of traumatic understanding, will continue to reverberate forever, beyond the end of Tolstoy's text and beyond the confessant's—and the author's—life or death.

> I only began to grasp it when I saw her in her coffin. . . . It was only when I saw her dead face that I realized what I'd done. I realized that I'd killed her. . . , and that there was no way of setting this to rights, not ever, not anywhere, not by any means. If you've never experienced that, you can't possibly understand. (118)

Conclusion, or Justice and Mercy

Like Pozdnyshev, O. J. Simpson has (purportedly) shared with the public his life story, under the teasingly confessional title, *I Want to Tell You.* Like Tolstoy, he has published this life story as a book and has made a celebrated publication of a celebrated autobiography. Unlike Pozdnyshev, O. J. Simpson has claimed he is innocent and has no murder story to confess to. Unlike Tolstoy, he has chosen (in his right as a criminal defendant) *not to testify.*[74]

It is, however, for a different kind of court and for a different kind of justice that Tolstoy has testified, and has left a confession that has,

---

74. The main difference, in effect, between the criminal trial and its legal repetition in the civil trial derived from the fact that in the civil trial, Simpson was *compelled to testify.* But his testimony, in its absolute denial of reality against all evidence ("I never owned such shoes—absolutely not;" "I never hit my wife—absolutely not"), still essentially continued to maintain his choice of legal silence (even in his courtroom speech) through his absolute *refusal to become a witness;* a witness not just to the crime, but *to the trial;* a witness to himself—and to the evidence.

perhaps, confessed for many others and that speaks, perhaps, for all of us: a confession that may well include, in Camus' terms, "a portrait of no one and of everyone";[75] a confession that (not by coincidence) no censor could stop, yet that no trial could contain; a confession that no legal argument could summarize, that no court could translate into coherent legal language, that no jury could hear, yet that no legal pro-hibition could reduce to silence; a confession that has spoken, and still speaks, outside the trial and despite the law to turn away from sub-terfuge; a confession that in fact has never ended and still does not end but begins again the endless trial; a confession that continues endlessly into the night of our culture, of our history.

> "Well, *prostite*, forgive me . . . "
> He turned away from me. . . . I went over to him in order to say good-bye . . .
> "*Proschayte*, goodbye," I said, offering my hand . . .
> "Yes, *prostite*, forgive me. . . ," he said, repeating the word with which he had brought his story to an end. (118)

"By nightfall on judgment day," wrote Francis X. Clines, "the national throng of juror-voyeurs was discovering that justice can be tempered with mercy, for it looked, at long last, as if the end of the O. J. spectacle was in sight":

> Such mercy was to be hoped for as the white minivan [in which O. J. Simpson was released from jail after the acquittal] returned the football star free and clear to his home, and *dragged an old image back* across the national memoryscape. Its fleet *recapitulation* of the white Bronco's via doloroso crawl, the van speeding along the L.A. freeways was *as inarticulate an attempt at closing a story cycle* as might have been scripted in the film factories beyond the Califor-nia hills.[76]

Stories like the O. J. Simpson trial, or the story of the murder of the wife of *The Kreutzer Sonata*, do not end. Their not ending is, perhaps, in some way, part of their poetic justice. They survive as narratives the life and

---

75. Camus, *La Chute* (Paris: Collection Folio, Gallimard, 1956), 148.
76. Clines, "Now, the Audience Rests," 4.

death of their narrators and the convictions or acquittals of their perpetrators.

The questions that Tolstoy's confession poses to our culture have outlived Tolstoy, as they will outlive the murderer of Nicole Brown-Simpson and of Ronald Goldman. The significance of the confession will survive the repercussions of the known and unknown stories of the double murder and its transformation into the spectacular court version of the trial of the century. "The verdict has exposed a chasm in place for generations. . . . People are reacting as if it's O. J. when it's really about themselves."[77] "People no longer greeted each other in the street with 'How are you?' but with 'Have you read *The Kreutzer Sonata?*'"[78]

"The definition of a writer," says Kafka, "of such a writer, and the explanation of his effectiveness, to the extent that he has any," is this:

> He is the scapegoat of mankind. He makes it possible for men to enjoy sin without guilt, *almost without guilt*.[79]

Have you read *The Kreutzer Sonata?*

In a situation in which justice is impossible, in a culture that does not forgive, a literary story puts the century on trial and begs for mercy that it cannot receive.

> I looked at the children, at her battered face with its bruises, and for the first time I forgot about myself, about my marital rights and my injured pride; for the first time I saw her as a human being. And so insignificant did all that had hurt me and made me jealous appear, and so significant what I'd done, that I wanted to press my face to her hand and say: "Forgive me!"—but I didn't dare to. (117)

> "Well, *prostite*, forgive me . . ."
> He turned away from me. . . . I went over to him in order to say good-bye . . .
> "*Proschayte*, goodbye," I said, offering my hand . . .
> "Yes, *prostite*, forgive me. . . ," he said, repeating the word with which he had brought his story to an end. (118)

---

77. Wilkerson, "Whose Side to Take," 4.
78. Troyat, *Tolstoy*, 664.
79. Franz Kafka, letter to Max Brod (Plana, July 5, 1922), in *The Basic Kafka* (New York: Pocket Books, 1971), 295.

Memory, Law, and Literature: The Cases of Flaubert and Baudelaire

Dominick LaCapra

One is supposed to remember the law, since ignorance of it is no defense. Whether Flaubert remembered the law against "outrage to public and religious morality and to good morals," which he was accused of infringing, is moot, but he was brought to trial nonetheless. Indeed his trial was intended to serve as a lesson to others and to increase the likelihood that they would remember the law. Baudelaire did not learn the lesson, for within months of Flaubert's trial, he too found himself before the bar on the same charge.

The publications for which Flaubert and Baudelaire stood trial are of course quite memorable. *Madame Bovary* and *Les Fleurs du mal* are hallowed classics of French literature, seemingly unshakable pillars of the literary canon not only in France but in world—or at least Euro-American—literature. The trials of their authors are less remembered. Yet Flaubert's trial is typically included in French editions of *Madame Bovary*, although it would seem to be relatively infrequently read or at least commented upon.[1] At least one important member of the legal profession, M. le conseiller Falco, did remember Baudelaire's trial precisely because it was in his eyes anomalous and even scandalous that an acknowledged classic of French literature could, in the year 1949, still have some of its poems under a publication ban. He noted that "the year 1857 was a year of great judicial prudishness *(pudeur)* that poorly

---

1. To remedy this state of affairs and thereby make Flaubert's trial more memorable was one purpose of my book, *"Madame Bovary" on Trial* (Ithaca: Cornell University Press, 1982).

chose its victims . . . Flaubert and Baudelaire."[2] And he successfully urged the court to overturn the prior decision against Baudelaire by stressing the need for a more enlightened understanding of civil liberties in relation to art. For him this required that the court understand more "symbolically"—by which he meant spiritually—poems that the 1857 judges had read and condemned in "realistic" terms. Yet it is noteworthy that the theoretical understanding of true art on which the 1949 court relied resembled that of the 1857 court. The judiciary's aesthetic remained idealistic. It demanded that a work of art provide purely symbolic and "spiritual" resolution of the problems it explored. What changed in 1949 was the judgment: certain portions of *Les Fleurs du mal,* once deemed offensive, were now found uplifting. And this change of view was facilitated if not dictated by the text's canonization in literary history and public opinion, which the court's revised decision itself recognized and sanctioned.

Still, whatever the embarrassment they caused to later, seemingly more enlightened and liberal commentators, including those in the legal profession, the trials of Flaubert and Baudelaire were not demonstrative "show" trials whose purpose was either to instill in memory, for the present and future, or to recall from the past, an event or series of events that insistently made demands on collective and individual remembrance and thus necessitated entry into the public sphere. Such were, in important ways, the Nuremberg trials soon after World War II or the trial in Jerusalem of Adolf Eichmann in the early 1960s and, more recently, the trial in France of Klaus Barbie. The trials of Flaubert and Baudelaire were primarily intended as warnings to those involved in literary life whose writings might nonetheless affect a broader public. Moreover, these trials in their own way are worthy of attention and recall in that they still pose questions to us and even bear on issues that remain objects of concern and debate in the contemporary world.

One may certainly ask whether the transmission of memory is a principal (or even a legitimate) function of the law, at least in court trials. One may argue that the transmission of memory, particularly in anything approximating a "show" trial, exists in tension with—and may even contradict—the primary function of a trial: the adjudication of particular cases and the rendering of justice to pertinent parties. The contradiction would pose a manifest problem when political or social

2. See the "Rapport de M. le conseiller Falco," in Charles Baudelaire, *Les Fleurs du mal,* ed. Claude Bonnefoy (Paris: Editions Pierre Belfond, 1965), 139.

pressure is exerted to achieve a desired result, when lawyers "grand-stand" to make a lasting impression, or when material is slanted or interpretations skewed for ideological reasons.[3]

Unlike a court case, historiography has an important and direct collective function in conveying knowledge to a community of inquir-ers as well as to a broader public. But whether historiography itself has the function of transmitting memory is debated by historians. Some—perhaps many—historians would assert a decisive binary opposition or sharp break between the two, placing history on the side of positive research seeking truth, and memory on the side of myth, liturgy, or fal-lible and faulty recollection.[4] Fewer historians would go to the opposite extreme of grounding history in memory as a crucial experience.[5] How-ever, there are historians with a less binary view who construe history and memory as having an open dialectical or dialogic relation in which memory, including its lapses and repressions, helps frame issues for history, while history tests memory and ideally makes it more informed and accurate.[6] Indeed one might contend that, to the extent history loses contact with memory, it addresses dead issues.

An object of research that remains invested with emotion and value—an intensely "cathected" object in psychoanalytic terms—is an object that poses problems for memory. Here one might argue that his-tory itself has at least two closely—and at times tensely—related objec-tives: the adjudication of truth-claims about the past and the transmis-sion of memory. In both senses it bears some resemblance to the law,

---

3. Henry Rousso concludes his discussion of the 1983 Klaus Barbie trial by noting the limitations of using courts primarily as psychodramatic stages for evoking and reshaping historical memory in contrast to their role in satisfying victims' needs for jus-tice. See *The Vichy Syndrome: History and Memory in France since 1944* (Cambridge: Har-vard University Press, 1991), 215.

4. See, for example, Pierre Nora, introduction, *Les Lieux de mémoire* (Paris: Galli-mard, 1984); Arno Mayer, *Why Did the Heavens Not Darken? The "Final Solution" in History* (New York: Pantheon, 1988), esp. 17; and Yosef Hayim Yerushalmi, *Zakhor: Jewish History and Jewish Memory* (New York: Schocken, 1987).

5. For a recent revival of this historicist tendency, see Patrick Hutton, *History as an Art of Memory* (Hanover, N.H.: University Press of New England, 1993). The turn to expe-rience is, however, a broad trend that has recently appeared in the discipline of history, in part as a reaction against the so-called linguistic turn. See, for example, John H. Zam-mito, "Are We Being Theoretical Yet? The New Historicism, the New Philosophy of His-tory, and 'Practicing' Historians," *Journal of Modern History* 65 (1993): 783–814.

6. See Saul Friedlander, *Memory, History, and the Extermination of the Jews of Europe* (Bloomington: Indiana University Press, 1993). See also my *History and Memory after Auschwitz* (Ithaca: Cornell University Press, 1998).

and the comparison of the historian to the magistrate is an old one. Yet it may be more plausible to claim that the transmission of memory is a principal—although not the only—function of history than it would be to ascribe such a status to cases at law. At least with respect to trials (in contrast, say, to legislation concerning basic aspects of social life that should be known and remembered), the transmission of memory would seem to be at most a side effect of rendering justice, and when it becomes central the aims of justice may be subverted or obscured. By contrast, transmitting memory in the proper way would seem inti-mately bound up with the historical attempt retrospectively to do jus-tice to historical agents (notably victims of traumatic events), to avoid more or less destructive repetitions of past events, and even to adjudi-cate truth-claims in a collectively effective manner (at least in the case of sensitive, emotion-laden issues).

Thus one may argue that, even if the transmission of memory is not—or should not be—a primary object of a trial itself, remembering the trial may still in certain respects be an important task of historical research and reflection. Moreover, it would clearly seem acceptable for a participant in a trial, such as Telford Taylor of the Nuremberg trials, to later take on the role of historian and address issues in a manner not suitable in a trial itself.[7] Here one seems to have an important distinc-tion between trials and historiography: the former are indentured to adjudicating particular cases and controversies in order to render jus-tice to individuals, while the latter is dedicated to adjudicating truth-claims, transmitting memory, and, at least in a figurative sense, render-ing retrospective justice to collectivities as well as to individuals. Hence, even in the Nuremberg trials, where the charge of crimes against humanity threatened to override distinctions applicable to an ordinary trial, it was specific individuals who were on trial and not the German nation as a whole or even a delimited collectivity such as the Nazi Party or the SS. Historians have, however, debated the issue of the criminality, liability, and even guilt of collectivities, including the ques-tion of whether one may incriminate an entire nation such as Germany or must restrict criminality and guilt to relatively circumscribed collec-tivities (the Nazi Party, the SS, and their supporters) even if one

---

7. See Telford Taylor, *Anatomy of the Nuremberg Trials* (Waltham, Mass.: Little, Brown, 1993).

ascribes limited liability for the past, including reparations, to a nation and its government.[8]

The literary text also transmits memory, but its relation to truth-claims presents a knotty problem. Literature presumably neither affirms nor denies and thus is beyond (or beneath) truth-claims. In any case, its "events" and characters do not have an existence subject to standard processes of verification and falsification. One might even question the sanity of someone who undertook archival research to establish the true characteristics of Emma Bovary in order to compare them with her features in Flaubert's novel. In fact one of the challenging inversions of *Madame Bovary* as a novel is Flaubert's tendency to provide detailed, seemingly realistic descriptions of imaginary places, such as Yonville, and to set real places, such as Rouen or, even more so, Paris, within a vague and imaginary setting that makes them objects of dream and longing. One may nonetheless maintain that a knowledge of actual or "real" features of Rouen and Paris as cities is necessary for certain of Flaubert's initiatives to have an effect on the reader. And, to the extent that a literary work addresses sensitive topics, notably limit-cases that still provoke controversy, emotion, and evaluative commitments, one may insist that it not radically distort the record established by historians and validated by collective memory—or at least that it frame its experiments that transform or depart from empirical truth in carefully conceived and acceptable ways. In this respect, *Madame Bovary* and *Les Fleurs du mal* do not pose the kinds of problems that a literary work treating the Holocaust or the bombing of Hiroshima might present. Still, certain larger problems at issue in Flaubert and Baudelaire, such as the nature and status of Christianity or "family values" in society, would concern certain—perhaps even many—readers today. And these were precisely the problems on which attention was riveted at their trials.

Moreover, the trials of Flaubert and Baudelaire are of further interest in that they pointedly raise questions about how a literary text was—and perhaps possibly can be—read in a court of law, especially in comparison and contrast with its readings in both literary criticism and historiography sensitive to problems of critical reading. Can readings

---

8. Such issues have swirled around the debate generated by Daniel Jonah Goldhagen's controversial book, *Hitler's Willing Executioners: Ordinary Germans and the Holocaust* (New York: Knopf, 1996).

in a court of law depart from certain expectations created by legal precedent, by the way applicable law is framed, and by what those sitting in judgment will accept as plausible or convincing? Must legal readings be normalizing at least insofar as lawyers are concerned with winning a case and are obliged to accept the legitimacy of what they apprehend as the existing state of law and society as their context or horizon of reading and interpretation? These questions are especially vexed, as we shall see, in the case of literary texts that are in some basic sense transgressive or strangely disconcerting, at least in the context of their own time.

A tradition of literary criticism may be similar to a certain kind of legal interpretation instantiated in a trial insofar as it canonizes a work and tends to suppress, deny, or repress its more disconcerting features in order to make it a vehicle for social values that are at least assumed to function in support of a status quo. By contrast, non- or anticanonical readings may strive, however unsuccessfully (notably when their reading or interpretive strategies become routinized), to bring out the ways even canonized texts may have noncanonical features that not only proved disorienting or uncanny in their own time but may still be able to raise provocative questions for later readers as well. It is conceivable that the most memorable literary texts are precisely those that negotiate a tense and problematic relation between being open to—even inviting—canonical uses and simultaneously presenting the most fundamental challenges to such uses. These are texts that are most likely to register with readers as having a power of contestation in posing "outrageous" challenges to certain normalized social values or routinized norms—challenges basic enough to bring about a defamiliarizing and potentially transformative rethinking of these values or norms and their cultural, social, or political functions.[9] In contrast to the canonizing and idealizing rationale offered the court by Falco, I would suggest that one see a basic tenet of civil liberties as maintaining that

---

9. More wildly experimental texts, especially if their experimentation takes place largely on the levels of form and style, may not be recognized—at least initially—as posing challenges to conventional expectations. They may simply leave the overwhelming majority of readers cold or be seen as pointless and have at best a cult following. Of course they should also receive the protection required by civil liberties, but they may paradoxically be less in need of it than more liminal or hybridized texts that unsettle, deconstruct, and rework conventional or normalized assumptions. It is doubtful, for example, that Flaubert's *Bouvard and Pécuchet* or even his *Salammbô* would come to trial. The same point might be made about James Joyce's *Finnegans Wake* in contrast to *Ulysses*.

precisely these texts, at least insofar as they do not present clear and present dangers on the level of incitement to harmful social action, should not be censored or their authors prosecuted.

The regime under which Flaubert and Baudelaire lived did not recognize civil liberties in this sense, but the one under which Falco lived presumably did, although one might question the idealistic or "symbolic" aesthetic of Falco and the court that recalled important dimensions of the trials of Flaubert and Baudelaire. Here one might argue that art is a relatively safe haven for experimenting with and exploring certain problems that one would not have experimented with or explored in the same way in ordinary life. Thus one might contend that the law might be justified in prohibiting or regulating in ordinary social life what it should not prohibit in art or literature. In this sense, authors of texts or other works of art fictively exploring certain issues should not be brought to trial even if they portray things that would be indictable in ordinary social life. Of course such a general principle would require further specification in any concrete situation, notably in terms of the law's tendency to apply universalizing rules or norms in contexts that are riven with differences in power, status, and wealth. Moreover, what things are allowable in art but not in ordinary life might change over time and create bases of conflict among social groups at any given time. Most people today in France or the United States would probably not defend literary censorship, much less legal sanctions, with respect to works representing—however favorably—adultery, although they might be more uneasy about other challenges to "family values" in Flaubert and Baudelaire. And certain religious or moral groups might indeed take a firm stand on adultery in ordinary life and even in literature to the point of demanding not only ethical condemnation but legal sanctions. Moreover, even more people might get uneasy about "outrages" to religion in art itself, as is demonstrated by recent controversies over the limits of art in this respect. We shall see that "family values" as well as religion were very much at issue in the texts and trials of Flaubert and Baudelaire, as the prosecuting attorney at their trials was at pains to point out.

In the trial concerning *Madame Bovary*, Flaubert was given a severe reprimand but acquitted by the court. The acquittal seemed anticlimactic, however, for the reasoning of the court appeared to agree with that of the prosecuting attorney until it reached the point of judgment. In the words of the court, Flaubert's work did "deserve stern censure, for the mission of literature must be to enrich and to refresh the spirit by improving the understanding and by perfecting character, more than to instill a loathing of vice by offering a picture of the disorders that may exist in society." Indeed "it is not permitted, under pretext of painting local color, to reproduce in all their immorality the exploits and sayings of the characters the writer has made it his duty to paint. . . . Such a system applied to the works of the mind as well as to the products of the fine arts would lead to a realism that would be the negation of the beautiful and the good, and that, in begetting works equally offensive to sight and mind, would be committing continual outrages against public morality and decency." Thus, for the court, the ideal and idealizing nature of art functioned to condemn the putative "realism" practiced by Flaubert. What is significant is that the court itself affirmed a stereotypically idealistic conception of art in order to censure Flaubert and, by implication, all other "realists." Flaubert, in the eyes of the court, had "insufficiently understood" that "there are limits that even the most frivolous literature must not overstep." But the court nonetheless concluded that the charges against Flaubert had been insufficiently proved, not explaining how its own seemingly absolute judgments could be converted into a matter of degree. Evidence of rather nominal acceptance of the norms and rituals of established society seemed to be enough for the court, at least in the case of this writer. The court satisfied itself with observing that Flaubert's novel was the product of much work, that the author affirmed his respect for decency, and that his sole aim was not the gratification of the passions. "He has committed only the fault of sometimes losing sight of the rule that no self-respecting writer should ever infringe and of forgetting that literature, like art, if it is to achieve the good that it is called upon to produce, must be chaste and pure not only in its form but in its expression."[10] Thus the court reprimanded Flaubert, provided him with what might be called (with a touch of Flaubertian irony) a "memorable" experience, and released him without awarding him the costs of the trial.

This decision very much upset Ernest Pinard, who was the prosecutor in the cases of both Flaubert and Baudelaire. Falco in 1949 sensed the closeness of the considerations at issue in the two trials and even intimated that in 1857 the minister of the interior (Adolphe Billault)

---

10. *Flaubert Oeuvres,* ed. Albert Thibaudet and René Dusmenil, vol. 1 (Paris: Gallimard, 1951), 682–83. Translations from the French, unless otherwise indicated, are my own, and further page references shall be included in the text.

may have insisted on bringing Baudelaire to trial as a vengeful compensation for the acquittal of Flaubert. Baudelaire's trial was in fact a miniaturized replay of Flaubert's, and it holds few surprises for anyone familiar with the earlier trial.[11] However, Baudelaire's lawyer (Chaix d'Est-Ange) offered a rhetorically less effective plea than Flaubert's (Marie-Antoine-Jules Sénard).[12] And, in spite of the fact that he won the case against Baudelaire, Pinard seemed decidedly less invested in Baudelaire's trial and text than in Flaubert's—perhaps because he judged *Les Fleurs du mal* to retain more saving vestiges of Christianity, which he believed to be the very foundation of Western civilization. In the case of Baudelaire, Pinard even successfully advised the court to tone down the charges and to consider only the offense to public morality while dropping that of outrage to religious morality.

The prosecution of Flaubert and Baudelaire was not exceptional under the Second Empire's regime of censorship. But the fact that works of more manifestly "prurient" (or "lascivious") interest and of markedly inferior aesthetic quality than *Madame Bovary* or *Les Fleurs du mal* escaped prosecution makes their trials distinctive. Flaubert and Baudelaire were indicted under the law of May 17, 1819, and the provisions of this law were rendered even more restrictive by the decree of February 17, 1852. In 1819 François Guizot had introduced the system of *cautionnement* whereby anyone who wished to start a newspaper had to deposit a sum of money with the Treasury—a sum that would be forfeited in case of successful prosecution. Under the 1852 press law, the

---

11. For this reason, I shall focus primarily on Flaubert's trial.

12. In a gesture that seems poised between the serious and the ironic, Flaubert dedicated *Madame Bovary* to Sénard: "To Marie-Antoine-Jules Sénard/ Member of the Parisian Bar/ Ex-President of the National Assembly, and/ Former Minister of the Interior/ Dear and Illustrious Friend,—/ Permit me to inscribe your name at the head of this book, and above its dedication: for it is to you, before all, that I owe its publication. By becoming part of your magnificent defence, my work has acquired for myself, as it were, an unexpected authority. Accept, then, here, the homage of my gratitude, which, however great, will never attain to the level of your eloquence and your devotion./ Gustave Flaubert" (I here use the suggestive translation of Paul de Man, which introduces six more commas than Flaubert himself used, thereby breaking up the flow of the prose and creating more gaps into which doubt and ironic hesitation may be introduced. See *Madame Bovary*, edited with a substantially new translation by Paul de Man [New York: Norton, 1965], 1). Flaubert here indicates that his novel has become part of Sénard's defense, as if the work of fiction could be integrated into a legal brief and somehow derive authority from this relationship. In fact the trial has become an appendage to the text of the novel, at least in all French editions. In either event, the scene is set for intertextual readings of the trial and the novel.

required deposit rose to an intimidating level (fifty thousand francs in Paris and slightly less in the provinces). Moreover, during the Second Empire, all cases brought under the 1819 act were to be treated in the same manner as offenses against the press laws. The accused no longer had the right to a jury trial. He or she went before a magistrate presiding over a *tribunal correctionnel* where common criminals such as pimps and prostitutes were the typical delinquents. Appearance before such a court was itself to some extent a ritual of degradation.[13]

While censorship under the Second Empire was strict, it was somewhat capriciously administered. It was most inquisitorial with respect to books and periodicals. But it lacked the techniques of surveillance and control that have been made familiar by more recent dictatorial regimes. Still, the effect of censorship was culturally stultifying, and it was an indication of the anxieties created by the increased dissemination of literature through commodification and the commercial market in books and periodicals. In 1857 the *Revue de Paris,* where *Madame Bovary* was first published in serial form, was an object of manifest political suspicion on the part of the government, and its editor, Maxime du Camp, as well as Flaubert himself, expressed the view that the prosecution of the novelist served as a pretext to repress the periodical. But the trials of both Flaubert and Baudelaire were overdetermined events, and the complex way repression operated linked a manifest political animus with more latent "literary" and sociocultural considerations.

In his diary, Pinard (the prosecuting attorney) tried to explain why Flaubert was brought to trial. The curious anomalies in his recollection of events are themselves so glaring that they attest to significant anxieties and suggest not simple errors but evasion and repression.

> The novel *Madame Bovary* reveals a true talent; but the description of certain scenes goes beyond all bounds *(toute mesure);* if we close our eyes, Flaubert will have many imitators, who will go even further in the same direction. In addition, the *Chambre correctionnelle* had just condemned Baudelaire's *Les Fleurs du mal;* it inflicted a

---

13. One may note that the trials took the highly stylized format of monologues by the prosecution and by the defense, followed by the judgment of the court. In Flaubert's trial, there were a few brief interruptions or interjections on the part of the prosecutor during the speech of the defense. There was no direct questioning of witnesses or cross-examination.

fine upon the author and ordered the suppression of certain passages. If we abstain [in Flaubert's case], one will say that we are easy on the strong and the heads of schools and that we are accommodating toward our own but inflexible for opponents. Baudelaire had many friends in the camp of the republicans [opponents of Napoleon III's regime under which Pinard served], while Flaubert was an assiduous, feted guest in the salons of Princess Mathilde [Napoleon III's cousin].[14]

This after-the-fact rationale of Pinard's is astounding. André Pasquet, who quotes it in his book on Pinard, which attempts to rehabilitate the latter's reputation and to counteract the tendency of literary critics to vilify him, nonetheless comments: "Ernest Pinard's memory betrayed him in an extreme way. It is difficult to accumulate more errors in a few lines."[15] What were these errors?

First, the condemnation of Baudelaire could not have influenced Pinard's decision because Baudelaire's *Fleurs du mal*, which appeared on June 25, 1857, was condemned on August 20 of that year, six months after the trial of Flaubert. Second, Flaubert's sustained relations with the Princess Mathilde began only in 1860, three years after the trial.[16] Third, Flaubert, at the time of the trial, was hardly a powerful *chef d'école*. He had published nothing. (He became a figurehead for "realists" and "naturalists," much to his dismay, only after the trial.)[17] Fourth, those responsible for the trial probably did not know of the social importance of Flaubert's family, a point that Flaubert commented upon in his letters and that his defense lawyer, Sénard, made much of at the trial. (One might add that Baudelaire's stepfather, Gen-

---

14. Quoted in André Pasquet, *Ernest Pinard et le procès de Madame Bovary* (Paris: Editions Savoir, Vouloir Pouvoir, 1949), 10.

15. Ibid., 11.

16. It should, however, be noted that Baudelaire himself believed that the princess had intervened for Flaubert, and this belief inspired him to try to get Madame Sabatier to perform a similar service on his own behalf.

17. Flaubert himself rejected a certain kind of photographic realism and was upset when others took him as the figurehead of a realistic movement in art. He thought realism was the death of art, and one of his strong beliefs was that the artistic imagination should strive to negate and transcend an ugly (especially bourgeois) reality through painful stylistic work *(les affres du style)*. In a sense Flaubert shared asceticism with Christianity and a version of the capitalist ethos, but he turned it against both orthodox salvation and the productive work ethic, at times holding out instead a problematic vision of redemption through pure art.

eral Aupick, had a national prominence greater than the more regional
fame of Doctor Flaubert and that the aesthetic views of Baudelaire and
Flaubert were quite similar—as they both immediately recognized.)
Pinard's "tricks" of memory were indicative of his unsettlement and
his ambivalent investment in the reading of *Madame Bovary*, a work that
he opposed so strongly because he himself could feel the temptations it
conveyed without being fully able to articulate them.

Pinard was clearly disturbed by the novel in a way that the defense
lawyer, Sénard, refused to be. Although there are many conventionalizing appeals to common sense in his argument, Pinard seemed open to
the allure of Emma Bovary herself, whose existence might be imaginary but whose effects could for him be quite real. Sénard's interpretation, on the contrary, made the novel out to be altogether conventional
and harmless if not beneficent in nature. In fact he took it to be less
risqué than acknowledged classics in the literary canon. (Sénard
delighted in comparing the famous fiacre or cab scene in *Madame
Bovary* to a scene in Prosper Merimée's *La Double Méprise* where the
novelist was indeed so bold as to describe what went on between an
amorous couple inside a closed cab—what Flaubert explicitly did not
do.) Unlike his legal colleague, Pinard experienced the novel's insinua-
tions and disconcerting potential despite his sustained effort to construe it in terms of simple deviance from established norms. At the very
least, Pinard may have been "poisoned" or contaminated by what he
saw as the "painting of passion" in the novel and, himself facing temptation, may have set out in a self-preservative quest to find a legal
answer to Flaubert's writing. Here the law was to function as the saving antidote to literature. Certain of Pinard's comments during the trial
lend themselves to this interpretation, for example, when he suggests
the possibility that even men may be "feminized" by literature and
evokes, in almost Platonic fashion, the image of the laws as the
guardians of public morality and religion.

> Who will read the novel of Flaubert? Will it be men who busy
> themselves with political or social economy? No! The light pages
> of *Madame Bovary* will fall into even lighter hands—into the hands
> of young women, sometimes of married women. Well, when the
> imagination will have been seduced, when seduction will have
> descended into the heart, when the heart will have spoken to the

senses, do you believe that a very cold reasoning will be very strong against this seduction of the senses and of sentiment? In addition, even men must not drape themselves too much in their force and virtue; men too harbor instincts from below and ideas from above and, with everyone alike, virtue is the consequence of effort, very often painful effort. Lascivious paintings generally have more influence than cold reasonings. (631–32)

Both Pinard and Sénard try to arrive at the meaning or message of the novel by attempting to define the intention or "thought" of the author. Yet, for Pinard, the title and subtitle provided by Flaubert—*Madame Bovary: Moeurs de province*—do not explain Flaubert's "thought"; only the subtitle gives some sense of it. The author, for Pinard, wanted to provide tableaux or pictures: the language of the novel is a "picturesque" one, and it depends on the "colors" of the picture for its effects. The portrait of the husband, Charles, begins and ends the novel. Yet, for Pinard, this fact does not give Charles a particularly important role in the narration. For the prosecutor, "it is evidently [the portrait] of Madame Bovary" that is the most "serious" one in the novel, the one that "illuminates" all the others (616). For Pinard, Emma is unquestionably the central, sunlike figure in the novel.

Pinard provides a conventional plot summary following the outline of the four principal scenes he will use as frames for his quotations and his general indictment of the novel and its author: (1) Emma's "fall" with Rodolphe, (2) the religious transition between the two adulteries, (3) the "fall" with Léon, (4) the death of Emma. On the basis of this summary, he offers a new title, a précis of the novel's meaning, and a delineation of its dominant "color."

The new and more accurate title is "The History of the Adulteries of a Provincial Woman" (618). The essential meaning is also the essential charge against the novel: "The offense to public morality is in the lascivious tableaux that I shall place before your eyes: the offense to religious morality is in the voluptuous images mingled with sacred things." The "general color of the author . . . is the lascivious color, before, during, and after the falls" (619). The author, employing "all the wonders of his style," has used these colors to paint Madame Bovary, and the result is a glorification of adultery and an undermining of marriage. For "the beauty of Madame Bovary is a beauty of provocation" (621).

The genre or school to which this use of language belongs is the "realistic" one: "the genre that Monsieur Flaubert cultivates, that which he realizes without the circumspection of art but with all the resources of art, is the descriptive genre: it is realistic painting." Realism for Pinard seems to encapsulate all that is disconcerting in the art of Flaubert. But it is more particularly related to Flaubert's "lascivious" colorations and to his lack of circumspection and *mesure* (measure or limits) in art.

Pinard was especially disoriented by a telling phrase in Flaubert's novel: "les souillures du mariage et les désillusions de l'adultère" [the defilements of marriage and the disillusions of adultery]. Pinard twice expressed his outrage, and in his second recrimination he noted: "Often when one is married, instead of the unclouded happiness one expected, one encounters sacrifices and bitterness. The word 'disillusion' might be justified; that of 'defilement' could never be" (625). Flaubert had turned things topsy-turvy, ascribing to marriage what might be expected of adultery and vice-versa.

In closing his argument, Pinard attempted to preempt a line of defense. "One will say as a general objection: but, after all, the novel is fundamentally moral, because adultery is punished." For Pinard, even if the ending were moral, it would not justify "lascivious" details in the book: if it did, anything would be justified by a moral ending. But even assuming this end or ending existed—an assumption Pinard denied— it would not justify the means. For "this would go against the rules of common sense. It would amount to putting poison in the reach of all and the antidote in the hands of a very small number, if indeed there were an antidote" (631).

The ending of *Madame Bovary* is not genuinely moral for Pinard. Emma dies, but her death conveys no moral lesson. Her death is not brought on as a punishment for her adultery. "She dies not because she is adulterous but because she wanted to die. She dies in all the splendor of youth and beauty" (632). Hence for Pinard Emma's death is as much a provocation as her adulterous life. Her self-poisoning is a willful, brazen act that compounds her infectiously poisonous crime rather than compensating for it.

Pinard concludes with general reflections on the immorality of the novel "from a philosophical point of view" (632). In his own way, he alludes to what later theorists would refer to as unreliable narration:

> Who can condemn this woman in the book? Nobody. Such is the conclusion. There is not in the book a character who can condemn her. If you find in it a wise character, if you find in it a single principle in virtue of which adultery may be stigmatized, then I'm wrong. Thus if in all the book there is not a character who can make her bend her head; if there is not an idea, a line in virtue of which adultery is scourged, then I am right: the book is immoral. . . . Would you condemn her in the name of the author's conscience? I do not know what the author's conscience thinks. (632–33)

Thus for Pinard there is no secure or reliable position within the novel—no Archimedean point—from which to condemn Emma. Conjugal honor is represented by a foolish husband who literally hands his wife over to her lovers—by insisting that she go riding with Rodolphe and stay over in Rouen to attend an opera with Léon. Public opinion is "personified in a grotesque being, the pharmacist Homais, who is surrounded by ridiculous people whom this woman dominates." Religion is incarnated in the priest Bournisien, "a priest about as grotesque as the pharmacist, believing in physical and never moral suffering, almost a materialist" (632). The author is so elusive that his moral position cannot be determined. What is left is the powerful personality of Emma and the harmful example she gives. Within the novel, "the only person who dominates is Madame Bovary" (633).

For Pinard the absence in the novel of an authoritative source of moral judgment and censure leads to the conclusion that one must look outside the text to a larger and more certain context—that of "Christian morality, which is the foundation of our modern civilizations." In its light, "everything becomes explained and clarified" (633). From this morality, one may derive solid, luminous principles through which the novel and its characters may be judged and by which the court itself must be guided in its deliberations. Only this Christian morality is a force strong enough to dominate Emma and put a stop to her poisonous influence.

> In its name adultery is stigmatized and condemned, not because it is an imprudence that exposes one to disillusionments and regrets, but because it is a crime for the family. You stigmatize and condemn suicide not because it is an act of madness—the madman is

not responsible—not because it is an act of cowardice—it at times demands a certain physical courage—but because it is the contempt for one's duty in the life that is ending and a cry of disbelief in the life that begins. This morality stigmatizes realistic literature not because it paints the passions: hatred, vengeance, love—the world lives on nothing else, and art must paint them—but when it paints them without brakes, without measure *(mesure)*. Art without rules is no longer art; it is like a woman who takes off all her clothes. To impose upon art the unique rule of public decency is not to subordinate it but to honor it. One can grow only in accordance with a rule. These are the principles that we profess. This is a doctrine that we defend conscientiously. (635)

Pinard here explicitly enunciates his belief in the manner in which public morality is grounded in the Christian tradition as well as his conviction that the mission of the legal system is to uphold that morality. The core of his argument is staunchly and unabashedly moral and religious. And the strength of his convictions in some sense enables him to be unsettled or shaken by aspects of the novel that the more insistently complacent and conventionalizing approach of the defense attorney will obscure or obliterate. For Sénard's defense will take the tack that Pinard's sense of outrage is entirely misplaced. The novel is not at all sacrilegious or nonconformist. On the contrary, it is the fully reputable and responsible confirmation of conventional morality.

Sénard begins by giving his own rendition of the intention or thought of the author. It is "an eminently moral and religious thought that can be translated by these words: the incitement to virtue through horror of vice *(l'incitation à la vertu par l'horreur du vice)*" (634). Sénard apparently does not notice that "incitement" is a strange word to apply to virtue since it would more plausibly be used in the case of vice or crime. Indeed Sénard is not only unself-conscious about aspects of his own discourse but notices little about the disconcerting movements in the novel itself, for his strategy is one of sustained and imperturbable conventionalization whereby the novel is made to confirm the most respectable and devout wishes of the solid citizen. In his hands, *Madame Bovary* becomes a provincial bildungsroman or even a *leçon de morale* that resoundingly reaffirms existing morality and society.

Sénard staunchly rejects Pinard's proposed subtitle for the novel.

His countertitle is inserted into his own rendition of the novel's essential meaning or message:

> No! The second title of this work is not *The Story of the Adulteries of a Provincial Wife;* it is, if you absolutely must have a second title, the story of the education too often given in the provinces; the story of the dangers to which it can lead; the story of degradation, of villainy, of a suicide seen as a consequence of an early transgression, and of a transgression that was itself induced by a first misstep into which a young woman is often led; it is a story of an education, the story of a deplorable life to which this sort of education is too often the preface. (636)

For Sénard, *Madame Bovary* recounts the sad but ultimately uplifting story of social maladjustment: a farmer's daughter, socially suited to a modest marriage, looks beyond her station in life because she receives an inappropriate education. From this dissonance between social position and unwarranted expectations, Sénard draws a socially conservative moral:

> Oh! God knows, those of our young women who do not find enough in honest and elevated principles or in a strict religion to keep them steadfast in the performance of their duties as mothers, who do not find it above all in that resignation, that practical understanding of life that tells us that we must make the best of what we have, but who turn their reveries outside, these most honorable and pure young women who, in the prosaic everydayness of their household, are sometimes tormented by what goes on around them—a book like this will, you can be sure, lead more than one of them to reflect. This is what Monsieur Flaubert has done. . . . The dénouement in favor of morality is found in every line of the book. (639)

Like Pinard, Sénard is preoccupied with the way the novel may be read by young women, but he draws from it symmetrically opposite conclusions for the young, particularly tender minds and hearts of the fairer sex. He also looks to what parents may derive from its tale. Indeed, for him, every line of the book poses the question: "Have you done all you should in the education of your daughters?" (677)

To establish the exemplary morality of the novel, Sénard turns to Flaubert's own character and family. "M. Gustave Flaubert is a man with a serious character, carried by his nature toward grave and serious things." His studies, "conforming to the nature of his spirit," were also serious and broad-ranging, and "they included not only all branches of literature but also the law" (635). (In light of Flaubert's pronounced and oft-proclaimed hatred for his early legal studies, Sénard's last point is a particularly nice touch.)

Sénard comes to Flaubert's defense for reasons of both conscience and friendship. Flaubert's father was his friend, and his own children are friends of Gustave, the good doctor's son. Sénard goes on to establish a genealogy of moral respectability for his client. But his boldest move is to postulate both a personal responsibility for Flaubert's text and a privileged access to the mind of its author, thus enabling him to speak in Flaubert's voice. "I know his thought; I know his intentions; and the lawyer has the right to present himself as the personal bondsman [or bail—*caution*] for his client" (635).

Early in his defense, Sénard mentions the phrase that caused Pinard difficulties: the seeming reversal of ordinary expectations in "les souillures du mariage et les désillusions de l'adultère." Sénard passes quickly over the first part of the phrase that stains marriage with the defilements of adultery, and he avoids the problem of reversal altogether. Instead he lingers over the second part of the phrase in isolation, and he provides a reassuring gloss of it. It demonstrates the way adultery will not bring a desired escape from the platitudes of marriage but only something worse and more disillusioning. Indeed Sénard resorts to a voice-over from on high and delivers his melodramatic interpretation through the clouds of a patronizing apostrophe to Emma Bovary herself and to anyone bemused enough to emulate her:

> There where you expected to find love, you will find only libertinage. There where you expected to find happiness, you will find only bitterness. A husband who goes quietly about his affairs, who puts on his nightcap and eats his supper with you, is a prosaic husband who disgusts you. You dream of a man who loves you, who idolizes you, poor child! That man will be a libertine who will have taken you up for a moment to play with you. . . . The man of whom you dreamed will have lost all his glamour; you will have rediscovered in love the platitudes of marriage, and you will have redis-

covered them with contempt and scorn, with disgust and piercing remorse. (638)

Sénard feels obliged to confront the view that Flaubert should be seen as a realist, for that view in Pinard took on the nature of an accusation. For Sénard Flaubert is a realist, but only in the most banal and moralistic of senses. "What Monsieur Flaubert wanted above all was to take a subject of study from real life and to create or constitute true middle-class types, thereby arriving at a useful result. Yes, what has most preoccupied my client in this study to which he had dedicated himself is precisely this useful purpose, and he has pursued it by setting forth three or four characters from present-day society living in real-life circumstances, and by presenting to the reader's eye a true tableau of what most often happens in the world" (636). He then poses the rhetorical question: "Can this book, placed in the hands of a young girl, have the effect of drawing her toward easy pleasures, toward adultery, or will it on the contrary show the danger of the initial steps and make her tremble with horror?" The answer is a foregone conclusion:

My God! There are nuances that may sometimes escape us given our habits, but they cannot escape women of great intelligence, of great purity, of great chastity. There are names that cannot be pronounced before the court, but if I were to tell you what has been said to Monsieur Flaubert, what has been said to me by mothers of families who read the book . . . (642)

Sénard's overall strategy in countering the prosecution is to argue that Pinard quoted out of context and that he need but quote from the novel more fully and in context to make his case. He even alludes to his project of publishing with Flaubert a *mémoire* that he himself would have cosigned with the author, composed of an annotated version of the entire text of *Madame Bovary* (647). Only an injunction directed against the explanatory notes prevented this venture where Sénard would actually have joined his name to Flaubert's in engendering a new version of the novel. In lieu of it, Sénard will quote extensively from the novel and use quotations to defeat and deflate all the contentions of the prosecution. Indeed his array of quotations fills thirty tightly packed pages of the Pléiade edition (650–80). The process of filling out and contextualizing the prosecutor's quotations can lead to one and only one conclusion: "The reading of this book cannot produce in you an impression other than that which it produced in us, that is, that this book is excellent as a whole and that its details are irreproachable" (680–81). Earlier in his plea, Sénard provided an appreciation of religion as it applied to the novel—an appreciation that could be read as an unself-conscious parody of Flaubert's explicitly parodic recitation, in the compromised, indeed despised voice of Homais, of Rousseau's *Profession of Faith of a Savorard Vicar:*

> As for myself, here is what I flatly declare: I know of nothing more beautiful, more useful, and more necessary to support us in the path of life [than religion]: not only for women, but also for men, who themselves have at times extremely painful trials to overcome. I know of nothing more useful and necessary, but the religious sentiment must be solemn and, allow me to add, it must be severe. I want my children to understand God, but not a God in the abstractions of pantheism, but a Supreme Being with whom they are in harmony, to whom they raise themselves in prayer, and who, at the same time, helps them to grow and gives them strength. (646)[18]

I have intimated that a principal charge against both Flaubert and Baudelaire in 1857 was realism—realism understood as an alluring representation of the ugly and the evil marked by a lascivious or prurient coloration and a lack of a legitimate sense of limits *(mesure).* It was a charge Sénard tried to deflect or defuse, and one that Pinard framed in memorable words: "Art without rules is no longer art; it is like a woman who takes off all her clothes" (635). Or as the court put it in their judgment, realism as practiced by Flaubert is "the negation of the beautiful and the good." In advocating the abrogation of the verdict against Baudelaire in 1949, Falco not only stressed the need for a more

---

18. Compare Homais: "I have a religion, my religion, and I even have more than all these others with their mummeries and their juggling. I adore God, on the contrary. I believe in the Supreme Being, in a Creator, whatever he may be. I care little who has placed us here below to fulfill our duties as citizens and parents; but I don't need to go to church to kiss silver plates, and fatten out of my pocket, a lot of good-for-nothings who live better than we do. For one can know him as well in a wood, in a field, or even contemplating the ethereal heavens like the ancients. My god is the God of Socrates, of Franklin, of Voltaire, and of Béranger! I support the *profession de Foi du Vicaire savoyard* and the immortal principles of '89!" (*Madame Bovary,* trans. de Man, 55).

enlightened understanding of civil liberties in relation to art and the possibility of a more "symbolic" (or what the court termed "spiritualistic") interpretation of a text that the court saw in "realistic" terms in 1857. He also suggestively noted that moderns might be "more blasé" in their relation to values, but he did not expand upon the point or relate it to the problem of civil liberties. As I noted, the judiciary's aesthetic, in 1949 as in 1857, was idealistic, and it demanded that a work of art provide purely symbolic and satisfyingly uplifting resolution of the problems it disclosed.

A trial is a crucial setting for the reception of texts (and other artifacts), and it affects both the artistic and the ordinary life of the artist. Particularly to the extent that lawyers and judges are rhetorically attuned to public mores, it is also one index of expectations and assumptions in the larger society at least on the level of "official" consciousness. What is striking is that prosecution, defense, and judges at the trials of both Flaubert and Baudelaire shared a great deal on the level of more or less unspoken assumptions and expectations. Aside from certain preconceptions about the nature of true art, they assumed that the larger sociocultural and political context of both trial and text was fundamentally legitimate. Hence they could not recognize the ways in which the texts they judged not only attested to but intensified a legitimation crisis by placing in question the very contextualized norms upon which the court relied to render judgment. In this sense, the "crime" of these texts was not ordinary but ideological—a kind of criminality that an existing legal system may not be able to recognize insofar as it points to a perceived "rottenness" (in Walter Benjamin's term) or illegitimacy in the social basis of the existing legal system itself. Both prosecution and defense were constrained to conceive in terms of a simple binary opposition between ordinary conformity (in the case of the defense) and ordinary deviance or crime (in the case of the prosecution) what involved elements of ideological and extraordinary "crime" or transgression. Thus they processed as either conformity or deviance what might be argued to be fundamental difference or nonnegotiable basic criticism.

It is noteworthy that the defense at both trials was more insistently conventionalizing, normalizing, or domesticating than the prosecution, for one of the primary tactics of the defense lawyers was to insist upon ways in which *Madame Bovary* and *Les Fleurs du mal* were less risqué in the treatment of certain themes—particularly erotic themes—than were many of the most cherished classics in French literature. The prosecuting attorney Pinard, especially in the case of Flaubert, threatened at times to stumble upon facets of the text that escaped the confines of simple or standardized deviance, notably with respect to the telling reversal of normal expectations in the phrase "les souillures du mariage et les désillusions de l'adultère" [the defilements of marriage and the disillusions of adultery].

If one departs from Pinard's premises, one might attempt to indicate the truly destabilizing import of Flaubert's telling chiasmus. For one might argue that the text of *Madame Bovary* does not simply praise adultery and condemn marriage (as the prosecution contended) or, conversely, attack adultery and defend marriage (as the defense maintained); it discloses a drastically unstable sociocultural and ethicopolitical context in which the very founding opposition between adultery and marriage threatens to become a distinction without a difference. In other words, the stable order and firm oppositions assumed by classical tragedy—and by the legal system in these cases—appear to be unavailable in Emma's world. A reason for her addled "tragedy" or predicament is that little of substance differentiates her husband from her lovers, her ordinary reality from her imaginings. Seeming opposites tend to crumble or to become deadly repetitions of one another, and the despised husband paradoxically both resembles her lovers and proves in the end to be the only one who loves her. Not only does he keep an adoring vigil at her coffin while others sleep or are absent. He ends his life imitating hers as he establishes Emma as an undefiled romantic idol in spite of all evidence to the contrary.

In *Madame Bovary,* moreover, the unsettling treatment of the family is conjoined with an often outrageous, satirical critique of religion. The binary opposition between the sacred and the profane proves to be as untenable as that between marriage and adultery. There is, for example, little to distinguish the priest Bournisien from his ridiculous, secular counterpart, the pharmacist Homais—a point epitomized in the fact that this loving couple finally "recognize" one another as they eat and sleep together over Emma's coffin.[19] Most subtly perhaps, Flaubert's very style of narration—including the so-called *style indirect libre,* or free indirect style—decenters the subject through modulations of narrative voice and perspective. Tropisms relate unreliable narration to the

---

19. To some extent the prosecutor Pinard recognized this point but did not draw certain unsettling conclusions from it.

unsettlement of the solid bourgeois individual as a presumed foundation of judgment and interpretation—a problem sensed by the prosecuting attorney when he exclaimed that there was no vantage point within the novel from which Emma Bovary could be forthrightly condemned. These tropisms are also the larger textual setting in which Flaubert's so-called free indirect style should be understood—a style that is inadequately interpreted as the monological rendition of the thoughts of a character in the words of the narrator, for the *style indirect libre* brings about a shifting, dialogical interaction of irony and empathy, proximity and distance, as the narrator weaves in and out of objects of narration.[20]

One may, however, note that conventionalizing readings are not altogether wrong and that a task for analysis—perhaps a type of analysis that cannot be housed within the confines of a trial or even given a recognizable place in the discipline of law—is to delineate the relations among symptomatic, critical, and potentially transformative aspects of a text. (Indeed a problem here is that a reading that attempts to trace and raise questions about the more uncanny movements of these texts may not find a settled place in any single discipline.) *Madame Bovary* and *Les Fleurs du mal* to some extent invite conventionalizing or symptomatic readings both because of the strategies they bring into play and

---

20. For this dimension of the novel, see my *"Madame Bovary" on Trial*, chaps. 6–7. Here is but one passage in which the tropisms in Flaubert's narrative, involving varying degrees of proximity and distance between narrator and characters, are particularly evident: "Charles was surprised at the whiteness of her nails. They were shiny, delicate at the tips, more polished than the ivory of Dieppe, and almond-shaped. Yet her hand was not beautiful, perhaps not white enough, and a little hard at the knuckles; besides, it was too long, with no soft inflections in the outlines. Her real beauty was in her eyes. Although brown, they seemed black because of the lashes, and her look came at you frankly with a candid boldness" (11). This passage begins with perceptions that seem plausible for Charles. But when one comes to the ivory of Dieppe, one has a comparison that may be too subtle or refined for him. With the observation that her hand was not beautiful, the narrator seems to intervene and to struggle with Charles for the right to describe (hence to possess linguistically or verbally dress and undress the fictive) Emma. The narrator almost seems implicitly to reprimand Charles and to tell him to forget about Emma's hands and look at her eyes! These eyes change color in the course of the narration—they are brown, blue, and black—and emblematize not only Emma but Flaubert's chameleon-like narrative style itself. The last sentence is also typical of certain movements in Flaubert: it seems to provide an explanation for the seeming blackness of Emma's eyes—which is really nonexplanatory—and it ends by veering off in a direction out of keeping with the rest of the passage, for it turns from physical description to a reaction of the viewer or reader and an implied imputation of a moral quality to Emma ("her look came at you frankly with a candid boldness").

because of their more questionable ideological investments. Both texts may be argued to be hybridized or liminal in the sense that they are situated between traditional expectations and experimentation as well as between a more or less hyperbolic "realism" and textual strategies that seem to escape realism (however it may be defined).

Les Fleurs du mal combines traditional poetic harmonies (amenable to the most classical analyses of form) with the disconcerting, poetically alchemical attempt to extract "beauty" from the ugly and the evil—an attempt that involves an ambivalent ("satanic-divine") fascination with transgression. To some significant extent, it enacts the double or "ironic" consciousness that for Baudelaire was definitive of the artist, more specifically, what he calls the "two simultaneous postulations, one toward God, the other toward Satan." This duality of the human being places in jeopardy the idea that evil comes purely from the outside or from a discrete, diabolical other. As Baudelaire recognized, this troubling duality recalls the notion of original sin—a notion embedded in a mythological narrative that purports to explain the human being's constitutive anxiety and propensity for evil.

In *Madame Bovary*, Flaubert puts into play an elaborate strategy of double inscription that indicates it is impossible fully to realize the desire to transcend an ugly, contaminating reality and to achieve radical transcendence. In Flaubert's novelistic practice, double inscription involves the re-citation and recycling of cliché—cliché that is simultaneously a linguistic definition of social reality and a manifestation of stupidity.[21] This work on (or play with) cliché as constitutive of novelistic practice indicates the writer's ineluctable implication in the discourse of an often—even typically—hated social reality. The writer may take distance from this reality (through ironic and parodic [re]citation) but can never quite achieve a desired total transcendence of it toward a realm or practice of pure beauty and style. This tension

---

21. Parodying Louis Althusser, one might even suggest the following oversimplified "dialectic" of the recycling of cliché in Flaubert. Stupidity I: the unself-conscious and sometimes awe-inspiring use of cliché in the scarcely articulate (for example, Catherine Leroux in *Madame Bovary* or, most poignantly, Félicité in *Un Coeur simple*). Stupidity II: the unself-conscious but self-parodic use of cliché among the highly articulate bourgeois who believe—to Flaubert's chagrin—that they are actually saying something (for example, Homais, Flaubert's own anxiety-producing enemy-double who also employs a language that seems to transcend ordinary reality but in the direction of technicity and bombast). Stupidity III: the parodic and ironic re-citation of cliché in art that may, at its most sublime, induce dream *(faire rêver)* and approach *l'indisable* (Flaubert's idiosyncratic spelling of *l'indicible*—the unspeakable)—one declared goal of Flaubert himself as artist.

between cliché (or social discourse in general) and artistic transcendence or autonomy was a problem Flaubert left to later writers (such as Samuel Beckett) who would address it through their own stylistic variations.

Still, the desire for transcendence was insistent and important in the thought and work of Baudelaire and Flaubert. Their most manifest antirealistic animus was enunciated in a shared project (or problematic commitment) that induced their mutual recognition of an elective affinity in aesthetic ideals: the (impossible) quest for pure art having a transcendent relation to any content, theme, or empirical implication it might harbor. In Baudelaire a "religion of art" sanctified the attempt in a *poésie pure* to transubstantiate the ugly into the beautiful (indeed the sublime). In Flaubert it induced an image of the artist as the Christ of art as well as the waking dream of a "livre sur rien" (a book about nothing)—one plausible interpretation of which is a book made up entirely of recycled clichés that had been transformed into "liberated signifiers" or secularly ritual blazons exchanged in independence of their "real" referents. Here is how Flaubert formulated his project:

> What seems beautiful to me, what I should like to write, is a book about nothing, a book dependent on nothing external, which would be held together by the strength of its style, just as the earth, suspended in the void, depends on nothing external for its support; a book which would have almost no subject, or at least in which the subject would be almost invisible, if such a thing is possible. . . . From the standpoint of pure Art one might almost establish the axiom that there is no such thing as subject, style in itself being an absolute manner of seeing things. (January 16, 1852)[22]

Both pure poetry and the book about nothing had a paradoxical status. They made use of the detritus of society, which they recycled or attempted to transform in art. Yet they also sought autonomy and flew in the face of conventional notions of productivity in either economics or ethics and law. They thus reformulated the relation between work and play in terms that resisted constructions of the latter as a mere pause that refreshes or a period of relaxation that restores one for the world of productive work.

---

22. Quoted in *Madame Bovary*, 309–10.

Seeing the texts of Baudelaire and Flaubert as enactments of their project of "autonomous" or "pure" art has generated a tradition of more or less restricted "formalist" analysis whose variations often take the form of different interpretations or readings of how their texts bring about—or at least approach—self-referentiality and an autonomous or "autotelic" status having little if anything to do with content, theme, or ordinary reality. Indeed the canonization of these texts has been attended by the canonization of formalistic readings of them. These readings may emphasize the defamiliarizing potential of autonomous art that refuses to be subordinated to a regime of production, but they may also function to contain art's more challenging, ambivalent, and disturbing potentials—both those that are sociopolitical and those that are less readily classifiable. Although they begin at a pole diametrically opposed to the readings typified by Pinard and Sénard, these readings may themselves threaten at times to become narrowly legalistic, especially when formalism itself becomes routinized and tends to focus on aesthetic technique or the internal play of literary language. The egregious (but perhaps necessary) mistake of the readings at the trials, from a formalistic perspective, would be a blindness to the specificity of "literary" language, its self-referential virtuosity, its intertextual relation to literary contexts (such as other novels or poems), and its ability to extricate itself from reference, notably through "figurality"—or at least to attempt such an extrication while falling back upon inevitable double binds and aporias in virtue of the referential residue of all language that is not purely technical.[23]

I shall simply mention some of the most powerful and impressive readings that provide important analyses of form but also at times tend in a formalistic direction in following Flaubert's lead concerning a "book about nothing." Naomi Schor, in her essay "Pour une Thématique Restreinte: Ecriture, Parole, et Différence dans *Madame Bovary*," argues that the various structural oppositions employed and undermined in *Madame Bovary* are "as if transcended *(dépassées)* by Flaubert's radical distrust of language in general."[24] Leo Bersani, in *Balzac to Beckett*, presents *Madame Bovary* as the realization of Flaubert's quest for

---

23. I would distinguish between formalism that understands literature in what are presumed to be purely literary terms and necessary formal and intertextual analysis that is problematically related to other concerns such as the broader contextual issues I have touched on.

24. *Littérature*, May 1976, 43.

pure art as purely autotelic language. "Flaubert's novels are most inter-estingly about . . . the arbitrary, insignificant, inexpressive nature of language. . . . Fundamentally, language refers to nothing beyond its own impersonal (and discouraging) virtuosity."[25] Jonathan Culler's objective in his important book on Flaubert is to combine Sartre's understanding of Flaubert's projects with a formal analysis of the way Flaubert's texts instantiate them.[26] In this sense, he may be seen as pro-viding the fourth volume of L'Idiot de la famille that Sartre left in a sketchy and incomplete state.

One curious feature of formalistic analysis, especially in its less cel-ebratory vein, is the tendency to converge in certain respects with the seemingly antiformalistic, politically committed approach of Jean-Paul Sartre. Sartre's ambitious effort includes—while attempting to dialecti-cally transcend—a formalistic understanding of literature and art, but it also shares with the readings at the trials a moral, aesthetic, and polit-ical vision that ultimately subordinates literature and art to some higher design. Indeed Sartre may be read as taking up on a higher level the project of the trials of Flaubert and Baudelaire, this time not in the interest of the status quo but of a more or less Marxist attempt to criti-cize and revolutionize it. Since Sartre's may be the most ambitious attempt to tell us how to remember Flaubert and Baudelaire while restaging in its own terms their trial—an attempt that even his critics and adversaries feel constrained to confront—I shall trace certain linea-ments of Sartre's expansive argument.[27]

For Sartre Baudelaire and Flaubert are themselves "formalists" who attempt to detach language from sociopolitical commitments and to bring about an aesthetic transcendence of the "real" world. Art in their hands becomes a secularized negative theology of transcendence that singularly fails to save or redeem. In Sartre this interpretation pref-aces a radical critique of Baudelaire, Flaubert, and the entire tradition of "formalist" writing and criticism (including recent "structuralist" and "poststructuralist" initiatives that have more or less problematic rela-tions to "formalism"). Indeed it is strikingly ironic that at the very time when the court was exonerating Baudelaire in 1949, Sartre published a terse and potent book that insistently retried him on existential

---

25. (New York: Oxford University Press, 1970), 144.

26. *Flaubert: The Uses of Uncertainty* (Ithaca: Cornell University Press, 1974).

27. On these issues, see my *Preface to Sartre* (Ithaca: Cornell University Press, 1978), 174–79, 183–218.

grounds.[28] If one accepts Sartre's analysis, one might see Baudelaire's belated legal victory as Pyrrhic, for it coincides with a broader existential and sociopolitical indictment and condemnation.

For Sartre, Baudelaire arrested himself at the negative moment of freedom as noninvolvement in the world and then sought escape from worldliness and committed freedom in trying to turn himself into a statue having the solidity of a thing. Sartre, in effect, presents Baudelaire as a "real-life" Antoine Roquentin or a specular image of the early Sartre as Sartre presents his early self in *Les Mots (The Words)*—a figure who saw through others' bourgeois bad faith but did not recognize his own. Baudelaire had a will to fail and to scandalize the solid citizens who lived in accordance with conventional criteria of success and respectability. But, like Antoine in *La Nausée (Nausea)*, he was only a rebel and not a genuine revolutionary. His attitude was parasitic on the status quo, which he needed for his own poses and role-playing. In Baudelaire, however, the fascination for the artificial and the affirmation of the antinatural led to the posture of the dandy. For Sartre, the role of the dandy has existential significance as the extreme exemplification of both a purely negative freedom that refuses to be implicated in, and contaminated by, the real world and a childish unwillingness to grow up and assume adult responsibilities.

For Sartre, Baudelaire's poems were at one with his life, having identical themes and encompassed within the same structure of intentionality. Baudelaire chose to be the *poète maudit* just as he chose to be the isolated child, in an attempt to reappropriate his otherness in negative freedom. The existential foundation of his poetry was the nihilation of the real, the escape from action, the immobilization of time, and the association of evil, beauty, and death. From the ashes of an ugly reality, he created imaginary flowers of evil. His will to fail enabled a poetic victory at the expense of life—what Sartre terms the game of "loser wins" *(qui perd gagne)* whereby a deeply intentional will to fail in life is the prerequisite for a paradoxical, sham victory in art. A resoundingly rhetorical conclusion—itself a bizarre tribute to the dead flowers of rhetoric that Baudelaire's poems have been revealed to be—brings Sartre's book to a dramatic close:

---

28. *Baudelaire* (Paris: Gallimard, 1947). Trans. Martin Turnell (Norfolk, Conn.: James Laughlin, 1950). Page references are to the French edition and shall be included in the text.

Every event was a reflection of that indecomposable totality that he was from the first to the last day of his life. He refused experience. Nothing came from outside to change him, and he learned nothing. General Aupick's death scarcely altered his relations with his mother. For the rest, his story is the story of a slow, very painful decomposition. Such he was at the age of twenty, such we shall find him on the eve of his death. He is simply gloomier, more nervous, less alive, while of his talent and his admirable intelligence nothing remains except memories. And such no doubt was his singularity, that "difference" which he sought until death and which was only visible to others. He was an experiment in a retort, something like the homunculus in the second part of *Faust;* and the quasi-abstract circumstances of the experience enabled him to bear witness with unequaled brilliance to this truth—the free choice that a man makes of himself is completely identified with what is called his destiny. (245)

With the massive, three-volume study of Flaubert and his times, *L'Idiot de la famille,*[29] Sartre's existential hermeneutic is both enriched and overburdened with Marxist and Freudian categories, and his critique (which is simultaneously a self-criticism of what Sartre would like to position and to exorcise as his early, mystified self) becomes more far-ranging and less amenable to summary. In overly simple terms, one might say that Sartre interprets texts as symptomatic both of more or less conscious projects (or ideologies), such as the quest for pure art, and of less conscious, murkier life processes and lived experience *(le vécu)*. On both counts Baudelaire and Flaubert are themselves neurotically symptomatic of some of the most negative and destructive tendencies in modern society: escapism, nihilism, and antihumanism. Their so-called realism is in reality a cover for hateful, indeed genocidal, tendencies, and "formalism" or pure art is a purely imaginary, ineffective attempt to derealize the real and realize the unreal. In either case, the result is a reinforcement of bourgeois dominance and an aggravation of what earlier theorists saw as bourgeois "decadence."

Sartre's militant interpretation, as well as the less politically oriented formalist interpretations that it encompasses, may be applicable to the most unqualified assertions of pure art in Baudelaire and

---

29. Paris: Gallimard, 1971–72.

Flaubert and to their texts only insofar as they instantiate these assertions. It may also apply to certain dubious tendencies particularly in
their later thought, including an elitist and antidemocratic bias, a bla-
tant animus against feminism and socialism, and an inclination to have
sociocultural critique shade into general misanthropy if not nihilism
(notably in Flaubert). What should be stressed, however, is the importance of certain considerations that return one to the problem of the
readings at the trials and the ways they apparently could not allow certain aspects of the texts to register. As Sartre himself at times seems to
intimate, pure art is itself not a simple ideology in either Baudelaire or
Flaubert; it is a tensely invested, even contradictory, idea, as any basic
and anxiety-ridden commitment tends to be. It is, moreover, rendered
more problematic or even countered both by other "projects" or tendencies in their thought and by the very way it is enacted or played out
in their texts.

As I have already intimated, both Baudelaire and Flaubert clearly
recognized pure art to be an impossible ideal—a secular displacement
of the anxious quest for a radically transcendent divinity. This recognition not only intensified the pathos of the ideal but helped to shift it in
the direction of transgressively immanent critique. This critique
allowed for situational, in contrast to total, transcendence, that is, the
possible transformation of the nexus linking society, culture, and art. I
have noted that total transcendence, however negative or nihilating,
was countered by the writer's paradoxical relation to cliché as the epitome of social discourse. It was more directly questioned (at least in
Flaubert) by a desire for mystical, pantheistic participation—or self-dis-
solving immersion—in the world. Moreover, certain analogues of transcendence might be problematized or even parodied (for example,
Emma's quest for romantic love, Homais's decontextualized, technocratic language, or Charles's fetishizing idolatry of Emma in spite of all
evidence negating his wife's claim to the status of idol). The very ideal
of art required a ritual, quasi-priestly, indeed ascetic status for the artist
and a special state of soul or spirit in artistic practice itself, in contrast
to a hypostatized, formalistic conception of the transcendent aesthetic
object. And it was bound up with an attempted transvaluation of values in this world that simultaneously countered the dominance of utility, technical rationality, and commercialism and affirmed the significance of art and its practice. Given the subdominant and increasingly
commercialized status of art in bourgeois society, this affirmation was

of course beleaguered and self-questioning—the writer being both semidivine and a clown for Flaubert and the poet both exemplary and accursed for Baudelaire—but the embattled affirmation was never simply renounced.

I would suggest that the texts of Baudelaire and Flaubert put into practice aspects of immanent critique of social and literary conditions (without being reducible to such critique), and this dimension of the texts was to some extent related to what might be called a "carnivalesque" project that appeared in different ways in the work of each writer. In a letter of November 22, 1852, Flaubert asserted that "[Rabelais] is the great fountain of French letters. Our strongest writers draw from him by the cupful. We must return to his spirit—to robust outrages." In a letter of December 16 or 17, 1852, he added: "What's missing in modern society is not a Christ, nor a Washington, nor a Socrates, nor even a Voltaire; it's an Aristophanes." Other letters struck similar notes.

In the world represented in *Madame Bovary* itself, "carnivalesque" phenomena are depicted as suppressed, repressed, or noxiously distorted, and festive occasions invariably go wrong (as in scenes involving the *comices agricoles*, the wedding, or the ball at Vaubyessard). Indeed the unavailability of the carnivalesque, other than in negative or deranged forms, is one thing direly objectionable in the world that forms the context of the novel, and the motif of the festival or celebration gone awry has become recurrent in modern literature. But modulations of narrative voice and perspective might be seen as linked to a desire to revive the possibility of the carnivalesque—a sublimated mode of stylistic carnivalization linked to a muted form of satire. In this distinctive form of satire, the narrator is relatively clear about what he rejects (for example, bourgeois stupidity or the repression of the carnivalesque in an increasingly utilitarian, technocratic society beset with an intolerant *esprit de sérieux*) but uncertain, self-critical, and clearly undogmatic about specific alternatives. In *Madame Bovary*, moreover, the critique of the family in the modern context is, as I noted, conjoined with an often outrageous critique of religion—indeed a critique of the presentation of the modern family itself as a consecrated or holy family.

One should resist the temptation to provide an inverted mirror image of the trials of 1857 by overemphasizing similarities in the textual operations of Flaubert and Baudelaire. Yet Baudelaire also indicated the extreme instability of reversible binary oppositions (*spleen*

and *idéal*, self and other, hell and heaven), and he combined the sub-
version of standard expectations with an attempt to reinscribe or
rearticulate them in significantly different ways. One may even suggest
that, in Baudelaire, one finds at least *en creux* a problematic general
apprehension of an alternative society—one that may easily be abused
not only in the traditional conservative if at times extreme formulations
of Joseph de Maistre (who, Baudelaire claimed, taught him how to
think) but, more pointedly, in the case of a later figure such as Ezra
Pound. But analogues of Baudelaire's concerns in the thought of Emile
Durkheim (notably in the form of an affirmation of limits as the necessary countervailing force to desires for excess and transgression) as
well as in the more intricate and vexed formulations of Georges Bataille
would perhaps be enough to indicate that Baudelaire's views retain a
certain power of contestation. For Baudelaire's very attempt to rehabilitate an ambivalent relation of attraction and repulsion toward transgression not only sat uncomfortably with an ideal of pure art. It also
required a society in which there was a deeply internalized sense of
legitimate normative limits, for when transgression meets little resistance and is generalized or banalized, one's response to it tends not to
be ambivalent and self-questioning but blasé, confused, equivocating,
or intolerant. Moreover, Baudelaire's approach required an ability to
conjoin seriousness with a "joking" relation to one's commitments as
well as a society that was characterized neither by the extreme alien-
ation and withdrawal of its critical intelligentsia nor by the numbing
prevalence of scapegoated "marginal" types—prostitutes, conspira-
tors, outsiders—with whom intellectuals and artists were (at times
histrionically) tempted to identify. As a partial elucidation of these
issues, a valuable theoretical supplement to *Les Fleurs du mal* is Baudelaire's essay of 1855, "De l'essence du rire."

In this essay, Baudelaire contrasts the "ordinary" or social comic
with the "absolute" comic, and both of these forms of the comic are in
turn contrasted with the "definitive absolute," a radically transcendent
ideal that itself is the analogue of the impossible quest for "pure poetry."
In paradise—the site of the definitive absolute or radical transcendence—
there is no laughter, for laughter is related to sin and the fall. "From the
point of view of the definitive absolute, there is nothing but joy."[30] (Here

---

30. *"De l'essence du rire,"* in Baudelaire, *Oeuvres complètes* (Paris: Editions du Seuil,
1968), 375.

one may recall Baudelaire's statement in *Mon Coeur mis à nu* that the criterion of true civilization is to be found in the diminution of the traces of original sin.) Ordinary or social laughter itself is negative, invidious, and satanic, and it is related to an unjustified sense of superiority over one's fellow man. One may supplement Baudelaire's account by noting that social laughter requires a distinct butt of the joke at whom others laugh and by laughing may conceal their own anxiety and weakness. True laughter related to the absolute comic is, however, not a sign of one's own weakness or of the unhappiness of one's fellow man. Nor is it invidiously related to the victimization of others. Rather it is the laughter caused by the grotesque, and this laughter provokes a mad hilarity and a feeling of vertigo, and it is linked by Baudelaire with *l'art pour l'art* and distinguished from the lesser laughter of the comedy of manners and ordinary social satire. Here Baudelaire unexpectedly associates art for art's sake not with transcendence but with elements of the carnivalesque (such as the grotesque) as well as with possibly more indeterminate elements (mad hilarity and a feeling of vertigo). But he insists that the absolute comic of the grotesque is absolute only relative to a fallen humanity and that the definitive absolute that would be pure joy is reserved for a higher being. It is equally significant that the entire argument of this text construes the contrasting forms of the comic not as pure binaries but as necessary supplements of one another and as forms that may be mixed or hybridized (as in the work of E. T. A. Hoffmann, who is presented as the epitome of the comic spirit). The point that may be derived for the present discussion is that art and its interpretation are not confined to the categories of ideology and sociocultural critique, but neither are they entirely disjoined from the latter, for sociocultural conditions are mutually implicated with other possibilities in literature and life, including those that Baudelaire referred to as the *comique absolu* or Flaubert as the *grotesque triste* (the sad grotesque that made him *rêver longuement*). As Flaubert put the point in a letter that indicates one of his clearest affinities with a later "stoic comedian," Samuel Beckett:

> For me the sad grotesque has an unheard-of charm. It corresponds to the intimate needs of my buffoonishly bitter nature. It does not make me laugh but dream at length *(rêver longuement)*. I take hold of it wherever it is to be found, and I, like everyone, carry it in me:

that is why I love to analyze myself. It's a form of study that amuses me. What prevents me from taking myself seriously, although I have a rather grave spirit, is that I find myself very ridiculous—not with that relative ridiculousness which is the theatrical comic but with that ridiculousness intrinsic to human life itself and that springs from the simplest action or from the most ordinary gesture. For example, never do I shave without laughing, so stupid (bête) does it seem to me. All that is very difficult to explain and must be felt. (August 21–22, 1846)

In performing my own variant of memory-work, I have tried to suggest that the trials of Baudelaire and Flaubert are well worth remembering as crucial indications that the problem for contemporary interpretation is to elicit the variable historical manner in which "literary" experimentation (which is recognized but at times hypostatized in a formalistic methodology) is bound up with broader political, legal, and sociocultural issues in the production, reception, and critical reading of texts. With respect to memory and the law, the related questions may be formulated as follows: what can a legal system, notably in trials, allow lawyers and judges to say and transmit about the work and play of literary texts? Must the legal system induce extremely reduced, unself-questioning, and tendentious readings—or even systematic misreadings—of literary texts insofar as these texts are judged in terms of standard conformity and deviance when, one may argue, they should at times be understood—in continually displaced and changing ways—as presenting more uncanny and less manageable forms of transgression or ideological crime that place in complex question the sociopolitical context that the law tends to assume as its own legitimate foundation? Would the legal recognition that art and literature are relatively safe havens for experimentation, including experimentation that poses certain challenges to social norms and to any overly secure definition of self or society, provide a perspective on civil liberties that might make different readings possible in legal theory sensitive to significant issues or even in courts of law in the event that certain works still came to trial in the aftermath of active recognition of their possibly disorienting but thought-provoking social and cultural role? In the American context, these questions might be seen as addressing the very meaning of the phrase "redeeming social value." Given the contemporary climate of rising religious fundamentalism and moral neoconservatism, these questions may be more pressing than one might like to believe.[31]

31. The present essay was completed before I read Pierre Bourdieu's *The Rules of Art: Genesis and Structure of the Literary Field*, trans. Susan Emanuel (1992; Stanford, Calif.: Stanford University Press, 1995). Bourdieu provides an extensive analysis of the "field" in which there emerged art for art's sake in Flaubert and Baudelaire. His conception of the field is a conceptually developed analogue of the notion of context that historians often employ in relatively "untheorized" ways, and Bourdieu elaborates it in a suggestive manner that brings out its theoretical and applied possibilities. Although he touches only briefly on the trials of Flaubert and Baudelaire, he provides much useful historical information and some daring sociological hypotheses or projects. His explanatory ambitions for the "field," however, are placed in jeopardy by his somewhat indeterminate conception of it with respect to conceptual or disciplinary considerations and the problem of institutionalization. His project includes the rather utopian attempt to arrive at an explanation of the insertion of the artifact in the field that, in its thoroughness, would furnish a generative formula reproducing the artifact or artwork in another (sociological) mode, thereby resulting in a kind of sociological clone that would "explain" the literary artifact. His major thesis is that one must not take art for art's sake (or autonomous art) at face value but instead elicit its sociological and historical conditions of possibility. My own approach agrees with Bourdieu's in critically framing the type of formalism that validates autonomous art and in seeking a reconstruction of the pertinent contexts of artifacts (although my understanding of pertinent contexts and of the relation of an artifact to them is explicitly more problematic and self-questioning than is Bourdieu's emphatically explanatory yet paradoxically indeterminate notion of the field). It may be useful further to indicate or even accentuate the differences between Bourdieu's influential approach and my own since they tend to divide the "field" of historical studies itself, and many historians might find their own views rendered explicit and ably defended by Bourdieu (for example, Roger Chartier, whose work Bourdieu praises as an attempt to apply his project). Bourdieu's analysis is insistently objectifying and "scientific" if not positivistic. He seeks explanatory models or formulas distanced from interpretation of the kind that tensely combines reconstruction of past contexts with an active, self-implicating exchange or dialogue with its artifacts. In fact Bourdieu sees the observer's transferential relation to, or implication in, the observed only as a threat to be warded off; he is thus in no position to thematize it as an inevitable problem that both limits objectification and opens possibilities of reading, interpretation, and self-understanding in coming to terms with the past and its artifacts. He thus does little to open new readings or interpretations of artifacts and primarily relies on the readings or interpretations of critics that he then situates or attempts to insert into sociological explanations. He also tends to cut history off from the problem of memory or, conversely, to construe memory only in terms of reconstruction and explanation of artifacts in their own time (as reconstructed and reproduced in truncated terms through an insistently objectifying methodology wary of anachronisms and unable to do justice to the problem of nonteleological belated effects and recognitions, for example, with respect to the workings of free indirect style). In addition, although he tries to historicize and explain it, Bourdieu himself accepts "art for art's sake" at face value as an ideology and by and large assumes that it is unproblematically instantiated in artifacts such as novels, poems, or paintings. By contrast, I think art for art's sake, even in its most significant, indeed ardent defenders (such as Flaubert and Baudelaire) is a problematic, internally divided commitment (not a simple ideology) both in its own terms and in relation to other projects (such as carnivalization).

It is rendered even further problematic by the way it is enacted and contested (not simply instantiated) in particular artifacts. The latter process can be elucidated only through the kind of close reading Bourdieu eschews or holds at arm's length. Bourdieu's own commitment to an objectifying sociology is itself closer to an unself-questioning ideological belief than is Flaubert's or Baudelaire's relation to art for art's sake, and it inhibits him from inquiring more fully into the self-reflexive question of his implication in the problems he treats—an implication that requires a more intricate mode of response articulating (objectifying) critical distance with an active recognition of one's involvement in certain problems such as voice, positionality in one's own field(s), ideological resonance, and normative judgment. Bourdieu's understanding of self-reflexivity is limited to self-objectification. By contrast, I think self-implication raises the question of how to recognize—and even to allow to register in one's account—the anxiety or uncertainty produced by the unavailability of a clear and distinct "field" of one's own and to work through it toward a rather different conception of the field and the institution from Bourdieu's. (Here Bourdieu may rely too uncritically on the prevalent conception of modernity in terms of the autonomization of separate spheres.) Finally, the intricate processes through which a commitment (such as art for art's sake) is both contested and affirmed, as it is elaborated in "theoretical" terms (for example, in paratexts such as letters) and "textualized" or woven into particular artifacts, imply that a field (such as autonomous art) may allow not only for internal conflict over positions, representations, or symbolic capital. It may itself be questioned and unsettled—at times radically—not simply by outsiders or critics (such as Marxists or social realists) but by the very figures who are crucial in its genesis and establishment. In other words, the very limits or even possibility of a field in any autonomous sense may be placed in jeopardy through the very operations by which it is being developed and set forth, and the understanding of modernity in terms of autonomous spheres may be both explored and placed in more or less extreme doubt. The process of problematization is especially pertinent (although not restricted) to a field such as the literary, which Bourdieu himself recognizes as relatively indeterminate and institutionalized only in limited ways. (Here my specific reading of Flaubert's *Sentimental Education* differs from that of Bourdieu, who sees it as enacting a vision of autonomous art and separate spheres. I see it in more complex terms that involve the exploration of the tenuousness and even fragility of spheres of modern life undergoing legitimation crisis, notably with respect to the private and public spheres. See my "Collapsing Spheres in Flaubert's *Sentimental Education*," in *History, Politics, and the Novel* [Ithaca: Cornell University Press, 1987], 83–110. Indeed the destabilization of spheres and the binary oppositions that subtend them is probably even more insistent in the blatantly excavated world of *The Sentimental Education* than in *Madame Bovary*.)

Collective Memory and the Nineteenth Amendment: Reasoning about "the Woman Question" in the Discourse of Sex Discrimination

Reva B. Siegel

The perception of racial classifications as inherently odious stems from a lengthy and tragic history that gender-based classifications do not share.

Justice Lewis Powell, *University of California v. Bakke*

For women . . . new choices are available largely because of technology, for blacks because of the success of the civil rights movement.

Robert Bork, *Slouching towards Gomorrah*

At a recent conference on affirmative action, I was struck by a characteristic, if not defining, feature of American conversations about race. Claims about race discrimination are located in national and constitutional history; they refer, whether explicitly or tacitly, to past wrongful acts of the American polity, particularly the law of slavery and segregation. Of course, claims respecting this history differ significantly: partisans may, for example, disagree about how best to expunge the nation's legacy of racial wrongdoing, or they may dispute the degree to which individual white Americans bear responsibility for it. But parties to disputes about racial equality share in common the understanding that, in matters of race, the nation has a legacy of wrongdoing that it has constitutionally committed itself to transcend.

By contrast, claims about sex equality lack this historical structure. Legal and popular disputes about sex equality often focus on asserted differences in women's nature or choices. And when claims about sex equality are couched in historical terms, the narrative they invoke differs significantly from the race discrimination narrative. Where claims about race discrimination invoke a lengthy national history of state-sanctioned coercion, claims about sex discrimination often refer to a history of social attitudes that are the product of custom and consensus. The story one might cull from debates over sex discrimination goes something like this. The relations of the sexes are in the process of gradual transformation toward some more enlightened state. We need to abandon "archaic" or "outmoded" stereotypical assumptions about the sexes and recognize deeper similarities between them.

Of course, we could tell a story about women's status that is structurally homologous to the race discrimination narrative. Such a story would emphasize the many legal disabilities that defined women as second-class citizens from the time of the founding until the modern era. And such a story would locate in the campaign for suffrage and the ratification of the Nineteenth Amendment a constitutional commitment to rectify this history of subordination—a commitment, like the constitutional commitments of the Reconstruction Era, initially betrayed, but then, over the last several decades, progressively respected.

To be sure, variants of this story do surface in legal and popular debates over sex equality. But the story tying questions of sex discrimination to national and constitutional history is not the organizing paradigm for debates about sex equality, as it is in matters concerning race equality. In this essay, I want to examine how interpretation of the Constitution both reflects and produces the narrative structures that organize our intuitions about questions of gender justice. Specifically, I will be examining how judicial interpretation of the Nineteenth Amendment and the equal protection clause of the Fourteenth Amendment has isolated questions of women's citizenship from narratives of national and constitutional history.

Today, the Nineteenth Amendment is scarcely ever mentioned in conversations about women's civic status and constitutional rights. There is a "common sense" explanation for this silence. The text of the

Nineteenth Amendment states a nondiscrimination rule governing voting with which we now comply. Because restrictions on the franchise are no longer used to regulate the social status of women as a group, the suffrage amendment is for all practical purposes an irrelevance.

But how have we come to read the Nineteenth Amendment as a rule rather than a source of norms—a piece of constitutional text that can be understood without reference to the debates and commitments that led to its ratification? This essay argues that the prevailing understanding of the suffrage amendment reflects habits of reasoning about gender relations that it in turn helps sustain. At the level of common sense, we do not understand gender relations to have a political history in anything like the way we understand race relations to have a political history: the narrative structures through which we explain the relations of the sexes depict gender arrangements as the product of consensus and custom rather than coercion and conflict. Our understanding of the Nineteenth Amendment both reflects and sustains these habits of reasoning. Because of these habits of reasoning, we read the suffrage amendment as a text shorn of the semantically informing context that an understanding of the struggles over its ratification might supply. And interpretive construction of the suffrage amendment as a rule, rather than a transformative constitutional commitment, in turn sustains the prevailing understanding of gender arrangements as the product of evolving social consensus rather than legal coercion and political conflict. In short, the "collective memory" of gender relations has shaped and been shaped by the practices of interpretation through which we give meaning to the Nineteenth and Fourteenth Amendments. If we approach the Constitution through the field of collective memory, we can thus analyze the interpretive history of the suffrage amendment as part of the larger narrative processes through which this society naturalizes gender arrangements and insulates them from political contestation.

I.   The Constitution as Vehicle of Social Memory

Many of our constitutive social understandings assume narrative form, and these narratives frequently involve stories about the past. By telling stories about a common past, a group can constitute itself as a group, a collective subject with certain experiences, expectations, entitlements, obligations, and commitments. The stories that help forge group identity also supply structures of ordinary understanding, frameworks within which members of a society interpret experience and make positive and normative judgments concerning it. In short, narratives about the genesis of social arrangements help constitute social groups as collective subjects and, in so doing, construct their commonsense intuitions about the actual and proper organization of social relations. Scholars call this narrative matrix "collective" or "social" memory.[1]

To appreciate how narratives about the past construct the identity and understandings of collective subjects, it might be helpful to consider the process through which the authority of the Constitution is produced. We might ask: why do Americans experience themselves as authors of a constitution that in turn binds the government that "represents" them? Wouldn't it be more reasonable to observe that Americans who are born under the Constitution are "subject" to its authority? The experience of citizenship as authorizing government depends on an act of identification with "the Founding Fathers"—those who drafted and ratified the Constitution that constitutes us as a nation. Stories about the drafting and ratification of the Constitution supply the basis for claims about the authority of the state. We tell and retell these stories over time, recreating from generation to generation the experience of identification with the acts of the "Founders" on which the authority of the national government rests.[2]

From this vantage point, we can see that when lawyers interpret the Constitution, they engage the task as carriers of social memory,

---

1. For an overview of some of the large body of literature on collective memory, see, for example, Susan A. Crane, "Writing the Individual Back into Collective Memory," *American Historical Review* 20 (1997): 1372; Natalie Zemon Davis and Randolph Starn, eds., "Memory and Counter Memory," special issue of *Representations* 26 (1989); Iwona Irwin-Zarecka, *Frames of Remembrance: The Dynamics of Collective Memory* (New Brunswick, N.J.: Transaction Publishers, 1994) (annotated bibliography); see also J. M. Balkin, *Cultural Software: A Theory of Ideology* (New Haven: Yale University Press, 1998), 203–15.

2. Of course, it is not the accounts that professional historians supply about the framing that dispose Americans to identify with the acts of the founding generation as acts of "We, the People." The disposition to identify with the Founders would seem to be part of a belief system learned at an early age. Each generation recounts the story of America's origins in an act of revolution (rupture) and constitution making (reintegration) to children at an early age. This story is part of the "civic religion" that each generation inculcates in its young, told in the family setting, at school, and in various national commemorative symbols, holidays, and rituals. See generally Michael G. Kammen, *A Machine That Would Go of Itself: The Constitution in American Culture* (New York: Knopf, 1986).

equipped with certain belief structures that will shape the way in which they understand law. But it also seems clear that when lawyers interpret the Constitution they are contributing to the stock of narratives that, passed from generation to generation, constitute our civic identity, norms, and purposes. Judicial decisions are thus products of social memory; at the same time, they are one of the many social institutions that produce social memory.

The same narrative processes that produce the national identity of "Americans" also play a crucial role in articulating relationships among Americans. Thus, for example, social memory plays a central role in the construction of racial identity—a dynamic readily apparent in the domain of constitutional interpretation. Racial understandings are transmitted from one generation to the next, often taking the form of stories about our nation's origins. A story of the founding as a compact among white, Anglo-Saxon, Protestant men defines nationhood and citizenship in race-exclusionary terms; the *Dred Scott* decision tells such a story about the founding compact.[3] Today, of course, American civic culture abjures this racialist account of the constitutional compact. That the original Constitution sanctioned slavery is depicted as a form of founding-error, a betrayal of the more fundamental principles that define the nation. We thus encounter an important modification of the founding narrative, one that has gained in currency in the decades since World War II. In this view, it took a war and major constitutional reform to redeem the nation from its morally compromised origins. When the nation's story of origins is retold in this fashion, a story about race is embedded in the travails of the nation's birth and bloody rebirth in the crucible of the Civil War.[4]

---

3. *Dred Scott v. Sandford,* 60 U.S. (19 How.) 393 (1856).

4. To illustrate, I quote a passage from *Bell v. Maryland,* 378 U.S. 226 (1963), a civil rights decision of the 1960s that overturned the convictions of a group of black students who were arrested for participating in a "sit-in" demonstration at a restaurant that discriminated against blacks. The opinion notes that the ideals of the Declaration of Independence were "not fully achieved with the adoption of the Constitution because of the hard and tragic reality of Negro slavery," and then goes on to observe:

The Constitution of the new Nation, while heralding liberty, in effect declared all men to be free and equal—except black men who were to be neither free nor equal. This inconsistency reflected a fundamental departure from the American creed, a departure which it took a tragic civil war to set right. With the adoption, however, of the Thirteenth, Fourteenth, and Fifteenth Amendments to the Constitution, freedom and equality were guaranteed expressly to all regardless of "race, color, or previous condition of servitude."

To be sure, stories about race and nationhood evolve with the political struggles of each generation. Stories about the meaning of the Civil War amendments told in the Supreme Court opinions of the Reconstruction Era differ from those of the 1960s, and these stories in turn differ from the stories told by the justices who sit today on the Court. In the 1960s, the Court identified slavery and segregation as the founding errors to be rectified through racial integration of the basic institutions of American life; but, in the 1990s, as these integrationist commitments have waned, the Court adverts to a "history of racial classification"[5] as the founding error the nation must expiate by restricting, or abolishing, race-conscious remedies.[6] Once the history of racial wrongs is abstracted to a "history of racial classifications," even Martin Luther King can be enlisted as an opponent of affirmative action.

Thus, as Americans tell and retell stories about race relations of the past, they are struggling over the narratives that rationalize race relations in the present: Stories about the past constitute racial groups as collective subjects who face each other with certain defining experiences, understandings, expectations, entitlements, and obligations. The central role that social memory plays in racial group construction is painfully visible in the debates over affirmative action. Consider, for example, the familiar objection to affirmative action, "My grandfather didn't own slaves," or a more sophisticated variant of this claim advanced by Justice Powell in *Bakke*, that we are "a Nation of minorities."[7] Such objections to affirmative action acknowledge that past gen-

---

> In the light of this American commitment to equality and the history of that commitment, these Amendments must be read not as "legislative codes . . . but as the revelation of the great purposes which were intended to be achieved by the Constitution as a continuing instrument of government." . . . The cases following the 1896 decision in *Plessy v. Ferguson* . . . too often tended to negate this great purpose. . . . [But since] *Brown* the Court has consistently applied this constitutional standard to give real meaning to the Equal Protection Clause "as the revelation" of an enduring constitutional purpose. 378 U.S. at 286–87 (Goldberg, J., concurring) (citations omitted).

5. See *Miller v. Johnson,* 515 U.S. 900, 922 (1995) (quoting *City of Richmond v. J.A. Croson Co.,* 488 U.S. 469, 501 [1989]).

6. See Reva B. Siegel, "Why Equal Protection No Longer Protects: The Evolving Forms of Status-Enforcing State Action," *Stanford Law Review* 49 (1997): 1142.

7. *Regents of the University of California v. Bakke,* 438 U.S. 265, 292 (1978) (footnotes omitted) ("During the dormancy of the Equal Protection clause, the United States had become a nation of minorities. Each had to struggle—and to some extent struggles still— to overcome the prejudices not of a monolithic majority, but of a 'majority' composed of various minority groups of whom it was said—perhaps unfairly in many cases—that a shared characteristic was a willingness to disadvantage other groups").

erations of white Americans inflicted injuries on black Americans that continue to have present effects in defining the social position of the races. Yet each seeks to rearticulate the subject position of white Americans with respect to that history so as to eschew responsibility for its rectification. The first repudiates individual responsibility by disclaiming lineal descent from the white persons who enslaved African Americans; the second repudiates collective responsibility by deconstructing the category of white persons understood as descendants of slave owners. In each case, the interposition of a "counter" historical narrative modifies racial genealogy so as to deny collective agency in matters of *racial* formation, while continuing to allow for the assertion of collective identity with respect to other features of the American past. Interestingly enough, each of these objections to affirmative action repudiates an understanding of white racial identity as entailing obligations to rectify past wrongs inflicted on African Americans without repudiating the commonsense understanding that the subordinate social position of African Americans is attributable to such historic injustices.

It is instructive to compare the complex struggles over the past that attend racial conflicts in American life with the narratives about the past that inform debates about gender justice. In this society, the forms of social memory that construct gender relations differ in kind from those that shape race relations. Justice Powell voiced this understanding when he observed in *Bakke*, "The perception of racial classifications as inherently odious stems from a lengthy and tragic history that gender-based classifications do not share."[8] While the history of race relations in this country is generally understood as a story of publicly and privately inflicted injury and imposition, the history of gender relations unfolds in the more diffuse realm of customary time, involving consensually inhabited mores that are assumed slowly to have evolved over the centuries. For the most part, law does not play a role in the social memory of gender relations. Because governing narratives about the genesis of gender arrangements do not focus on acts of legal coercion, even those trained in law are disinclined to view law as playing a significant role in defining the social position of the sexes.

An anecdote or two might suffice to illustrate. Some years ago when I began work on a project concerning the common-law doctrine that gave a husband property rights in his wife's labor, I encountered diverse forms of resistance among legal academics to the very notion

---

8. *Bakke*, 303.

that household labor had a legal history. The family, I was told, was not a proper object of legal-historical inquiry because law did not exert social force in the family as it did in other arenas. There might be anti-quated forms of family law "on the books," but family life was more importantly shaped by tradition and affect, custom and consent. The view that law exerted little constraining force in family affairs recurred in diverse forms. When I pointed out that nineteenth-century laws giving wives rights in their earnings did not abolish the common-law doctrine of marital service because the law continued to vest a husband with rights in the labor his wife performed for the family, I was told that it was ahistorical for me to expect total abolition of the common-law rule; no woman in the nineteenth century would have sought property rights in her household labor. (As I have since demonstrated in some detail, in the decades before and after the Civil War, the woman's rights movement in fact energetically advocated reforms that would have given wives rights in their household labor.)[9] On one occasion I was presenting a paper concerning wives' claims to earnings for work performed in keeping boarders—a problematic area of litigation because courts appreciated that recognizing wives' earnings claims for household work performed for nonfamily members might legitimate claims for remuneration of the same work performed for family members. As I pointed out how courts deciding the boarder cases had struggled to preserve a husband's right to his wife's household services, one legal historian in the audience criticized my modernization thesis, remarking, "My mother kept boarders and she never wanted any of the money." Like the claim that no woman in the nineteenth century would have demanded property rights in the labor she performed for the family, this claim also asserted that the expropriation of women's household labor was fundamentally a consensual affair.

In this context, it is interesting to consider Robert Bork's recent account of the genesis of contemporary gender arrangements:

> Once such things as the right to vote and the right of wives to hold property in their own names had been won, the difference in the opportunities open to women has been largely due to technology. I am old enough to remember my grandmother washing work

---

9. See Reva B. Siegel, "Home as Work: The First Woman's Rights Claims Concerning Wives' Household Labor, 1850–1880," *Yale Law Journal* 103 (1994): 1073.

clothes on a scrub board, mashing potatoes by hand, and emptying the water tray from the bottom of the ice box. There was simply no possibility that she could have had both a family and a career. Were she young today, she would find that shopping, food preparation, laundering and much else have been made dramatically easier so that she could, if she wished, become a lawyer or a doctor or virtually anything that appealed to her.[10]

In Bork's view, "For women the new choices are available largely because of technology, for blacks because of the success of the civil rights movement" (228). In short, law plays at best an incidental role in the social memory of gender relations, which are assumed to result from custom and consent; if constraints on women's choices appear in such narratives at all, they are frequently depicted as an impersonal effect of technology, rather than coercive legal or social arrangements. Again and again in such narratives, the possibility that conflict or coercion has played a role in defining women's lives is repressed and women appear as figures who give of themselves selflessly and without protest. The social memory of gender relations thus elaborates a scene that is private, consensual, and naturalized, that is to say, outside the public realm where matters of law and governance are conducted. For this reason, claims about collective agency that play so prominent a role in disputes over racial justice are notably lacking in disputes over gender justice. The claim "my grandfather didn't own slaves" differs from the claim "my mother kept boarders and she never wanted any of the money." The first acknowledges that publicly and privately inflicted injury occurred but disclaims responsibility for rectifying it; the second denies that publicly and privately inflicted injury ever occurred.

It is of course possible to tell a very different story about the genesis of gender arrangements. If, for example, one consults the pages of nineteenth-century woman suffrage journals, one encounters detailed accounts of the ways that law enforces women's subordination in the public and private spheres. Consider this 1875 narrative—striking for present purposes because it understands family relations as simultaneously affective and coercive, private and public:

10. Robert H. Bork, *Slouching towards Gomorrah* (New York: Regan Books, 1996), 195.

As a mother, a woman goes through the tragedy of giving birth to her son, watches over and cares for his helpless infancy, brings him through all the diseases incident to childhood, is his nurse, physician, seamstress, washerwoman, teacher, friend, and guide, spending the cream of her days to bring him up to be a voter with no provision in law for her own support in the mean time, with not so much as "I thank you." Then he leaves home and marries a wife, whom it took some other mother twenty-one years to raise, educate, and teach to cook his meals, to make and wash his clothes, to furnish him with a bed, and to fill the house with comforts, of which he has the larger share, at her own expense. And all this done for him up to this period of his life without any cost to himself. Then he votes to help make a law to disfranchise his wife and these two mothers, who have unitedly spent forty-two years of the prime of their days for his benefit, without any compensation. And then he makes another law to compel his wife to do all the same kind of drudgery which his mother had done, with the addition of giving birth to as many children as in his good pleasure he sees fit to force upon her. And all her earnings and the fruit of her labor are his, his wife being the third woman who spends her life to support him. It takes three, and sometimes four women to get a man through from the cradle to the grave, and sometimes a pretty busy time they have of it, too. It is time we stated facts and called things by their right names, and handled this subject without kid gloves.[11]

As this woman suffrage advocate reminds us, acts of public and private coercion have long played a role in organizing the social relations of the sexes. Law does not stop at the family circle, but plays an important role in constituting it—defining women's lives in matters of sex and work, love and money, as well as affairs of state.

Viewed from this standpoint, questions of sex discrimination could easily be situated within a narrative of national wrong and rectification. Women were, after all, second-class citizens at the time of the founding, ineligible to speak as "We, the People" because denied the right to vote, subordinated in the family, and constrained in diverse spheres of social life. After demanding equal civic status over the

11. "A Wife's Protest," *Woman's Journal*, March 6, 1875, 74.

course of several generations, women finally persuaded the nation to repudiate its foundational understandings and to amend the Constitution to allow them to vote as equal citizens under law. In according constitutional protections to women's rights, the Court often draws analogies between race and sex discrimination. Yet it does not invoke this story of founding error and rectification, whether in construing the suffrage provisions of the Nineteenth Amendment or in interpreting the equal protection clause of the Fourteenth Amendment—the current constitutional "home" of doctrines protecting women's rights.[12]

The prevailing understanding of the Nineteenth and Fourteenth Amendments thus illustrates how the social memory of gender relations shapes and is shaped by acts of constitutional interpretation. In the quest for the vote, generations of American women resisted their pervasive legal disempowerment and raised core questions about the organizing principles and institutions of American life. Their struggle provoked wide-ranging debate that explored the relations of the sexes, both in the family and in the state. This national, multigenerational debate about the norms that should structure public and private life ultimately produced a constitutional commitment to revise foundational structures of the Republic. During the 1920s, at least some courts responded to the ratification of the Nineteenth Amendment in ways that reflected the social meaning and institutional preoccupations of the woman suffrage campaign. But this response was both hesitant and fleeting, and the meaning of the suffrage struggle soon faded from popular and legal consciousness. When, decades later, the Court finally began to develop a body of constitutional doctrine protecting women's rights under the Fourteenth Amendment, it did not build upon the memory of the woman suffrage campaign, but instead proceeded to elaborate a body of sex discrimination doctrine that is fundamentally indifferent to the history of women's struggles in the American legal system. Thus, the very body of law that currently protects women's rights is elaborated in terms that (1) efface the history of women's resistance to legal imposition and (2) obscure the specific institutional sites of that struggle. Lost, with this history, is a narrative matrix for reasoning about the social relations of the sexes and for conducting public conversations about the normative commitments they implicate.

---

12. In a recent sex discrimination case, the Court has finally broken this pattern, as I discuss in part V of this essay.

Examining how the social memory of gender relations is expressed in contemporary constitutional law reveals one mechanism by which this society insulates the prevailing gender order from political contestation. Our propensity to explain the relations of the sexes through stories of evolving custom and consensus rather than conflict suggests that, as a society, we remain normatively invested in the naturalization of present gender arrangements and will do much to repress the normative dissonance that confrontation with their history would produce. At the same time, examining how the social memory of gender relations is made and sustained in law raises important questions about the possibility of its remaking through law. Thus, after exploring how interpretation of the Nineteenth and Fourteenth Amendments has isolated questions concerning women's status from narratives of national and constitutional history, this essay will conclude by considering what difference it might make for the Court to rejoin questions about sex discrimination to the history of American law and governance.

II. The Campaign for Woman Suffrage

The Nineteenth Amendment provides that "[t]he right of citizens of the United States to vote shall not be denied or abridged by the United States or by any State on account of sex," and further provides that "Congress shall have the power to enforce this article by appropriate legislation." The amendment was ratified in 1920, 133 years after the founding and over 70 years after women first organized to demand suffrage. For generations, "the woman question"—as the debates precipitated by the campaign for woman suffrage were called—occupied a place in the national political imagination akin to the civil rights movement of the 1950s. Yet no consciousness of this history informs contemporary understandings of the Constitution. An anecdote should suffice to illustrate the point. Some years ago when I was teaching at the University of California–Berkeley law school, a colleague asked me about my research; I replied that I was thinking about the significance of the Nineteenth Amendment, and my colleague—a nationally prominent constitutional law scholar—replied, "Which one is that?"

Women's right to vote was not obtained by stealth or acclamation. Rather, it was steadfastly demanded, and denied, for seven decades, as Americans mocked and then, with growing earnestness, debated the "woman question." For the generations of Americans who debated the question, gender restrictions on the franchise were tied to fundamental principles organizing government and family both. But the significance of denying, or granting, women the vote has disappeared from constitutional cognizance because of the manner in which courts have interpreted the amendment. Courts have adopted a rule-based construction of the amendment that reads its language acontextually—without reference to the sociopolitical commitments of those who opposed and advocated reform of the Constitution. Consequently, as currently interpreted, the Nineteenth Amendment bars sex-based restrictions on voting—no more.

This result, of course, was not inevitable. As a brief discussion will illustrate, the woman suffrage campaign concerned considerably more than voting, and the question of women voting was itself was understood to raise core questions concerning the structure of the family. These larger normative concerns of the suffrage campaign did play a role in shaping the Nineteenth Amendment's meaning for a brief period in the aftermath of its ratification, when courts in a number of cases interpreted the suffrage amendment to speak to questions other than voting. But, as I show, these interpretive understandings were only intermittently expressed, and ultimately gave way to the modern, acontextual interpretation of the amendment as a rule governing voting. I begin, then, by briefly revisiting the terms of the suffrage debate, before turning to examine how courts interpreted the woman suffrage provisions of the Constitution—in the immediate aftermath of ratification and then, decades later, in the course of developing the modern law of sex discrimination.

Today we understand the right to vote as a basic incident of citizenship in a democratic polity; the demand for woman suffrage was itself premised on this modern or "universal" conception of the franchise. From this modern standpoint, it is difficult to appreciate the conception of voting that supported the original, gendered definition of the franchise. More was at stake than stereotypical assumptions about the roles of the sexes. Gendered restrictions on the franchise rested on a particular understanding of government and family structure both.

At the time of the founding, the franchise was restricted to those thought to have sufficient independence to exercise wisely the prerogative to govern the new republic: white, property-holding men, generally heads of households.[13] In the view of the founding generation, the independence of judgment necessary to vote responsibly could only be achieved through property ownership. As John Adams explained,

> [V]ery few men who have no property, have any judgment of their own. They talk and vote as they are directed by some man of property, who has attached their minds to his interest. . . . [They are] to all intents and purposes as much dependent upon others, who will please to feed, clothe, and employ them, as women are upon their husbands, or children on their parents.[14]

In short, persons in relations of dependency were unfit to govern because they were governed by others.[15] The relations of governance and dependence Adams described were household relationships, and the concepts of authority he invoked were simultaneously economic and legal. During the eighteenth century, most propertyless people were dependents in a propertied household, a group that included wives, children, slaves, servants, apprentices, journeymen, and hired laborers.[16] Law amplified the effects of economic inequality. In this era,

---

13. See generally Robert Steinfeld, "Property and Suffrage in the Early American Republic," *Stanford Law Review* 41 (1989): 335. Thus, Thomas Jefferson wrote to a friend in 1776 that he favored "extending the right of suffrage (or in other words the rights of a citizen) to all who had a permanent intention of living in the country. Take what circumstances you please as evidence of this, either the having resided a certain time, or having a family, or having property, any or all of them." Jefferson to Pendleton, August 26, 1776, in *The Papers of Thomas Jefferson,* ed. Julian Boyd et al., 60 vols. (Princeton: Princeton University Press, 1950), 1:503–5, quoted in Joan R. Gundersen, "Independence, Citizenship, and the American Revolution," *Signs* 13 (1987): 64.

14. Letter from John Adams to James Sullivan, May 26, 1776, *The Works of John Adams,* ed. C. Adams (1864), 9:376–77, quoted in Steinfeld, "Property and Suffrage," 340.

15. For a closer examination of this question during the Revolutionary Era, see Gundersen, "Independence, Citizenship," 63–65 ("For American leaders who abandoned virtual representation for direct representation, the association of women with dependency provided the way to disqualify women as voters").

16. See Steinfeld, "Property and Suffrage," 344 ("for the most part, inequality between the property owners and the propertyless was a domestic affair"); see also Toby L. Ditz, "Ownership and Obligation: Inheritance and Patriarchal Households in Connecticut, 1750–1820," *William and Mary Quarterly* 47 (1990): 236–37 ("The independence and civic standing of men in family-farm areas also rested on the capacity to marshal the labor of women, children, servants, and occasionally slaves. The status of independent proprietor thus entailed its complement, the status of household dependent: a person who lacked the formal capacity to participate in public life and who was subject to the authority of household heads").

the common law structured the "domestic relations" (husband/wife, parent/child, and master/servant, or apprentice) hierarchically, as relations of private governance between a head of household and his dependents.[17] The master of the household was to support and represent his dependents, who in turn were to serve him.

It was upon this understanding of "family government" that women's legal disabilities in marriage rested. At common law, a husband acquired rights to his wife's paid and unpaid labor and most property she brought into the marriage. A wife was obliged to serve and obey her husband, and a husband was subject to a reciprocal duty to support his wife and to represent her in the legal system. A wife was unable to file suit without her husband's consent and participation; he, in turn, was responsible for his wife's conduct—liable, under certain circumstances, for her contracts, torts, and even some crimes.[18] The common law thus made a married woman the legal ward of her husband, dependent upon him for representation in both public and private affairs.

To say the least, there was a degree of tension between the relations of dominance and subservience constituting the "domestic relations" and the principles of equality uniting household heads in the new republic. As Christopher Tomlins observes:

Legal relations of household mastery were inscribed on what otherwise now professed itself a "free" contractarian legal and political culture. On the face of it, this was a meeting between incompatible tendencies. But those incompatibilities were resolvable along the lines of demarcation between polis and household, public and private, that already structured political and social life. The public realm was where economically independent heads of households met, their participation sanctified, democratized, and to a degree equalized in the polity's civic guarantees. Relations within households (master/servant, parent/child, husband/wife), in contrast, occurred within a separate domestic realm. These were

---

17. See Nancy Fraser and Linda Gordon, "A Genealogy of Dependence: Tracing a Keyword of the U.S. Welfare State," *Signs* 19 (1994): 13; Christopher Tomlins, "Subordination, Authority, Law: Subjects in Labor History," *International Labor and Working-Class Historian* 47 (1995): 70.

18. See Norma Basch, *In the Eyes of the Law: Women, Marriage, and Property in Nineteenth-Century New York* (Ithaca: Cornell University Press, 1982), 47–55, 70–112.

not relations between heads of household; rather, they were relations between heads and dependents. They were household head's
private business, their hierarchical character more or less impervi-
ous to revolutionary discourses of *public* liberty.[19]

In this social framework, distribution of the franchise both recognized and conferred a special form of standing in the community.[20]
And by the dawn of the nineteenth century, status-based restrictions
on the franchise had become a point of controversy among men,
with property-based restrictions challenged throughout the opening
decades of the century, and race-based restrictions becoming a focal
point of controversy in the aftermath of the Civil War.[21] It was during
these nineteenth-century campaigns to extend the franchise among
men that women first organized to demand the vote.

The woman's rights movement grew out of evangelical movements of the early nineteenth century, especially movements for tem-
perance and abolition of slavery.[22] As the abolitionist movement began
to supplement tactics of moral suasion with demands for political and
legal reform, women in its ranks found themselves disabled from participating, and began more self-consciously to consider their own dis-
franchised position within the legal system.[23] It was a group of abolitionists who first convened at Seneca Falls, New York, in 1848 to protest
women's disfranchisement and demand reform of the common-law
marital-status rules. These early woman's rights advocates used ready-
to-hand tools to challenge the gender-hierarchical organization of family and state: They claimed that family and state ought be organized in
accordance with the egalitarian principles that ordered relations
among male heads of household in the Republic. Indeed the movement
announced its demands for suffrage and marriage reform in a Declaration of Sentiments that was explicitly modeled on the Declaration of

---

19. Tomlins, "Subordination, Authority, Law," 74.

20. See Judith N. Shklar, *American Citizenship* (Cambridge: Harvard University
Press, 1991), 2, 27–28.

21. On challenges to property-based restrictions to suffrage, see Steinfeld, "Property and Suffrage," 353–60; see also Jacob Katz Cogan, "The Look Within: Property,
Capacity, and Suffrage in Nineteenth-Century America," *Yale Law Journal* 107 (1997): 473.

22. See Eleanor Flexner, *Century of Struggle: The Woman's Rights Movement in the
United States* (Cambridge: Belknap Press, Harvard University Press, 1959), 41–52, 181–86.

23. See Paula Baker, "The Domestication of Politics," *American Historical Review* 89
(1984): 634; Lori D. Ginzberg, *Women and the Work of Benevolence* (New Haven: Yale University Press, 1990): 91–97.

Independence.[24] Woman's rights advocates continued to work within abolitionist organizations until the immediate aftermath of the Civil War. They believed that constitutional reform during the Reconstruction Era would institutionalize principles of universal suffrage. It was only when the Republican Party expressly refused to include woman suffrage in postwar constitutional reform that the movement began to develop its own organizational structure.[25]

As the Republican Party drafted the constitutional and statutory provisions that would emancipate the slaves and protect the basic civil rights of freedpersons, its leadership was well aware that this new body of civil rights law would grant basic family-law rights to the newly emancipated slaves[26] and, in so doing, might call into question various forms of marital-status law.[27] Republican leaders such as Thaddeus Stevens took the position that while the Fourteenth Amendment might govern family law, provisions such as the equal protection clause would not disturb traditional forms of marital-status regulation.[28] But the architects of Reconstruction were more alarmed about giving women political than civil rights; they specifically drafted the Fourteenth and Fifteenth Amendments so as to enfranchise freedmen without enfranchising women.[29] To justify this partial extension of the

24. See "Declaration of Sentiments," in *History of Woman Suffrage,* ed. Elizabeth Cady Stanton et al. (Salem, N.H.: Ayer, 1985), 1:70–73; see also Linda K. Kerber, "From the Declaration of Independence to the Declaration of Sentiments: The Legal Status of Women in the Early Republic, 1776–1848," *Human Rights* 6 (1977): 115.

25. See Ellen Carol DuBois, *Feminism and Suffrage* (Ithaca: Cornell University Press, 1978), 55–66.

26. See Jill E. Hasday, "Federalism and the Family Reconstructed," *University of California Law Review* 451 (1998).

27. See Hasday, "Federalism and Family Reconstructed"; Patricia Lucie, "On Being a Free Person and a Citizen by Constitutional Amendment," *Journal of American Studies* 12 (1978): 350; Nina Morais, "Sex Discrimination and the Fourteenth Amendment: Lost History," *Yale Law Journal* 97 (1988): 1157 and n. 21; and Amy Dru Stanley, "Conjugal Bonds and Wage Labor: Rights of Contract in the Age of Emancipation," *Journal of American History* 75 (1988): 480.

28. See *Congressional Globe,* 39th Cong., 1st sess., 1064 (1866) (statement of Rep. Stevens) ("When a distinction is made between two married people or two femmes sole, then it is unequal legislation; but where all of the same class are dealt with in the same way then there is no pretense of inequality"); see also Hasday, "Federalism and Family Reconstructed"; Morais, "Sex Discrimination," 1157 and n. 21.

29. See Ellen Carol DuBois, "Outgrowing the Compact of the Fathers: Equal Rights, Woman Suffrage, and the United States Constitution, 1820–1878," *Journal of American History* 74 (1987): 836–52, and *Feminism and Suffrage,* 58–62, 162–63. For an account of the strategic considerations underlying the Republican Party's decisions about expanding the franchise during the Reconstruction Era, see Joellen Lind, "Dominance and Democracy: The Legacy of Woman Suffrage for the Voting Right," *U.C.L.A. Women's Law Journal* 5 (1994): 154–67.

franchise, congressmen invoked the understanding that women were represented in the state through the male heads of household. As one Republican Congressman put it:

> *To constitute the required form of government, therefore, it is necessary that every citizen may either exercise the right of suffrage himself, or have it exercised for his benefit by some one who by reason of domestic or social relations with him can be fairly said to represent his interests.* In one of these cases he is directly represented in the government, and in the other indirectly. The indirect representation is that possessed by women, children, and all those under the legal control of others.
>
> However desirable it may be that every free agent should have by law an equal voice in the common government, yet the fact that women do not vote is not in theory inconsistent with republicanism. *The primary and natural division of human society is into families.* All forms of religion, all systems of law, recognize this arrangement. *By common consent or common submission, whether founded on reason and justice or not, is not material to the argument, the adult males are supposed to represent the family, and the government is not bound to look farther than this common consent or submission.* It receives as representation of the family those whom the family sets up in this capacity.[30]

Claims of this sort recurred throughout the debates on Reconstruction.[31]

Thus, in the nineteenth century, opposition to woman suffrage did not limit itself to the objection that (1) women were, by nature (divinely

---

30. *Congressional Globe,* 40th Cong., 2d sess., 1956 (1868) (Sen. Broomal) (emphasis added).

31. See, for example, *Congressional Globe,* 38th Cong., 1st sess., 2243 (1864) (Sen. Howe) ("I am willing to deprive those who are not males of the right of suffrage, because they exercise it by proxy, as we all know. Females send their votes to the ballot-box by their husbands or other male friends"); *Congressional Globe,* 39th Cong., 2d sess., 56 (1866) (Sen. Williams) ("[A]s a general proposition it is true that the sons defend and protect the reputation and rights of their mothers; husbands defend and protect the reputation and rights of their wives; brothers defend and protect the reputation and rights of their sisters"); and *Congressional Globe,* 39th Cong., 2d sess., 307 (1866) (Sen. Sherman) ("So far as the families, the women and children, are concerned, we know that they are represented by their husbands, by their parents, by their brothers, by those who are connected with them by domestic ties").

and biologically ordained), different from and subordinate to men, hence unsuited to vote. Other core objections to woman suffrage arose from the interlocking conception of state and family upon which the government of the early Republic was premised: (2) women did not need the vote because they were already represented in government by and through men, and (3) woman suffrage would destroy the family by introducing domestic discord into the marital relation and distracting women from their primary duties as mothers.[32]

In short, objections to woman suffrage grew out of an interdependent understanding of nature, family, and state. For example, in his popular tract *Women's Suffrage: The Reform against Nature* (1869), Horace Bushnell argued that "masculinity carries, in the distribution of sex, the governmental function" and depicted "the natural leadership, the decision-power, the determining will of the house and the state, as belonging to men," observing that "happily, it is just as natural to women to maintain this beautiful allegiance to the masterhood and governing sway-force of men, both in the family and in the state, as we could wish

---

For sources discussing the tradition that equated independence with household headship in the nineteenth century, see, for example, Rowland Berthoff, "Conventional Mentality: Free Blacks, Women, and Business Corporations as Unequal Persons, 1820–1870," *Journal of American History* 76 (1989): 757 ("[O]nly men . . . free to sustain the commonwealth ought to be citizens—not their dependent wives, children, tenants, employees, servants, or slaves"); Nancy F. Cott, "Marriage and Women's Citizenship in the United States, 1830–1934," *American Historical Review* 103 (1998): 1440, 1452 ("Independence . . . for the male household head existed in counterpoint to the dependence of others. Having and supporting dependents was *evidence* of independence"); and Laura F. Edwards, "'The Marriage Covenant Is at the Foundation of All Our Rights': The Politics of Slave Marriages in North Carolina after Emancipation," *Law and History Review* 14 (1996): 83 (In the antebellum South, "The figure of a household head was an adult, white, propertied male. . . . Dependency tainted all those who lacked sufficient property to control their own labor and maintain households of their own").

32. As one historian puts it: "Three categories of arguments emerge from a survey of anti-suffrage rhetoric. These were arguments regarding man's and woman's nature as ordained by nature and God; arguments about the nature of representative government, and arguments that detailed the consequences of voting on women, their families, and society" (Martha Ann Hagan, "The Rhetoric of the American Anti-Suffrage Movement, 1867–1920," Ph.D. diss., Washington State University, 1993, 106). Aileen Kraditor puts it a bit more acerbically: "Close to the heart of all antisuffragist orators, particularly congressmen, was a sentimental vision of Home and Mother, equal in sanctity to God and the Constitution. Although all four entities regularly appeared in antisuffragist propaganda, it was the link of woman to the home that underlay the entire ideology." *The Ideas of the Woman Suffrage Movement, 1890–1920* (New York: Norton, 1981), 15.

it to be."[33] Bushnell thus contended that "the male and female natures together constitute the proper man, and are, therefore, both represented in the vote of the man" (67), substantiating his claim about nature by pointing to the institution of marriage (where, under concepts of marital unity, women "are already represented in and by the vote of their husbands") (68). At the same time, he confidently dismissed the objection that many women are "single persons . . . and have therefore no husbands by whose vote their rights may be protected" with a rejoinder from nature: "What we have to say is, that all women alike are made to be married, whether they are or not" (70–71). From this standpoint point it was self-evident that woman suffrage "loosens every joint of the family state, and is really meant to do it, as we plainly see by many of the appeals set forth" (154).

Without disputing the question of gender difference (or disputing it only in degree), suffragists asserted that women were the equal of men in natural entitlement and capacity to exercise the franchise—a position explicitly premised on repudiating the republican conception of the state as an aggregation of households. As Mary Putnam Jacobi was to define the revolutionary core of woman suffrage, the movement understood the state as based on "individual cells," not households: "Confessedly, in embracing this conception as women, we do introduce a change which, though in itself purely ideal, underlies all the practical issues now in dispute. In this essentially modern conception, women are brought into direct relations with the state, independent of their 'mate' or 'brood.'"[34] Of course, suffragists did not rest their case on theory alone. They repeatedly—and heatedly—countered arguments that men represented women by pointing to women's subordi-

---

33. Horace Bushnell, *Women's Suffrage: The Reform against Nature* (New York: Charles Scribner, 1869), 52, 53, 54. For an example of antisuffrage discourse from the decade prior to the war that weaves arguments from nature, family, and the state in a remarkably similar fashion, see Cogan, "The Look Within," 488–89 (quoting speaker at the Massachusetts constitutional convention of 1853).

34. Mary Putnam Jacobi, *"Common Sense" Applied to Woman Suffrage* (New York: Putnam, 1894), 138. See also Elizabeth Cady Stanton, "The Solitude of Self (1892)," reprinted in Beth M. Waggenspack, *The Search for Self-Sovereignty* (New York: Greenwood Press, 1989), 159–60 ("In discussing the sphere of man we do not decide his rights as an individual, as a citizen, as a man [by] his duties as a father, a husband, a brother, or a son, relations some of which he many never fill. . . . Just so with woman. The education that will fit her to discharge the duties on the largest sphere of human usefulness, will best fit her for whatever special work she may be compelled to do").

nation in the state, the family, market, education, and church, asserting that the record uniformly demonstrated men's *in*capacity to represent fully and fairly women's interests.[35] Finally, suffragists sought in various ways to demonstrate that suffrage did not disrupt the family order, rightly conceived. The vision of family life they defended was not, of course, that of the common law: the movement was simultaneously seeking reform of the common-law rules of marriage that subordinated wives to their husbands. Rather, in various ways, the suffrage movement was exploring new, more egalitarian conceptions of the family that contemplated for women a far more prominent role in the nation's economic and political institutions.[36]

The challenge that suffrage advocacy posed to the gendered institutions of American life was a deep one. As the movement contested claims of virtual representation and undertook to demonstrate why women needed the vote, advocates offered an account of women's subordination that ranged well beyond the fact of disfranchisement. To cite but a few examples: Suffragists protested the sex-based restrictions on employment and compensation that impoverished women and drove them into marriage.[37] They deplored women's legally enforced dependency in marriage, particularly property rules that vested in husbands rights to their wives' earnings and to the value of wives' household labor.[38] They decried law's failure to protect women from physical coercion in marriage, including domestic violence, marital rape, and "forced motherhood."[39] They protested double standards of sexual propriety that punished one sex for conduct in which both were engaged.[40] And they challenged the exclusion of women from juries

---

35. See "Declaration of Sentiments," in Stanton et al., *History of Woman Suffrage,* 1:70–73.

36. See Siegel, "Home as Work," 1116 ("The joint property claim thus repudiated the rhetoric of protection in a bid for equal governance rights in the household, much as the movement's suffrage arguments repudiated claims of virtual representation in a bid for equal governance rights in the polity").

37. See, e.g., id., 1121.

38. See generally Siegel, "Home as Work."

39. See, e.g., id., 1104–6; DuBois, "Outgrowing the Compact," 842–43; and Reva B. Siegel, "'The Rule of Love': Wife Beating as Prerogative and Privacy," *Yale Law Journal* 105 (1996): 2117.

40. See Jane E. Larson, "'Even a Worm Will Turn at Last': Rape Reform in Late Nineteenth-Century America," *Yale Journal of Law and the Humanities* 9 (1997): 8–10.

convened to judge the fate of those in the criminal justice system.[41] Over the decades, as the movement developed from a fringe protest group to a respectable voice in the spectrum of American political opinion, its arguments for the vote changed, to a degree, in political complexion. By the turn of the century, the movement was arguing that women needed the vote for purposes of "social housekeeping," detailing a range of progressive reforms that would improve the health and welfare of families living in America's growing cities.[42] At the same time, as it broadened its class base, the movement began to emphasize with greater vigor the range of social reforms needed to improve the lot of working-class women.[43]

III. Interpreting the Nineteenth Amendment

In 1920, some seventy years after women first demanded the right to vote at Seneca Falls, and over a half century after the Republican Party refused to include woman suffrage on the agenda of Reconstruction reform, the movement developed a sufficiently wide-ranging coalition to amend the Constitution. Ratification of the Nineteenth Amendment was the capstone of a multigenerational effort to change the terms of the original constitutional compact so that women might count, equally with men, among the ranks of "We, the People."[44] Why then has the amendment disappeared from legal and popular consciousness?

----

41. See Deborah Rhode, *Justice and Gender* (Cambridge: Harvard University Press, 1989), 48–50. For examples of movement rhetoric protesting women's exclusion from juries, see Stanton et al., *History of Woman Suffrage*, 1:597–98 (1881) (Elizabeth Cady Stanton discussing the plight of women charged with infanticide in a speech before the New York Legislature); and id., 2:648 (1882) (Susan B. Anthony protesting her conviction for voting unlawfully); see also Siegel, "Home as Work," 1144 (demand for right to serve on juries figuring prominently in resolutions of the Tenth National Woman's Rights Convention).

42. See Kraditor, *Ideas of the Woman Suffrage Movement*, 66–71; see also Jane Addams, "Why Women Should Vote," in *One Woman, One Vote*, ed. Marjorie Spruill Wheeler (Troutdale, Ore.: NewSage Press, 1995), 195–202.

43. On the expansion of the class base of the suffrage movement in the first decades of the twentieth century, see Ellen Carol DuBois, *Harriot Stanton Blatch and the Winning of Woman Suffrage* (New Haven: Yale University Press, 1997), 94–106.

44. It was this understanding of the amendment that, in the view of some opponents, rendered it unconstitutional, as exceeding the legitimate scope of Article 5 amending processes. See George Stewart Brown, "The Amending Clause Was Provided for Changing, Limiting, Shifting, or Delegating 'Powers of Government.' It Was Not Provided for Amending 'the People.' The 19th Amendment Is Therefore Ultra Vires," *Virginia Law Review* 8 (1922): 237. The Supreme Court upheld the woman-suffrage amendment against such claims in *Lesser v. Garnett*, 258 U.S. 130 (1922). See Reva B. Siegel, "She, the People: Reading the Nineteenth Amendment as Norm and Rule," typescript, May 1998.

The answer would seem to lie primarily in the domain of constitutional interpretation. If the Nineteenth Amendment fails to speak
to us today, it is because courts have construed the amendment as a
rule governing voting whose meaning can be adduced without reference to the normative commitments leading to its adoption. It is
taken to be a matter of common sense that because the text of the
amendment states a nondiscrimination rule governing voting, the
amendment concerns matters of voting only: As Frank Michelman
recently remarked of the country's experience with the Nineteenth
Amendment, "Has any of us heard of a lawyer or judge suggesting
that it has any bearing on constitutional law respecting sex discrimination beyond the question of the vote . . . ?"[45] But it is by no means
inevitable that the amendment should have been construed this way.
The "rulelike" character of the suffrage amendment is not an intrinsic property of its text, but instead arises from the way courts have
interpreted its text.

To illustrate the point, we might briefly consider another amendment whose text might be characterized as "rulelike" in character.
The Eleventh Amendment provides that "[t]he Judicial power of the
United States shall not be construed to extend to any suit in law or
equity, commenced or prosecuted against one of the United States by
Citizens of another State, or by Citizens or Subjects of any Foreign
State." Yet, in *Hans v. Louisiana*,[46] the Court read the Eleventh Amendment to apply to suits against a state brought by one of its own citizens, and in *Monaco v. Mississippi*,[47] to suits brought by a foreign state
against one of the states of the union. In extending sovereign immunity doctrine beyond the express terms of the Eleventh Amendment,
the *Monaco* Court reasoned: "Manifestly, we cannot rest with a mere
literal application of the words of § 2 of Article III, or assume that the
letter of the Eleventh Amendment exhausts the restrictions upon suits
against non-consenting States. *Behind the words of the constitutional provisions are postulates which limit and control.*"[48] This interpretive pro-
viso is entirely commonplace. In adducing the meaning of constitu-

---

45. Frank Michelman, "Saving Old Glory: On Constitutional Iconography," *Stanford Law Review* 42 (1990): 1344 n. 24.

46. 134 U.S. 1 (1890).

47. 292 U.S. 313 (1934).

48. Id., 322 (emphasis added). The Court has recently reiterated its understanding that the principles giving rise to the Eleventh Amendment and not the Amendment's text alone should govern its meaning. See *Seminole Tribe of Florida v. Florida*, 116 S. Ct. 1114, 1129–30 (1996) (criticizing "blind reliance upon the text of the Eleventh Amendment").

tional language, courts generally refer to the norms and purposes for which the text was adopted.[49] Thus, the clause of Article 1 that gives to Congress the power "to make Rules for the Government and Regulation of the land and naval forces" (sec. 8, cl. 14) is uncontroversially interpreted to give Congress the power to regulate the air force, as well.[50] Reasoning from norms and purposes, the Supreme Court has given restrictive and expansive construction to the language authorizing Congress to enact legislation enforcing the Thirteenth Amendment's prohibition on slavery and involuntary servitude.[51] And in fact, in the immediate aftermath of the Nineteenth Amendment's ratification, at least some courts read the suffrage amendment in light of the normative commitments leading to its adoption, and so concluded that it had constitutional significance in matters other than voting. Indeed, the Supreme Court's first substantive discussion of the Nineteenth Amendment suggested that it articulated a normative commitment of wide-ranging constitutional significance.

In short, during the 1920s and 1930s the Nineteenth Amendment was read as a text arising out of a particular historical context: the product of a lengthy debate on the status of women in the American legal system. So construed, the amendment was understood by at least some courts to have normative implications for practices other than voting. Most intriguingly, a few courts understood the suffrage amendment to speak to matters concerning marital-status law, while others understood it to affect a variety of political rights women might exercise, such as office holding and jury service. But, as the case law reveals, these intuitions about the meaning of the constitutional amendment were only intermittently expressed, and ultimately gave way to the modern, functional understanding of the amendment, as governing matters of voting only. In short, in the period after ratification, we can observe the Nineteenth Amendment undergoing interpretive construction, initially read as a text arising out of a particular sociohistorical context and then

49. Cf. *Hans v. Louisiana*, 134 U.S. 1, 12–14 (1890) (analyzing the framer's understanding of state sovereignty in the course of interpreting the Eleventh Amendment). For one overview of the literature on purposive interpretation of the Constitution's text, see Robert Post, "Theories of Constitutional Interpretation," *Representations* 30 (1990): 21–23.

50. See Post, "Theories of Constitutional Interpretation," 21–22.

51. Compare *The Civil Rights Cases*, 109 U.S. 3 (1883) (holding that the Thirteenth Amendment does not authorize Congress to prohibit race discrimination in public accommodations) with *Jones v. Alfred H. Mayer Co.*, 392 U.S. 409 (1968) (holding that the Thirteenth Amendment authorizes Congress to prohibit private discrimination in real-estate dealings).

progressively being stripped of its context to emerge as a rule capable of being applied without reference to the normative debates and commitments that led to its adoption.

The Supreme Court offered its first commentary on the meaning of the Nineteenth Amendment in 1923.[52] The occasion was the Court's decision in *Adkins v. Children Hospital*,[53] striking down the District of Columbia's minimum-wage law for women and children. While the Court had severely restricted protective labor legislation for men in substantive due-process cases such as *Lochner v. New York*,[54] it had upheld a minimum-hours law for women in the 1908 case of *Muller v. Oregon*.[55] On the face of it, *Adkins* presented a question concerning the application of substantive due-process doctrine, but, as we will see, this question in turn tacitly raised issues concerning the continuing authority of common-law marital-status traditions in the wake of the Nineteenth Amendment's ratification.

During the Progressive Era, substantive due-process doctrine protected employees' freedom to contract along sex-differentiated lines. In *Lochner*, the Court held that legislation restricting the hours that men might work infringed upon their liberty of contract, but in *Muller*, the Court reasoned that legislation restricting the hours of women's employment was a constitutional exercise of the police power, justified in view of important physical differences between the sexes, particularly women's role in bearing children.[56] *Muller* presented this new constitutional rationale for regulating women's employment as an extension of the ancient common-law tradition that restricted the contractual capacity of married women. Even if the old coverture rules governing wives' contractual capacity were now being repealed, *Muller* reasoned, differences in women's physical and social roles warranted continuing differential treatment of the sexes.[57]

---

52. The Supreme Court upheld the constitutionality of the amendment against federalism objections in *Lesser v. Garnett*, 258 U.S. 130 (1922).

53. 261 U.S. 525 (1923).

54. 198 U.S. 45 (1905).

55. 208 U.S. 412 (1908).

56. *Muller*, 422–23 ("The two sexes differ in structure of body, in the functions to be performed by each. . . . This difference justifies a difference in legislation").

57. The Court began its opinion in *Muller* by noting, "The current runs steadily and strongly in the direction of the emancipation of the wife" and observed that Oregon had reformed the common law to allow wives to make contracts as if single (id., 418). But the Court then asserted that even if legislatures were reforming the marital-status rules of the common law, there was still reason to treat women's contracts differently than men's: "Though

The question presented in *Adkins* was whether the Court would apply *Muller*'s reasoning to uphold a sex-based minimum-wage law or strike the statute down on liberty-of-contract grounds generally applicable to men. Opponents of labor-protective regulation and at least some proponents of women's rights pointed to the ratification of the Nineteenth Amendment as reason for questioning the continued viability of a sex-differentiated constitutional rule—a position adopted by the lower court in striking down the statute.[58] Of course, if the case for sex-differentiated analysis of protective labor legislation rested on the basis of physiological difference alone, passage of the Nineteenth Amendment would seem to have scant bearing on the question; but if in fact, *Muller*'s discussion of women's physiological differences perpetuated, in new idiomatic form, the ancient marital-status traditions of the common law,[59] then ratification of the Nineteenth Amendment might well signify the obsolescence of this normative regime.

In *Adkins,* the Supreme Court held the sex-based minimum-wage statute unconstitutional in an opinion written by the newly appointed justice George Sutherland. Before joining the Court, Sutherland had advised Alice Paul of the National Women's Party on the campaign for woman suffrage as well as the drafting of an equal rights amendment,[60] and his opinion for the Court emphasized women's evolving legal status as a basis for distinguishing *Muller* and analyzing the sex-based minimum-wage statute in accordance with the same liberty-of-contract principles that governed men's work:

---

limitations upon personal and contractual rights may be removed by legislation, there is that in her disposition and habits of life which will operate against full assertion of those rights" (id., 422). As I have elsewhere argued, "In Muller, the Court employed claims about women's bodies to reach a result which some decades earlier it might have justified by invoking the common law of marital status." See Reva B. Siegel, "Reasoning from the Body: A Historical Perspective on Abortion Regulation and Questions of Equal Protection," *Stanford Law Review* 44 (1992): 323.

58. See Joan Zimmerman, "The Jurisprudence of Equality: The Women's Minimum Wage, the First Equal Rights Amendment, and *Adkins v. Children's Hospital, 1905–1923*," *Journal of American History* 78 (1991): 188; *Children's Hospital of the District of Columbia v. Adkins,* 284 F. 613, 618 (1922) ("No reason is apparent why the operation of the law should be extended to women to the exclusion of men, since women have been accorded full equality with men in the commercial and political world. Indeed, this equality in law has been sanctioned by constitutional amendment").

59. See Siegel, "Reasoning from the Body," 322–23.

60. See Zimmerman, "The Jurisprudence of Equality," 212–13, 219–20.

But the ancient inequality of the sexes, otherwise than physical, as suggested in the Muller case, has continued "with diminishing intensity." *In view of the great—not to say revolutionary—changes which have taken place since that utterance, in the contractual, political, and civil status of women, culminating in the Nineteenth Amendment, it is not unreasonable to say that these differences have now come almost, if not quite, to the vanishing point.* In this aspect of the matter, while the physical differences must be recognized in appropriate cases, and legislation fixing hours or conditions of work may properly take them into account, *we cannot accept the doctrine that women of mature age, sui juris, require or may be subjected to restrictions upon their liberty of contract which could not lawfully be imposed in the case of men under similar circumstances.* To do so would be to ignore all the implications to be drawn from the present day trend of legislation, as well as that of common thought and usage, by which *woman is accorded emancipation from that old doctrine that she must be given special protection or be subjected to special restraint in her contractual and civil relationships.*[61]

Thus, in *Adkins,* the Court read "the great—not to say revolutionary—changes . . . in the contractual, political, and civil status of women, culminating in the Nineteenth Amendment"[62] as expressing a transformative constitutional commitment to recognize women as men's equals in the American legal system. But the opinion does not discuss this emergent sex-equality norm in abstract or formal terms. Rather, it construes the "changes . . . culminating in the Nineteenth Amendment" *sociohistorically,* as repudiating "the ancient inequality of the sexes" and "accord[ing]" women "emancipation from th[e] old doctrine[s]" of the common law.[63] The entire logic of the *Adkins* opinion depends on this finding of normative conflict between the suffrage amendment and marital-status law. In separately authored dissents, Justice Taft and Justice Holmes each argued that "[t]he 19th Amendment did not change the physical strength or limitations of women upon which the decision in Muller v. Oregon rests."[64] But this commonsense objection has force

---

61. *Adkins v. Children's Hospital,* 261 U.S. 525, 553 (1923) (emphasis added).

62. Id.

63. Id.

64. Id., 567 (Taft, J., dissenting); see also id., 569–70 (Holmes, J., dissenting).

only if one reads *Muller*'s discussion of physiological sex differences acontextually, ignoring the connections *Muller* draws between the gender norms of the coverture tradition and women's family role. It is because the majority in *Adkins* read *Muller*'s argument for regulation of women's employment as giving new expression to the marital-status traditions of the common law that the *Adkins* majority concluded that the case for a sex-differentiated approach to liberty-of-contract doctrine had been eroded by the transformations in women's legal status culminating in ratification of the Nineteenth Amendment.

Adkins does not apply the Nineteenth Amendment to matters of employment or marital-status law in any simple sense. Rather, *Adkins* invokes the commitments of the woman's rights campaign that culminated in ratification of the suffrage amendment and then treats this positive account of the ratification campaign normatively: as a reason for similarly transformative interpretation of the due-process jurisprudence of the Fourteenth Amendment. So construed, the suffrage amendment both reflects and embodies emancipatory commitments with implications for the interpretation of diverse bodies of law.

The Supreme Court was not the only court to read the Nineteenth Amendment expansively or to suggest that ratification of the suffrage amendment amounted to a repudiation of the marital-status norms of the common law. At least one federal district court concluded shortly after the *Adkins* decision that the suffrage amendment of its own force disestablished coverture doctrine. The judge refused to apply the common-law doctrine absolving a wife of responsibility for crimes committed jointly with her husband, reasoning that "since the adoption of the Nineteenth Amendment to the Constitution, it seems to me that the rule of common law has no application to crimes committed against the United States."[65] A judge concurring in a federal tax case reached a similar conclusion, rejecting the government's claim that under common-law coverture principles a wife's tax domicile was her husband's.[66] Quoting *Adkins* to the effect that "woman is accorded emancipation from the old doctrine that she must be given special protection or be

---

65. *United States v. Hinson*, 3 F.2d 200, 200 (S.D.Fla. 1925).

66. *McCormick v. United States*, T.D. 43804, 57 Treas. Dec. 117, 125–26 (1930) (Cline, J., concurring); see also Sophonisba P. Breckinridge, *Marriage and the Civic Rights of Women: Separate Domicile and Independent Citizenship* (Chicago: University of Chicago Press, 1931), 4–5. I am indebted to Gretchen Ritter for drawing my attention to this decision.

subjected to special restraint in her contractual and civil relationships,"[67] the judge asserted that the Nineteenth Amendment "covers
the right of a woman to select and establish a residence wherever she
chooses to vote."[68] Other courts deciding questions concerning coverture law invoked the suffrage amendment as authorizing liberalizing
interpretations of the common law. For example, a New Jersey
chancery court concluded that the legal changes culminating in ratification of the Nineteenth Amendment warranted giving a narrow construction to a clause in the state's married women's property act that
preserved coverture restrictions on a wife's capacity to contract.[69]
While the New Jersey statute still required wives to obtain a husband's
joinder for contracts involving the sale of land,[70] the court reasoned
that traditions in equity allowing a wife to act as a separate agent with
respect to her separate property had been "enlarged and extended by
both courts and legislative bodies to the point where, since the adoption of the Nineteenth Amendment to the federal Constitution, practically all of the disabilities of women, both married and single, have
been removed, so that to-day she has practically all the rights and privileges of the male citizen."[71] The New Jersey court invoked the Nineteenth Amendment both positively and normatively: It described ratification of the suffrage amendment as the culmination of efforts to
disestablish traditional forms of gender status regulation and then
treated ratification of the suffrage amendment as normative authority
justifying the extension of these egalitarian commitments in private
law, much as *Adkins* gave effect to the normative commitments of the
suffrage amendment in the interpretation of public law. The court thus
allowed enforcement of a divorced woman's contract for sale of land,
even though the contract appeared to be invalid under state law
because the woman entered the agreement during the life of her marriage without her husband's consent.

---

67. *McCormick*, 125 (quoting *Adkins*, 261 U.S. at 553).

68. Id. The majority reasoned within common-law principles, concluding that the
woman had established a domicile for tax purposes that was separate from her husband's
because the husband had consented to the arrangement.

The Virginia Supreme Court also concluded that a married woman had the right to
select her own domicile for state tax purposes, in passing giving weight to the concern
that continued adherence to the marital-unity principle would be "subversive of the
statutory right of voting." See *Commonwealth v. Rutherfoord*, 169 S.E. 909, 913 (Va. 1933).

69. *Hollander v. Abrams*, 132 A. 224 (Ct. Chancery N.J. 1926).

70. Id., 228.

71. Id., 229.

But such decisions were exceptional. Few courts read the Nineteenth Amendment as authorizing further extension of sex-equality norms in the private-law arena. To illustrate, one federal court expressed its astonishment that the "law of Tennessee, as to tenants by the entirety is purely the old common law," announcing, "in this age of the Nineteenth Amendment, rights of women, feminism, women office holders, and general emancipation of the sex, it is almost shocking to learn that in one form of conveyancing, 'the husband and wife are one person in law.'"[72] While the court recognized a deep normative conflict between the suffrage amendment and the common-law coverture rules, it voiced this sense of normative dissonance without treating the suffrage amendment as authorizing a liberalizing interpretation of the common law. In this regard, it assumed what was shortly to become the "common sense" view of the amendment: that it had no direct bearing on matters concerning the interpretation of marital-status law. Indeed, shortly after its decision in *Adkins* striking down a sex-based minimum-wage law, the Supreme Court upheld a New York statute prohibiting nighttime employment of women in restaurants, weakly distinguishing *Adkins* and resting its decision on the authority of *Muller v. Oregon*.[73]

It is possible to detect this same ambivalent dynamic at work in the legislative arena. Immediately after ratification of the Nineteenth Amendment, Congress, at the urging of the women's movement, adopted the Cable Act, which provided that women who married certain foreign nationals would retain their American citizenship.[74] This move to restrict the application of the coverture domicile rules to matters of national citizenship was self-consciously presented as warranted by the ratification of the Nineteenth Amendment.[75] As one congressman put it: "in my judgment there was no particular force in the demand for this bill until the nineteenth amendment became part of the

72. *McNeil v. Connecticut Fire Ins. Co.*, 24 F.2d 221, 223 (W.D.Tenn. 1928).

73. See *Radice v. People of the State of New York*, 264 U.S. 292, 294–95 (1924).

74. See Act Relative to the Naturalization and Citizenship of Married Women, ch. 411, 42 Stat. 1021 (1922). According to the act, an American woman still lost her citizenship if she married a foreigner who was ineligible for United States citizenship, for example, an Asian man. On the exceptions to the Cable Act and thus the persisting connection between women's marital status and citizenship, see Cott, "Women's Marriage and Citizenship," 26–27.

75. See Cott, "Women's Marriage and Citizenship," 25–26; Virginia Sapiro, "Women, Citizenship, and Nationality: Immigration and Naturalization Policies in the United States," *Politics and Society* 13 (1984): 1, 12–13.

organic law of the land. . . . At that moment the doctrine of dependent or derived citizenship became as archaic as the doctrine of ordeal by fire."[76] But, the Cable Act repealed the doctrine of dependent citizenship for some American women only; those who married men of the "wrong" race or nationality remained subject to the old common-law domicile rules, and forfeited their American citizenship.[77] Similarly, in this period, state law reform of the coverture domicile rules was generally quite limited. A number of states adopted legislation allowing married women to choose their own domiciles for purposes of voting; these state statutes repealed the common-law principles governing the domicile of married women in matters of voting *only*, otherwise leaving the common-law rule intact.[78]

Thus, as we have seen, in the period after ratification the Supreme Court and the United States Congress interpreted the suffrage amendment as reflecting and embodying a commitment to disestablish the gender-status norms of the common law; but neither the Court nor the Congress acted consistently on this understanding. A few federal and state courts interpreted the suffrage amendment as disestablishing the marital-status traditions of the common law. But this understanding of constitutional reform never gathered significant momentum. During the 1920s and 1930s, the Nineteenth Amendment was, however, given effect outside the voting context in matters deemed to concern "political" rights, such as the right to hold office and to serve on juries.

At least some state courts understood the suffrage amendment to embody a general sex-equality norm in matters concerning political participation. So, for example, the Supreme Court of Maine declared that after ratification of the Nineteenth Amendment, the governor could appoint a woman justice of the peace.[79] While the state legislature had responded to the ratification of the Nineteenth Amendment by enacting a statute declaring that the right to hold state office could not be denied on account of sex, the state's constitution had earlier been interpreted to bar office holding by women. The Maine Supreme Court declared this

---

76. Quoted in Sapiro, "Women, Citizenship, and Nationality," 12.

77. See note 74 above.

78. See, e.g., 1929 Me. Acts 268; 1922 Mass. Acts 315–16; 1927 N.J. Laws 235; 1929 N.Y. Laws 984; 1923 Ohio Laws 118–19; 1923 Pa. Laws 1034; Va. Code Ann. sec. 82a (Michie 1924). For a discussion of these laws, see Breckinridge, *Marriage and Civic Rights,* 4–5. I thank Gretchen Ritter for drawing my attention to these laws.

79. See *Opinion of the Justices,* 113 A. 614 (Me. 1921).

prior construction of the state constitution superseded by the Nineteenth Amendment. Among the several reasons given was the pronouncement, "Every political distinction based upon consideration of sex was eliminated from the Constitution by the ratification of the amendment. Males and females were thenceforth, when citizens of the United States, privileged to take equal hand in the conduct of government."[80]

Similarly, in the years following ratification, the Nineteenth Amendment was interpreted in a series of cases concerning sex-based restrictions on jury service, restrictions long complained of by the women's movement. The common law barred women from serving on juries, excluding women, as Blackstone observed, "propter defectum sexus"—on account of defect of sex.[81] Did ratification of the Nineteenth Amendment eliminate this ancient restriction on women's participation in the civic life of the community? In some states, legislatures responded to the suffrage amendment by revising the statutes governing juror qualifications to indicate that women were now eligible to serve. (As one court observed: "The spirit of equality of the sexes which [the Nineteenth Amendment] breathes moved the Legislature of New Jersey in 1921 to amend our act concerning jurors so as to include . . . women as well as men.")[82] In jurisdictions where the legislature took no such action, courts divided about the effect of the suffrage amendment on juror eligibility. Some courts concluded that, after ratification, women should serve as jurors because state statutes directed that jurors be drawn from the pool of electors—even if the relevant statutes referred to those eligible as "men."[83] But in other states, courts ruled

80. Id., 617. For other office-holding cases, see, for example, *In re Opinion of the Justices*, 135 N.E. 173 (Mass. 1922) (by striking sex restriction on voting from Massachusetts constitution, Nineteenth Amendment removed only source of law that might have precluded women from holding office); *Preston v. Roberts*, 110 S.E. 586 (N.C. 1922) (woman qualified to serve as notary public and deputy clerk of the superior court; disqualification to hold public office removed by Nineteenth Amendment); *Dickson v. Strickland*, 265 S.W. 1012, 1023 (Tex. 1924) (wife of former governor not disqualified from holding public office by reason of sex or marital status, citing Nineteenth Amendment). But see *State ex Rel. Buford v. Daniel*, 99 So. 804 (Fla. 1924) (upholding statute providing that county welfare board shall be composed of five men and four women, over dissenting opinion arguing that rule is unconstitutional under the Nineteenth Amendment).

81. William Blackstone, *Commentaries on the Laws of England* (1768; reprint, Chicago: University of Chicago Press, 1979), 3:362.

82. *State v. James*, 114 A. 553, 556 (N.J. 1921).

83. See, for example, *State v. Walker*, 185 N.W. 619, 625–26 (Iowa 1921); *Cleveland, C., C. & St. L. Ry. Co. v. Wehmeier*, 170 N.E. 27, 29 (Ohio 1929); and *Browning v. State*, 165 N.E. 566, 567 (Ohio 1929); see also *Palmer v. State*, 150 N.E. 917, 919 (Ind. 1926) (no gender referent in statute setting forth juror qualifications; ratification of the Nineteenth Amendment made women electors, hence eligible for jury service).

that the Nineteenth Amendment concerned the franchise only and did not affect other political and civil disabilities imposed on women. Thus, in construing an 1895 statute specifying that jurors were to be drawn from "male residents of the parish," the Louisiana Supreme Court reasoned that ratification of the Nineteenth Amendment might make women electors, but it did not make these new electors jurors: "The Nineteenth Amendment . . . refers not to the right to serve on juries, but only the right to vote."[84] The court emphasized that "[t]here is no statute of Louisiana declaring women eligible to serve on juries," and pointed out that "[a] trial by jury, at common law, and as guaranteed by the Constitution, has been universally declared to mean a trial by jury of men, not women, nor men and women." (418) Reasoning along similar lines, the Supreme Court of Illinois read a gender restriction into a *gender-neutral* statute that declared electors were to serve as jurors, reasoning, "The word 'electors,' in the statute here in question, meant male persons, only, to the legislators who used it."[85] The fact that the Constitution had been amended to make women electors was, in this court's view, irrelevant: "The Nineteenth Amendment to the Constitution of the United States makes no provision whatever with reference to the qualifications of jurors."[86] This view of the Nineteenth Amendment as a rule governing voting *simpliciter* was to prevail in the ensuing decades—and was, in later years, tacitly adopted by the Supreme Court, which never mentioned the Nineteenth Amendment in its cases upholding, and then striking down, statutes providing women automatic exemptions from jury service.[87]

Apart from the decisions just described, there is little other case law discussing the significance, or practical force, of the amendment in the ensuing decades. Not surprisingly, it is not until the late 1960s, with the rise of the so-called second-wave feminist movement, that discus-

---

84. *State v. Bray*, 95 S. 417, 418 (La. 1923).

85. *People ex rel. Fyfe v. Barnett*, 150 N.E. 290, 292 (Ill. 1926).

86. Id., 291.

87. See *Hoyt v. Florida*, 368 U.S. 57, 61–62 (1961) (upholding statute giving women absolute exemption from jury service unless they expressly waive the privilege, reasoning that "[d]espite the enlightened emancipation of women from the restrictions and protections of bygone years, and their entry into many parts of community life formerly considered to be reserved to men, woman is still regarded as the center of home and family life"); *Taylor v. Louisiana*, 419 U.S. 522 (1975) (statute providing women automatic exemption from jury service, waivable in writing, is unconstitutional under the Sixth and Fourteenth Amendments). *J.E.B. v. Alabama ex rel. T.B.*, 511 U.S. 127 (1994) (holding that state's use of gender as basis for peremptory strikes in jury selection is unconstitutional under equal protection clause).

sion of the Nineteenth Amendment begins to appear in the case law again. These initial scattered references suggested that the Nineteenth Amendment had force *outside* the voting context—again, intriguingly, in matters concerning marital-status law. For example, in 1968, a prominent federal jurisdiction decision rejected cases equating a wife's domicile with her husband's for diversity-jurisdiction purposes. In the court's view, the jurisdiction cases impermissibly perpetuated old common-law doctrines of marital status: "Whatever the ancient doctrine, a wife is capable of acquiring a domicile separate from that of her husband; at least to this extent legal equality of the sexes is embodied in the Fourteenth and Nineteenth Amendments."[88]

In this period, it was still not at all clear what form constitutional protection of women's rights might take. While momentum was developing for a new constitutional amendment guaranteeing women equal rights under law, litigants continued to pursue alternate constitutional strategies. And, as the Supreme Court had not yet struck down a sex-based law on equal-protection grounds, plaintiffs raising sex discrimination claims based them on both Fourteenth and Nineteenth Amendment grounds.[89] In this period, plaintiffs also invoked the Nineteenth Amendment as a constitutional basis for challenging criminal abortion statutes, arguing, for example, that "the effect of [a criminal abortion] statute in compelling them to bear unwanted children is to perpetuate an inferior status which the Nineteenth Amendment was intended to

---

For an argument that the Nineteenth Amendment should be read to bestow on women the full complement of political rights (for example, the right to hold office, serve on juries, and even serve in militias), see Akhil Reed Amar, "Women and the Constitution," *Harvard Journal of Law and Public Policy* 18 (1994): 471–72, and "The Bill of Rights as a Constitution," *Yale Law Journal* 100 (1991): 1202–3; see also Vikram David Amar, "Jury Service as Political Participation Akin to Voting," *Cornell Law Review* 80 (1995): 241–42. For a historical account of the Nineteenth Amendment's interpretation in the jury cases, see Jennifer K. Brown, "The Nineteenth Amendment and Women's Equality," *Yale Law Journal* 102 (1993): 2175; Gretchen Ritter, "A Jury of Her Peers: Citizenship and Women's Jury Service after the Nineteenth Amendment," typescript, May 1997.

88. *Spindel v. Spindel*, 283 F.Supp. 797, 813 (E.D.N.Y. 1968); see also *Gill v. Gill*, 412 F.Supp. 1153, 1154 (E.D.Pa. 1976) (quoting and following Judge Weinstein's opinion in *Spindel*).

89. See, for example, *Ex Parte Mathews*, 488 S.W.2d 434 (Ct.Crim.Ap.Tex. 1973) (striking down sex-differentiated age-of-majority law in juvenile code on equal-protection grounds that was challenged on Fourteenth and Nineteenth Amendment grounds); *Johnson v. State*, 476 P. 2d 397, 398 (Okla.Crim.App. 1970) (upholding sex-differentiated age of majority law in juvenile code against Fourteenth and Nineteenth Amendment challenge); accord *Benson v. State*, 488 P.2d 383, 384 (Okla.Crim.App. 1971); *Coyle v. State*, 489 P.2d 223, 224 (Okla.Crim.App. 1971).

eradicate."[90] The claim may sound strange today, but at the time it was advanced the Court had not yet held that women have a constitutional privacy right that protects decisions about abortion, nor had it yet given shape to sex discrimination jurisprudence under the equal protection clause. (In retrospect, the Nineteenth Amendment challenge to criminal abortion statutes is especially striking because it asserts a right against state action imposing an *inferior status,* reasoning about equality in sociological rather than formal terms.)

In 1970, a law review article appeared, entitled "Women and the Constitution: Some Legal History and a New Approach to the Nineteenth Amendment."[91] Its author suggested that courts had construed the amendment narrowly in the wake of its ratification—just as the Reconstruction amendments had been construed—but that the time was ripe to reconsider its meaning. He then reviewed the history of the suffrage campaign, and concluded that "the 19th amendment really had very little to do with the vote, but instead established the total equality of women with men. Under such an interpretation, there is a national right in all women to suffer no discriminations of any kind *because of their sex*" (50). In this view, "The 19th amendment to the Constitution, while on its face dealing only with women's suffrage, can be interpreted as an emancipation proclamation which extends the guarantees of all three Civil War amendments to all women" (26). As Justice Ginsburg recalls, "[T]here was always a view that once the Nineteenth Amendment was passed and it made women full citizens, that was, in effect, an Equal Rights Amendment. . . . Many people thought that you could put the Fourteenth Amendment together with the Nineteenth Amendment and that was essentially the Equal Rights Amendment. But it didn't happen."[92]

In short, during the opening years of the ERA campaign, it was still uncertain how women's claims for equal civic status would find constitutional grounding. But, by the early 1970s, the new campaign to amend the Constitution and secure for women equal rights under law

---

90. *Young Women's Christian Ass'n v. Kugler,* 342 F.Supp. 1048, 1056 (D.N.J. 1972). For discussion of the abortion litigation strategy, see Sylvia A. Law, "Rethinking Sex and the Constitution," *University of Pennsylvania Law Review* 132 (1984): 970–73 and n. 55; see also W. William Hodes, "Women and the Constitution: Some Legal History and a New Approach to the Nineteenth Amendment," *Rutgers Law Review* 25 (1970): 51 n. 101.

91. Hodes, "Women and the Constitution."

92. Comments of Justice Ruth Bader Ginsburg in *John Marshall Law School Alumni News,* December 1994, 45.

had moved the Court to find a constitutional basis for protecting women's rights that it had not discerned in the previous century. That constitutional basis proved to be, not the Nineteenth Amendment, but instead the equal protection clause of the Fourteenth Amendment.

IV. Burying "the Woman Question" in the Discourse of "Sex Discrimination": Heightened Scrutiny under the Equal Protection Clause

As we have seen, by 1970 there was a sketchy body of precedents that viewed the Nineteenth Amendment as recognizing women's equal civic status. Building from these fragments, or returning to the history of the suffrage campaign itself, the Court might have employed the suffrage amendment as a basis for developing a more substantial body of constitutional protections for women's rights. Instead, beginning in 1971, the Court struck down, for the first time, a sex-based statute under the equal protection clause of the Fourteenth Amendment.[93] In retrospect, the Court's choice to ground constitutional protections for women's rights in the equal protection clause is not terribly surprising. In the wake of the civil rights movement of the 1950s and 1960s, the Court had construed the clause expansively, to give unprecedented protections against race discrimination to African Americans and other minority groups. Equal-protection jurisprudence was alive and growing at a prodigious pace, while the Nineteenth Amendment had languished mute for decades.[94]

What is striking, however, is the Court's failure to link the Nineteenth and Fourteenth Amendments in developing a body of constitutional protections for women's rights. There was ample precedent for this kind of synthetic interpretation of the Constitution's provisions. To cite one prominent example, when the Court ruled in *Brown v. Board of Education* that the equal protection clause of the Fourteenth Amendment forbade de jure race discrimination in public education, it declared that the same principles of equal protection binding the states under the Fourteenth Amendment bound the federal government under the due process clause of the Fifth Amendment. The Court's ruling in *Bolling v. Sharpe*[95] thus "incorporated" a twentieth-century inter-

---

93. *Reed v. Reed*, 404 U.S. 71 (1971).
94. This same set of circumstances would have influenced litigators as well.
95. 347 U.S. 497 (1954).

pretation of a nineteenth-century amendment into a constitutional provision dating from the late eighteenth century. Along very different lines, the constitutional right of privacy that the Court was developing in the late 1960s and early 1970s was held to rest on the "penumbras" of several constitutional provisions. Employing a synthetic interpretive approach, the Court might have held that the Nineteenth Amendment's grant of equal civic status to women would find substantive elaboration under the equal protection clause of the Fourteenth Amendment.[96]

Had the Court proceeded in this fashion, it might have returned to the ratification history of the suffrage amendment and observed that generations of Americans had debated the way law should regulate women's status in diverse spheres of social life. It might then have recalled the core objection to woman suffrage: that woman were represented in the state through male household heads and that women's participation in matters of civic governance was fundamentally inconsistent with their role as wives and mothers. The Court could then have pointed out that, after seven decades of protest, Americans finally amended the Constitution, decisively repudiating the republican conception of the state as an aggregation of male-headed households and recognizing that women were entitled to participate directly in democratic self-governance, as equal citizens under law. Had the Court proceeded to give effect to the normative commitments of the Nineteenth Amendment through the equal protection clause of the Fourteenth Amendment, it would have grounded equal-protection jurisprudence in the history of women's struggle for equal rights, acknowledging that women resisted their pervasive disempowerment over the centuries, identifying the specific social sites of that struggle, and recognizing that, in ratifying the Nineteenth Amendment, the nation had made a commitment to transform the basic ordering principles of the Republic.

---

96. For similar observations about the interpretation of the Nineteenth Amendment, see Amar, "Women and the Constitution," 472 (reading Nineteenth Amendment to alter Article 2 references to president as "he"); Amar, "Bill of Rights," 1202–3 (discussing synthetic or holistic interpretation of the Constitution with specific reference to the Nineteenth Amendment).

Bruce Ackerman has advanced a richly developed theory of synthetic constitutional interpretation, engagement with which is beyond the scope of this essay. For his most recent elaboration of his views, see Bruce Ackerman, *We the People: Transformations* (Cambridge: Harvard University Press, 1998); see also Bruce Ackerman, "Constitutional Politics/Constitutional Law," *Yale Law Journal* 99 (1989): 515–47.

The question of emancipating women from the status constraints of the family would have been central in that narrative, as it was in the *Adkins* opinion. So conceived, the equal protection jurisprudence would have been grounded in a sociohistorical understanding of women's subordination in the American legal system.

But the Court did not proceed in this fashion. Instead, in the early 1970s, the Court began haltingly to construe the equal protection clause to bar certain forms of sex-based legislation, and it did so without reference to the debates over women's status that culminated in ratification of the Nineteenth Amendment. Considered from this vantage point, the modern law of sex discrimination was founded in an act of historical erasure. What is more, in basing constitutional protections for women's rights on the equal protection clause, the Court never revisited the ratification history of the Fourteenth Amendment in an effort to determine whether, or to what extent, its framers understood the language they had adopted to protect women against sex discrimination. A credible case can in fact be made that the authors of the Fourteenth Amendment understood Section 1 to employ language of sufficient generality that it might reach certain forms of gender status regulation.[97] Given that, since *Brown,* the Court had been interpreting the equal protection clause in ways that quite arguably exceeded expectations of its framers, this return to the ratification history of the Fourteenth Amendment would at least have had the salutary effect of grounding its protections in the history of the struggle for women's rights. But the Court did not look to history. Rather, it proceeded on what is still the "commonplace" assumption, that the framers of the Fourteenth Amendment gave no thought to questions of women's rights. Unfortunately, this view is often held without careful analysis of the historical record (concerning, for example, the intentions of move-

---

97. For one such argument, see Morais, "Sex Discrimination," 1153. There is no doubt that the framers of the Fourteenth Amendment understood that it could have implications for groups other than African Americans. See William E. Nelson, *The Fourteenth Amendment: From Political Principle to Judicial Doctrine* (Cambridge: Harvard University Press, 1988), 163 ("Those who discussed the amendment were aware of its implications for other groups, such as Chinese, Indians, women, and religious minorities"); Mark G. Yudof, "Equal Protection, Class Legislation, and Sex Discrimination: One Small Cheer for Mr. Herbert Spencer's Social Statics," *Michigan Law Review* 88 (1990): 1387–89, 1396–97 (discussing scattered references to women in debates over the Fourteenth Amendment). See also pp. 147–48 of this essay. Evaluating the significance of the framers' statements and intentions for contemporary understandings of the Fourteenth Amendment is, however, a complex undertaking, beyond the scope of this essay.

ment allies in the Republican Party, prevailing distinctions between civil and political rights, congressional floor debates on the reach of the amendment, etc.), and generally seems to reflect the presentist assumption that the campaign for women's rights began in earnest sometime in the late 1960s.

Thus, while not as significant as its neglect of the Nineteenth Amendment, the Court's decision to extend the protections of the equal protection clause to women without considering the ratification history of the Fourteenth Amendment once again effaced the struggles of the woman's rights movement. Of course, reckoning with that history would have exposed weaknesses in the intentionalist case for interpreting the equal protection clause to prohibit sex discrimination; yet those deficiencies might have been cured by synthetic interpretation—by implementing the Nineteenth Amendment's commitment to sex equality through the equal protection clause of the Fourteenth Amendment, reading the later amendment to modify the normative framework of its predecessor, much as the Court has implemented the equal protection commitments of the Fourteenth Amendment through the due process clause of the Fifth Amendment.[98] On this view, the struggle for constitutional recognition of women's rights begun in the era of the Civil War was resolved in 1920, resulting in a national commitment to disestablish gender inequality as carefully deliberated as the commitment to disestablish race inequality expressed in the Reconstruction amendments.

But the Court built the case for applying the equal protection clause to sex discrimination in very different terms. The best account we have of the reasons underlying the Court's decision to review sex-based state action with heightened scrutiny appears in a plurality opinion authored by Justice Brennan in the case of *Frontiero v. Richardson*.[99] In this opinion, Justice Brennan argued that under the equal protection clause, sex-based state action should be reviewed with "strict scrutiny," just as race-based state action was. Such a holding would have created a strong, virtually irrebuttable presumption that all sex-based legislation was unconstitutional. (Brennan, however, failed to secure a majority of the justices to join his opinion; several took refuge in the argument that as the ERA was currently being considered for ratification, it

---

98. Cf. Amar, "Women and the Constitution," 471–72.
99. 411 U.S. 677 (1973).

would be unseemly for the Court to interpret the Constitution in a manner that would effectively preempt state decisions about whether to amend the Constitution.)[100]

In his *Frontiero* opinion, Justice Brennan made the case for strict scrutiny of sex-based state action on the grounds that sex discrimination was sufficiently like race discrimination so as to warrant similar constitutional treatment. History did play a role in this argument. Justice Brennan began his argument by announcing, "There can be no doubt that our Nation has had a long and unfortunate history of sex discrimination";[101] yet, Justice Brennan's purpose in invoking the history of women's treatment in the American legal system was to establish an analogy between the case of race and sex discrimination. Pointing to expressions of separate-spheres ideology in the opinions of the Supreme Court ("The paramount destiny and mission of woman are to fulfill the noble and benign offices of wife and mother. This is the law of the Creator"),[102] Justice Brennan then observed:

> As a result of notions such as these, our statute books gradually became laden with gross, stereotypical distinctions between the sexes and, indeed, throughout much of the 19th century the position of women was, in many respects, comparable to that of blacks under the pre–Civil War slave codes. Neither slaves nor women could hold office, serve on juries, or bring suit in their own names, and married women traditionally were denied the legal capacity to hold or convey property or to serve as legal guardians of their own children. . . . And although blacks were guaranteed the right to vote in 1870, women were denied even that right . . . until adoption of the Nineteenth Amendment half a century later.[103]

It is striking that, even as Justice Brennan recounts the nation's "long and unfortunate history of sex discrimination," he represents the history of women in the American legal system as legally relevant only insofar as their "position . . . was . . . comparable to blacks." It is the collective memory of *race* relations that makes women's experience in the

---

100. See id., 691–92 (Justices Powell, Burger, and Blackmun, concurring).

101. Id., 684.

102. Id., 685 (quoting *Bradwell v. State,* 16 Wall. 130, 141 [1873] [Bradley, J., concurring]).

103. Id., 685.

American legal system visible as a "history of sex discrimination" and invests that history with normative significance it is otherwise assumed to lack. Thus, the race/gender analogy generates a narrative that simultaneously represents and effaces the history of women's treatment in the American legal system, even as it completely occludes the historical experiences of women of color.

This dynamic of recognizing and effacing history is replicated at the level of constitutional doctrine, as well. In the quoted passage, Justice Brennan invokes the history of women's treatment in the American legal system in order to demonstrate the similarity of race and sex discrimination, an analogy he completes by arguing that sex, like race, is "an immutable characteristic determined solely by accident of birth" and "frequently bears no relation to ability to perform or contribute to society."[104] In short, the history Justice Brennan recites has no independent constitutional significance; it is recited only to construct the analogical nexus between race and sex discrimination and thus to establish a constitutional basis for reviewing sex discrimination claims otherwise presumed not to exist under the equal protection clause. Consistent with this, in the two decades of cases decided after *Frontiero,* the Court never again revisited the nation's "long and unfortunate history of sex discrimination" or referred to the Nineteenth Amendment—a pattern unbroken until decisions of the past several terms, as I will discuss below. Instead, development of the Court's sex discrimination jurisprudence proceeded without grounding in the nation's legal or constitutional history.

It was not until 1976 that a majority of the Court concluded that sex-based state action warranted heightened or "intermediate scrutiny" under the equal protection clause—a standard like, but somewhat less rigorous than, the "strict" scrutiny standard the Court employs in reviewing race-based state action. The Court chose what can at best be described as a curious case in which to make this historic pronouncement. In *Craig v. Boren,*[105] a teenage boy argued that an Oklahoma statute prohibiting the sale of "nonintoxicating" 3.2 percent beer to males under the age of twenty-one and to females under the age of eighteen discriminated against him on grounds of sex. Against the history detailed in Justice Brennan's *Frontiero* opinion, the "injury" the

104. Id., 686.
105. See 429 U.S. 190 (1976).

plaintiff "suffered" was appallingly trivial. Even given the ACLU's strategy of bringing sex discrimination claims raised by men as well as women,[106] the Court had before it other, more significant cases in which it could have announced this new, heightened standard of equal-protection review. In the years between *Frontiero* and *Craig*, the Court had upheld a statute denying employment disability insurance to pregnant women (reasoning infamously that pregnancy classifications were not sex classifications because they divided the world into pregnant and nonpregnant persons).[107] The Court had, without so much as mentioning the Nineteenth Amendment, struck down a statute exempting women from jury service.[108] It had addressed questions concerning gender-differentiated social security benefits, marital inheritance rights, and age-of-majority statutes, as well as women's service in the military.[109] Any of these cases raised issues concerning the history of women's treatment in the American legal system more pressing than those at issue in *Craig*.

Nonetheless, it was on these facts—concerning the right of a teenage boy to purchase watered-down beer when girls of his age could—that the Court announced the new standard to govern sex discrimination claims under the equal protection clause. For the government to regulate in a sex-based manner, it would henceforth have to demonstrate that the sex-based classification bore a "substantial" relationship to an "important" government interest.[110] In announcing this standard, Justice Brennan's opinion for the Court did not so much as mention the legal and constitutional history he had invoked in the *Frontiero* opinion; indeed, given the plaintiff and the injury at issue in the

---

106. See David Cole, "Strategies of Difference: Litigating for Women's Rights in a Man's World," *Law and Inequity Journal* 2 (1984): 54–58.

107. See *Geduldig v. Aiello*, 417 U.S. 484, 496–97 n. 20 (1974) ("The program divides potential recipients into two groups—pregnant women and nonpregnant persons. While the first group is exclusively female, the second includes members of both sexes").

108. See *Taylor v. Louisiana*, 419 U.S. 522 (1975).

109. See *Kahn v. Shevin*, 416 U.S. 351 (1974) (upholding statute granting widows a property tax exemption not granted to widowers); *Winberger v. Wiesenfeld*, 420 U.S. 636 (1975) (striking down provision of Social Security Act that granted survivors benefits based on earnings of a deceased man to his widow, but provided no survivors benefits based on earnings of a deceased woman to her widower); *Stanton v. Stanton*, 421 U.S. 7 (1975) (striking down age-of-majority statute requiring a parent to pay child support to girls until eighteen and boys through the age of twenty-one); *Schlesinger v. Ballard*, 419 U.S. 498 (1975) (allowing differential treatment of male and female naval officers, in view of restrictions on women's eligibility for service and combat).

110. *Craig*, 197.

Craig case, it would have been somewhat difficult to state the relevance of this history. Instead the opinion fleshed out the new standard of review by enumerating a list of constitutionally impermissible attitudes. Government actors could no longer engage in sex-based regulation when such regulation "foster[ed] 'old notions' of role typing" or relied on "'archaic and overbroad' generalizations" about the sexes.[111] As the Court summarized the logic of its new sex discrimination cases: "increasingly outdated misconceptions concerning the role of females in the home rather than in the 'marketplace and world of ideas' were rejected as loose-fitting characterizations incapable of supporting state statutory schemes that were premised on their accuracy."[112]

Thus, in explaining its new standard of review, the *Craig* opinion refers to history, but not to the nation's legal or constitutional history. Instead, the opinion's prohibition on sex discrimination is situated in a history of evolving social attitudes: the Court exhorts state actors to shed "'old notions' of role typing," "archaic and overbroad generalizations," and "increasingly outdated misconceptions" concerning the sexes. Testing sex-based state action for evidence of such "outdated misconceptions" is the announced purpose of *Craig*'s heightened standard of review. Henceforth, for state actors to regulate on the basis of sex, they would have to defend their use of sexually discriminatory means by demonstrating that it was substantially related to an important government purpose. By requiring a showing that sex classifications in law rationally advance permissible ends, rather than reflect archaic stereotypical norms, the standard of heightened scrutiny aims to free the nation from what the *Frontiero* opinion referred to as its "long and unfortunate history of sex discrimination." Indeed, in this view, heightened scrutiny performs a kind of commemorative act, tacitly invoking a regrettable past the nation is aspiring to transcend.[113] But the history the doctrine of heightened scrutiny strives to transcend remains utterly unparticularized, lying in the realm of what we might call "old-fashioned ways of thinking." No examination of this history guides the operations of heightened scrutiny. History plays no role in

---

111. Id., 198.

112. Id., 199.

113. See, for example, *J.E.B. v. Alabama ex rel. T.B.*, 511 U.S. 127, 136, 1425 (1994) (nation's "'long and unfortunate history of sex discrimination' . . . warrants the heightened scrutiny we afford all gender-based classifications today"); *United States v. Virginia*, 116 S.Ct. 2264, 2274 (1996) ("Today's skeptical scrutiny of official action denying rights or opportunities based on sex responds to volumes of history").

identifying the group of plaintiffs heightened scrutiny protects or the kinds of state action it prohibits.

As the Court understands sex discrimination, anyone, male or female, may be its victim; indeed most of the major sex discrimination cases were brought by male plaintiffs.[114] How is it that men, as well as women, may complain that they are the victims of sex discrimination? To recall: the *Frontiero* plurality opinion pointed to two kinds of rationales for subjecting sex-based state action to heightened scrutiny—that women had suffered a history of discrimination and that sex was an immutable trait bearing no relation to ability to perform. While the "immutability" and "history of discrimination" rationales for heightened scrutiny are generally viewed as complementary, they in fact reflect two competing impulses in contemporary antidiscrimination law. The history-of-discrimination rationale is concerned with the treatment of particular social groups (racial and ethnic minorities, women), while the immutability rationale is concerned with the treatment of individuals (all who possess a "race" or "gender"). The impulse giving rise to the history-of-discrimination rationale seeks to remedy, or at least to alleviate, entrenched patterns of group-based subordination, while the impulse giving rise to the "immutability" rationale seeks to eliminate distinctions among citizens predicated on group membership.[115] It is in fact the immutability rationale, and not the history-of-discrimination rationale, that best explains the body of equal-protection doctrine the Court has elaborated. *Heightened scrutiny protects individuals against sex-based classification by the legal system.*

The Court has made no effort to connect the kinds of state action triggering heightened scrutiny to the history of women's treatment in the legal system. To the contrary: Heightened scrutiny is triggered by *any* form of state action that employs a sex-based classification. All state action employing sex-based classifications receives the same degree of scrutiny, whether the law regulates access to 3.2 percent beer, institutions of higher learning, or women's bodies. Moreover, the Court has

---

114. As explained in *Virginia,* "the Court . . . has carefully inspected official action that closes a door or denies opportunity to women (or to men)." *United States v. Virginia,* 116 S.Ct. 2264, 2275 (1996).

115. Other criteria *Frontiero* invokes to build the case for heightened scrutiny can be similarly distinguished. "Political powerlessness" is an indicator of group-based subordination, while the high "visibility" of the sex characteristic is, like immutability, relevant to building the case that sex discrimination subjects individuals to arbitrary distinctions on the basis of group membership. See *Frontiero v. Richardson,* 411 U.S. 677, 684–86 (1973).

defined the type of regulatory distinctions that count as sex-based classifications without attention to history or social meaning. Reasoning formalistically, it has ruled that policies regulating pregnancy do not employ sex-based classifications because such policies discriminate between pregnant women and nonpregnant persons (a group including both men and women); hence laws excluding pregnant women from employment or criminalizing abortion do not receive heightened scrutiny under the equal protection clause.[116] Similarly, the Court has ruled that statutes awarding civil-service employment preferences to veterans are not sex-based, because the preferences advantage a group, at the time of the Court's decision, virtually, but not exclusively, male.[117]

And when the state regulates on what the Court deems to be a "facially neutral" basis, the Court adopts an exceedingly deferential posture in reviewing the legislation. In such cases, the Court has announced that it will defer to legislative judgments about social policy so long as there is no evidence that the facially neutral state action was motivated by a discriminatory purpose, a concept that the Court has defined as tantamount to malice (state action undertaken "at least in part 'because of,' and not merely 'in spite of,' its adverse effects" on women).[118] In so defining the triggers for heightened scrutiny, the Court has made no effort to consult the history of women's treatment in the legal system. It matters not that many nineteenth-century doctrines of marital-status law were couched in "facially neutral" terms (e.g. the doctrine of interspousal tort immunity that precluded "spouses" from suing each other for battery).[119] Nor is it relevant that, under the pressure of heightened scrutiny, many of the most infamous marital-status doctrines of the common law have recently been redefined in gender-neutral terms. A rule exempting spouses from criminal prohibitions on rape or treating spousal battery more leniently than other forms of assault or valuing "homemaker" services or defining child support will not trigger heightened scrutiny, no matter how closely its history may be tied to the marital-status rules of the common law.[120]

---

116. See *Geduldig v. Aiello*, 417 U.S. 484, 494–97 (1974).

117. See *Personnel Administrator of Massachusetts v. Feeney*, 442 U.S. 256, 280–81 (1979).

118. Id., 279.

119. See Siegel, "The Rule of Love," 2156–58.

120. See id., 2188–96.

In its preoccupation with formal acts of classification, the law of sex discrimination in fact converges with the modern law of race discrimination as that body of doctrine was "tamed" in the 1970s;[121] as I have elsewhere argued, both bodies of equal-protection doctrine now define discrimination without attention to history—in particular, ignoring the ways that disestablishing a body of status law may cause status-enforcing state action to evolve in rule structure and justificatory rhetoric.[122] Yet, the tendency to equate discrimination with classification took decades to become fully entrenched in the law of race discrimination. The modern law of race discrimination began with a several-decade struggle over the disestablishment of America's apartheid system, in public education and elsewhere. In hundreds of cases, minority plaintiffs challenged overt practices of racial classification, but they also challenged apartheid's less formalized manifestations, contesting the state's claim to have eradicated the legacy of segregation ("present effects of past discrimination") in diverse social institutions.[123] It was not until the 1970s that the Court began restrictively to equate race discrimination with racial classification,[124] and, again, not until this era, that the Court began, with considerable hesitation, to treat the race discrimination claims of white plaintiffs as commensurable with the race discrimination claims of minority plaintiffs. By contrast, at no point in the litigation of sex discrimination claims was there ever a sustained effort to disestablish entrenched status relations in particular social institutions. For the most part, it would seem, the eradication of formal gender classifications was taken by itself to signify the eradication of historically subordinating practices. (Thus, the law of marriage was taken to be cleansed of sex discrimination when stripped of sex classifications, although the governing norms of the institution remained unexamined and, now, effectively immunized from equal-

---

121. It was not until 1976 that the Supreme Court ruled that plaintiffs challenging "facially neutral" state action that had a disparate impact on a subordinated group would have to prove that the challenged action was motivated by discriminatory purpose. See *Washington v. Davis*, 426 U.S. 229 (1976); see generally David A. Strauss, "Discriminatory Intent and the Taming of *Brown*," *University of Chicago Law Review* 56 (1989): 935; Siegel, "Equal Protection," 1129–46.

122. Siegel, "Equal Protection."

123. See, e.g. Daniel J. McMullen and Irene Hirata McMullen, "Stubborn Facts of History—the Vestiges of Past Discrimination in School Desegregation Cases," *Case Western Law Review* 44 (1993): 75.

124. The Court struggled with the question as early as the 1970s but did not decisively resolve it until its decision in *City of Richmond v. J.A. Croson*, 488 U.S. 469 (1989).

protection scrutiny.)[125] Further, as I have observed, from the beginning, men as well as women figured as sex discrimination plaintiffs, with the result that claims of sex discrimination were often only tenuously connected to an historically subordinated group and the history of its treatment in the legal system. No doubt, those who litigated the early sex discrimination cases share responsibility for this along with the Court. But no matter how one allocates responsibility, the result remains: the modern law of equal protection understands sex discrimination formally, as involving practices of sex-based classification, and has never critically scrutinized the institutions and practices that have played an historic role in perpetuating women's secondary status in the American legal system.

In short, doctrines of heightened scrutiny may serve a commemorative function, recalling a past they aspire to transcend; but the past that doctrines of heightened scrutiny construct has little to do with the history of gender status regulation in the American legal system. It may be that "our Nation has had a long and unfortunate history of sex discrimination," but as the Court has elaborated equal-protection doctrine, it has not tied the "history of sex discrimination" to the institutions and practices that generations of suffragists protested, and generations of Americans defended, as they debated "the woman question."

V. What Difference Would Remembering Make?

The interpretive judgments I have described both reflect, and perpetuate, social memory of a certain sort. The justices who forged sex discrimination law in the 1970s were no doubt raised in a world where few would have had cause to know much about the history of women's subordination in the American legal system or the history of the quest for women's rights. With women's access to the academy and the bar severely restricted throughout most of the twentieth century, both scholarly and popular consciousness about such matters was scant. These same conditions shaped the understandings of those advocates who argued sex discrimination claims before the Court.

Thus, it was not as an advocate before the Court, but over two decades later as a member *of* the Court, that Ruth B. Ginsburg would

---

125. See Siegel, "The Rule of Love," 2193 and n. 275.

self-consciously situate claims about the law of sex discrimination in an historical framework.[126] Her opinion for the Court in the *Virginia Military Institute* case,[127] decided in 1996, broke with prior case law and grounded the doctrine of heightened scrutiny in national and constitutional history, revisiting the Founding through a narrative of wrong and rectification:

> Today's skeptical scrutiny of official action denying rights or opportunities based on sex responds to volumes of history. As a plurality of this Court acknowledged a generation ago [in *Frontiero*], "our Nation has had a long and unfortunate history of sex discrimination." Through a century plus three decades and more of that history, women did not count among voters composing "We the People"; not until 1920 did women gain a constitutional right to the franchise. . . . And for a half century thereafter, it remained the prevailing doctrine that government, both federal and state, could withhold from women opportunities accorded men so long as any "basis in reason" could be conceived for the discrimination. . . .
>
>   In 1971, for the first time in our Nation's history, this Court ruled in favor of a woman who complained that her State had denied her the equal protection of the laws.[128]

In her *Virginia Military Institute* opinion, Justice Ginsburg does not invoke history to demonstrate that sex discrimination resembles race discrimination. But she does employ a mode of reasoning about equal protection often encountered in the Court's opinions about race discrimination. The *Virginia Military Institute* decision invokes a history of constitutional wrongs to demonstrate why the nation has a deep moral obligation to protect women's constitutional rights. It took some two

126. Some of Justice Ginsburg's pathbreaking sex discrimination briefs for the ACLU invoke the "history of discrimination" argument to establish the race/gender analogy adopted in *Frontiero*, but the history of women's treatment in the American legal system remains peripheral to their main constitutional arguments. See, e.g. Brief for Appellant, 15–16, *Reed v. Reed*, 404 U.S. 71 (1971); Brief of American Civil Liberties Union Amicus Curiae, at 11–20, *Frontiero v. Richardson*, 411 U.S. 677 (1973) (beginning argument with a section entitled "Historical Perspectives" that compares the law's treatment of women and blacks in a passage from which Justice Brennan's opinion drew, nearly verbatim).

127. *United States v. Virginia*, 116 S. Ct. 2264 (1996).

128. Id., 2274–75.

decades, and more than twenty-five opinions, for the Court to ground equal-protection analysis of sex discrimination questions in a narrative emphasizing collective agency and responsibility in this way. Differently put, it took the appointment of a nationally prominent woman's rights advocate to the Court for the Court to reason about questions of sex discrimination this way. If we analyze the dynamics of social memory at work in the Court's sex discrimination cases, it would appear that the analytical framework of equal protection law has been deeply shaped by relations of gender inequality the doctrine purports to rectify.

What difference would a memory of constitutional wrongs make to the adjudication of women's constitutional rights? To begin with, the memorialization of wrongs is itself a symbolic practice of rectification, for when a community voices collective acknowledgment of collective wrongdoing, it defines itself in opposition to its own past practices. Considered in the best light, equal-protection law functions in just this way; unlike other bodies of constitutional doctrine, equal-protection law defines the nation *against* its own "history and traditions," and almost exclusively through its aspirational ideals.[129] If we consider the ways that law functions as a vehicle of social memory, it is possible to see how this process of redefining national identity might work. Were the Court to recount the narrative of constitutional wrong and rectification it tells in the *Virginia Military Institute* case in its equal-protection opinions of the next decade, the social memory of future generations of Americans might well differ from the memory of those who inaugurated modern sex discrimination jurisprudence.

Would such narratives of collective agency ultimately engender a deeper sense of national responsibility in matters of women's rights? We can only speculate about the answer to so large a question, with intuitions, in all likelihood, reflecting our judgments about the nation's conduct in matters of race during the last few decades. But the significance of memorialization does not hinge on this "big" question alone. Social memory shapes collective intuitions about gender justice in more local and particularized ways.

Stories about the past shape our "common sense" intuitions about

---

129. It is for this reason that considerations of past practice lack the authority in matters of equal protection that they possess in other bodies of constitutional doctrine. Cf. Cass R. Sunstein, "Homosexuality and the Constitution," *Indiana Law Journal* 70 (1994): 1.

the present; more concretely, the stories we tell about gender relations in the past shape our understandings of gender relations in the present. As Vicki Schultz has demonstrated, the nation is inclined to view racial segregation in the workplace within a framework of discrimination, while it assumes that gender segregation in the workplace is the product of women's choices.[130] Consider an example or two drawn from the Court's sex discrimination cases of the 1980s. In a case evaluating an affirmative action plan for a county road-dispatcher position for which no woman had ever been hired, Justice Scalia observed: "It is absurd to think that the nationwide failure of road maintenance crews, for example, to achieve . . . female representation is attributable primarily, if even substantially, to systemic exclusion of women eager to shoulder pick and shovel. It is a 'traditionally segregated job category' . . . in the sense that, because of longstanding social attitudes, it has not been regarded *by women themselves* as desirable work."[131] Along similar lines, Justice Powell defended sex segregation at a state university by observing, "Coeducation, historically, is a novel educational theory. . . . [M]uch of the Nation's population during much of our history has been educated in sexually segregated classrooms," and then observed of that history: "The sexual segregation of students has been a reflection of, rather than an imposition upon, the preference of those subject to the policy."[132] As these opinions should illustrate, stories explaining how the world came to be organized profoundly affect commonsense intuitions about the justice of the social order, exculpating or implicating a wide range of institutional practices. The view that gender relations are the product of an evolving social consensus remains quite prevalent today, continuing to obscure the role that more coercive forces play in maintaining the gender stratification of social life.

Because narratives about the past can raise questions about the legitimacy of particular institutions and practices, they can also identify ways in which the social forms of gender injustice vary from, and intersect with, the social forms of racial injustice. At present, American antidiscrimination law rests on an analogy between race and sex dis-

---

130. See Vicki Schultz, "Telling Stories about Women and Work: Judicial Interpretations of Sex Segregation in the Workplace in Title VII Cases Raising the Lack of Interest Argument," *Harvard Law Review* 103 (1990): 1749.

131. *Johnson v. Santa Clara County*, 480 U.S. 616, 668 (1987).

132. *Mississippi University v. Hogan*, 458 U.S. 718, 736–37 (1982) (Powell, J., dissenting). This Powell opinion supplied the framework for the legal arguments the Virginia Military Institute recently employed to justify its gender-exclusionary admissions policy.

crimination in which it only halfheartedly believes. In constitutional parlance, sex discrimination deserves heightened scrutiny because it is like race discrimination, but sex discrimination only deserves "inter-mediate" rather than "strict" scrutiny because, in the last analysis, sex discrimination is in fact unlike race discrimination. Intuitions about the difference between race and sex discrimination, and intersections between them, might more usefully be informed by an understanding of the particular social processes whereby race and gender inequality have been enforced.

Modern equal-protection jurisprudence understands discrimina-tion as a practice of classification—a conceptual artifact, perhaps, of the struggle to disestablish Jim Crow.[133] But, dimly, equal-protection doc-trine also grasps that discrimination is an expression of status relations. When we think about discrimination in a status framework, it is clear that different kinds of status relations are enforced through different networks of meanings, institutions, and practices; further, persons who are members of multiple status groups are subordinated in distinctive ways. Finally, as I have elsewhere argued, status regulation is dynamic, continually changing shape as it is contested.[134] Pursuing this inquiry in the case of gender, we would find that family law played a central role in subordinating women and has enforced the status position of women of different class, ethnic, and racial backgrounds in various ways that have in fact changed shape over the centuries.

We might arrive at this understanding by interpreting the Four-teenth Amendment's guarantee of equal protection sociohistorically, rather than formally. But we could also arrive at this understanding by asking ourselves, in simple narrative form, what was at stake in the protracted struggle over "the woman question." Exactly what commit-ment did the nation make when, after seven decades of protest, it finally broke with the foundational understandings of the Republic and amended the Constitution to make women equal citizens with men? Not surprisingly, the story of the debates over the Nineteenth Amend-ment would lead us to the same sites of status conflict—prominent among them, the family—that sociohistorical analysis under the equal protection clause would. In this way, recovering the story of "the woman question" from "our nation's long and unfortunate history of

133. Cf. Siegel, "Equal Protection," 1142–44.
134. See, for example, id. 1116–19, 1141–48.

sex discrimination" might well alter our judgments about the nature of "sex discrimination" itself—a regulative concept that operates far beyond the courtroom walls.

No doubt, the ways that contemporary generations of Americans would give concrete social meaning to the normative commitments of the Nineteenth Amendment might vary from understandings of those who ratified it. This is as it should be in a nation that celebrates its highest constitutional moments in opinions like *Brown v. Board of Education*. The struggle of each generation to make sense of the nation's foundational constitutional commitments, and to take responsibility for its compromised record of respecting them, is a crucial part of the American tradition, one that gives meaning to the Constitution as a constitutive institution in the nation's life.[135]

---

135. With such a synthetic reading of the Nineteenth and Fourteenth Amendments, we might ask: Even if the nation has abandoned most sex-based forms of regulation, has it yet emancipated women from the status constraints of the family? In what ways does state regulation of family life *still* presuppose, and perpetuate, duel standards of citizenship for "independent" and "dependent" household members? We could ask such question in matters concerning work, parenting, and the distribution of property, or the physical security of persons in intimate relations.

Held in the Body of the State: Prisons and the Law

Joan Dayan

Gaining unexpected admission and granted interviews that were marked exceptions to Arizona Department of Corrections policy, I began traveling to the prisons in Arizona three years ago. My sources consist of interviews with correctional officers, wardens, and classification specialists, as well as the formal policies, standard operating procedures, and regulations of the Arizona Department of Corrections. These tales are remembered—albeit in new forms, as if dreamed again—in the legal cases to which I refer. I will move through a few narratives: (1) spectacles of chain and the tales that accompany them; (2) the Special Management Unit I (the model for Pelican Bay) and Special Management Unit II in the Eyman Complex, Florence, Arizona (a locus of control, security, and categorization that circumvents previous offender classification codes and substitutes the fact of incapacitation and punishment with the illusion of penological justification); and, finally, (3) law libraries, the right to counsel and court intervention in the civil rights of prisoners. The accompanying legal narratives are drawn primarily from the ten-year struggle between the federal district court and the State of Arizona, culminating in Lewis v. Casey, *in which the question of access to the courts was answered in a precedent-setting decision by the Supreme Court in June 1996.*

Legitimacy, reasonableness, and necessity. These words recur throughout the Code Noir of the French islands, the West Indian slave laws of the eighteenth century, the black codes of the American South, and contemporary legal decisions maintaining prison security. The language of

I thank Hendrik Hartog, Austin Sarat, members of the Amherst Seminar, Mark Batik, Daniel Pochoda, and Donald McNutt for their comments, research leads, and inspiration.

the law, amid the current spectacle of chain gangs, control units, and executions, preserves the memory of slavery. What is remarkable in reading these past slave codes together with contemporary prisoner litigation is the divorce between intention, law, and reality. As a set of legal acts that has its own history, the law defines how material considerations and a concern for order and discipline can produce the juridical nonexistence of the person through degrees of deprivation.

The absolute separation between the formal existence of the law and the day-to-day records that underpin the law's authority makes the decisions of the court read as incantation: founded on precedent, repeated, and gaining in force with each repetition. Like ritual, the more banal the enunciation, the more tried and used, the more authority it has. As fading, elusive, and deathly as Locke's memory, the law is a tomb of dead ideas. Yet what refreshes and sustains the law, what keeps it from wearing away, is its ability to mobilize history. Changing circumstances, immobilized as precepts, become the lifeblood for the constancy, the deathlessness of legal inquiry.

A seemingly vague phrase, a general conceptual structure, an impersonal tradition, gains concrete significance and even a power to summon practice, through its history of applications. There is something terrifying about a formality that fears the figurative and yet makes its existence possible in reality. Though incomplete as descriptions of practice, judicial opinions are integral as structures of thought. What Robert Cover called "the task of construing broad constitutional language" summons a history memorialized so precisely that while certain facts are repressed, the emblems of power and privilege endure. Narratives of the past, once remembered in law, demarcate a semantic genealogy of slavery and involuntary servitude.

Chains

I remember seeing, as a child growing up in Atlanta, men wearing zebra stripes working along the highway. These chain gangs continued—in spite of protestations by Georgians to the contrary—until the mid-1960s. While in Tucson during the spring of 1995, I heard that chain gangs were returning to Arizona as part of Governor Fife Symington's "get tough on crime" philosophy.[1] I was intrigued by the

---

1. "Chain Gangs to Begin in Arizona," *ADC News Release,* Arizona Department of Corrections, May 12, 1995.

transport of a past idea to the contemporary Southwest: how images of denigration, the chain and rock busting popularized in film and fiction, could construct a new phantasm of criminality. What Orlando Patterson has called the "full mechanics" of "appropriation" is accomplished by controlling the "appropriate symbolic instruments . . . by exploiting already existing symbols" or by creating "new ones."[2] The use of chain is the exploitation of a powerful symbol. Once attached to inmates, it claims them as characters in a drama of denigration and abuse: a memorial to slavery and the convict lease system.[3]

Nowhere is the slick packaging of spectacles of punishment as apparent as in Sheriff Joe Arpaio's Maricopa County Jail chain gangs. Arpaio calls the inmates in his jails his "extras," part of his "film crew," for unlike the chain programs in the state prison system, Arpaio's local reforms—tent cities, posses, "last chance" chain gangs—have been aired on *Hard Copy, Sixty Minutes, Donahue, 20/20*, and French, English, German, and Australian TV, and discussed in a wide range of newspapers and magazines.[4] Unlike inmates in prisons, those in the county jails either have not been sentenced and await trial or they have been sentenced for a year or less. Arpaio's presentation of crime and punish-

---

2. Orlando Patterson, *Slavery and Social Death: A Comparative Study* (Cambridge: Harvard University Press, 1982), 37.

3. The unequal incarceration and execution of African Americans takes us beyond the symbolic, and the figures are chilling: Of the over one million inmates held in prisons in the United States, six hundred thousand are African Americans. African Americans are six times more likely than white Americans to be incarcerated (a rate of 1,947 per 100,000 African American citizens compared to a rate of 306 per 100,000 for white citizens). They comprise 40 percent of those executed. In Arizona, African Americans are overrepresented in the prison population (17.3 percent) compared to the state's general population (2.9 percent), as are Hispanics (31.1 percent) compared to the general population (18.8 percent). See Randall Kennedy's discussion in *Race, Crime, and the Law* (New York: Pantheon Books, 1997), 128–35, of "the darkening of jail and prison populations during the past twenty years" and the increasing "terrors of incarceration."

4. Mark Fisk, "Modern Wild West Sheriff Packs Prisoners into Tents in the Scorching Desert," *National Enquirer*, October 25, 1994, 1; Marc Cooper, "Law of the Future: Meet the Phoenix Posse," *Village Voice*, January 18–24, 1995, 30; Richard Grant, "The Mean Machine: Meet America's Toughest Cop—and Don't the Voters Love Him," *Sidney Morning Herald*, June 10, 1995, 8–9; Seth Mydans, "Taking No Prisoners, in Manner of Speaking, *New York Times*, March 4, 1995, 1; William Neuman, "America's Toughest Sheriff: Proud His Jail Is a Living Hell," *New York Post*, May 30, 1995, 8–9; Bob Ford, "America's Most Wanted: A Guy Who'll Get Tough with Lowlifes," *Philadelphia Inquirer Magazine*, June 18, 1995, 18–27; Carol J. Castaneda, "Arizona Sheriff Walking Tall, but Some Don't Like His Style," *USA Today*, May 26–29, 1995, 7; Jonathan Freedland, "Pride and Prejudice of Sheriff Joe, the Meanest, Cheapest, Harshest Jailer in America," *Guardian*, May 23, 1995.

ment draws on images deep in the psyche of the American Dream: a fantasy so at risk that the transport of post-Emancipation criminal codes and convict labor from the New South to the contemporary Southwest has made Arpaio the most popular politician in the state.

On September 19, 1996, fifteen women—ten of them African American—wearing bright orange jumpsuits and chained together picked up trash along a Phoenix street. Arpaio calls himself an "equal opportunity incarcerator" and boasts that women in his jails can take the hundred-degree heat as well as men.[5] The solicitude for gender that cost Alabama corrections commissioner Ron Jones his job—when he envisioned putting women inmates to work in leg-irons—bites the dust in Arizona. Chained together at the feet by one-quarter-inch proof coil, one of these women, who called herself "Princess," said she had put on makeup for the event, glad to "do publicity for Joe." Another woman in her early twenties had been arrested for prostitution—on the street she now walked in chains—by Arpaio's posse in their crusade "Operation Adopt a Whore," more popularly known as the "Pussy Patrol." Turning away from the cameras, she asked me if I would like to change places with her. "This is bullshit," she said, "nothing but a publicity stunt. The chains, makeup, and video cameras get all the attention, not the showers with worms, the stun guns, hog-tying, and rotten food." The show matters less for what it accomplishes in terms of correction, than for how it works as performance. Arpaio has recently outfitted his chain crews in white pants and trousers with horizontal black stripes. They are accompanied by dogs.

It is more difficult, and indeed critical, to know how to speak about the less sensational chain crews that have become part of corrections and deterrence at the Arizona State Prison. Arpaio knows his antics make no sense, giving his hot pink inmate undershorts—signed by "Sheriff Joe" on sale at Wal-Mart—and his green bologna sandwiches a zany theatricality. But the director of corrections, wardens, and officers in the prison system try to make sense of their thematization of chain. According to some officers, servility thus institutionalized preserves order in the prison. To my mind, obedience thus assured marks the most concerted effort since the end of the first Reconstruction to create a class of citizens subordinate to and separate from those outside the prison walls.

---

5. Eun-Kyung Kim, "Maricopa County Sheriff Plans 1st Female Chain Gang," *Arizona Daily Star*, August 26, 1996, 1.

What one warden called "the public display of chain" is the new representational event: not only stigmatizing those whose "nature" demands this "behavior" or "attitude" adjustment—what one officer called "involuntary compliance"—but creating for the public, and more seriously for the keepers and the kept, a visualization of domination and duress. Hard labor has always been a part of prison programs. According to an Arizona statute passed in 1983, inmates must work forty hours a week.[6] Depending on custody level and classification, the kind of work and the amount of hourly pay varies. The chain crews, however, are a different kind of labor. Those on chain do not produce goods—for example, clothing, licenses, bedding, furniture, or crops— nor do they participate in prison construction, maintenance, or renovation.

A group of about twenty male inmates stand shackled. They carry hoes, sickles, and rakes. Eight correctional officers survey the scene. In what begins to seem like a choreographed movement through dust, brush, and stones, I hear an officer shout, "Hard labor, get into it." Though they are apparently clearing brush and debris from the shoulder of the road between the interstate and the prison, nothing that they pick up or pile up makes any difference. The ground, as far as the eye can see, is nothing but dirt and gravel. They are ordered to clear one section of rocks, weeds, and waste, and then move on. After two hours, there is still no difference in the landscape, no matter how far they have walked, no matter how diligently they work.

Nowhere is the violence of futile work so well demonstrated as in the internal hard-labor program set up for "the worst of the worst." Inside the razor-wired exterior fence of the Complex Detention Unit at the Arizona State Prison at Tucson, eighteen prisoners are breaking rock with sledgehammers. Two are standing, chained to a rail as a disciplinary corrective for refusing to work. Given hot water to drink in 110-degree heat, a few prisoners shout, "Agua caliente." When I return two months later, men are still working. Instead of the letters "CDU" made out of small rocks on the ground, now the words are spelled out

---

6. Article 3, "Labor by Prisoners," of the *Arizona Revised Statutes*, Title 31, reads: "The director has the authority to require that each able-bodied prisoner under commitment to the state department of corrections engage in hard labor for not less than forty hours per week, except that not more than twenty hours per week of participation in an educational, training or treatment program may be substituted for an equivalent number of hours of hard labor as prescribed by the director of the state department of corrections."

in even smaller, broken rocks: "Complex Detention Unit." Some officers joke about the senseless exercise: "How many did they do today? Are they just busting on the same rock?" As one officer explained:

> They do a rock a week. Big rock to little rocks. And where do these rocks come from? We have literally to go to Fort Grant, load up a semi, and drag rocks here. You don't see any rocks in the desert, do you? They were to be used for rip-rapping the washes, for erosion control. But Pima County says they don't want them. These rocks are too little to do any good. We don't know what to do with these little rocks. What are we going to do with these rocks, now that we've got a whole lot of them?[7]

On December 7, 1995, the Death Row Chain Gang began. Arizona is the only state that *requires* condemned inmates to work. They till the nineteen-acre vegetable field inside the yard of the Arizona State Prison Complex at Florence. When fights break out with garden hoes, the officers fire beanbag-like projectiles, BB-sized rubber pellets, or larger rubber pellets called "three-ball stingers" that do not break the skin or spray like the birdshot that officers formerly used. Meg Savage, the new warden of Florence and the first woman warden in the state, confided: "It's very heartwarming looking out in that garden. I drive around. The men are happy to be out there. We've got tomatoes."[8]

There are two kinds of chain crews—officially called "inmate hard labor programs"—operating in the prisons of Arizona: an exterior program along state highways and interstates (doing roadside cleanup) for inmates who have "demonstrated behavior and attitude problems" and an interior program, breaking rock or cutting railroad ties, for those whose crimes make them a danger to public safety. Both groups work four days a week, eight hours a day, and are paid ten cents an hour. They wear leg restraints with chains attached to both ankles, but they are not chained together.[9] Inmates are transported to and from the work site in handcuffs, upper restraints, and belly chains.

---

7. Interview with officer (name withheld), Arizona State Prison Complex, Tucson, August 10, 1995.

8. Interview with Meg Savage, warden, Arizona State Prison Complex, Florence, April 5, 1996.

9. "Management Order #32, Inmate Hard Labor Program," memorandum from Samuel A. Lewis, director, Arizona Department of Corrections, to wardens, deputy wardens, unit administrators, May 11, 1995, 1–4.

Explanations of the chain initiative by the Department of Corrections give a rationale for chain that depends on a rhetorical appeal to the rehabilitative properties of labor: earning self-discipline through "meaningful work" instills "an improved work ethic" in inmates.[10] But the official narrative bears no resemblance to the drudgery of nonproductive labor, nor does it capture the smug reasonableness of prison administrators. For Charles Ryan, the former warden of the Florence/Eyman Arizona State Prison Complex (and now deputy director of the Department of Corrections in Phoenix), the "new science of chain" that "contains" "troublemakers" should not be confused with "romantic" images of chain gangs as "cruel, vicious, mean, and whatever." Instead, according to him, the approach is pragmatic:

> I can tell you unequivocally that we have just about mastered chain gang technology. I mean I think we've covered just about every angle to insure that we are humane and that we are not doing this to be abusive to prisoners. We're saying "Prisoner, it's a hard labor program." The use of chain and the decision to shackle them individually means that first and foremost in our minds is officer safety and efficiency; secondly, if you really take a look at the chain and see what the chain and those leather restraints are about—because we had staff walk around in them for a couple of days, and we had our doctors wear them to ensure their comfort. "Well, whadya think, doc?" "Well, it's just a snug leather binding." It does not cut into the skin and it does not cause discomfort on the ankle. . . . I mean look at it, if you've ever felt it, it's relatively pliable. It's not bad, it doesn't hurt you. Just put it on your ankle. Wrap it around your pants leg, because that's the way it is, and all you do is snug it up, as tight as you can, and then you run the chain in the lock. Now you could walk around like that all day log. You can walk, but you can't run. Now all this is just a security restraint.[11]

Emphasizing the benevolence of painless restraint, Ryan characterizes the "new penological objective" as "necessary" and "reason-

10. Telephone interview with Michael A. Arra, public information officer, Arizona Department of Corrections, May 26, 1995.

11. Interview with Charles Ryan, senior warden, Arizona State Prison Complex, Florence/Eyman, August 25, 1995.

able." The implements of control consist of padded, leather shackles
with the imprint "Humane Restraint," two-foot-long lightweight steel
chains, and a red, plastic padlock. Wanting to know more about the
philosophy behind this regulatory indulgence, I called Humane
Restraint Co., Inc. in Waunakee, Wisconsin. Since the company began
in 1876, when it was called Lynch Manufacturing Company, their
designs have been implemented in order to carry out Lynch's "idea of
humane restraint, and his goal of providing comfortable security."[12]

For the Department of Corrections, the simple desire to get lazy
troublemakers to work necessitates the amiable bondage of chain. Ryan
emphasizes the relative comfort of fetters, the lack of physical brutality
in this kind of behavior modification. How does the brute dispossession summoned by the use of chain get supplanted by kindly, if necessary, coercion? The contempt for criminals as unworthy of rehabilitation, but deserving only of incapacitation, pervades the reasoning of
Terry Stewart, the current director of the Arizona Department of Corrections. Even in films made about inmate work programs, chain
gangs, and Arizona Correctional Industries, he refuses to use talking
inmates, but presents instead what he calls "mythical inmates," photographic stills of prisoners. Such muteness is necessary, for "What can
inmates say? They're liars, they're thieves, they're cheats. Who would
believe an inmate, anyway?"[13]

Director Stewart stresses the "humanity" of the program: the
"humane setting" replete with water, bagged lunches, porta-potty,
straw hats, sunscreen, and a "reasonable" wage of ten cents. While
admitting that busting rock and cutting railroad ties are "menial tasks,"
he rationalizes: "Those are the people who won't do productive work
by doing public works, something that will benefit the community, so
busting rocks is fine with me."[14] Stewart's simulation of chain causality
can be succinctly paraphrased. Because you are in prison, you are a
criminal, and because you are a criminal, you are lazy, and because you
are lazy, you must work, but because of your personality, you are a
threat to security, and because your are a threat, you must be restrained
in chains. Or, as Warden Ryan had put it, somewhat more succinctly:
"Murderer, you're illiterate, you're a dummy, you have opted to be a

---

12. *Humane Restraint*, catalog, faxed, September 1, 1995, 2.

13. Interview with Terry Stewart, director, Arizona Department of Corrections,
Phoenix, July 10, 1996.

14. Ibid.

criminal because it was easy for you, and now we're gonna' try and instill in you an education and a work program to give you other choices."[15]

What counts is the indignity of submission. For there is no significance to chain other than its ability to stigmatize. And not surprisingly, it is this symbolic power of chain that Stewart refuses to recognize. When I suggested that using chain had changed the former Arizona gun gangs from work crews to dehumanizing display, thus recalling the southern legacy of slavery and convict leasing, he countered:

> That is a very superficial level of analysis. And so thinking people ought to say, "Well, of course, that's a symbol, and it has its racial overtones and all that, but let's look at it in reality, and the fact is that this department and every other department in the United States has gun gangs who work on public highways or on public works projects. No one contends that they are degrading. What we're saying is that we can now get work out of people we previously didn't get work out of. We have chain because there are some who by virtue of their crime or because of their refusal to work must be made to work. It serves a legitimate penological interest, both in terms of punishment and in terms of complying with the law: every able-bodied inmate must work forty hours a week.[16]

Symbolic power is, according to Stewart, nothing compared to the pragmatic use of chain. He laments that nothing but an emotive response might be expected of the general public, but adds, as he smiles: "I would expect anyone who wants to be a sincere critic to rationally evaluate what's happening and to get past the symbolism."[17]

Yet the Department of Corrections relies on this symbolism. *Doin' Time on the Arizona Gun Gang*, the department chain gang video (produced by the Arizona Department of Corrections as a teaching device in prisons outside Arizona), uses images of Paul Muni in the 1932 film *I Am a Fugitive from a Chain Gang* as if documentary footage, though set to an upbeat country western tempo. Set against the gas guns, shotguns, AR-15s, rock busting, weeding, shackles, upper restraints, and

15. Ryan, interview.
16. Stewart, interview.
17. Ibid.

belly chains in the desert, the film footage seems like fantasy. Nothing in the muted pastness of Muni's pain quite prepares the viewer for the shock of mimicry in the video: the dismembering of the black body. In one of the first scenes, two black hands come out through the open tray slots of the cell. Nothing else can be seen, only two white hands applying the "upper restraints"—wrist chains and cuffs—to outstretched black hands. At the end of the video, the black hands are offered to the viewers again, this time at the end of the day, when they are again shackled in preparation for transport back to the cell.

Confinement

> . . . . before it was the Special Management Unit it was the adminis-
> trative unit at CB6. They changed the name and they changed the
> location, but the game is the same, as it were. I mean what they're
> doing is the same thing.
>
> Alice Bendheim, lawyer for the plaintiffs,
> *Casey v. Lewis*, Phoenix, May 25, 1995

The United States penitentiary on Alcatraz Island, "The Rock," is now part of the Golden Gate National Recreation Area. In 1963, after twenty-nine years, the federal government closed Alcatraz, the most infamous of maximum-security facilities, thus ending, as the guide on an unseasonably warm Sunday in November announced, "a grim era in America's penal history." As I walked along "Agave Walk," struck by the odor of sage, the sight of yucca, ferns, ivy, and flowers that I had never seen before, I heard a father talking with his daughter: "What were *your* crimes? You killed *your father?*" The joke, funny because inconceivable, said much about how completely the harshness of Alcatraz and solitary confinement, also known as "the hole" (actually, cells 9–14 in D Block) had become entertainment. The "Self-Guiding Information" brochure, called "Discover Alcatraz," welcomes visitors with the promise of a theme park: "Alcatraz has something to give you— gifts of place, of the past, and of the American experience."[18]

The myth of Alcatraz makes what has never disappeared from the American prison a relic of days gone by. The United States penitentiary at Marion, Illinois (where the term "control unit" was coined), opened the year Alcatraz closed. I bought a copy of the revised 1956 "Institu-

---

18. Eileen Campbell, Michael Rigsby, and Tacy Dunham, *Discover Alcatraz: A Tour of the Rock* (Golden Gate National Parks Association, 1996).

tion Rules and Regulations" for inmates at Alcatraz. I read rule 6, "*Disciplinary Action* may result in loss of some or all of your privileges and/or confinement in the Treatment Unit." I read rule 7, "*Treatment Unit* is the segregation section of the Institution where privileges may be restricted to a minimum." I read about the daily routine, the work details, yard recreation, and dining-room rules. I read about the objects allowed in the cell, the property items and supplies that inmates could retain, medical attention, auditorium rules, library rules, and movies.[19] Considering the utter deprivation of the new, super, maxi-maximum security prisons—where the isolation once limited to the "disciplinary cell," "solitary," or "dry cell" has been extended to encompass an entire prison complex—the mythification of atrocity in the ruins of Alcatraz ensures the continuation of even harsher practices.

The history of solitary confinement began in 1823 at the Eastern State Penitentiary in Philadelphia, also known as "Cherry Hill." In what became known as the "separate system" (as opposed to the congregate system of penitentiary organization at Auburn State Prison and Sing Sing in New York), prisoners were confined to individual cells for the entire period of their incarceration. Silence, labor, and discipline were understood to be the basis of reformation. In *American Notes for General Circulation,* Dickens condemned the separate system of prison discipline as "this slow and daily tampering with the mysteries of the brain . . . immeasurably worse than any torture of the body."[20] When Cherry Hill closed in the 1970s, new control units for violent offenders continued to be built or added to existing high-security prisons, often without disclosure to the public.

What used to be called "solitary confinement," which had legal limits of duration, has now become the penal philosophy behind entire prison facilities, built to detain "incorrigibles" for indefinite periods of time.[21] Under the sign of professionalism and state-of-the-art technology, idleness, deterrence, and deprivation constitute the "treatment" in

---

19. *Institution Rules and Regulations,* United States Penitentiary, Alcatraz, California, Paul J. Madigan, warden, revised 1956 (Copyright Golden Gate National Parks Association, 1983).

20. Charles Dickens, *American Notes,* 1842, 1:238–39.

21. In *Hutto v. Finney* 437 U.S. 678 (1978), the Supreme Court upheld a lower court's order limiting the length of stay in the punitive segregation unit of the Arkansas prison system to thirty days. But there is no agreed-on time limit beyond which confinement in isolation can be judged cruel and unusual. In other cases, such as *Adams v. Carlson,* 488 F.2d 619 (7th Cir. 1973) and *Sostre v McGinnis,* 334 F.2d 906 (2d Cir. 1964) indefinite confinement was sustained.

these control units (also called administrative-segregation units, isolation units, special-housing units, or special-treatment units). Though never a place for tourists—nor named for condemnation in the numerous recent publications trying to put an end to mass incarceration—Special Management Unit I in the Eyman Complex in Florence, Arizona, was the model for Pelican Bay State Prison in California, the best known of these supersecurity prisons.[22] Opened in October 1987, SMU (a 768-bed structure that now houses 960 inmates), the highest maximum security unit in Arizona, was considered the model of "efficiency and security."[23]

SMU I is a cement building of unremitting monotony. Skylights in the hall give indirect access to natural light. Each windowless cell is eighty square feet and is equipped only with a built-in bunk and a toilet sink unit. The doors of the cells are made of heavy gauge perforated metal. The cement walls and ceilings in the halls are unpainted. Human contact is reserved for what is known as "cell extraction." When an inmate refuses a transfer to another cell or fails to return his food tray, four or five guards in riot gear immobilize him. The procedure officially sanctions unnecessary and excessive force, containing brutality

---

22. Pelican Bay State Prison, which includes the Security Housing Unit, commonly referred to as the "SHU," opened in 1989, two years after SMU I. And while the recently completed Florence Control Unit ("the Administrative Maximum Facility" or Ad Max) in Florence, Colorado, also called the "Alcatraz of the Rockies" or "the harshest hole ever constructed," is always mentioned, both SMU I and SMU II, which opened in June 1996, are ignored. The striking absence of reference to the control units in Florence, Arizona, is especially surprising in the long list in "From Alcatraz to Marion to Florence—Control Unit Prisons in the United States," published on the internet by CEML (Committee to End the Marion Lockdown), <http://www-unix.oit.umass.edu/~kastor/ceml.html> (November 1995).

In *Madrid v. Gomez*, 889 F.Supp. 1146 (N.D.Cal. 1995), the court ordered injunctive relief, concluding that prison officials had demonstrated deliberate indifference to medical, dental, and mental health care needs. Of specific import to the much-publicized Pelican Bay case was the use of lockdown as a means of dealing with seriously mentally ill inmates. The ignoring of the Arizona SMU units in otherwise exhaustive accounts of control has, I believe, much to do with the decision of the Department of Corrections never to allow news media access to their prisons. Cautious about what kind of information is fit for public scrutiny, the department allows interviews with no one but Michael Arra, the department spokesperson. (I seem to have been the exception.) James McFadden, former warden of SMU I and now warden of SMU II, explained during our first interview, June 7, 1996, "I would never allow *60 Minutes* into my unit. They called us before they called Pelican Bay, and we said 'no.' They're a trash company. They're not interested in doing a story that is fair. There were problems in Pelican Bay. They had done things. I can't comment on them. But I read the lawsuit."

23. Interview with Anthony W. Zelenak, lead project manager, Facility Activation Bureau, Arizona Department of Corrections, Phoenix, August 14, 1996.

in the redesignation of tasers and gas guns as "nonlethal weapons."[24] Inmates are moved from their cells with restraints that include at a minimum handcuffs or belly chains (chains fastened at the back with cuffs for the hands). A small exercise pen with cement floors and walls twenty feet high, virtually another cell, provides the only access to fresh air.

Special Management Unit I has been surpassed by Special Management Unit II (a 768-bed structure); completed in 1996, it cost taxpayers 40 million dollars. It is one of the most advanced maximum-security prison designs in the nation. The two-page leaflet of introduction to SMU II lists "Project Data," as if to emphasize exhaustive security and massive restriction. The mechanical details and the prodigious numbers create the effect of the incommensurate. Disorientation ensures our recognition of the enormity, even grandeur of this project of impregnable incarceration, a product of earth, concrete, masonry, and steel:

> 390,690 cubic feet of concrete; 2,295,000 cubic feet of earth moved; 22,000,000 pounds of gravel; 11,000,000 pounds of asphalt; 2,363,138 pounds of reinforcing steel used in foundation and walls; 1,408,000 pounds of security steel used in cell door bars security systems; 254,000 masonry blocks placed on site; 1,100 security keys; 183,000 lineal feet of security caulking "no-pick" placed throughout the facility.

Situated on forty acres of desert, SMU II is surrounded by two rings of twenty-foot high fence topped with razor wire. As in SMU I, there is no paint on the poured-concrete walls. Nothing can be put on the walls. There is nothing in the cells that can be moved or removed. The cells are eight feet by ten feet. The cell doors are covered with thick steel plates pierced with small ventilation holes, 3/8 inches in diameter, punched very close, so that it looks, as Anthony Zelenak, the Department of Corrections architect, put it, "like irregular-shaped swiss cheese."[25] The steel mirror, sink, and toilet are fastened with adhesives

---

24. See William F. Schulz, "Cruel and Unusual Punishment," *New York Review of Books*, April 24, 1997, 51–55, for the use of electronic shock devices in jails and prisons in the United States, as well as their export for torture in countries including Egypt, Mexico, Russia, Saudi Arabia, and China.

25. Zelenak, interview.

that cannot be chipped. The water supply (to toilet and sink) can be shut off from a nearby control booth.

Deputy Warden James McFadden (former warden of SMU I), who supervised the design, construction, and opening of SMU II and, as warden, now manages an operating budget of $4.5 million, elaborated for me the import of water control:

> The water control device that we came up with allows us to electronically control every water device in SMU II. Your hot water in your sink, your cold water in your sink, your toilet, all electronically monitored. And they can be set as a group or individually. I can individually see each cell. I can individually set each device in each cell. Hot will run for one second; cold will run for fourteen seconds. Fifteen seconds of water. The inmate must then wait five minutes before using water again, or it will be turned off for an hour. $800,000 is the cost of the water control system. They were killing us with flooding.[26]

Not only is the inmate isolated in his cell, where he spends twenty-three hours a day, but each cell is further isolated in a separate, steel-door-enclosed enclave of five or six similar cells. The cell hallways radiate from a central pod, where a guard can always see each door.[27] An officer manages each pod of sixty cells from a sealed control booth. (There are six pods in each cluster; ten inmates in each pod—five on top, five on bottom; sixty inmates in each cluster.) From the booth, officers can direct inmates to the shower or exercise pen. Officers and prisoners can talk via intercom, giving new meaning to the popular trinity of detention, incapacitation, and control.

---

26. McFadden, interview. The most impressive prison administrator I've met, McFadden will be leaving SMU II to become complex warden at the Arizona State Prison Lewis Complex, located thirteen miles south of Buckeye on State Route 85. When completed, the Lewis Complex—named for Samuel Lewis, former director of the Department of Corrections—will be the state's largest prison complex, on 337 acres with 4,150 beds.

27. The blueprint for SMU I and II, with blocks of separate cells (or wings) that radiate from the central monitoring station, from which cells and corridors can be observed, looks like the ground plan for the nineteenth-century prison, laid out for security, ease of control, and, as far as possible, the total separation of one prisoner from the next. The layout owes much to the experiments of Jeremy Bentham's Panopticon design, where the radial plan made possible (at least hypothetically) total surveillance. Despite similarities of geometry, it could be argued that in form and use the SMU units are closer to a series of connected, polygonal panopticons than to the single hub and straight ranges of cells of a true radial plan.

The cell doors have traps through which food trays can be passed, when, as McFadden put it, "they feed." Second-floor hallways have steel-mesh floors so that the hallway below is visible. Above, the skylights intensify the spectacle of light and immaculateness. The black doors of the cells are reflected in the ultra-shined floors, commented on by Warden McFadden: "Looking good. From now on I'll have to wear sun glasses." McFadden says the computer system is "absolutely state-of-the art, probably more advanced than any in the country." As McFadden explained:

> Because of "condition of confinement" cases, we must keep track of everything an inmate does. By computer we electronically log in "the condition of confinement." There are two recording capabilities. If cell number 60 leaves his cell for recreation, shower, or law library, the officer pushes 60 for computer log-in. Then the icon comes up: "open/stop/close." Another officer watches as the inmate goes to recreation or exercise. The second kind of capability has to do with the log-in screen that automatically logs in when each inmate goes for shower or exercise.[28]

When an officer uses the touch-screen monitor to let an inmate out of his cell to go to the bare exercise pen (where they can spend about forty-five minutes, if they bother to go) or shower (usually under ten minutes), he logs these activities into the computer. An icon specifies the location of the prisoner. Like Bentham's panopticon, but making reality out of the fiction of constant observation, this tracking system allows officers at each station to know where every inmate is at any moment, but further, as McFadden "we explained," We have a history of where he was for his entire stay here."[29]

The room that controls all of SMU II is called "Count and Movement." On one wall is a list of types of inmates, matched with color codes. Making taxonomies for those incarcerated assumes the rightness of labels, the categorical certainty of description. SMU II, designed to "house the state's most serious criminal offenders" (described in its "Mission Statement" as "extreme management cases, prison gang members, and violence oriented maximum custody inmates") is precisely delineated inside the prison. The seven categories are High Risk,

---

28. McFadden, interview.
29. Interview with James P. McFadden, October 21, 1996.

Death Row, Protective Segregation, STG (Security Threat Group) Member, Juvenile, Special Needs Area (Mental Health), and the Violence Control Unit (called "Special Cautionary Unit" in SMU I). This last unit includes another container for holding those who remain dangerous once confined to SMU. (Then there is a special area in the VCU, a more severely restrained receptacle, called the "Warden's Hold," where no inmate can be moved outside—even for an emergency, even if he has a heart attack—without the warden's okay. As McFadden admitted, "I'd rather he die than harm someone else.")[30]

The architectural form is made possible by the law's model for the lawful prison. The tautology is telling. There is a legal grammar to the spatial structure. If you can establish what are "basic" or "fundamental" human needs, then you can build deprivation into construction methods. What is judged legitimate and reasonable turns what was punitive or disciplinary action into a necessary administrative regulation. Atrocity becomes ordinary. The more the law got involved in prisoners' rights, the more prison regulations carried the power of redefining these very rights.

And these regulations became essential to the logical end of classification—a classification that does away with gradations of classification: the special receptacle for the storage of many men. A building that takes confinement, trauma, and deprivation to its extreme is rationalized as a "general population" unit (the general population of those judged to be the worst inmates who repeatedly offend), necessary for security, order, and discipline. The Special Management units depend on the typology of a particular kind of prisoner, who has attained the status of "the worst of the worst." Because of that status and the collective anonymity associated with it, an ever more inclusive population can be housed in SMU.

Classification

I have been describing certain rituals of memory. Punishment, and the legal assurance that it be *reasonably* sustained, depends on the selective forfeiture of remembrance. How did what used to be known, in the days of the Eastern Penitentiary, as the "separate system," and then "individual treatment," which was not a form of punishment, become

---

30. McFadden, interview, October 21, 1996.

confounded with "solitary confinement," which was? Further, how did punitive or disciplinary segregation, once renamed as "administrative segregation," give a changed label the power to continue a practice?[31] The courts demanded due-process procedures for disciplinary action, so the prisons segregated inmates just as harshly as before, with just as many loss of privileges and threat of psychological decompensation, but called it by another name.[32] Once called "administrative," the transfer carried with it justification, for it served a legitimate need of the prison, or more incredibly, it suggested the near mystical ability of prison officials to predict ("informed predictions" in *Meachum v. Fano*)[33] what would best serve institutional security or (in *Hewitt*) to possess a "general knowledge of prison conditions and tensions, which are singularly unsuited for 'proof' in any highly structured manner."[34]

In *Wolff v. McDonnell*,[35] the court required that prisoners, when accused of disciplinary misconduct and faced with the loss of good-time credits or isolation, receive a detailed written notice of charges, a hearing, an opportunity to present witnesses, or a written explanation of reasons for disciplinary action. But the amount of process required in cases of administrative, as opposed to disciplinary segregation, is sub-

---

31. Case law tends to require that conditions in protective custody and administrative segregation be demonstrably different from those in the disciplinary unit and/or that they be similar to those provided the general population. See American Correctional Association, *Model Correctional Rules and Regulations* (College Park, Md.: ACA Correctional Law Project, 1979). But, most noticeably in the Rehnquist court, in cases like *Hewitt v. Helms*, 459 U.S. 460 (1983) and *Sandin v. Connor*, 515 U.S. 472 (1995), no importance is attached to the difference between disciplinary and administrative transfers. It makes no difference whether the transfer resulted from "classification" or from "discipline," thus eliding the distinction between a normal procedure of prison order, applicable to all prisoners, and a special situation, affecting only prisoners who have misbehaved. Rehnquist distinguishes between disciplinary and administrative segregation in *Hewitt*, 464 n. 1, only to "assume for purposes of this case that the conditions in the two types of confinement are substantially identical." In *Sandin*, 486, he argues that "disciplinary segregation, with insignificant exceptions, mirrored those conditions imposed upon inmates in administrative segregation and protective custody."

32. Rules claim that "special management" is not disciplinary and inmates in close management are not being "punished." Bill Bradley, classifications specialist at the Arizona Department of Corrections called SMU I and SMU II "general-population units." But general population means inmates who are not placed under any "extraordinary restrictions and not in lockdown" (A Human Rights Watch Report, *Prison Conditions in the United States* [1991], 44). Through these terminological qualifications, the conditions of SMU become normative, and confinement open-ended.

33. 427 U.S. 215, 225 (1976).

34. *Hewitt*, 477 n. 9.

35. 418 U.S. 539, 559 (1974).

stantially less.[36] The amount of due process, then, depends on whether the prisoner's transfer, even to a special-management unit, is characterized as disciplinary or administrative. In "American Prison Law after 25 Years, 1962–1987," Jonathan Willens argues: "The deprivation of liberty requires process; less deprivation requires less process." I am suggesting that the depth of deprivation is determined by a mere name, not substance.[37]

With the new name, an old method continued, but without the detailed due-process proceedings required in *Wolff*. Then, with the turn to "status" or "nature" the prison authorities did away with even these distinctions, normalizing the Special Management Unit as a "general-population unit" that *resembles* mainline living. As Stewart, director of the Department of Corrections, explained, "The Special Management Unit requires conditions and services essentially equal to those available in the general population."[38] Harol "Hal" Whitley, deputy warden of SMU I, explained: "This isn't isolation in here. They still have TV, they have newspapers, magazines."[39]

But in giving inmates the boon of television privileges, some wardens get the chance to demonstrate even greater control. Inmates may have the privilege, but they are not entitled to use it. As Deputy Warden McFadden of SMU II explained to me:

> As long as they have their own TVs, they can watch TV in the hours we say it's OK. We actually captured the television station here in this facility. We have our own productions, so that when we don't want them to watch something, they can't watch it. We're looking at it from a programming aspect. It will probably become standard in corrections. We have modern technology. So we can

---

36. See *Barnett v. Centoni*, 31 F.3d 813, 815 (9th Cir. 1994) (quoting *Toussaint v. McCarthy*, 801 F.2d 1080, 1099 (9th Cir. 1986): "Due process, in the administrative context, merely requires that the prison officials present the inmate with 'some notice of the charges against him and an opportunity to present views to the prison official charged with deciding whether to transfer [the inmate] to administrative segregation.'"

37. Jonathan Willens, "American Prison Law after 25 Years, 1962–1987," *American University Law Review* 37 (1987): 131.

38. Stewart, interview.

39. Interview with Harol Whitley, deputy warden of SMU I, Arizona State Prison Complex, Florence, October 21, 1996. Captain Whitley was plaintiff in *Whitley v. Albers*, 475 U.S. 312 (1986). He used excessive force against an inmate during a riot at Oregon State Penitentiary, and the majority of judges found it to be justified.

do anything we want. And we buy canned programs; there's a program called "Cage Your Rage."[40] They have sixteen channels they can watch, actually seventeen now, because we have the SMU II channel. We can shut them off when we want, individually or in a group.[41]

Cruel? Unusual?[42] The more channels inmates are given, the more keenly felt the deprivation when they are taken away. Imagine inmates, locked up for twenty-three hours a day, looking forward to watching a program, only to discover the channels have been locked down. All they can get in their cage is "Cage Your Rage."

The techniques employed to dehumanize criminals are in part rhetorical, and these rhetorical strategies initiate new forms of containment, which are, to a large degree, determined by recent judicial decisions. If the prisoner must expect deprivation once in custody, there is no place for an ethical tradition that would accord the incarcerated individual the right to be treated with dignity.[43] Further, if a legal limit could be set to the amount of time an inmate could be kept in solitary confinement, then a structure could be invented that would put everyone in solitary. A rare and special disciplinary condition thus becomes a normal and general condition for those held under "close," "special," or "secure" management.[44]

If there is something about the Special Management units in Florence that makes me mute, I find a voice, a way of speaking about the

---

40. *Cage Your Rage: An Inmate's Guide to Anger Control Video Package* (1993, 75 minutes), is based on the best-selling workbook by Murray Cullen, published in 1992 by the American Correctional Association.

41. McFadden, interview, June 7, 1996.

42. See *Estelle v. Gamble*, 429 U.S. 97, 105 (1976): "After incarceration, only the 'unnecessary and wanton infliction of pain' constitutes cruel and unusual punishment forbidden by the Eight Amendment."

43. In *Meachum*, 233, Stevens argued in his dissent (citing his 1973 decision in *Miller v. Twomey*, 479 F.2d 701 [7th Cir. 1973]), "The deprivation of liberty following an adjudication of guilt is partial, not total. A residuum of constitutionally protected rights remain." For Stevens, "the right to be treated with dignity" should play some part in determining conditions of confinement.

44. The special-management units in Florence are the ultimate form of classification, with each prisoner assigned to his own category, but rationalized as "general population" of repeatedly offending worst-case inmates. See the description of special management in Richard A. McGee, George Warner, and Nora Harlow, *The Special Management Inmate*, in the series Issues and Practices in Criminal Justice, National Institute of Justice, U.S. Department of Justice (March 1985).

unspeakable, in the law. The law sets limits to permissible deprivation, and in its generalizing tactics, the law goes so far as to obviate the need for sanctions or "disciplinary" actions in order to impose the penalty of segregation. How, to adopt the language of *Sandin v. Connor*, do we define "the ordinary incidents of prison life?" What kind of rule can be used to ascertain whether a deprivation "imposes atypical and significant hardship on the inmate?" When is a sanction that is atypical and significant not also cruel and unusual? Faced with the necessities of institutional security, and the preservation of order and discipline, the U.S. Supreme Court has decided—in a series of decisions, especially during the past ten years—to limit or remove the constitutional rights of prisoners. How this has been done, how new labels have been invented for historic abominations, is what matters here.

In thinking about how the necessities of imprisonment legitimate irrational decisions, I am reminded of the logic of the Caribbean black codes: the law of containment necessary to control uncontrollable masses of slaves. Bryan Edwards, writing about the British colonies in the West Indies, understood the unrelenting order the institution of slavery demanded:

> In countries where slavery is established, the leading principle on which the government is supported is fear: or a sense of that absolute coercive necessity which, leaving no choice of action, supersedes all questions of right. It is vain to deny that such actually is, and necessarily must be, the case in all countries where slavery is allowed.[45]

The Rehnquist Court, when confronted with the "danger" or "perils" of the prison, depends on the "subjective" expertise of prison administrators or "deference" to their special knowledge. In so doing, the historic substance of imprisonment, the purpose, principles, or rationale of which can be found in varying slave laws, gets a new garb and answers to new names. Because of their nature, criminals, like slaves, must realize that hardship, even if intolerable, is within the bounds of incarceration.

---

45. Bryan Edwards, *The History of the British Colonies in the West Indies*, quoted in Goveia, *The West Indian Slave Laws* (Washington, D.C.: Howard University Press, 1980), 35.

A conception of prisoners' rights—the right to some minimal dignity—loses out to formalism, to a legal history driven by its own precedents. It is not so much an appeal to legal tradition, as to an assumption about what defines that entity called "prisoner"—much like what it means to be a slave—that makes inevitable the turning of the prisoner into "a creature of the State," dispossessed of any claims to personhood except those that "specific laws or regulations" confer upon him, as Stevens's characterized it in his dissenting opinion in *Meachum*.[46]

The directives for creating a structure for the Special Management Unit, the least lawful lawful prison, were laid out in the law. The dangers of arbitrary action on the part of prison officials are recognized, but efforts to prevent inmates from being the subject of arbitrary action remain futile. Even when prisoners' rights are acknowledged, they have no means of enforcing their rights. This ability of the law to give with one hand what it takes away with the other, to tell double stories, gives near omniscience to prison officials, while making inmates nonpersons who must expect all kinds of deprivation. The winnowing away of the substance of incarceration (what actually happens to the body and soul of a person in custody) in favor of an increasingly vague, if more adamant pragmatics of forms, rules, and labels, allows increasingly abnormal circumstances to be normalized once in prison.

Although the prisoner's rights movement seemed first to succeed in limiting the prerogatives of penal bureaucrats, such judicial oversight and scrutiny actually provided the terms by which conditions of incarceration could, by miming the language of the law, assure that old abuses and arbitrary actions were masked by vague standards and apparent legitimacy. While apparently applying rational legal principles, the lawful prison capitulated to irrational power. In other words, the necessities of imprisonment legitimate irrational decisions. The new legal analysis ensures that discretion is expertise and deprivation is part of prison. As Rehnquist concluded in *Atiyeh v. Capps*, "nobody promised them a rose garden."[47]

I turn to the language of three cases—from the late seventies to, most recently, 1995—that concern the legality of prison conditions: where an inmate is placed and where he might end up. These cases demonstrate that the law tells its own history, or to be more precise,

---

46. *Meachum*, 230.
47. 449 U.S. 1312, 1316 (1981).

misconstrues a past narrative of rights and privileges, while apparently having no recollection of it. What is critical is who controls the issue at hand, who frames the necessary questions, and who does the defining. According to the *Meachum* opinion, written by Justice White, "confinement"—no matter where or why—"in any of the state's institutions" is considered "within the normal limits or range of custody, which the conviction has authorized the state to impose."[48] Even if harm comes to the prisoner in being transferred—and some transfers amount to a death sentence—transfer is part of imprisonment, and thus implicates no liberty interest nor any grievous loss. Harm is not subject to judicial review. What is startling about Justice White's reasoning is his recognition that, first, an inmate's "conduct" or "behavior" is often a factor in transfer. But then he moves from linking necessity of transfer to serving "the State's penological goals," in order to trigger a surprising turn away from certainty into official "discretion to transfer prisoners for any number of reasons." That "discretion" is loaded with arbitrary power: "Their discretion is not limited to instances of serious misconduct." There seems to be no limit to permissible deprivation. Even if a prisoner behaves and thus expects to stay where he is, that expectation "is too ephemeral and insubstantial to trigger procedural due process protections as long as prison officials have discretion to transfer him for whatever reason or for no reason at all."[49]

Stevens's dissent depends for its force on his condemnation of the Court's "rationale," which reconceives the meaning of "liberty" in order to make it inapplicable to the person in the penitentiary. The history that matters for Stevens is the amelioration of the harshness of the Thirteenth Amendment, a trend that culminates for him in *Morrissey v. Brewer*[50] as he emphasizes the "residuum of constitutionally protected liberty" possessed by an individual, even within prison walls. Appealing to "ethical tradition" and the substance of "liberty" and "custody" as being mutually adaptable, Stevens clinches his argument by pitting "prison regulations" against "protected liberty interests."[51] If what the state allows becomes the yardstick for liberty, thereby erasing claims to "dignity" and "worth," then, he concludes, an inmate "is really little more than the slave described in the 19th century cases."

---

48. *Meachum*, 225.
49. Ibid., 228.
50. 408 U.S. 471 (1972).
51. *Meachum*, 232.

When Rehnquist writes his opinion in *Hewitt*, he decides to answer Stevens's appeal to treatment of the prisoner as a person by introducing the prisoner as a special kind of property, deprived of any rights prison administrators think necessary in order to preserve order and maintain security. And if Stevens complains of the "narrow holding" in *Meachum*, Rehnquist trivializes constitutional claims by a methodology of "semantic due process," privileging mandatory predicates (a medley of "shall," "will," or "must") over guides to discretion (conditions of confinement and institutional practices).

For Rehnquist, "administrative segregation is the sort of confinement that inmates should reasonably anticipate receiving at some point in their incarceration."[52] Then Rehnquist, in a subtle maneuver, evades due-process concerns by removing the distinction between administrative custody and punitive isolation ("the two types of confinement are substantially identical"), except for one particular: "Unlike disciplinary confinement the stigma of wrongdoing or misconduct does not attach to administrative segregation."[53] Arguing that the inmate's "private interest is not one of great consequence," the Court then concludes: "He was merely transferred from one extremely restricted environment to an even more confined situation."[54] It is as if the tougher, the more restrictive the prison, the greater the discretion to move inmates into another, even more restrictive, locale. After all, everything is in a name: if you use a different name, you remove the stigma, and then you can treat an inmate who is not guilty of misconduct the same as an inmate who is. But the Court ends up granting the inmate a "liberty interest"— giving back what it has taken away—because, as Stevens puts it so beautifully in his dissent:

> Pennsylvania's written prison regulations display a magical combination of "substantive predicates" and "explicitly mandatory language." . . . [T]he Court seems to assume that after his conviction a prisoner has, in essence, no liberty save that created, in writing, by the State which imprisons him. Under this view a prisoner crosses into limbo when he enters into penal confinement.[55]

---

52. *Hewitt*, 468.
53. Ibid., 473.
54. Ibid.
55. Ibid., 482 (Stevens, J., dissenting).

In *Sandin v. Connor,* Rehnquist's language is stronger, and the stakes higher. He borrows Stevens's argument in *Hewitt* in order to do away with *Hewitt's* methodology, but for quite different ends. Turning against the language of "a particular regulation" and back to "the nature of the deprivation" (and apparently away from the state's regulations in favor of the inmate's condition), Rehnquist then deviates from the mechanical methodology he had instituted, in favor, it seems, of the "nature" of the interest, the concern with the prisoner's conditions of confinement, the substance of liberty that mattered so much to Stevens. But this is a parody of rights, mere rhetoric. For Rehnquist distinguishes between superficial form and weighty substance only to give more deference to prison officials than they had before. No matter that he appears to contradict his own words in *Hewitt,* for no sooner does he get to punishment of the incarcerated, repeating Stevens's repetition that "prisoners do not shed all constitutional rights at the prison gate," then he clarifies that liberty by further restricting it, in the words of the dissent: "It therefore imposes a minimum standard, namely that a deprivation falls within the Fourteenth Amendment's definition of 'liberty' only if it 'imposes atypical and significant hardship on the inmate in relation to the ordinary incidents of prison life.' "[56]

Deprivation and containment are the basis of the Court's holding. Although it appears that the Court aims to set limits to brutality, its curious logic makes a fiction of protection: allowing for an ominous leeway that was a salient feature of slave codes. In *Sandin,* for example, thirty days in Hawaii's "hole" is not a very grievous loss. Rehnquist, in turning on his own mandate in *Hewitt,* has given inmates a new bottom line in terms of conditions of confinement: "restraint," with the certainty that new hardships calling for due process will have to be ever more extreme to get the attention of the courts. Further, Rehnquist depends upon a qualification of punishment that makes possible the aggravation of a loss that has already occurred, without the inmate who is claiming a grievous loss gaining any chance of success, if the prison is just marginally within the nondemanding parameters of cruel and unusual punishment. Here, then, is the reasoning:

> This case, though concededly punitive, does not present a dramatic departure from the basic conditions of Conner's indetermi-

---

56. *Sandin,* 496 (Breyer, J., joined by Souter, J., dissenting).

nate sentence. . . . We hold that Conner's discipline in segregated confinement did not present the type of atypical, significant deprivation in which a state might conceivably create a liberty interest. The record shows that, at the time of Conner's punishment, disciplinary segregation, *with insignificant exceptions,* mirrored those conditions imposed upon inmates in administrative segregation and protective custody.[57]

What the dissenting opinion identifies as a dangerous "middle category" somewhere between the due process clause and a prison code ("The State may create a liberty interest" . . . when "atypical and significant hardship [would be borne by] the inmate in relation to the ordinary incidents of prison life") results in this compelling question: "What design lies beneath these key words?"[58] What the Court has done in matching "atypical and significant" with "ordinary" is to level the distinction, to make it impossible to prove when the due process clause should kick in: how atypical must something be in order to be extraordinary?

The Court's rationalization of custody and control legitimizes terms of imprisonment that reconstitute "cruel and unusual punishment." No longer called the "hole" or "solitary," but adapting the legal language of decorum and the vocabulary of decency, these places are renamed, engaging language in legality to the extent that the new prison plantations are recast as "state-of-the-art" facilities for the incapacitation of those now known as "strategic threat groups." If three years in solitary confinement appears as an unimaginable crime committed against Henry Young in *Murder in the First,* how do we begin to talk about the new, clean and well-lit control or security units, where inmates are locked down for days, months, or years?

Prison administrators in Arizona, especially the wardens at the Special Management units in Florence, are quite prepared to play with terminologies, as they create a maxi-maxi prison that obviates the need for due-process procedures involving penalty of segregation. In a lengthy interview in 1996, I asked Deputy Warden McFadden of SMU II about cases of inmates losing their minds because of lack of human contact. He avoided answering me by discussing programs for mental-

---

57. Ibid., 485–86; emphasis added.
58. Ibid., 490 (Ginsburg, J., joined by Stevens, J., dissenting).

health inmates. I tried to press him to talk about the other cases, those who are not predisposed, but whose mental state worsens because they are being locked down for an unspecified amount of time, undergoing "indeterminate incapacitation," to use the phrase favored by Director Stewart.

McFadden, aware of the complex ruling against Pelican Bay in *Madrid v. Gomez*,[59] again deftly deflected my question. He replied, "I guess I'll let the social scientists figure it out. If I have to treat seven hundred pretty tough so that twenty-two thousand can survive, then I'll do that to the seven hundred. And at some point in time I will be told that I can't do this anymore. This wave that we're riding right now of 'lock 'em up and throw away the key and they ain't got nothing coming' will change." He explained that because control units are becoming more popular, with each state developing its own, he is "absolutely" certain that the Supreme Court will be asked to clarify control, and he concluded:

> It will be interesting. You know, there are inmates in this facility that are so violent, we have to take *extraordinary* measures to protect other inmates and staff. I don't know if the courts someday will recognize these as extraordinary measures for extraordinary situations or as overstepping the bounds of decency.[60]

I suspect that, as the language of the majority in the Supreme Court continues to defer to the rules and regulations of state prison authorities, there will be no danger of a word like "decency" interfering with "discretion." Further, if *Sandin* introduced the test of a liberty interest as limited to undue restraint in relation to ordinary conditions, the Special Management units are built to fit the description of the ordinary: clean, safe, and well-lit, three meals, toilet and sink. The granting of bare necessities, or as one officer boasted, "the minimal constitutional rights," allows the transfer into what nevertheless remains solitary confinement.[61]

---

59. 889 F.Supp. 1146 (N.D.Cal. 1995).

60. McFadden, interview, October 21, 1996.

61. Note that in *Madrid*, though judging against the defendants—the California Department of Corrections and the administrators of "Pelican Bay"—the court still determined that the security housing unit—and conditions of "extreme social isolation and reduced environmental stimulation"—did not violate the Eighth Amendment in regard to *all* inmates, but only when imposed on certain inmates "at risk of developing an injury

As I have argued, classification is key. Its formality, no matter whether the intricate typology actually fits the person upon whom it is imposed, "stands," as William Bailey, the classifications specialist at the Department of Corrections in Phoenix, explained, "the test of the courts." Yet, this tallying allows officials to be unaccountable in the exercise of their power. A ruse of objectivity removes the opportunity of appeal, as Bailey put it:

> There are certain kinds of things that are not subject to appeal. There is no case law that requires us to address the issue of housing. Inmates cannot appeal where they are moved, unless they are placed in a facility that's higher than their custody level, but we can do that in a facility override. But normally, placements fit a particular table in the back of the manual. Every placement based on the relative institutional risk scores, the matrix, is not subject to appeal. Score changes that are based on the normal procedures built into the manual for disciplinary violations are not subject to appeal.[62]

Since 1986, when the Arizona Department of Corrections *Classification Operating Manual* was created, according to Bailey, there has not been one case of an inmate winning a case about transfer. "It's in complete accord with case law. Before the inmates could win, because the system could be called 'arbitrary and capricious.' The classification system is a response to objective criteria."[63] These criteria become the most fluid and, in the hands of some correctional officers, the most coercive means of control. There is a great deal of the haphazard in simulated order. Inmates get "ordered," "placed," "combined," or "separated." They change or get "contaminated" as they are moved, put in proximity to

---

to mental health of *sufficiently serious magnitude*" (1265). There is nothing *improper* about segregating inmates, and further, prison officials not only can impose conditions that are "restrictive and even harsh," but may "emphasize idleness, deterrents, and deprivation over rehabilitation." The Court has, in spite of its judgment against prison officials, sanctioned the new penology of fear and divestment so reminiscent of the old order demanded by the institution of slavery.

62. Interview with William Bailey, classifications specialist, Arizona Department of Corrections, Phoenix, August 14, 1996. The Offender Classification system is based on the Correctional Classification Profile (CCP). The two major scores are the public-risk score and the institutional-risk score: the first is based on the crime and the second on management possibilities within the prison.

63. Ibid.

what once, in the world outside, would have been judged their opposites.

Within the walls of the prison what some might judge to be the debris of a culture is perpetually "re-amalgamated." The residue of past methods of punishment is systematized in order to insure that powerful images of vagrants, social outcasts, and misfits can be transmitted to a receptive public. The generality of "the criminal type" is all that matters. What Ian Hacking calls "dynamic nominalism" produces the possibilities of action: "What is curious about human action is that by and large what I am deliberately doing depends on the possibilities of description. . . . [A]ll intentional acts are acts under description. Hence if new modes of description come into being, new possibilities for action come into being in consequence."[64] For those incarcerated, intangible terms like *nature, attitude,* or *personality* demand "behavior modification" or "attitude adjustment" and qualify the inmate for incapacitation in lockdown. Those having too many disciplinary tickets, no matter what kind—for talking back or bad attitude—might find themselves in one of the Special Management units with those termed "predators," best known for throwing feces, urine, or darts at officers, or for mutilating other inmates.

The institutional-risk score (ranging from 1 to 5) is based on behavior *after* entering in prison, and this is the score that matters. As inmates move up the chain of scores, always related to their disciplinary reports, they lose privileges, until they wind up in one of the two Special Management units that give new meaning to the word *privilege.* Yet for Bailey, *discipline* and *classification* must be kept distinct. "We're not involved in that disciplinary process at all. That's a completely separate, independent process. We respond only to documented behavior. He dismisses the obvious and logical connection between classification and disciplinary procedures: "Classification is nonpunitive in every single way. We only deal with the relative risk the inmate represents. We don't have any punitive measures anywhere in the classification system. In fact, there are no provisions in that manual that even allow us to lock an inmate up."[65]

---

64. Ian Hacking, "Making Up People," in *Reconstructing Individualism: Autonomy, Individuality, and the Self in Western Thought,* ed. Thomas C. Heller, Morton Sasna, and David E. Wellbery (Stanford, Calif.: Stanford University Press), 231.

65. Bailey, interview.

Yet an inmate gets into a specific unit because of his classification, and classification is behavior- and discipline-based: the type of crime, how you get along in prison, the number of disciplinary tickets you receive. In aiming to distinguish between disciplinary and administrative transfers (which are usually distinct in name only), prison officials have been able to claim that the proceedings were for "classification" not "discipline"; and that, therefore, they are not punitive (and do not fall under either the Eighth or the Fourteenth Amendment). An expert in using words in such a way that they change meaning in the flash of a hat, Bailey answers my query about administrative segregation: "The category really doesn't exist anymore, except as a broad, general term." As if paraphrasing Rehnquist in *Hewitt* ("The phrase 'administrative segregation' . . . appears to be something of a catchall"), he maneuvers his meaning by reappropriating legal language: "If you take administrative segregation to mean any time an inmate is segregated from the rest of the population, there are probably any number of conditions that apply."[66]

The force of terms, properly, shall we say, legally manipulated, to decide an inmate's fate becomes clearer as Bailey speaks. I cite him in full, since his vagueness says much about how SMU I and SMU II can become—first, rhetorically, and then, actually—general-population units: holes from which no inmate can claim deprivation or deserve due process.

> Technically from a . . . how should I put this . . . it's referring to administrative segregation as the ACA [American Correctional Association] would define it, as uh, when uh . . . Let's say that administrative segregation in our department had a very specific definition at one time. That went out about November of 1984 or 1985. Then it meant strictly that if the inmate did certain things, they would be put in isolation. That hasn't even existed for a long time. Since the advent of this classification system and our high-custody facilities that house level-5 inmates, we don't need that designation anymore. Inmates who were once in that category are now simply housed in SMU I or SMU II in the general population. There's no specific category now.[67]

---

66. Ibid.
67. Ibid.

Categorization erases the need for categories. If there was a problem in *Hewitt* in denying due process to inmates transferred into administrative segregation, prison administrators in Arizona, decided—within less than two years after the Court's decision in 1983—to build SMU I and SMU II.

No more disciplinary or administrative units are necessary, because any inmate who scores I-5, the top of the line for institutional risk, no longer receives individual punishment in a "detention unit." Those in detention units, for example, are awaiting a transfer that will take them out of general population, but Bailey reasons:

> SMU I and II are general-population units. They are simply those general-population units that house the highest-risk inmates. They're not detention units, they're not punishment units, contrary to what inmates would like you to believe. They are normal, ordinary, general-population units. The difference is that they're for the highest-risk inmates. When they have gotten to the highest risk score, that's the normal place they're sent. That's published, that's just where they're all put together. In a lot of respects, they're just regular places.[68]

This wrangling about names reduces what is most "human" about the prisoner, while making it impossible for the prisoner—cast as abnormal, violent, or threatening—to appeal to behavior or to claim any loss. How can there be anything atypical about what is so normal?

McFadden, who has been in court many times, as deputy warden of SMU I and then deputy warden of SMU II, knows that, as he put it, "It's semantics." He gives a history to the concept of the Special Management Unit that reveals how crucial Stevens's dissent in *Hewitt* became to judges, such as Judge Carl Muecke in the Arizona district court, who had become a thorn in the side of a state determined to ignore federal court rulings:

> Historically, we put inmates in what was termed "administrative segregation." And because it was then considered to be a special, lockup-type process—you lost privileges—every state in the union

---

68. Ibid.

had the courts on their backs. We had a special master over our administrative-segregation units. In a 1985 case called *Black v. Ricketts*, Judge Muecke gave us all kinds of rules and regulations. It got to the point that we weren't controlling our own destiny.[69]

McFadden then gives an example of an inmate who is a real danger, in lockdown in a detention unit. Classification usually occurs every six months. At that time, in McFadden's not-so-hypothetical hypothetical case, as he put it: "We'd say, 'You're a dangerous dude, you're staying.'" But then the courts stepped in, in this case Muecke, and decided that because the inmates' life was so restrictive, the officials had to demonstrate what he had done *in the last six months* that made him so dangerous.[70] So, as McFadden explained: "Well," we said, "he hasn't done anything in the last six months, but he killed two people nine months ago, and that's good enough for us."

McFadden admits that it was, in his words, "our own fault":

We had created some liberty interests by putting him in segregation, because he wouldn't earn any good time, no release credits. So we did away with administrative segregation, said there *is* no such thing. The Central Detention units (CDUs) are only temporary lockdown units, but if you're a big enough butthead, you go to SMU I or II, general population. Just really strict rules, but you still earn good time, so you have no liberty interest. But you ain't going anywhere. So it was our response to court issues, how to get around that problem of a guy who's a triple murderer in prison, but he hasn't done anything in the last year. So I can't keep him under this tight reign, unless I give him general privileges. So he

---

69. McFadden, interview, October 21, 1996. This formalizing of classification followed Judge Carl Muecke's order in the Stipulated Settlement Agreement, *Black v. Ricketts*, No. CIV 814-111-PHX-CAM (D.Ariz. 1985). The defendants—the Arizona Department of Corrections, the superintendent of the Arizona State Prison at Florence, and the warden of Cell Block 6, Florence—and the plaintiffs in this class action lawsuit agreed to a Stipulated Settlement Agreement (1985), in which *a written classification system* was to be implemented, in order to "govern placement into, and release from, administrative segregation."

70. A direct reference to Stevens's complaint in *Hewitt*, 492, regarding the question of an inmate's unchangeability: "Even if Helms was a threat to safety on December 8, 1978, it cannot be taken for granted that he was still a threat to safety on January 8, 1979."

has general privileges under a banner of tight security, and the courts are comfortable with that. "Okay," the courts say, "he can still earn good time. He gets very little exercise, has very little human contact, but that's good security practice, and it doesn't affect his liberty interest."[71]

McFadden's articulation of legal reasoning shows how much can be gotten away with in the name of security. What gets distilled by the court in its apparently seamless logical argument gets fleshed out by McFadden, who remembers what other state officials choose to forget: how the ruses of terminological change justify the new penology of divestment.

Cages

Security is like liberty in that many are the crimes committed in its name.

Justice Jackson, United States ex rel. *Knauff v. Shaugnessy*[72]

On January 12, 1990, *Casey v. Lewis* was filed by twenty-two inmates of various prisons operated by the Arizona Department of Corrections. The plaintiffs alleged that ADOC was depriving them of their rights of access to the courts and counsel protected by the First, Sixth, and Fourteenth Amendments. The case came before Judge Carl Muecke, who for twenty of his thirty years on the federal bench had ruled in favor of prisoners' constitutional rights in cases ranging from what became known as the "three-package rule" for prisoners' Christmas mail;[73] to ordering an end to overcrowding, as well as a review of inmate security classifications at Florence State Prison in 1977; to the overturning of the Arizona death penalty statute in 1978 as unconstitutional;[74] to the 1988

---

71. McFadden, interview, October 21, 1996.

72. *Knauff v. Shaugnessy*, 338 U.S. 537, 551 (1950).

73. In the civil rights action that began the lawsuit in 1973, the inmates alleged violations of their First and Fourteenth Amendment rights concerning the Arizona Department of Corrections mail policies. The lawsuit and the consent decree (approved by the court on October 19, 1973) generated controversy, especially the question of Christmas food packages.

74. *Richmond v. Cardwell*, 450 F.Supp. 519 (D.Ariz. 1978). In *Knapp v. Cardwell*, 513 F.Supp. 4 (D.Ariz. 1980), Muecke decided in favor of death row prisoners who challenged a sentencing statute.

ruling against the state in *Gluth v. Kangas,* which ordered that Central Unit at Florence State Prison provide adequate access to the courts.[75]

On June 26, 1990, the U.S. district court in Arizona certified a class comprised of "all adult persons who are now or who in the future will be in the custody of or under the supervision of the State of Arizona Department of Corrections." These plaintiffs sought declaratory and injunctive relief on behalf of the class, which consisted of more than twelve thousand prisoners, for inadequate access to the courts; improper classification procedures leading to unconstitutional transfers; discrimination against handicapped prisoners; denial of contact visits between inmates and attorneys, and of medical, dental, and mental-health care; and denying food-service jobs to HIV-positive inmates.[76]

75. See *Gluth v. Kangas,* 773 F.Supp. 1309 (D.Ariz. 1988),which found major access to the courts inadequacies in the Central Unit at Florence, and ordered injunctive relief, including the so-called "Muecke List" of books necessary in the law library. *Casey v. Lewis,* 834 F.Supp. 1553 (D.Ariz. 1992), extended the *Gluth* orders to the entire Arizona prison system. Dan Pochoda, who served as special master in the *Gluth* case, was appointed to *Casey,* to "investigate and report about a proper remedy." The result was a comprehensive, extremely detailed injunctive order.

76. Judge Muecke decided against plaintiffs in consideration of inmate classification and administrative segregation policies, *Casey v. Lewis,* 837 F.Supp. 1009 (D.Ariz. 1993). In *Casey v. Lewis,* 834 F.Supp. 1569 (D.Ariz. 1993), Muecke concluded that defendants did not discriminate against handicapped inmates in violation of Section 504 of the Rehabilitation Act of 1973, yet determined that failure to provide accessible bathrooms, showers, and cells to handicapped inmates and delays in receiving hearing aids violated Eighth Amendment rights to be free from cruel and unusual punishment. Allegations of deliberate indifference to mental-health needs, violating the Eighth Amendment, as well as unequal treatment of male and female inmates, thus violating female inmates' equal protection, as well as their Eighth Amendment rights, led to injunctive relief ordered by Judge Muecke, *Casey v. Lewis,* 834 F.Supp. 1477 (D.Ariz. 1993). In *Casey v. Lewis,* 773 F.Supp. 1365 (D.Ariz. 1991), Muecke granted summary judgment in favor of prisoners and enjoined ADOC from obstructing contact visits between inmates and their attorneys (August 31, 1991); but the United States Court of Appeals for the Ninth Circuit overturned Muecke's decision, *Casey v. Lewis,* 4 F.3d 1516 (9th Cir. 1993). The issue of access to the courts was settled in district court by Muecke, who held, after a three-month bench trial, that the state was not complying with constitutional standards for ensuring prisoners access to the courts, ruling that the law libraries and legal assistance programs were inadequate, *Casey v. Lewis,* 834 F.Supp. 1553 (D.Ariz. 1992). The Ninth Circuit upheld most of Muecke's order for injunctive relief, *Casey v. Lewis,* 43 F.3d 1261 (9th Cir. 1994). Then, in June 1994, the Department of Corrections was successful in obtaining relief from compliance with the plan from the Supreme Court, until such time as all appeals had been exhausted. On May 22, 1995, the Supreme Court agreed to hear the defendant's appeal over the judge's legal-access plan. On June 24, 1996 the Supreme Court overturned the district court's decision and reversed the court of appeals in *Lewis v. Casey,* 518 U.S. 343, 116 S.Ct. 2174 (1996), thus marking the end of *Casey,* a setback for prisoners' fundamental right of access to the courts, and a major victory for states' rights.

Depositions taken in this action range from narratives of a law librarian fired from Central Unit in Florence for obeying court orders for inmate access; to an inmate attorney nearly hit by a truck driven by a uniformed officer in the parking lot of SMU I; to a black woman, imprisoned for ten years for assault, held in lockdown for six months, without her prescribed psychotropic drugs, as a substitute for psychiatric care; to an epileptic, assigned to an upper bunk, when transferred, despite his protests; to a blind and crippled inmate, who found a dead mouse under his eggs and scorpions in his bed.[77] I could continue, for the narratives of individuals denied even the most basic rights, and the retaliation against those who argued on behalf of these disenfranchised, are voluminous in the records—records that would be ignored in *Lewis v. Casey*, the final Supreme Court decision in favor of the Arizona Department of Corrections—when they confronted only one part of this history, the issue of "access to courts."

The documents in the legal-access component of *Casey v. Lewis*—the most costly, heavily litigated, and contentious case in Arizona state history—tell a story of relentless circumscription. Within the courtroom, inmate witnesses were ignored, or their tales blatantly misconstrued, while accounts of restraint—usually unjustifiable restriction—got lost in the voluminous legal narratives. I have selected only one story, a small piece of the precedent-setting case. It is, in a sense, the least dramatic of tales rendered, but in its relation of one seemingly legitimate prison regulation—which prescribed noncontact visits with attorneys for inmates in Cell Block 6 (CB6) and the Special Management Unit—it reveals cruelty under the guise of security. In moving from the recitation of inmates to the judgment of the law, we can understand how details that would matter most in making sense of a human condition are expunged in a fiction of reasonableness and legitimacy. The deprivation of inmate access to the courts, the most fundamental and basic of our constitutional rights, begins here, in a tale of cages.

By 1990, CB6 at the Arizona State Prison in Florence housed approximately 162 inmates, half of whom were sentenced to death, "on the row of the dead," as the inmates say. The remaining prisoners awaited disciplinary hearings, classification, or transfer to another facility. The cages in CB6 measure approximately seven feet high, four feet wide, and three feet deep, or more exactly, eighty-one inches tall,

---

77. Of the twenty-two representative plaintiffs in the access to the courts part of *Casey*, eight were women.

by forty-six inches wide, by thirty-four inches deep, about the size of a telephone booth. They are constructed of perforated steel or screen mesh that crisscrosses the entire area. The heavy wire mesh of the cages has been painted over so often that the tiny holes are difficult to see through. The cages have food trap doors of thirteen inches by five inches, located approximately forty inches from the floor, through which legal documents are passed. When seated in the cage, a prisoner who is shorter than five feet, five inches tall has no part of his face visible through the open food trap door. Whether or not parts of the faces of prisoners or attorneys can be viewed through the trap door while both are seated depends on their height and the height of their chairs. The only light in the room is located on the attorney's side of the cage.

From the time *Casey v. Lewis* was filed on January 12, 1990, until February 1, 1991, plaintiff's attorneys from the ACLU National Prison Project were allowed contact visits with the prisoners in CB6. When the Department of Corrections unexpectedly decided to refuse attorney-client contact visits, the prisoners could not see their attorneys unless seated in a cage. Plaintiffs requested that the court issue a preliminary injunction, and on May 9, 1991, the district court enjoined defendants from implementation of this policy. Plaintiffs then requested that the court's ruling apply to all the facilities that prohibit contact visits, not just CB6, but also SMU, the Alhambra Reception Center, and the other facilities where prisoners are kept in lockdown status.[78]

In considering the constitutional right to contact visits, ACLU attorneys raised questions concerning decency, dignity, and logic.[79] Not only could the correctional officers overhear conversations between inmates and lawyers, but in the case of the SMU glass visitation booth, the wavy slot in the concrete partition for transfer of legal documents allowed only two or three pages at a time to be exchanged. Larger packets were conveyed from attorney to client by an officer,

---

78. Noncontact visitation policy at the Special Management Unit had been in place since the inception of the facility in 1987. Although many of the inmates of SMU, given their record of assaults and violence, might not reasonably be granted contact visits, there was never sufficient evidence for a blanket denial of contact attorney visitation. Some of these inmates had an institutional-risk score of 3 and were in SMU, while awaiting transfer to another facility.

79. See Declaration of ACLU attorneys James Wilber and Adjoa A. Aiyetoro, Plaintiff's Exhibit 8 and 9, submitted in Statement of Facts in Support of Plaintiffs' Motion for Summary Judgment on the Issues of Contact Attorney Visitation and the Denial of Prison Jobs in Violation of Section 504 of the Rehabilitation Act, July 22, 1991.

who, if available, took from five to seven minutes to deliver the documents to the inmate. Because the wavy slot is located on the opposite side of the booth from the telephone, prisoners could not deliver and retrieve documents while at the same time talking to their attorney. Stephen Bishop, already held in SMU for three years at the time of *Lewis* (even though his institutional-risk score was 2), provided the facts as if a reiteration of impairment.

> I am separated by a partition with a glass window.
> I am locked in on the prisoner side of the attorney visitation room, and a guard is able to look at me through the window in the door at all times.
> I am unable to review at the same time legal documents with my attorney.
> A narrow slit in the wall is provided to allow me to pass my legal documents to my attorney.
> I cannot exchange more than a few pages of legal documents at a time through the narrow slit in the concrete partition.
> Whenever I attempt to pass more than one page at a time, the pages tear.
> In order to pass more than a few pages or my legal documents to my attorney, an ADC guard must be given my documents.
> On or about November 1990, I arrived at the prisoner side of the noncontact visitation room. When I got there my legal documents were already there. They were left there by a guard and had not been placed in an envelope.
> When the guard disappears with my documents, I become anxious that he is reviewing them, whether or not they are placed in a sealed envelope.[80]

Physical obstructions, as well as the waiver of confidentiality and debasement of the attorney-client relationship, thus made a sham of the due-process rights of access to the courts. "The defendants," as the attorneys for the plaintiffs wrote in their answer to defendants' opposing motion, "have erected a significant barrier to adequate legal representation by placing prisoners in a setting that depicts them as subhu-

---

80. Declaration of Stephen Bishop, July 16, 1991, Plaintiff's Exhibit 7, submitted in Statement of Facts in Support of Plaintiffs' Motion for Summary Judgment, July 22, 1991 (numbering omitted).

man."[81] This barrier between counsel and client, making their interaction virtually impossible, became fit metaphor for the curtailment of prisoners' rights. The denial eradicated what is most human about the inmate, as surely as the voice distortion in the SMU booth, and the obliteration of facial expression and physical demeanor in the CB6 cage.

At no point during the legal proceedings did defendants provide proof of the noncontact regulation's purpose or demonstrate how it furthered any legitimate penological concerns. Nor did they offer any evidence that contact attorney visits resulted in escapes or assaults in any of the facilities. Indeed, no assaults had occurred in the history of CB6, and the department's search and observation procedures were already sufficient to protect prisoners, attorneys, and staff. What defendants presented as a sound preventive measure was not based on evidence, but official surmise. "The primary rationale," the defendants stated, "for the non-contact visitation policy at lockdown unit is to prevent escapes, assaults on attorneys and staff and hostage taking."[82] In addition, defendants allowed some CB6 prisoners to have contact visits with their families, while offering no evidence that attorneys, as officers of the court, were more likely than were family members to pass on contraband, assist in escapes, or be assaulted. In spite of expressed official concern, the cage's food trap door was large enough to pass dangerous contraband. The only evidence of an escape presented by defendants was perpetrated with the assistance of family members. Apart from a rumor that later became part of the documentation presented by defendants—a female attorney hugging and kissing a male inmate—the Arizona Department of Corrections provided no justification in support of its decision to deny contact visits.[83]

Plaintiff's attorneys, on the other hand, emphasized the seriousness of this arbitrary and punitive abridgment of civil rights. In capital cases, the impossibility of the simultaneous review of legal documents

---

81. Plaintiffs' Reply to Defendants' Memorandum in Opposition to Plaintiffs' Motion for Temporary Restraining Order and Preliminary Injunction, April 5, 1991, 1.

82. Defendants' Statement of Facts in Support of Defendants' Opposition to Plaintiffs' Motion for Summary Judgment, August 7, 1991, 6.

83. Depositions of J. C. Keeney, Director, Adult Institutions, Arizona Department of Corrections, Phoenix, November 14, 1990 and Roger W. Crist, Warden, Cell Block 6, Phoenix, March 22, 1991. See also the affidavits of Keeney and James McFadden, then Deputy Warden of Special Management Unit I at Florence, appendix, *Casey v. Lewis,* 4 F.3d 1516, 1542 (9th Cir. 1993).

by prisoner and attorney, and the impediments to viewing clients' expressions and gestures—not being able to gauge the meaning of silence—can literally make the difference between life and death. Plaintiffs' attorneys repeatedly asked prison officials, including Samuel Lewis, then director of the Department of Corrections, for evidence that this infringement of effective access preserved security.[84] What is fascinating about the responses of prison officials is how little they need to say, to prove, or to demonstrate. The language of the law is present, and the formulas are certain and as secure as the cages, the containers into which inmates are led.

Even more telling than the defendants' specious documentation of the applicability of a reasonableness test to their restrictive policy was their characterization, sometimes implicit, of the prisoners: for example, inmates incarcerated in CB6 are sentenced to death, "and they have little to lose." They are not deprived of physical contact, since they can shake hands with attorneys through the food slot. Most inmates are "illiterate or mentally deficient." In not being able to read and review documents with their attorneys, their "inconvenience . . . does not rise to the level of irreparable harm."[85]

The testimony of prison officials, and especially Director Samuel Lewis, demonstrates an astonishing disregard for facts in claiming as necessary and rational what remains contingent and biased. They talk about their opinion, base their beliefs on what might happen, and repeat lines from *Turner v. Safley:* "when a prison regulation impinges on inmates' constitutional rights, the regulation is valid if it is *reasonably related* to legitimate penological interests."[86] Rather than providing specific reasons for his policy change, Lewis states his personal opinion:

> I feel that the United States mail service, the telephone system and non-contact visits provide adequate means for communication between the attorney and his or her client, and that there is no need

---

84. See Proposed Findings of Fact and Conclusions of Law Re: Plaintiffs' Motion for Temporary Restraining Order and Preliminary Injunction on Issue of Contact Attorney Visitation in Cellblock 6 (CB6), April 3, 1991; and Plaintiffs' Reply to Defendants' Memorandum in Opposition to Plaintiffs' Motion for Temporary Restraining Order and Preliminary Injunction, April 5, 1991.

85. Legal memorandum in opposition to Plaintiff's Motion for Temporary Restraining Order and Preliminary Injunction, April 3, 1991 and Deposition of J. C. Keeney, Phoenix, Arizona, November 14, 1990.

86. 482 U.S. 78, 89 (1987).

to have contact visits. Because no one has *demonstrated to me* the value or need.[87]

Pressed about the problem of classification in CB6, which was once an administrative-segregation unit, but is no longer, Lewis admitted that after SMU was built, CB6's "mission has been changed. We have a whole different type of inmate in there now."[88] What he neglected to mention was that the present inmates are far less threatening than those housed there when it served as a detention unit.[89] In the most dismissive answer of any of these legal narratives, Lewis avoided noting specific problems in attorney-prisoner contact visits in CB6, saying instead:

> I would have to go back and refresh my memory. . . . But I guess I simply would repeat that I think just because attorneys or any other citizen wants to do something doesn't mean that I necessarily have to accommodate what their wants are.[90]

As if to underscore the inflexibility of the Arizona Department of Corrections, present at one of the first inmate depositions in Florence, Arizona (September 18, 1990), in CB6 were a court reporter; Alice L.

---

87. *Casey v. Lewis,* 4 F.3d 1516, 1541 (9th Cir. 1993) (Pregerson, J., concurring in part and dissenting in part). See also Pregerson's sharp analysis of Lewis's testimony in his dissent on the subject of contact visitation.

88. Deposition of Samuel A. Lewis, Phoenix, February 28, 1991, Exhibit 7, submitted in Defendants' Objections to Plaintiffs' Statement of Facts (emphasis added). In an interview (October 27, 1996, Arizona State Prison, Florence), Ernest J. Trujillo, associate deputy warden of CB6, who looked more like a bureaucrat than a warden, explained to me that CB6 used to be the old administrative segregation building, but the words "administrative segregation" were "too inflammatory, you know, '*we* are segregating *you*.' Now, we have the Special Management units, and we identify problem inmates as management problems; they're grouped accordingly; and no one minds."

89. During the first week of August 1997, following an escape attempt on the death row chain gang in which a condemned inmate and his wife were killed, Arizona's 115 death row inmates were moved to Special Management Unit 2, what Corrections Department Director Stewart describes as "a super maximum-security fortress" (*Arizona Daily Star,* August 4, 1997). In just seven years, the Department of Corrections has changed from distinguishing death row inmates in CB6 from inmates in SMU, to caging death row inmates, as if they were as dangerous as those in SMU, and finally, to moving them into SMU 2 with the "worst of the worst."

90. *Casey v. Lewis,* 4 F.3d 1516, 1541 (9th Cir. 1993) (Pregerson, J., concurring in part and dissenting in part). See *Ching v. Lewis,* 895 F.2d 608 (9th Cir. 1989), where the Ninth Circuit held that a prisoner's right to access to the courts encompassed the right to contact attorney visits.

Bendheim, for the plaintiffs; Kathleen L. Wieneke, for the defendants; and Steven C. James, an inmate in CB6 in a cage. Bendheim made a statement for the record, objecting to the witness being caged, which not only hid most of his face, but meant that she could only confer with him by asking others to leave the room, if she chose to ensure their right to confidentiality. "I believe that this deposition could have been conducted in a true contact setting without the necessity of the witness being caged up this way."[91] The deposition took place just twelve weeks after Judge Muecke had ordered an end to noncontact visits throughout the Arizona prison system. The Arizona Department of Corrections demonstrated the refusal to comply with court orders that would characterize then-governor Symington and Director Lewis's subsequent fight against the federal government and their "intrusion" into the prisons.

The Arizona Department of Corrections appealed Judge Muecke's order on November 5, 1992. On September 23, 1993, the United States Court of Appeals for the Ninth Circuit vacated the injunction, reversed Muecke's order granting summary judgment for the inmate class, and ordered summary judgment in favor of the Arizona Department of Corrections.[92] The appellate court's tolerance of a barrier between attorneys and inmates, as Judge Pregerson declared in his dissent, "in effect has drawn an iron curtain between prisoners and the Constitution."[93]

The court of appeals adopted "reasonableness" as the standard of review and gave total deference to prison authorities. Reviewing the four factors cited in *Turner v. Safley* proposed to determine what is "reasonable" or "rational" about prison policies,[94] the appellate court makes some astonishing surmises: (1) "Prison officials need merely 'put forward' a legitimate government interest," thereby erasing the necessity of even minimal evidence. What the majority calls "a prophylactic security measure," if founded only on "belief" or "anticipation," should be seen as one of a set of "innovative solutions to the intractable

91. Deposition of Steven James, Florence, Arizona, September 18, 1990, 3, attachment to Proposed Findings of Fact and Conclusions of Law Re: Plaintiffs' Motion for Temporary Restraining Order and Preliminary Injunction on Issue of Contact Attorney Visitation in Cellblock 6 (CB6), April 3, 1991.

92. *Casey v. Lewis*, 4 F.3d 1516 (9th Cir. 1993).

93. Ibid., 1524 (Pregerson, J., concurring in part and dissenting in part), citing *Wolff v. McDonnell*, 418 U.S. 539, 555–56 (1974).

94. *Turner*, 89–90.

problems of prison administration." Further, the district court "placed an unduly onerous burden on the Department of Corrections" and should have recognized that mere concern, even absent actual cause, "is entitled to significant deference."[95] (2) Instead of discriminating among degrees or kinds of deprivation, the appellate court now rules that this particular deprivation is reasonable because inmates are not *totally* deprived of access to the courts. They cite *Bounds v. Smith,* which provides for "adequate law libraries or adequate assistance from persons trained in the law."[96] (3) In the most surprising turn, the court of appeals turns the question of "exaggerated response," which should apply to prison officials, on its head, instead putting the burden of proof on prisoners: "It is incumbent upon the prisoners to point to an alternative that accommodates their rights at de minimis cost to security interests."[97]

Pregerson responds to the reversal of Muecke's decision by demonstrating that the appellate court has redefined the "rational relationship" between prison policy and justifiable need, granting defendants the ability to imagine *any* rationale, no matter how ill-justified the restriction is in fact. Inmates, who already have been deprived, must now be involved in a virtually meaningless exercise. They are asked to provide alternatives to a gratuitous policy, to show why an illogical regulation is illogical. This burden of proof becomes at best a cynical expectation by the court, and at worst an absurd decree. While prison officials need not offer any evidence to support their belief that prisoners' activities would disrupt prison operations, prisoners must offer substantial evidence to demonstrate a deprivation of their constitutional rights. How can inmates respond to a legal decision when they cannot even obtain adequate interviews with their legal counsel? How can a court that affirms their need to be in cages command that they must demonstrate the unreasonableness of noncontact visitation?

By crediting unsupported allegations, the court, according to Pregerson, not only disregards the Ninth Circuit's interpretation of *Turner,*[98] requiring prison officials to *prove* that their justification is the

---

95. *Casey v. Lewis,* 4 F.3d 1516, 1520–21 (9th Cir. 1993).

96. Ibid., 1521–22, citing *Bounds v. Smith,* 430 U.S. 817, 828 (1977).

97. Ibid., 1523.

98. See ibid., 1525, where Pregerson remarks, "I dissent from the majority's opinion with respect to the 'access to the courts' claim because the majority has, in effect, abandoned the *Turner* 'reasonableness' standard of review in favor of the 'toothless' rational basis standard of review."

"actual basis" for a challenged regulation, but sharply narrows the right of access to the courts, as defined through fifty years of U.S. Supreme Court decisions.[99] Pregerson demonstrates that particularity is demolished by generality, individuality by anonymity. The "automatic and permanent denial" of attorney contact visits, regardless of whether a particular prisoner has violated a particular rule regarding visitation, becomes yet another means by which classification demolishes difference.[100] Pregerson is startled that units housing the prison's lowest-security-risk prisoners, as well as those whom officials imply are the most violent and uncontrollable, would in a credo of overdetermination, administer a blanket ban on contact visits. An already oppressive placement for first-time, nonviolent offenders is rendered even more hopeless when their right to counsel is vitiated. Pregerson explains that "the evidence indicates that housing assignment is a poor surrogate for a determination that a particular prisoner poses a security risk."[101] What this case reveals is the ominous blurring of categories, the shifting locales for incapacitation, the arbitrariness of classification, even in the most distinctive, supposedly special and categorical of units.

When I last visited CB6 at Florence in the summer of 1996, Ernest J. Trujillo, the new associate deputy warden of CB6, who calls himself a "senior administrator," responded only vaguely to my questions about the cages for attorney and client visits. He said, "They are used sometimes, for some attorneys and some inmates. It all depends on prisoner criteria." He then turned the conversation to a new plan for cages. Because the fenced-in recreation area for CB6 inmates is outside the perimeter wall, inmates will be moved inside. "The cages will be smaller, but things will be more secure."[102]

Civil Death

I understand why people have to be locked up; I certainly don't believe some of the people who are in prison should be out, but while they're there I think they have a right to be treated with dignity as human beings and consistent with the Constitution of the

---

99. Ibid., 1529 (Pregerson, J, concurring in part and dissenting in part).
100. Ibid.
101. Ibid., 1534.
102. Trujillo, interview.

United States. So that's the best I can say and I've said it in the form
of this case.

Judge Carl Muecke, *Casey v. Lewis*, Phoenix, December 1991[103]

In 1870, Woody Ruffin, a convicted felon, committed murder while
working in chains on the Chesapeake and Ohio Railroad. Though the
crime occurred in the county of Bath, Virginia, Ruffin was tried in the
circuit court of the City of Richmond. Found guilty of murder in the
first degree, he was sentenced to be hanged on May 25, 1871. The prisoner applied to the circuit court for a writ of error. His counsel claimed
that he was not tried by a jury of his vicinage, as authorized by the Bill
of Rights. In *Ruffin v. Commonwealth*,[104] Justice Christian, delivering the
opinion of the court, portrayed the convict, no matter where he might
be—whether in the county of Bath or the city of Richmond, whether
working in the penitentiary or for an outside contractor—as "civilly
dead," ever entrapped in the "restraints and regulations" of the "eye of
the law."

Let us read part of the narrative.

> Though at the time of the commission of the murder of which he
> was convicted, he was not within the walls of the penitentiary, but
> in a distant part of the State, he was yet, in the eye of the law, still
> a convict in the penitentiary; not, indeed, actually and bodily
> within its walls, imprisoned and physically restrained by its bars
> and bolts; but as certainly under the restraints of the laws, and as
> actually bound by the regulations of that institution, as if he had
> been locked within one of its cells. These laws and regulations
> attach to the person of the convict wherever he may be carried by
> authority of law . . . as certainly and tenaciously as the ball and
> chain which he drags after him.[105]

The degradation and defilement of the slave, though the analogy is
repressed, become the basis for the characterization of the inmate. Once
convicted of a crime, the criminal is no longer a person, but "the slave

---

103. *Casey v. Lewis*, Transcript of Bench Trial before the Honorable Carl A. Muecke,
Phoenix, Arizona, 5.

104. 62 Va. (21 Gratt.) 790 (1871).

105. Ibid., 793–94.

of the State."[106] The statutes of the Virginia criminal code provided for a change of venue and, when necessary, authorized a convict's case to be sent to any county in the state. Moreover, as Christian argued, whereas the Bill of Rights "govern[s] a society of freemen," state statutes ordain the status "of convicted felons and men civilly dead."[107] Civilly dead, the inmate exists outside the pale of human relation and empathy. The prison walls circumscribe the prisoner in a fiction that, in extending the bounds, the balls and chains, of servitude, becomes the basis for the negation of rights, thus reconciling constitutional strictures with the codes of slavery.

There is a history to this obsession with containment. In the eighteenth-century United States, thoughts of emancipation had become coterminous with necessities of evacuation. If the myth of an Anglo-Saxon America demanded rather heavy-handed figurative strategies of prejudice, neatly codified in constitutional law, the fact of a place like Haiti—locale for the only successful revolution of slaves in the New World—forced the rhetoric of coercive necessity and public order to shed its figurative trappings. A group of blacks in Haiti rose up against their oppressors to make themselves a nation and the presence of blacks here acquired the status of things that had to be handily removed. Haiti was judged, in Jefferson's words, as an alternate Africa: the appropriate place to contain "that race of men."[108] But it was Lincoln, addressing a "Committee of Colored Men" in Washington, D.C., on August 14, 1862, who demonstrated how imbricated social necessity and social identity had become, positing inequality as the definitive relation between free blacks and hypervaluated whites: "But even when you cease to be slaves, you are yet far removed from being placed on an equality with the white race. The aspiration of men is to enjoy equality with the best when free, but on this broad continent, not a single man of your race is made the equal of a single man of ours. Go where you are treated the best, and the ban is still upon you."[109]

What is at stake here is the power of competing analogies to redefine "liberty." *Ruffin* was decided in November 1871. Ratification of the Thirteenth Amendment to the Constitution had been announced in December 1865. The Thirteenth Amendment, Section 1, outlawed slav-

106. Ibid., 796.
107. Ibid.
108. Thomas Jefferson, *Writings*, ed. Merill D. Peterson (New York: Library of America, 1984), 1096–98.
109. *The Collected Works of Abraham Lincoln*, ed. Roy P. Blaser (New Brunswick, N.J.: Rutgers University Press, 1953), 372.

ery and involuntary servitude "except as punishment of crime whereof the party shall have been duly convicted." The legal exception became the means for terminological slippage: those who were once slaves were now criminals, and "forced labor" became a new form of degradation. The parenthetical expression guaranteed enclosure, a bracketing of servitude that revived slavery under cover of removing it. Such an amendment literally amounted to nothing less than an escape clause, a corrective that left the vestige of enslavement intact.

During the second session of the Thirty-ninth Congress (December 12, 1866–January 8, 1867), debates centered on the meaning of the exemption in the antislavery amendment, since punishment for crime found fit locale not only within the walls of prisons, but also on the auction block. Senator Charles Sumner, objected to "the phraseology" of the amendment, as "an unhappy deference . . . to an original legislative precedent at an earlier period of our history." Fearing what he saw as the congressional sanction of servitude, he had still hoped that the words "involuntary servitude, except for crime" applied only to "ordinary imprisonment." Noting, however, that what had seemed "exclusively applicable" had been "extended so as to cover some form of slavery," he asked that Congress "go farther and expurgate that phraseology from the text of the Constitution itself."[110] Throughout the recently disbanded Confederacy leased prisoners maintained plantations and rebuilt public places. Slave codes shaped the language of contracts for convict labor, and plantations turned into prisons. The new narratives of servitude and punishment were articulated by prison architecture, criminal dress codes, and the trappings of slavery transported to the new South: chains, dogs, whips, and other forms of corrective torture.[111]

---

110. *Congressional Globe,* 39th Cong., 2d sess. (Dec. 19, 1866), in *The Reconstruction Amendments' Debates,* ed. Alfred Avins (Richmond: Virginia Commission on Constitutional Government, 1967), 258.

111. Begun in the late 1860s, the convict lease system allowed private individuals to rent convict labor. As David M. Oshinsky argues in *"Worse Than Slavery": Parchman Farm and the Ordeal of Jim Crow Justice* (New York: Free Press, 1996), the postemancipation criminal code was thus established as a vehicle of racial subordination. See also Alex Lichtenstein's *Twice the Work of Free Labor: The Political Economy of Convict Labor in the New South* (London: Verso, 1996), a study of convict lease and the public chain gang that replaced it during a period of modernization during which not only impoverished African Americans, but "all prisoners, vicious, petty, and innocent alike" were reduced "to a commodity" (xvi). Lichtenstein makes crucial connections between political, economic, and penal suppression in the New South (especially Georgia) and contemporary criminalization of the poor in the expanding prison state.

There are certain things about personhood, about what it means to be a person, that are not lost with conviction, even if the Thirteenth Amendment, read strictly, puts prisoners outside the bounds of civil rights. To push the idea of penal forfeit further, we might reconsider the concept of civil death in terms of its ruling metaphors: "corruption of blood" or "forfeiture of property."[112] The English common-law fiction of strict civil death, to be "dead in law"—forfeiting property, as well as personal rights—though generally rejected as a rule of American common law, was adopted by some states.

Justice Christian's use of civil death legally to confine the prisoner beyond actual prison walls remains effective because of a working dichotomy that construes both persons and privilege: not only the opposition between natural (read physical) death and unnatural (read legal) death, but also the strategic and classificatory agenda implied in the distinction between natural rights and civil rights. One can, hypothetically, retain natural rights, but still be disabled by statutory abridgment, condemned by societal (or civilized) needs. Once the legal terminology of blood taint or disability was surcharged with racial prejudice—Ruffin's definition of the convict as "slave of the State"—then the claim for personal rights became shifting and tentative, as the inmate became something like a synthetic or artificial slave: incapacitated, and hence barbaric.

The constitutional equation of the institutions of slavery and imprisonment—in spite of those statutory provisions that made incomparable the rights of slave and prisoner—amplified control and compulsion. And, now, as an increasing number of citizens, redefined as criminals, are imaginatively recolored to match, or more precisely, to embody retrospectively the figure of the slave, the legal status of prisoners matters more than ever. The figures of containment and deprivation enunciated here as fundamental to the order and protection of society, once maintained in time as precedent, create the possibilities for the "walls," metaphorized by the law as if "reasonable," to ensure the "literal construction" of contemporary locales for punishment. It is not surprising that *Ruffin* became a memorial spot of time recalled by Justices Marshall, Brennan, and Stevens.[113]

---

112. I refer here to *Platner v. Sherwood*, 6 Johns. Ch (NY) 118 (1822).

113. See, for example, the dissents in *Jones v. North Carolina Prisoners' Labor Union, Inc.*, 433 U.S. 119 (Marshall, J., dissenting, joined by Brennan, J.); *Meachum v. Fano*, 427 U.S. 215 (Stevens, J., dissenting, joined by Brennan, J. and Marshall, J.); *Lewis v. Casey*, 518 U.S. 343, 116 S.Ct. 2174 (Stevens, J., dissenting).

What constitutes the idea of the person in prison? What is necessary to maintain that personal identity?[114] What, in other words, are the norms governing the exercise of power within prisons? What are the legitimate rights of the state over the interests of the incarcerated? The contemporary accoutrements of slavery—chains, cages, the diminution of access to the courts, hard labor, and elimination of personal property—recuperate the memory of servitude and provide a vehicle for reconceptualizing the status of inmates. Are they slaves of the state, wards of the state, or do they occupy some other status, perhaps "criminal aliens," in the words of the 1996 Antiterrorism and Effective Death Penalty Act?[115] In considering the more or less unbroken momentum of law and history that carried peonage and servitude into the present, a cautious legal historian might consider the relationship between slave and prisoner's rights as rather simpler than I make it out to be. Simply put, conviction for crime means that a prisoner falls outside the bounds of the Thirteenth Amendment. And once you equate slavery and imprisonment, then due process is not relevant. But *what* must we discount in order *not* to question the equation of slavery and incarceration in the Thirteenth Amendment?

In my attempt to argue the elusive concept of rights when applied to the convicted felon, I consider the normative assumptions of prison discourse and its relation to, and even reciprocity with, legal inquiry. Terminology and changing definitions matter a great deal, since the assessment of criminality and control of the confined is in large part a rhetorical endeavor. Discursive obfuscation spares one the need to confront the extreme practices subsumed under the name of "corrections": when *solitary confinement* is retermed *special management* or when those carrying out executions are known as the *special operations team*. The very notion of "security," like "person," "labor," "hardship," "pain," and "punishment," is redefined within the walls of the prison and in

---

114. In his introduction to *Democracy and Punishment: Disciplinary Origins of the United States* (Madison: University of Wisconsin Press, 1987), Thomas L. Dumm asserts that in "America, everyone is free; prison is the negation of that freedom." He continues, even more generally: "Hence the prison experience is a negation of the conditions which allow one to define oneself as a person" (3). Dumm's totalizing theory demonstrates the problem with taking Foucault's disciplinary valence in *Discipline and Punish*, trans. Alan Sheridan (New York: Vintage, 1995), as indicative of the experience of the incarcerated, while it ignores the substantial ambiguity in the legal scrutiny of conditions of confinement.

115. 104th Cong., 2d sess., S. 735, April 29, 1996. See Title IV, "Terrorist and Criminal Alien Removal and Exclusion," Sec. 440, 62.

the conclusions of law. The delimitation of liberty required, in what one officer described to me as "this other world"—and what Justice Brennan cautioned against as "power exercised in the shadows"[116]—produces an environment of language unlike any other. Judicial rhetoric turns to the form of law as the rule of action and the practice of memory: a judge's self-justification through what Cover calls "law language," the rules of which "are arrived at primarily by examining the way language is spoken in the past."[117]

What is the status of prisoners under the law? It is customary to begin discussing prisoners' rights—their right to dignity and humane treatment—with what some deem the ahistorical miscalculations of the Warren Court in the 1960s. With the curtailing of these opportunities in the 1980s, as well as the deconstruction of rights language as mystifying and ahistorical in critical legal studies, I take risks by relying on and referring to terms like *person, liberty,* and *rights.* In appealing to what could be seen as construed, transcendent values, I do not mean to imply a direct relation between the language of court decisions and actual practice inside the prisons. I am suggesting, however, that the functions of language and labeling keep legal opinions and correctional actions in dialogue.

In *Ruffin v. Commonwealth* Justice Christian delimited general principles such as "property" and "personhood" (yoked in the language of the Fourth, Fifth, and Fourteenth amendments) and employed an analogy to slavery for dislodging constitutional claims. But by the 1900s, the severity of his decree was tempered by a series of cases that dealt with convicts forced to labor without compensation as punishment for their crimes. Although the exact status of prisoners in this respect was never fully defined by the courts, in these turn-of-the-century Thirteenth Amendment decisions, both the limits of "involuntary servitude" and the means by which such servitude could be accomplished demonstrated that the recent past of slavery weighed heavily on the argument for basic rights.[118] The appearance of the word *rights* in these

---

116. *O'Lone v. Estate of Shabazz,* 482 U.S. 342, 355 (1987) (Brennan J. dissenting).

117. Robert Cover, *Justice Accused: Antislavery and the Judicial Process* (New Haven: Yale University Press, 1975), 126.

118. The fact of slavery as crucial to "the development of an alternate, rights conscious interpretation of the federal constitution" is crucial to Hendrik Hartog's discussion of categorical enslavement and emancipatory claims in "The Constitution of Aspiration and 'The Rights That Belong to Us All,'" *Journal of American History* 74, 3 (December 1987): 1016–25.

early cases thus casts into a new light arguments against the intrinsic rightness of rights in contingent and arbitrary social contexts.

I suggest, then, that the proximity to the customs, practices, and attitudes of "the peculiar institution" articulated the differing senses of rights not as some timeless principle, but rather as being fixed in the specifics of locale and consequently as responsive to changes over time.[119] Confronting the pressures of an all-too-recent history, the memory of degradation and want, these cases reveal a grit and concreteness lacking in legal decisions today. In cases such as *Kenyon v. Saunders*,[120] *Nugent, Superintendent v. State of Arizona Improvement Company*,[121] *Westbrook v. The State*,[122] and *Anderson v. Salant*[123] judges grappled with the specificity of rights and the possible violation of the constitutional provision forbidding slavery. A number of judicial decisions of this time state, or at least assume, that a "convict is neither civilly dead, nor deprived of his rights of property; and, if this be so, he should be entitled to enforce such right when it is necessary to do so."[124] *Anderson* hinged on deciding how definitive was the transformation of the plaintiff's condition—once contracted to labor as punishment—"from convict into that of slave."[125] Even though conviction imposed "a duty of servitude," that residue of rights "which a slave lacks"[126] remained critical in the court's decision.

Westbrook is the most unsettling and instructive of these cases. While working on a chain gang in Tift County, Georgia, Cleveland Westbrook killed the man next to him on the "squad chain," after J. M. Davis, the warden, set upon him with a strap. While checking on what sounded like a disturbance, Davis saw Westbrook with a knife and warned: "You have been cutting up some little bit, and I will have to correct you." Westbrook responded, "No sir, you won't. . . . [Y]ou ain't going to whip me," and refused to give up his knife. Davis ordered one of the trusties, "Eugene Wilson, a big negro," to take the knife away.

---

119. See *Bailey v. Alabama*, 219 U.S. 219 (1911) for the crucial Supreme Court decision at this time, declaring that statutory peonage laws violated the Thirteenth Amendment prohibition against involuntary servitude.

120. 18 R.I. 590 (1894).

121. 173 U.S. 338 (1899).

122. 133 Ga. 578 (1909).

123. 38 R.I. 463 (1916).

124. *Kenyon v. Saunders*, 592. See also *Willingham v. King*, 23 Fla. 478 (1887) and *Dade Coal Co. v. Haslett*, 83 Ga. 549 (1889).

125. *Anderson*, 467.

126. Ibid., 475.

According to the warden's testimony, "the boys" on the chain got scared, pulled away, and tightened the chain on Cleveland, and Cleveland stabbed the man next to him.[127]

Justice Mitchell ruled that the convict is not a mere chattel like a slave but has the same rights with regard to his person as any other man, with some qualifications: "He is not mere property without any civil rights, but has all the rights of an ordinary citizen which are not expressly or by necessary implication taken from him by law."[128] Although we can infer that even without such a provision by statute in the Georgia Penal Code, there could be no limitation of the warden's power—and obviously, wardens often administered corporal punishment with impunity—Mitchell's words regarding the warden's "assault," even under pressure, are crucial:

> Upon conviction the convict may lose his liberty for the time being, and may be required to perform hard labor, but he does not lose security of his person against unlawful invasion. The security of person, except as expressly provided by statute, remains his right; and if it be unlawfully invaded, he may resist such unlawful invasion as if there had been no conviction.[129]

The form in which Mitchell, a Tift County judge, articulated "reasonableness," "authority," and "the convict's right of personal security" must be recalled when turning to recent court decisions concerning "infliction of pain" and "use of force." In *Whitley v. Albers,* for example, "unreasonable" or "unnecessary" force is literally qualified out of existence, its meaning confounded, as the Supreme Court concludes that malice and sadism must be added to the "unnecessary and wanton" standard in order to establish a constitutional violation.[130]

Rehistoricizing the law of prisoners' rights has the benefit of allowing us to reconceive the cunning indirectness of certain contemporary

---

127. *Westbrook,* 579, 580.

128. Ibid., 585.

129. Ibid., 583.

130. Surely one of the more curious justifications in the majority opinion occurs in the temporal dislocation of the present judgment for future readers: "the infliction of pain in the course of a prison security measure . . . does not amount to cruel and unusual punishment simply because it may appear *in retrospect that the degree of force authorized or applied for security purposes was unreasonable, and hence unnecessary in the strict sense*" (ibid., 319; emphasis added).

judicial opinions. Though risking comparison of a Georgia with a Supreme Court case, I suggest the early narrative offers real continuities with the particulars of contemporary decisions regarding excessive force. In contrast to *Westbrook*, for example, the qualifications and evasiveness of *Whitley* mask a system of dominance that remembers the substance of slavery. That memory, though suppressed in fastidious distinctions and noncommittal formulas, reconstructs the necessary conditions for institutional dehumanization. It is no accident, then, that during the past twenty years what the majority has repressed—the continuum between being declared dead in law, made a slave (or senseless icon of the human), and judged a criminal—has been exposed by dissenting judges.

More than any other case in contemporary Supreme Court rulings, the 1996 *Lewis v. Casey* demonstrates how the Court's discursive maneuvering effectively preserves the identity of the slave in the person of the prisoner. In this instance, the U.S. Supreme Court responded to the appeal filed by the Arizona Department of Corrections and its director, Samuel Lewis, bringing to a close the legal access component of *Casey v. Lewis*.[131] Associate Justice Antonin Scalia, who delivered the majority opinion, reversed the district court's finding of liability, greatly narrowing the possibility of filing an injunction and making it almost impossible to prove a constitutional violation. According to Scalia, the prisoners did not demonstrate actual injury. Judge Muecke's legal-access injunction (affirmed by the Ninth Circuit Court of Appeals),[132] had mandated detailed, systemwide changes in the prison law libraries and legal-assistance programs, and the operative thrust of the Court's ruling was to demolish the fundamental right of access to the courts by arguing that the obvious problems in legal access in the Arizona State Prison system were really not injurious.

The Supreme Court strongly criticized the district court for imposing an injunction that the Supreme Court described as "inordinately—indeed wildly—intrusive . . . the ne plus ultra of what our opinions have lamented as a court's . . . becoming enmeshed in the minutiae of

---

131. *Casey v. Lewis*, 834 F.Supp. 1553 (D.Ariz. 1992).

132. *Casey v. Lewis*, 43 F.3d 1261 (9th Cir. 1994), Pregerson, J. Over a year after Pregerson's dissenting opinion in *Casey v. Lewis*, 4 F.3d 1516 (9th Cir. 1993), Pregerson, now the presiding judge, upheld Muecke's order of injunctive relief, claiming that ADOC's legal-access program unconstitutionally denied inmates meaningful access to the court.

prison operations."[133] The state victory over the federal courts might more accurately be termed "Lewis v. Muecke," for it ended the ten-year battle between Judge Muecke and Director Lewis.[134] In the course of the struggle, Lewis was cited with two contempt of court violations for refusing to obey court orders about the prisons;[135] Judge Muecke faced threats of impeachment by former governor Fife Symington; the Arizona legislature passed and Symington signed into law a measure to halt paychecks to special masters; and the state paid over two hundred thousand dollars in attorney's fees in order to avoid paying a court-appointed special master thirty-seven thousand dollars.

These facts only scratch the surface of the Arizona prison system's transformation under the stewardship of Director Lewis. He eliminated nearly all educational programs throughout the prisons; declared hot plates contraband; banned personal clothing inmates bought with their own funds, as well as fans, CD players, and tape recorders (especially tough on the approximately 72 percent of inmates who are illiterate and whose only means of family communication is on correspondence tape); implemented no early release credit if accused of minor infractions, charged for medical care and electricity (called a "plug-in" charge for appliances); and confiscated artwork from cells in most units. Lewis also reduced the number of items sold in commissaries. A list of items available that was once four pages long has now been reduced to less than one page.

In October 1996, three months after the Supreme Court decision in *Lewis v. Casey* (and six months after passage of the Prison Litigation Reform Act), the Ninth Circuit Court of Appeals modified a 1973 consent decree (arising out of the inmate suit *Hook v. State of Arizona*) that included regulations about mail policies.[136] The consent agreement contained a

---

133. *Lewis v. Casey*, 518 U.S. 343, 116 S.Ct. 2174, 2185 (1996).

134. See "Lewis and Muecke Clash over Operation of Prisons," *Courts and Corrections*, July 29, 1994, 4 and "District Judge Muecke Places Law over Popularity," *Arizona Republic*, November 11, 1995, A1, A14.

135. In 1994 Lewis was held in contempt for violating the 1973 stipulated consent decree regarding inmate mail and Christmas packages (followed by a 1990 injunction by Muecke and affirmed on appeal in *Hook v. Arizona*, 972 F.2d 1012 (9th Cir. 1992), when he ordered a ban on pornographic magazines such as *Playboy* and *Hustler*. In 1995, Lewis was again found in contempt for refusing to pay "special masters" appointed to monitor prison conditions. Muecke asked that an out-of-state judge be appointed to referee the dispute. Judge David Ezra of U.S. District Court in Honolulu concluded: "The record and file in this case shows an extraordinary history of non-compliance" ("No Fine for Lewis—This Time," *Arizona Republic*, November 4, 1995, A12.

136. *Hook v. Arizona*, 120 F.3d 921 (9th Cir. 1997)

provision allowing inmates to receive—between December 10 and December 31—up to three twenty-five-pound food packages for Christmas. The department celebrated the appellate court's repudiation of a long-standing decree, which had been affirmed on appeal.[137] As Lewis had reminded his critics just a year before: "There is no constitutional right to Christmas food packages, and inmates have no right to burden the department, its staff and the taxpayers."[138] Until Lewis became director, the *Internal Management Policy and Procedure Manual* read:

> The Department of Corrections recognizes and encourages holiday festivities and specifically inmates receiving additional items and/or money as gifts during the Christmas season. Because of problems associated with contraband, it is necessary to exercise some control in this process.[139]

---

137. See *Hook v State of Arizona*, 972 F.2d 1012 (9th Cir. 1992). The Prison Litigation Reform Act (PLRA) (part of the Omnibus Consolidated Rescissions and Appropriations Act of 1996, 104th Cong., 2d sess., H.3842, H.3861, April 25, 1995), signed into law on April 26, 1996, claiming to curtail frivolous prisoner lawsuits, actually limits the federal courts' jurisdiction or ability to enter effective remedies for constitutional violations in prisons. Besides noting the inappropriateness in subsuming such a serious congressional bill in an omnibus appropriations bill, thus leading to only a single hearing in the Judiciary Committee—and almost no media attention—Senator Kennedy warned: "I note with great concern that the bill would set a dangerous precedent for stripping the Federal courts of the ability to safeguard the civil rights of powerless and disadvantaged groups" (142 *Cong. Rec.* S.2292 [March 19, 1996]). Most seriously, the PLRA calls into question the validity of all existing consent decrees in prison and jail cases where there has been no finding that the relief is narrowly drawn, extends no further than necessary to correct the violation of the federal right, and is the least intrusive means necessary to correct the violation of the federal right. Since such statements were never felt to be necessary, these newly required recitations did not appear in consent decrees. The PLRA (introduced by Arizona Republican senator John Kyle) could be read as a response to *Casey v. Lewis*, especially to the testimony of the Arizona attorney general Grant Woods before the Supreme Court, and to the media blitz concerning Muecke's intrusive orders, "micromanaging" the prison system, and most of all, to the fight over the payment of special master's fees between the Arizona legislature, legislating on behalf of the Department of Corrections, and Judge Muecke, who would be supported by outside U.S. district judge David Ezra, who ruled Lewis in contempt of court for failing to pay special masters monitoring Arizona prisons. Ezra also declared unconstitutional a state law halting payments to the special masters appointed to investigate allegations related to three civil rights lawsuits filed by inmates in the state prison system. The PLRA shifts payment obligation to the federal courts, while seriously limiting the powers and duties of the special master. For example, the master may not talk with counsel for either side or with any of the defendants or staff of the institution unless counsel for both parties are present.

138. Samuel Lewis, "Let's Let Your Readers Decide Who the Real 'Grinch' Is," letter to *Arizona Republic*, October 10, 1995, p 2A.

139. "Christmas Packages for Inmates," ADOC *Internal Management Policy and Procedure Manual*, effective November 1, 1980.

Perhaps the best way to represent the dispossession, or more precisely, the institutionalizing of servility legislated by Lewis during his years as director is to speak the language of property. Eliminating the right to possess becomes fit backdrop for delegitimizing the right of access to prison law libraries and legal help.[140] The history of the district court's minutely detailed injunctive order, dealing with every conceivable issue of access to the courts, lies in Lewis's vision of inmates as state property. His "property policy," a massive attack on inmates' ownership of things, intimated the treatment of human as thing. If property gives a person identity, then ensuring that inmates can make nothing their own—not knowledge, not vocation, not dress—secures their status as isolate bodies, so much material exposed to lack.[141] In rendering its decision in *Lewis v. Casey*, the Supreme Court ignored the record of deprivation and abuse and tacitly rewarded the Department of Corrections for its contempt for court orders.

The question we must ask is which history do we look at as history, or ultimately, whose story matters. For Judge Muecke and the plaintiffs, the history is one of obstruction, recalcitrance, and resistance. This story will be omitted from of the majority opinion in *Lewis v. Casey*, which blamed the district court for not giving proper deference to the Department of Corrections, for not giving the state "ample opportunity to participate in the process of fashioning a remedy," as Souter wrote.[142] The memos, lengthy hearings, and statements by correctional officers, library staff, and inmates, however, tell another story. If inmates testified against prison officials, their typewriters were confiscated. As becomes clear in depositions of some of the library staff, who risked their jobs by telling the truth, they had read Muecke's decision, and they had begun to or were willing to make the necessary changes in library hours, access, and photocopying of documents.

How the majority could blame Muecke for not giving the Department of Corrections enough time to propose an adequate remedy is at best bewildering, and at worst a shocking example of judicial manipu-

---

140. This two-pronged right of access—through prison libraries *or* legal assistance—was the core of *Bounds v. Smith*.

141. For two distinct, but crucial articles on property, personhood, and privilege, see Margaret Jane Radin, "Property and Personhood," *Stanford Law Review* 34 (1982): 957–1015; and Cheryl I. Harris, "Whiteness as Property," *Harvard Law Review* 106 (1993): 1709–91.

142. *Lewis*, 518 U.S. 343, 116 S.Ct. 2174, 2203 (Souter, J., joined by Ginsburg and Breyer, concurring in part, dissenting in part, and concurring in the judgment).

lation. In his dissent, Stevens begins by recalling the Fourteenth Amendment, contrasting how *Ruffin* represented "the prison inmate" as "a mere 'slave of the State'" with a more recent history that claims a "residuum of liberty" for inmates, with "the 'well-established' right of access to the courts" as fundamental.[143] He further reminds the Court that such an opinion could only be made by ignoring the record. While agreeing that the order is excessive and flawed because of a breakdown in court-supervised negotiation, thus justifying a remand, Stevens disagrees with *how* the Court characterizes the guilty party. Declaring that "Much of the blame for its breadth . . . can be placed squarely in the lap of the State," Stevens returns to the strategic delays and "diversionary tactics" that "forced [the court] to take extraordinary measures."[144] For nearly two pages, Stevens recalls what the majority chose to ignore. After his analysis of the state's "lack of interest," "sparse objections," and "piecemeal and belated challenges to the scope of the proposed plan,"[145] it seems incredible that anyone could believe that, given the opportunity, the Arizona Department of Corrections would have articulated a remedial plan. Not only had the department never taken seriously meaningful court access for inmates, but even with the *Gluth* decision, it had tried to avoid responsibility for carrying out court orders.[146]

In refusing to fashion a constructive remedy at every stage of this case, the defendants were supported by the Supreme Court, which contrived a revisionary history. This remembrance helped to characterize what Stevens ironically calls a "railroaded," "browbeaten" state, so put upon by an overweening judge, that, cowed into silence, it could only wait for the chance to appeal, at which time it would regain its voice.[147]

Here, then, is one narrative. In October 1992, Judge Muecke, for the District Court of the State of Arizona, issued findings of fact and conclusions of law, finding violations of access to the courts; determining that the *Gluth* injunction, with legitimate modifications requested by the defendants, would be appropriate for systemic relief; and, given their prior unwillingness to cooperate, appointed Dan Pochoda, the

---

143. 116 S.Ct., 2206 (Stevens, J., dissenting).

144. Ibid., 2209.

145. Ibid., 2210.

146. *Gluth v. Kangas,* 773 F.Supp. 1309 (D.Ariz. 1988), aff'd, 951 F.2d 1504 (9th Cir. 1991).

147. *Lewis,* 518 U.S. 343, 116 S.Ct., 2209, 2210 (Stevens, J., dissenting).

special master from the *Gluth* case, to consider the parties' request and propose injunctive relief for remedying the constitutional violations. According to Pochoda, *Gluth* was a natural starting point, having been accepted by the Ninth Circuit virtually in its entirety with no further appeal by the defendants.[148] The parties were given six months to propose modification to the *Gluth* injunction (accepted by defendants in 1992, after the Ninth Circuit had affirmed it) in order to allow for differences in prisons within the state.

Instead of working with Pochoda, the defendants filed only insignificant modifications to the *Gluth* order, a number of which Pochoda accepted. Defendants did not argue against any major elements of the injunction, nor did they suggest replacing it with a new order of their own devising.[149] After the comment and objection period had ended, the district court considered and implemented the permanent injunction on October 8, 1993.[150] On December 6, 1993, Janet Bliss, the assistant special master, filed memoranda regarding numerous violations of the injunction. The court asked defendants to respond to alleged violations, warning that if defendants continued to circumvent the injunction, they would be found in contempt.

In an attempt to achieve compliance with the federal court order and to allow defendants to demonstrate progress, the district court ordered defendants to file monthly status reports, beginning January 31, 1994, within which they were to state what had been done, who was in charge of making changes and following up on changes, and attaching copies of policy changes to the report. The district court further ordered the defendants to make the changes requested by the special master by January 31 to show some compliance with the injunction. On January 31, 1994 defendants filed their initial status report, affirming that no policy changes had been made. The court ordered that prior to the February 28, 1994 status report the Department of Corrections post an order in the law libraries stating that the injunction was effective and must be obeyed or contempt could occur and then ordered defendants to take specific actions. On February 28, 1994, the defendants filed a status report and again stated that no policy changes had been made.

Because the defendants had taken no action to implement its

---

148. Interview with Dan Pochoda, Brooklyn, April 14, 1997.

149. Ibid.

150. *Casey v. Lewis*, "Permanent Injunction Access to the Courts Issues," No. CIV 90–0054-PHX-CAM. Pochoda's "Proposed Order" had been submitted July 12, 1993.

injunction, the district court issued an Order to Show Cause on March 3, 1994. The court concluded that, as found by the special master's office, and then acknowledged by Arizona Department of Corrections personnel throughout the state, no compliance would occur in the absence of orders and directives from the director and from the central office in Phoenix. Director Lewis ordered employees not to comply with the permanent injunction until *he* issued policy changes: "In summary, you are to do nothing to implement any portion of *Casey* until you receive direction from this office."[151] Yet, the Department of Corrections never made any attempt to comply with the injunction, and existing DOC legal-access directives and procedures that violated the injunction remained in effect with the director's approval. During the contempt hearings conducted by Pochoda in March 1994, Lewis, displaying indifference and disdain, admitted that he had issued three memos, advising (1) in January, that wardens and employees do nothing to implement any part of the *Casey* order; (2) in February, that employees maintain "security" and "chain of command," and that in doing so they could not be fined or held in contempt, even if following this order involved noncompliance with federal law; and (3) in March, that if held in contempt, their fines would be paid by risk management.[152]

The district court and the Ninth Circuit denied requests by the defendants for a stay of the injunction. The defendants then petitioned the Supreme Court for a hearing, and after the five-day hearing on contempt in March, while the special master awaited transcripts of the hearings, the Supreme Court, in an unusual move, granted a stay. The oral argument was heard before the Supreme Court on November 29, 1995. Seven months later, at the end of June 1996, the Supreme Court answered the question of access to the courts, by substituting a negative obligation for an affirmative duty: going back fifty years to *Ex parte Hull*, which ordered that state officials cannot block an inmate from getting to the courts.[153]

The precedent-setting decision of *Lewis v. Casey* chose form over substance, presenting a juggernaut of past deprivations as models for

---

151. Memorandum from Samuel A. Lewis to all wardens, Re: *Casey v. Lewis:* Legal Access Status, Arizona Department of Corrections, January 5, 1993.

152. *Casey v. Lewis,* "Transcript of Proceedings," No. CIV 90–0054-PHX-CAM, Phoenix, March 31, 1994, 4:5–40.

153. *Ex Parte Hull,* 312 U.S. 546 (1941).

the present. Since the U.S. Supreme Court found the lower court's finding of liability erroneous, the other complaints—such as the breadth or
intrusiveness of Judge Muecke's order—were legally unnecessary but
politically valuable. In light of a particular history, what is only minimally constitutional becomes utterly reasonable. By the time the majority of the Supreme Court justices, in their varying opinions, decided the
case, plans had been laid to gut the already existent libraries in the Arizona prison system and to substitute forms, pencils, and bilingual paralegals for law libraries, legal assistants, and the right to conduct
research or to request the state for assistance.

Scalia, delivering the majority opinion of the Court, disclaimed the
rights or needs of prisoners to discover grievances and to litigate effectively once in court: to "transform themselves," as he put it, "into litigating engines."[154] The majority, which ranged from five to nine justices depending on the issue being considered, based its reversal on the
failure of the court to show widespread actual injury. The expansive
remedy—described as "gross overreaching" by Thomas—should have
been limited only to correcting the inadequacy that caused injury, and
proper deference should have been given to the judgment of prison
officials. In discussing the actual injury requirement, Scalia claimed
that denying an inmate the ability to pursue a "frivolous" claim does
not violate the right of access to the courts. But how can inmates show
that a lawsuit has legal merit when they can no longer perform preliminary research, if they no longer have access to a law library or other
assistance? And who decides, or defines what is meritorious, and
when? As Souter reminded the Court: "Bounds recognized a right of
access for those who seek abdication, not just for sure winners or likely
winners or possible winners."[155]

But as disturbing as the substance of the majority opinion might
be, the style and assumptions of Justice Thomas's concurring opinion
are far more unsettling. The story Thomas relates depends on rituals of
diminution: where the intervention of the law is most required, it will
have the least effect. Suggesting that he has "constitutional text, history, or tradition" on his side, Thomas—through a judicious forgetting
of the local history of *Lewis v. Casey*—produces an image of the prisoner

---

154. *Lewis*, 518 U.S. 343, 116 S.Ct., 2182.
155. Ibid., 2203–4 (Souter, J., joined by Ginsburg and Breyer, concurring in part, dissenting in part, and concurring in the judgment).

that is aligned with that of the poor and disenfranchised. For his defense of the state's obligation to its indigent citizens and to its incarcerated criminals turns on the demolition of those cases, "rooted," as he puts it, "in largely obsolete theories of equal protection."[156] A new tradition is codified by Thomas, and customs made coherent by the mechanisms of state power that he recalls and reclaims.

It took a certain kind of remembrance to engender such a sweeping reassessment of prisoners' relation to and protection by the courts. What Thomas accomplished in his concurring opinion was to prove just how little a prisoner needs access to the courts, implying that the incapacity of criminals to read, to judge, to be heard, is proper, or to put it another way, historically sound. If Thomas succeeds at all in his argument, it is because he locates the historic substance of imprisonment in the slave past, without ever having to mention it.

Pushing his narrative aggressively into the past, Thomas uses a language of ultimate right: his words become vessel of a tradition brought down by a disruptive multitude of criminals filing frivolous lawsuits and an "unbridled" federal judiciary. Thomas summons rites of civility and control to do battle with the onslaught of fanaticism—calling the district court's opinion and order "a striking arrogation of power," the "virtually unbridled equitable power that we have for too long sanctioned."[157] Redefining the past with the help of what he calls "basic common sense" and "a healthy sense of realism," he sets limits to what he sees as the "virtually limitless right" that the decision in *Bounds* permitted.[158] The majority decision "engaged," as Thomas puts it, "in a loose and selective reading of our precedents as it created a freestanding and novel right to state-supported legal assistance, . . . a major departure both from precedent and historical practice."[159]

In his dissent, Justice Stevens returned to the language of the Fourteenth Amendment and summoned the ghost of *Ruffin*, not called by name, but evoked in the phraseology of servitude: "While at least one 19th-century court characterized the inmate as a mere 'slave of the State,' . . . in recent decades this Court has repeatedly held that the convicted felon's loss of liberty is not total. The 'well-established' right of

---

156. Ibid., 2193 (Thomas, J. concurring).
157. Ibid., 2198, 2196.
158. Ibid., 2199, 2197, 2194.
159. Ibid., 2188.

access to the courts . . . is one of these aspects of liberty that States must affirmatively protect."[160] Thomas does not adopt the metaphors of *Ruffin*, turning the laws and regulations of the land into the bars, bolts, and chains of the prison, but the unmentionable ensures that he can accomplish the circumscription of those considered unfit or stigmatized. For those in that narrow circle of the condemned, the "general principles" of the Constitution must be interpreted in a reasonable rather than a literal construction. Thomas extends the rationale of divestment to the indigent as well as the criminal. His new story, really a very old one, suggests that anyone who has no property or who commits a crime, no matter what it is, has forfeited all their claims to an identity that might protect or validate the request for protection. The force of Thomas's argument lies in its step-by-step curtailing of not just the power of the federal courts, but his gutting of those prisoners' rights cases that had provided a bit of liberty for the convicted felon. He celebrates what he calls the "traditional, pre-Bounds view of the law with regard to the State's obligation."[161] In taking away the state's duty to provide libraries—the core of *Bounds*—Thomas returns to a tradition of incapacity or incompetence. The story he tells might be put like this: The presumptive fiction is that inmates are rightfully confined. They have been judged by those empowered to judge, and are incapable of comprehending the law that binds them. Ill equipped to understand what those trained in the legal profession know, it would be unreasonable to give them access to the tools of the trade: law libraries or legal assistance.

While Thomas recalls cases harkening back to what he claims as pre-*Bounds*, overtly claiming a historical record dated as prior to the 1950s, or "the early part of this century," there, is, I suggest, a subtext to this inquiry. The unspoken tradition recalls the civil death of penal servitude, and the gist of that representation lies in the theory and practice of the black codes. Here, the indigent, the criminal, and the slave are joined in, and delimited by, the law. To put it another way, the laws of the state hold the slave, because of absolute necessity, in a degraded state. In this condition, the slave is reared in ignorance. It would thus be unreasonable for a slave to contract legal obligations, to be treated as a competent witness, to be party in a lawsuit, to contract into matrimony—in other words, to have access to the courts.

---

160. Ibid., 2206 (Stevens, J., dissenting).
161. Ibid., 2195 (Thomas, J., concurring).

Now, although Thomas says he agrees with providing prisoners what the Constitution minimally allows—right of access to the courts—the substance of his opinion, and the lower court decisions he invokes, eliminates that right. "Whether to expend state resources to facilitate prisoner lawsuits is a question of policy and one that the Constitution leaves to the discretion of the States."[162] No one can actively stand in the way of an inmate lodging a claim in a court, but this negative obligation removes what it seems to grant. For how, in the absence of assistance, can illiterate inmates articulate their complaints to the courts? Such apparently "trivial" violations, in Thomas's words, such as photocopying access, even paper, pens, and stamps, can effectively prevent prisoners from filing even habeas petitions. Further, since prisons "are inherently dangerous institutions," Thomas restricts the rights of the most restricted inmates. He suggests that alleged violations for inmates in lockdown, those most isolated and often most in need of pursuing court action, are not only minimal; they are not violations at all.[163]

Although *Bounds* left a number of questions unanswered, Muecke's injunction tried to clarify—even if too minutely—what had been left vague. For Thomas, this case is not only "remarkable," but "alarming."[164] Warning against what he calls "wholesale takeovers of state correctional facilities" by federal district courts,[165] Thomas converts a fundamental right into financial aid. He states at the outset that the case is not about access to the courts, but about how much the Constitution requires a state to spend "or otherwise assist a prisoner's efforts to bring suit against the state and its officials."[166]

The restrictions endorsed by Thomas finally come down to the question of money. Throughout the hearings in the district court, Muecke repeatedly had to remind prison officials and their attorneys that "the cost of protecting a constitutional right cannot justify its total denial." But once within the walls of the prison, expenses are seen as indulgences that must be curbed. Thomas makes impractical the practical exercise of access: " 'prison regulations are not required to provide prisoners with the time, the correspondence privileges . . . materials or

162. Ibid., 2195.
163. Ibid., 2200.
164. Ibid., 2196, 2198.
165. Ibid., 2186.
166. Ibid., 2187.

other facilities'" in order to utilize their access to the courts.[167] When Thomas turns to how prior cases had been "recharacterized almost beyond recognition," he bases that disfigurement on a new right granted prisoners after *Bounds:* "to have the State pay for law libraries or other forms of legal assistance without regard to equality of access."[168] In a prison where discrimination and disadvantage are the rule rather than the exception, Thomas's argument against "absolute equality or precisely equal advantages"[169] becomes the means by which he demolishes *any* chance for *any* prisoner to expect affirmative protection while incarcerated. Instead, in Thomas's prisoner code, the entitlement of rights can only be enforced by the state that has in fact eliminated them.

In June 1997, the Arizona Department of Corrections decided to close thirty-four of the thirty-five libraries in the state by August 4. The library in Central Unit at Florence would remain open, since the 1988 ruling against the state in *Gluth v. Kangas* is still in effect. Instead of publicly announcing the closures, Director of Corrections Terry Stewart issued a memo on June 2 to inmates, explaining that he would be "implementing Department Order 902 which completely revamps and streamlines inmate access to the courts." He affirmed that "the law libraries are being eliminated because the U.S. Supreme Court has said that they are not required for inmate legal access."[170]

Taking the lead from Thomas's narrative of forfeiture, Stewart returns to an anachronistic and mandatory deprivation of rights, privileges, and capacities. "Insight," the "Legal Issues" section of *Directions,* the official newsletter of the Arizona Department of Corrections, clarifies the "salient features of the new system": The new inmate legal access to court system will be a 'fact-based system,' with heavy reliance on 'forms' rather than a generalized legal research system with heavy reliance on law books." The concept of indigency, "in respect to this inmate access to court system, is essentially eliminated. All inmates, regardless of financial status, will have to pay for the photocopying of

---

167. Ibid., 2196, quoting *Lee v. Tahash,* 352 F.2d 970, 973 (8th Cir. 1965).

168. Ibid., 2190.

169. Ibid., 2191, quoting *San Antonio Independent School Dist. v. Rodriguez,* 411 U.S. 1, 24 (1973).

170. "Inmate Legal Access to the Courts," memorandum from Terry L. Stewart, director, Arizona Department of Corrections, to all inmates, June 2, 1997.

both their legal and non-legal documents and will also have to pay for their legal supplies."[171] Forms substitute for libraries, and paralegals, contracted by the Department of Corrections, replace inmate legal assistants. Telephone calls to attorneys on nonrecorded lines are eliminated, and photocopying of legal documents—for which inmates pay—are controlled and monitored.[172]

In addition to eliminating law libraries, Department Order 902 establishes 226 new rules governing court access. Paralegals provide assistance for filling out "forms" for the initial filing of "qualified legal claims." Only direct appeals from current conviction, habeas and section 1983 cases, determined to be "non-frivolous," are considered "qualified legal claims." But without access to research cases cited in opposition motions and briefs, how can prisoner-plaintiffs defend their claims? The request for a paralegal is given to designated staff, who may be defendants named in the claims. Department Order 902 also targets jailhouse lawyers and bans "all formal use of Inmate Legal Assistants and Law Clerks."[173]

These devices, coupled with the increasing subordination of the judiciary to the wishes of prison authorities, work to fashion the novel rudiments of civil death in Arizona. From 1864 (the first territorial legislative assembly) until 1977, the state's civil death and disability statute meant that imprisonment for life deprived the prisoner of "all civil rights," without specifying which rights were affected. The statute commanded forfeiture of "public offices and private trusts, authority,

---

171. *Directions*, May 1997, 5.

172. Monitored by ADOC staff, phone calls are tape-recorded and limited to fifteen minutes. All outgoing mail must be inspected by ADOC staff before it is sealed. The cost of photocopies has doubled to ten cents a page. The fee for a notary is one dollar, whereas before notary services were free. The average pay for Arizona prisoners able to work is eighteen dollars a month, from which prisoners must purchase their hygiene items, writing materials, and three-dollar medical copayments.

Two prisoners at the Arizona State Prison in Florence filed lawsuits contesting the contracted paralegals and photocopying monitoring. On July 1, 1997, District Judge Roger Strand dismissed the plaintiff's legal-access claims, a ruling that, according to *Prison Legal News*, October 1997, "essentially closed the book on *Lewis*."

173. See O'Neil Stough, "Experiment in Access: Law Libraries Eliminated in Arizona Prisons," *Prison Legal News*, October 1997, 1–3. For an update on fraud and mismanagement in the contract paralegal system, see "Arizona DOC Paralegal Fraud: Law Libraries Closed, Replaced by Scam Artists," *Prison Legal News*, October 1998, 1–4.

or power."[174] In the same year that *Bounds* determined that prisoners must have "meaningful" access to the courts, the state legislature repealed the civil-death statute and replaced it with a new statute of civil-right loss. The fiction of a coherent legal order has now broadened the scope of the penal law, extending the range of disabilities once imposed by the civil-death statute. Although the statutory provisions relating to civil death have been removed, the retroactive orders of the Arizona Department of Corrections have disabled *all* prisoners incarcerated in the state prison system.

Though repealed, the Arizona civil-death statute has returned under cover of *Lewis v. Casey*. The statute deprived prisoners of the right to be a plaintiff in a civil action, when the cause of action arises during imprisonment. Prisoners could not sue civilly to protect their property, to enforce contracts, to dissolve their marriages, or for any other reason. Department Order 902, which imposes disabilities without any statutory basis, disqualifies claims that include divorce proceedings, probate, child custody matters, wills, civil-property matters, disciplinary infractions, and a number of other significant legal issues. The redefinition, or rather curtailing, of procedures for photocopying legal materials, the monitoring of attorney phone calls and legal mail, as well as the obvious incapacity resulting from lack of access to legal materials such as federal or state case law reporters or annotated statutory material, amount to nothing less than depriving prisoners of their due-process rights, rendering them "dead in law."

The formal appearances of the rule of law have energized the maintenance of a servile order, now unmoored from its racialized episteme in order to resurface, transmuted, under guise of an essentialized criminal agency. Once those incarcerated are circumscribed by lack and characterized by their disregard for property, life, or rules of order, they have entered the purgatory of civil death, embodied as "a creature of law."[175] The rubric of penal legality has kept civil death alive in the United States; at least, its terms underwrite the network of images that sustain such antinomies as civility and brutality, ability and deficiency, natural and unnatural: the rules for a modern concept of servility. This working strategy of domination and control, producing noncitizens

---

174. *Arizona Revised Statutes*, 43–6116 (1939). See Danny E. Adams, "Arizona's Living Dead: Civil Death and Disabilities in Arizona, *Arizona State Law Journal* 137 (1975): 137–53.

175. *Holmes v. King*, 113 So. 274, 276 (1927).

outside the bounds of society, has proved too powerful an apparatus to lose. The rules for turning a person into a thing, the production of chattel slavery so crucial to the redefinition of criminality, were prepared for by the terminology of civil death: the connection between the condition of *being attainted* and *having in law stained and corrupted blood*. From the false derivation, corruption of blood became the essence of attainder, which would be identified as the stain or taint of a convicted felon.[176]

Nearly two years ago, before I was told not to speak to prisoners, an inmate told me that he could no longer be called by his first name. Instead, a new regulation had ordered officers to address inmates as "Mr. Jones" or "Inmate Jones." As he put it: "We're being turned into pieces of furniture. This creates lots of hostility. We don't like being a capital piece of furniture."[177] In order to legitimize the relations of domination in the prison, human beings must continually be reduced to pieces of property. With the decision in *Lewis v. Casey*, the Supreme Court gave the Department of Corrections more than it had asked for: the right to do away with the only sanctum of learning left in the prison. After the books had been sold or destroyed and the librarians fired, an officer confided to me: "Prisoners don't have any rights. They don't need books, and they certainly don't need to waste time filing suits and wasting our money."[178] I could only answer, "Reason not the need."

---

176. Current correctional policy and the legal decisions that support the continued disenfranchisement of convicted felons amount to nothing less than the most radical redefinition of personhood and property since slavery in the Americas. In October 1998, Human Rights Watch and The Sentencing Project published *Losing the Vote: The Impact of Felony Disenfranchisement Laws in the United States*, 1–2, which explicitly links "civil death" and contemporary disenfranchisement laws "that may be unique in the world": "in fourteen states even ex-offenders who have fully served their sentences remain barred for life from voting." The impact of these laws in the United States is shocking: "an estimated 3.9 million U.S. citizens are disenfranchised, including over one million who have fully completed their sentences. . . . Thirteen percent of African American men—1.4 million—are disenfranchised, representing just over one-third (36 percent) of the total disenfranchised population."

177. Interview with inmate (name withheld), Arizona State Prison Complex, Florence, April 5, 1996.

178. Interview with officer (name withheld), Arizona State Prison Complex, Florence, November 15, 1997.

Stigmas, Badges, and Brands: Discriminating Marks in Legal History

Brook Thomas

This history contains one clear lesson. Under our Constitution, the government may never act to the detriment of a person solely because of that person's race. The color of a person's skin and the country of his origin are immutable facts that bear no relation to ability, disadvantage, moral culpability, or any other characteristic of constitutionally permissible interest to government. . . . In short, racial discrimination is by definition invidious discrimination. The rule cannot be any different when the persons injured by a racially biased law are not members of a racial minority.

> Justice Stewart, dissenting in a
> 1979 Supreme Court
> case upholding a federal affirmative
> action program in the construction industry

I never thought that I would live to see the day when the city of Richmond, Virginia, the cradle of the Old Confederacy, sought on its own, within a narrow confine, to lessen the stark impact of persistent discrimination. But Richmond, to its great credit, acted. Yet this Court, the supposed bastion of equality, strikes down Richmond's efforts as though discrimination never existed or was not demonstrated in this particular litigation. Justice Marshall convincingly discloses the fallacy and shallowness of that approach. History is irrefutable, even though one might sympathize with those who—though possibly innocent in themselves—benefit from the wrongs of past decades.

> Justice Blackmun, dissenting in a
> 1988 Supreme Court
> case prohibiting a local affirmative
> action program in the construction industry

I

In his infamous opinion in *Dred Scott* Justice Roger Brooke Taney
denied United States citizenship to all blacks, free or slave. Various discriminatory legislation enacted by states against free blacks had, he
claimed, "stigmatized" them by impressing upon them "deep and
enduring marks of inferiority and degradation." Since there was only
one class of citizens in a republic and since, at the moment of founding,
states had "deemed it just and necessary thus to stigmatize" those of
African descent, they were excluded from the community that originally constituted the sovereign people of the nation.[1]

Dred Scott of course caused immediate controversy, and it is probably the most condemned decision in Supreme Court history. If Taney
claimed that blacks had been stigmatized, Chief Justice Charles Evans
Hughes implied that Taney's decision had stigmatized the Court when
in a memorable phrase he called it one of the Court's "self inflicted
wounds."[2] As condemned as it was, however, federal judge John Minor
Wisdom argued in 1968 that it was not until *Brown v. Board of Education*
that *Dred Scott* was "erased." In saying that *Brown* finally erased *Dred*
Judge Wisdom did not mean that in *1984*-fashion *Dred* had been
deposited in a "memory hole" and lost from human record. Instead he
meant that only with *Brown* were blacks no longer treated by the law as
" 'beings of an inferior race'—the *Dred Scott* article of faith."[3]

But Judge Wisdom might have been a bit hasty in his pronouncement. Derrick A. Bell Jr. has noted that *Dred* is "the most frequently
overturned decision in history."[4] Judge Wisdom's announcement was
perhaps one more in a long history of claims that *Dred* has been over-

---

1. 19 How. 393 at 416 (1857).
2. Charles Evans Hughes, *The Supreme Court of the United States* (New York: Columbia University Press, 1928), 50. Hughes of course was not the first to argue that *Dred* had
hurt the credibility of the Court. For instance, in 1898 D. P. Baldwin listed *Dred* along with
the legal-tender cases, the income tax case, and the *Slaughter House* case as the most
important "blunders" of the Court. *Dred*, he argued, was a "monstrous" decision,
"honey-combed with the virus of slavery" "Some Blunders of the United States Supreme
Court," *Indiana Law Journal* 2 [1898]: 97). Hughes's phrase captured more people's attention in part because of Hughes's importance and in part, no doubt, because of the appro-
priateness of his image for a decision concerned with the power of marking.
3. Quoted in Don E. Fehrenbacher, *The Dred Scott Case* (New York: Oxford University Press, 1978), 582.
4. Derrick A. Bell Jr., ed., *Race, Racism, and American Law* (Boston: Little, Brown,
1973), 21.

turned.[5] For instance, in the same year that Judge Wisdom made his remark Justice Douglas observed, "Some badges of slavery remain today. While the institution has been outlawed, it has remained in the minds and hearts of many white men. Cases which have come to this Court depict a spectacle of slavery unwilling to die."[6] Since slavery contributed to the country's racism, is it possible that *Dred*'s article of faith has not been completely erased even today?

A symptom of the extent to which the law is still in the wake of *Dred* is how both sides of the affirmative action debate focus on the potential for racial classifications to stigmatize. Writing for the four justices in *Bakke* who defended the affirmative action admission's policy of the University of California, Davis, Medical School, Justice Brennan cited "the cardinal principle" that racial classifications that are prohibited are those that "stigmatize" because "they are drawn on the presumption that one race is inferior to another or because they put the weight of government behind racial separation and separatism."[7] Nonetheless, he believed that "benign" racial classifications exist that do not necessarily stigmatize because their purpose is to achieve long-term racial equality and harmony.

Brennan did not rule out a risk of stigmatization. For instance, he admitted that race, like "gender-based classification[,] too often [has] been inexcusably utilized to stereotype and stigmatize politically powerless segments of society." He also admitted that "State programs designed to ameliorate the effects of past discrimination obviously create the same hazard of stigma, since they may promote racial separatism and reinforce the views of those who believe that members of racial minorities are inherently incapable of succeeding on their own." Nonetheless, he believed that a "carefully tailored" policy could "avoid these vices."[8] In contrast, opponents of affirmative action programs

---

5. Fully aware of the difference in racial attitudes between members of the *Brown* Court and Justice Taney, Judge Richard A. Posner notes that by thrusting the Court into the "midst of a power struggle between the southern and nonsouthern states" *Brown* in this limited sense "could be thought a reprise of the Dred Scott decision." *Overcoming Law* (Cambridge: Harvard University Press, 1995), 63.

6. *Jones v. Mayer Co.*, 392 U.S. 409 at 445 (1968).

7. *Regents of the University of California v. Bakke*, 438 U.S. 265 at 357–58 (1977).

8. *Bakke*, 360. Brennan's comments on stigma are similar to one he made in *United Jewish Organizations v. Carey*, 430 U.S. 144, 173–74: "Even preferential treatment may act to stigmatize its recipient groups, for although intended to correct systemic or institutional inequities, such a policy may imply to some the recipients' inferiority and especial need for protection."

deny the possibility of avoiding stigma. For instance, in the recent *Hopwood* case, in which the United States Court of Appeals for the Fifth Circuit invalidated the University of Texas Law School's affirmative action admission's policy, the court cites Professor William Van Alstyne's claim that "a new badge of implied inferiority" results as "an incident of governmental noblesse oblige" when programs involve lower and separate standard's of selection.[9] The *Hopwood* court does not go as far as some opponents and argue for a "color-blind" Constitution that would forbid all racial classifications, but it does dramatically limit the situations in which affirmative action programs are allowed.

Supporters of affirmative action often accuse opponents of ignoring the consequences of a history of legally sanctioned racial discrimination. But as my opening quotations indicate, people on both sides of the affirmative action debate enlist history for their cause. For instance, in *Maryland Trooper's Association v. Evans*, judges in the Fourth Circuit insist, "The case against race-based preferences does not rest on the sterile assumption that American society is untouched or unaffected by the tragic oppression of its past. Rather, it is the very enormity of that tragedy that lends resolve to the desire to never repeat it, and [to] find a legal order in which distinctions based on race will have no place."[10]

In this essay I will look at the history the Court's use of metaphors of racial marking in order to provide insight into how both sides of the affirmative action debate claim the authority of history. I also hope to suggest possible connections between the Court's use of history and its use of those metaphors. I will end with speculation on their effectiveness for people intent on evoking history to defend the goals of affirmative action.

II

Alfred H. Kelly identifies various uses of history by the Supreme Court. The two most obvious are the appeal to precedent and the examination of circumstances surrounding earlier judicial expositions of the law. To these two Kelly adds two more: "the creation of history a priori by what may be called 'judicial fiat' or 'authoritative revelation'" and "resort to

---

9. William Van Alstyne, "Rites of Passage: Race in the Supreme Court, and the Constitution," *University of Chicago Law Review* 46 (1979): 787 n. 38.

10. 993 F.2d 1072 at 1079 (4th Cir. 1993).

the extended essay in constitutional history."[11] Both of these allow the Court to claim historical constancy while in fact allowing for innovation.

The need for history by simple fiat, according to Kelly, "arose out of the all but universal assumption throughout the entire history of the Court, at least until very recently, that the Constitution was a static instrument whose absolute meaning did not change, but from which derivative truths unfolded through judicial exposition in particular cases." By simply declaring original intent the "Court could maintain with a minimum of difficulty the myth of historical continuity, i.e., the conception of an essentially static and absolute Constitution. . . . In a sense, by quoting history, the Court made history, since what it declared history to be was frequently more important than what the history might actually have been."[12] The primary use of the extended historical essay, Kelly claims, has been to challenge existing precedent by purporting to "return to the aboriginal meaning of the Constitution." Drawing on historical evidence "far beyond the narrow confines of judicial precedent," the Court used an appeal to history "to achieve a paradox: breaking precedence while rendering obeisance to the doctrine of constitutional continuity."[13]

This paradox is similar to one identified by Owen Barfield in an essay called "Poetic Diction and Legal Fiction." In a strict sense, Barfield notes, law should have no history. "It is the very essence of law that it should apply to every case. . . . If there is a different law for every case that arises, then what is being administered is simply not law at all but the arbitrary (though not necessarily unjust) decisions of those who govern us. But that is exactly what the law *means*—something which will be *the same* for the next case as it was for the last." Law's need to remain the same, Barfield claims, comes into conflict with its social function "to serve, to express, and indeed partly to *make* the social life of the community." Whereas law is supposedly unvarying, life varies. How can an institution that is supposed to apply the same in every case serve life that constantly changes? One answer is legislation, which explicitly alters the body of law. The other, according to Barfield, is fic-

---

11. Alfred H. Kelly, "Clio and the Court: An Illicit Love Affair," *Supreme Court Review* (1965): 122.

12. Kelly, "Clio and the Court," 122 and 123.

13. Kelly, "Clio and the Court," 126.

tion. Barfield quotes Sir Henry Maine's *Ancient Law:* "Without the Fiction of Adoption . . . it is difficult to understand how Society would ever have escaped from its swaddling clothes." As Maitland put it, legal fictions allow the law "to get modern results out of medieval premises."[14]

What Barfield does not note is that judges can solve the paradox that he identifies by generating new interpretations of existing legal documents, like the Constitution. Kelly shows that the Court can do so by using history; I want to show that it can do the same through using metaphor. Indeed, the history of the Court's use of metaphors of marking reveals one of its most interesting uses of history: one that changes the course of legal history without explicitly evoking it. That metaphor can be used this way should not be surprising when we remember that Barfield evokes legal fictions to illuminate the working of poetic diction, which, because of its metaphoric nature, has been called the language of paradox.[15] Metaphor, as we shall see, allows for innovative interpretations that paradoxically claim to stay true to the meaning of the text at hand. It does so in two ways. First, precisely because the meaning of metaphors is more suggestive than fixed, judges can interpret them innovatively. Second, judges can use metaphors in their decisions as a way of giving new meaning to precedent while continuing to honor it.

But if metaphor allows for innovation, it also helps to explain the difficulty in "erasing" *Dred Scott.* Strategic use of metaphor can help alter the course of legal history, but metaphors, like that of stigmatization, give the law a sort of memory that cannot simply be erased. Thus it should come as no surprise that the history of attempts to get out from under the history of racial discrimination is marked by metaphors from the history that it would escape. But to get to that part of my story, I have to start at the beginning.

III

My starting point is Taney's use of the metaphor of stigma in *Dred Scott.* Although my story begins here, Taney made no inaugural claim for his

---

14. Owen Barfield, "Poetic Diction and Legal Fiction," in *Essays Presented to Charles Williams* (New York: Oxford University Press, 1947), 122–23 and 124.

15. Cleanth Brooks, "The Language of Paradox," in *The Well Wrought Urn* (New York: Harcourt, Brace and World, 1947), 3–21.

opinion. On the contrary, he produced a prime example of what Kelly calls the Court's use of the extended historical essay. Taney used history to turn the Constitution's distinction between free and slave into one between white and black. Attacks on his use of history began with Justice Curtis's dissent and culminated with Don E. Fehrenbacher's exhaustive exposure of Taney's flawed use of historical evidence. A strategic flaw had to do with his use of metaphor.

It is commonplace to argue that Taney's decision helped to bring about the Civil War. But Taney by no means wanted to feed sectional conflict.[16] To be sure, he was intent on defending a southern point of view. It is also likely, as Fehrenbacher claims, that he wrote the decision in anger against antislavery sentiment. He did not, however, want to divide the nation. Why, then, did he choose metaphors that were bound to evoke one of the most commonplace images in abolitionist rhetoric: marks left on the slave's body by brands and the slaveowner's lash? In *Uncle Tom's Cabin,* for instance, Harriet Beecher Stowe uses the scars on both George Harris's and Roxy's bodies as emblems for the horrors of slavery. Taney's metaphor could easily have seemed to antislavery forces a callous endorsement of slavery's inhumanity.

Taney's metaphor might have fed sectional antagonism, but it was not, I suspect, chosen without reflection. Very likely he was attempting a subtle appropriation of abolitionist rhetoric. For abolitionists those stigmatized were not the blacks who bore marks, but the whites who produced them. In turn, Southerners resented being declared morally inferior by people who espoused the equality of man. As Justice Daniel wrote Martin Van Buren in 1847, for many Northerners, Southerners carried a "moral taint" that signaled their "degrading inequality or inferiority."[17] Taney's metaphor challenged that northern assumption. Pointing to northern laws denying free blacks equal political and civil rights, Taney implied that legislative acts of North and South alike were more important in marking blacks as inferior than the lashes of slaveholders.

Taney's strategy backfired. Even so, his metaphor of stigma marked the body of American law in such a way that anyone hoping to overcome the effects of his opinion had to reckon with it. Trying to balance a history of oppression, reformers fashioned the Thirteenth, Four-

---

16. Fehrenbacher, *The Dred Scott Case,* 561–67. Fehrenbacher notes that Taney's role in actually causing the war is sometimes overexaggerated.

17. Fehrenbacher, *The Dred Scott Case,* 561.

teenth, and Fifteenth Amendments with Taney's decision and other repressive acts in mind. In Senate debates Lyman Trumbull of Illinois alluded to the 1850 Fugitive Slave Law when he noted, "Surely we have the authority to enact a law as efficient in the interests of freedom, now that freedom prevails throughout the country, as we had in the interest of slavery when it prevailed in a portion of the country."[18] Another senator found "poetic justice" in using constitutional powers previously used to support slavery to support the rights of freedmen.[19]

The most obvious way in which the Thirteenth Amendment attempted to balance the wrongs of the past was to eliminate slavery. But for some of its supporters it went further. If Taney had used a flawed account of history to establish precedent for a constitutional distinction between blacks and whites, there were those who argued that fully to eliminate slavery the Thirteenth Amendment also had to undo that distinction. In order to do so it had to remove the marks of stigma that Taney claimed were impressed upon all "of those persons who are the descendants of Africans who were imported into this country, and sold as slaves."[20]

Soon after the amendment was passed Justice Swayne on circuit in *United States v. Rhodes* nullified a Kentucky law that forbade blacks from offering testimony adverse to whites. "Slaves," he wrote, "were imperfectly, if at all protected from the grossest outrages by the whites. Justice was not for them. The charities and rights of the domestic relations had no legal existence among them. The shadow of the evil fell upon the free blacks. They had but few civil and no political rights in the slave states. Many of the badges of the bondman's degradation were fastened upon them. Their condition, like his, though not so bad, was helpless and hopeless."[21] According to this precedent the Thirteenth Amendment called for the elimination, not only of slavery, but also of all badges of slavery and servitude. In Senate debates over the 1866 Freedman's Bureau Bill and Civil Rights Act, Trumbull labeled all legislation unfriendly to blacks a "badge of servitude."[22]

---

18. Quoted in Robert J. Kaczorowski, "To Begin the Nation Anew: Congress, Citizenship, and Civil Rights after the Civil War," *American Historical Review* 92 (1987): 59.

19. Quoted in Charles Fairman, *Reconstruction and Reunion, 1865–1888*, vol. 6. of *History of the Supreme Court of the United States*, Oliver Wendell Holmes Devise (New York: Macmillan, 1971), 1170.

20. *Dred Scott*, 403.

21. Quoted in Harold M. Hyman and William M. Wiecek, *Equal Justice under Law* (New York: Harper and Row, 1982), 505.

22. Fairman, *Reconstruction and Reunion*, 1165 and 1173.

Swayne and Trumbull took clear aim at Taney's declaration of African inferiority, but they also agreed with him on an important point. For them, as for Taney, the institution of slavery marked not only slaves but also free blacks. To be sure, Swayne made a few important distinctions. One of Taney's most controversial claims was that when the Constitution was written blacks were considered so inferior that "they had *no* rights which the white man was bound to respect" and that "This opinion was at that time fixed and universal in the civilized portion of the white race."[23] Swayne declared that free blacks had but *"few* civil and no political rights in the *slave states"* (emphasis added). In confining his remark to the slave states, Swayne was guilty of a bit of northern bias, since he ignored how many northern states also restricted the rights of blacks. Nonetheless, by indirectly acknowledging that even in slave states free blacks had a "few" civil rights, he undercut a crucial part of Taney's argument.

But Swayne's use of metaphor was even more important than his use of "few." For Taney slavery stigmatized even free blacks by *marking* them as inferior and degraded. In contrast, Swayne described how the bondman's badges of degradation had been *fastened upon* free blacks. *Stigma* is related to the Greek *stizein,* meaning to prick or mark. Originally it was a brand made with a burning iron upon criminals or slaves. From this use it took on the meaning of a mark of infamy or disgrace.[24] A badge is also a distinctive mark, but one that is worn rather than incorporated into the body. By using the metaphor of a badge Swayne disputed Taney's claim that the stigmatizing marks of slavery were "deep and enduring" and implied instead that they could be removed. Indeed, whereas Swayne along with Taney acknowledged that slavery affected people's attitudes toward free blacks, for him it did so by casting a "shadow" of "evil." Shadows can temporarily mark a body by covering it, but they do not create permanent scars. For Taney the institution of slavery had so marked the body of blacks that even the status of freedom could not eliminate their stigma of inferiority; for Swayne, once slavery had been eliminated, the Court's job was to guarantee complete emancipation by removing the lingering effects of the institution's "shadows."

If the Court had rigorously enforced Swayne's interpretation of the Thirteenth Amendment, we would have a very different history. But it

---

23. *Dred Scott,* 407.

24. A famous study of stigma is Erving Goffman, *Stigma: Notes on the Management of Spoiled Identity* (Englewood Cliffs, N.J.: Prentice-Hall, 1963).

did not, which is one reason why the Fourteenth Amendment has taken on more and more importance. In one respect, however, the Fourteenth Amendment is more limited than the Thirteenth. The last three clauses of Section 1 of the Fourteenth Amendment—the privileges and immunities, the due process, and the equal protection clauses—prohibit state action, not actions by private citizens or the federal government. The Thirteenth Amendment does not have this limitation. Thus, if it had been interpreted inclusively, it would have given the federal government much more power to prohibit discriminatory acts linked to the heritage of slavery by all parties.[25]

This latter limit is illustrated by *Civil Rights Cases* (1883), in which by an eight to one majority the Court declared unconstitutional the 1875 Civil Rights Act that forbade many acts of discrimination by private citizens. Writing for the Court, Justice Bradley ruled that the act overstepped federal authority since the Fourteenth Amendment confined itself to state action. He acknowledged that the Thirteenth Amendment had no such limit; nonetheless, he refused to accept a Thirteenth Amendment defense of the act. Mere discrimination based on color, he argued, did not stamp blacks with a badge of servitude linked to the institution of slavery since free blacks in the antebellum period had also experienced discrimination. Declaring an end to what he saw as the federal government's paternal protection of blacks, he pronounced, "When a man has emerged from slavery, and by aid of beneficent legislation has shaken off the inseparable concomitants of that state, there must be some stage in the progress of his elevation when he takes the ranks of a mere citizen, and ceases to be the special favorite of the law, and when his rights as a citizen or a man are to be protected in the ordinary modes by which other men's rights are protected."[26]

Bradley's attempt to end the "paternal" protection of blacks is notable for ignoring the historical condition of blacks. For him a mere eighteen years after the end of slavery, blacks were supposed to give up their position of "special favorites of the law" and take their place as

---

25. Another possible authority for federal protection against acts of discrimination by individuals was the Civil Rights Act of 1866. But the Court began to interpret it retrospectively through the Fourteenth Amendment to apply to state action only. See Barry Sullivan, "Historical Reconstruction, Reconstruction History, and the Proper Scope of Section 1981," *Yale Law Journal* 98 (1989): 541–64; and Robert J. Kaczorowski, "The Enforcement Provision of the Civil Rights Act of 1866: A Legislative History in Light of *Runyan v. McCrary*," *Yale Law Review* 98 (1989): 565–95.

26. 109 U.S. 3 at 13 and 25 (1883).

equals in United States society. Nonetheless, his opinion was not devoid of other appeals to history. Like Taney and Swayne before him, he admitted that free blacks as well as slaves were discriminated against in the antebellum period. But he used that historical fact to different effect. As we have seen, in order to give an expansive interpretation of the Thirteenth Amendment Swayne needed substantially to agree with Taney that the institution of slavery had marked free blacks as inferior and degraded. Their metaphors for those marks were different—badges rather than stigmas—but the link between racial discrimination and slavery was accepted by both. In contrast, Bradley's narrow interpretation depended on offering an account of racial discrimination directly at odds with Taney's. For him discrimination against free blacks in the antebellum period was not linked to slavery. Because it was not, mere discrimination against blacks after emancipation could not be connected to the Thirteenth Amendment's prohibition against slavery or involuntary servitude.

The *Civil Rights Cases,* therefore, have a disconcerting lesson for those who think that issues of racial politics can be resolved by an appeal to history. It would be comforting to think that, if we could only agree on what happened in the past, we would know how to act in the present. In fact the past tends to suggest that shared agreement about it does not necessarily result in shared agreement about present politics. Indeed, in the years after the Civil War progressive racial politics on the Court seemed to depend on agreement with Taney's link between racial discrimination and slavery—as in the case of Swayne—rather than disagreement with it—as in the case of Bradley. This irony is played out again in the notorious case of *Plessy v. Ferguson.*

IV

In upholding the constitutionality of a "separate but equal" law, the majority in *Plessy* was accused by Justice John Marshall Harlan, the lone dissenter, of rendering a decision "as pernicious as the decision made by this tribunal in the *Dred Scott case.*"[27] Harlan's *Plessy* dissent repeated a number of points that he made as the lone dissenter in the *Civil Rights Cases.* Like Swayne thirty years earlier, Harlan wrote with *Dred Scott* clearly in mind. Also like Swayne, he assented in part to Taney's description of the historical situation of blacks. Echoing

---

27. 163 U.S. 537 at 559 (1896).

Swayne's echo of Taney, he noted that prior to the Civil War, "colored people had very few rights that the dominant race felt obliged to protect."[28] The purpose of the Civil War amendments, he asserted, was to "eradicate" *Dred Scott*'s principle of racial superiority from the law. They did so when they "obliterated the race line from our governmental systems."[29] By maintaining that line the Louisiana law perpetuated *Dred Scott*'s principle of white supremacy.

Harlan's dissent has so much moral force that most today unquestionably accept his historical narrative that sees *Plessy* as an extension of the logic of *Dred Scott*. Insofar as *Plessy* legitimated a system that assumed the superiority of the white race, he was certainly right. The Court should have been able to see through what Harlan called the "thin disguise" of the law's guarantee of equal accommodations and recognize its assumption of white superiority. Nonetheless, the fact that the framers of the law had to resort to this disguise suggests that the legal principles upheld by the Court were different from those of *Dred Scott*, which straightforwardly declared the inferiority of blacks. Certainly, members of the majority did not feel that they were perpetuating *Dred*'s logic. Neither did the many people between *Plessy* and *Brown*, like Justice Hughes, who condemned *Dred* but not *Plessy*. To make this point is not to condone the principles upheld by *Plessy*. We should, however, try to understand them. We can do so by turning to the writings of Justice Horace Gray, a member of the majority in both the *Civil Rights Cases* and *Plessy*.

Gray had made a name for himself at the age of twenty-nine by writing a devastating criticism of Taney's use of history to support his *Dred Scott* decision. Born in Massachusetts, Gray was especially intent on challenging Taney's claim that at its founding as a state (not a colony) Massachusetts denied citizenship to blacks. Gray in part based his argument on his knowledge of the Massachusetts constitution. But he also took issue with Taney's claim that a Massachusetts antimiscegenation law marked blacks as inferior and thus denied them citizenship. The law, Gray argued, was not a sign of degradation, but simply a "prohibition founded on purely physiological grounds."[30]

---

28. *Plessy*, 563.

29. *Plessy*, 560 and 563.

30. Horace Gray, *A Legal Review of the Case of Dred Scott as Decided by the Supreme Court of the United States from the Law Reporter for June, 1857* (Boston: Crosby, Nichols, 1857), 15.

Although Harlan accuses the *Plessy* majority of perpetuating *Dred Scott*, Justice Henry Billings Brown's opinion relies on Gray's, not Taney's, view of antebellum Massachusetts legislation. For instance, wondering why Plessy depended so much on the Thirteenth Amendment, Brown, sounding very much like Gray in his refutation of Taney, claimed that "A statute which implies merely a legal distinction between the white and colored races—a distinction which is founded in the color of the two races, and which must always exist so long as white men are distinguished from the other race by color—has no tendency to destroy the legal equality of the two races, or reëstablish a state of involuntary servitude."[31] From the Court's point of view, to ask legislatures to ignore natural differences based on color would be to ask too much. "Legislation," declared Brown, "is powerless to eradicate racial instincts or to abolish distinctions based upon physical difference."[32] All that the Court could do was to make certain that in recognizing this natural difference states did not violate the equal political and civil rights of any group.

To be sure, Brown did not completely rule out the possibility of racial inferiority. "If one race be inferior to the other socially," he concluded, careful not to designate which race he had in mind, "the Constitution of the United States cannot put them upon the same plane."[33] But for the Court, enforcement of social equality, unlike that of political and civil equality, was beyond the scope of governmental powers. "In the nature of things" the Fourteenth Amendment could "not have been intended to abolish distinctions based upon color" or to "enforce social, as distinguished from political equality."[34] Although Brown admitted that one group might be socially inferior to the other, he also made clear that, if such inferiority existed, it should not be attributed to the law in question. The "underlying fallacy" of Plessy's argument, he wrote, consisted in the "assumption that the enforced separation of the two races stamps the colored race with a badge of inferiority. If this be so, it is not by reason of anything found in the act, but solely because the colored race chooses to put that construction upon it."[35]

Such logic was too much for Justice Harlan. Admitting that noth-

---

31. *Plessy*, 543.
32. *Plessy*, 551.
33. *Plessy*, 552.
34. *Plessy*, 544.
35. *Plessy*, 551.

ing in the law explicitly declared the inferiority of blacks, Harlan responded that everyone knew that its real purpose was "not so much to exclude white persons from railroad cars occupied by blacks, as to exclude colored people from coaches occupied by or assigned to white persons."[36] As a result, it did indeed stamp blacks with a badge of inferiority. Our sympathy with Harlan's argument should not, however, blind us to the differences that the *Plessy* Court had with Taney. Those differences force us to distinguish among three positions on the rights afforded to free blacks. All three in turn depend upon different interpretations of the condition of free blacks in the antebellum period.

First, there is Taney's that organically linked discrimination against free blacks with the institution of slavery and declared that all blacks were stigmatized by enduring marks of inferiority. Second, there is Swayne's and Harlan's that, like Taney's, linked discrimination against free blacks to the institution of slavery, but implied that marks of inferiority could and should be removed with the help of the federal government that once lent its support to the institution. Third, there are the majority opinions in both the *Civil Rights Cases* and *Plessy* that implicitly denied Taney's link between slavery and discrimination against free blacks. According to this view, discrimination based on color was not what today the Court would call "invidious" discrimination so long as it had a basis in nature and did not abridge guaranteed political and civil equality. It did not rule out the possibility of invidious discrimination, but it did make its occurrence very difficult to prove. Furthermore, when it occurred between private citizens rather than as the result of state action, its remedy was left up to the states. Indeed, since such discrimination was not linked to the institution of slavery that had received federal support, the federal government had no obligation to stop it.

To identify these three positions is to show how difficult it is to make definitive political judgments based on interpretations of history. For, paradoxically, it was precisely those judges who adopted a view of the past at odds with Taney who hurt the cause of freedmen, while Swayne and Harlan, who accepted a crucial part of Taney's account, promoted it. What is at stake, then, is not a particular interpretation of the past, but the uses that can be put to it. Swayne and Harlan might have agreed with Taney's link between slavery and markings of black

---

36. *Plessy,* 557.

inferiority, but they altered its significance through a creative use of metaphor. By evoking badges rather than stigmas, they could continue to link implications of racial inferiority to slavery while appealing to the Thirteenth Amendment to forbid discrimination of various sorts.

The extent to which Harlan self-consciously appropriated Taney's use of history is indicated by a story told by his wife. Noticing the difficulty that her husband was having composing his dissent in the *Civil Rights Cases*, she placed Taney's inkstand—a prized memento of the couple—in a noticeable position on his desk. Overcoming writer's block, Harlan used Taney's pen, and his dissent began to flow. But Harlan's metaphoric appropriation of Taney's use of history failed. The majority did not endorse Taney's account, but it did subscribe to a view of the past that severely limited the force of the Thirteenth Amendment. Indeed, in his *Civil Rights Cases* dissent Harlan accused the majority of rendering the amendment a "phantom of delusion."[37] Then in 1906, when the Court in *Hodges v. United States* denied Harlan's dissenting claim that freedom from slavery's "incidents or badges" was a universal right guaranteed by the Thirteenth Amendment, the Court stripped it of its potential as a civil rights weapon.[38]

By rendering the Thirteenth Amendment "such a weak reed,"[39] the Court forced those intent upon detecting discrimination to emphasize another set of metaphors. Because legal discrimination was no longer explicit, the problem became one of seeing marks of discrimination through the "thin disguise" of guaranteed equality. As a result, we need to discriminate, not only among the Court's use of metaphors of marking, but also among its metaphors of how to detect such marks, if they exist. In his *Plessy* dissent, for instance, Harlan implied that the Court's vision had been so impaired that it had lost the capacity to see how imposition of the color line continued to mark blacks as inferior. Not to see such marking was to violate the intent of the Constitution, which through the Civil War amendments had overturned Taney's flawed view of the Constitution as perpetuating a division between blacks and whites to create a "color-blind" Constitution.[40]

The metaphor of color-blindness is, of course, a crucial one in pres-

---

37. *Civil Rights Cases*, 34.
38. 203 U.S. 1 at 27 (1906). Harlan was joined in this dissent by Justice William Day.
39. Hyman and Wiecek, *Equal Justice under Law*, 505.
40. *Plessy*, 559.

ent debates about affirmative action.[41] But even before that debate, the question of how to detect the effects of discrimination was central to the landmark case of *Brown v. Board of Education*. Before turning to *Brown*, however, I need to complicate my own account of the history of marking.

So far I have emphasized that those advocating the cause of blacks after the Civil War were able to turn Taney's use of history to their advantage through a strategic use of metaphor that displaced his notion of permanent stigmatization with that of badges of servitude. But it is important to note that some of these same advocates also used the metaphor of "brands." For instance, in his *Plessy* dissent Harlan claimed that the Louisiana law "puts the brand of servitude and degradation upon a large class of our fellow citizens."[42] Plessy's attorney, the lawyer/novelist Albion W. Tourgée, used the same metaphor in his fiction. For instance, in his first novel a mulatto woman passing as white during the Civil War comes upon her wounded master and lover in a prison camp. She nurses him to health, only to have him betray her, when in front of others he adopts the voice of master, which she answers "instantly, with the inimitable and indescribable intonation of the slave: 'Sir?' That was all she said. It was enough. It revealed all. The brand showed."[43] In another Tourgée novel a character proclaims, "Slavery was never half so great a curse as that brand of infamy which stamps the soul at its birth with ineradicable inferiority."[44]

To call marks of discrimination brands rather than badges was to question the possibility of their removal. Indeed, it was to come extremely close to Taney's metaphor of stigmatization, especially when combined with the notion of infamy acquired at birth. Certainly, a brand more than a badge suggested greater difficulty in remedying the effects of discrimination. But it might also have given a more accurate

---

41. On the metaphor of color-blindness, see Andrew Kull, *The Color-Blind Constitution* (Cambridge: Harvard University Press, 1992); Neil Gotanda, "A Critique of 'Our Constitution Is Color-Blind,'" *Stanford University Law Review* 44 (1991): 1–68; and Brook Thomas, *American Literary Realism and the Failed Promise of Contract* (Berkeley and Los Angeles: University of California Press, 1997), 206–7, 332 n. 31, and 332–33 n. 32, and Thomas, ed., *Plessy v. Ferguson: A Brief History with Documents* (Boston: Bedford, 1997), 169–76.

42. *Plessy*, 562.

43. Albion W. Tourgée, *A Royal Gentleman and Zouri's Christmas* (New York: Fords, Howard, and Hulbert, 1881), 78.

44. Albion W. Tourgée, *Pactolus Prime* (New York: Cassell, 1890), 45.

description of the effects that a history of discrimination can have on those discriminated against. In dramatizing psychological effects of discrimination on blacks, Tourgée's examples anticipated W. E. B. Du Bois's famous description of double consciousness, first articulated the year after the *Plessy* decision. A complicated psychological state, double consciousness can lead among others things to a state of interiorized inferiority in blacks forced to measure themselves by the standard of whites who consider them degraded. As dramatized by Tourgée and articulated by Du Bois, it exposed the fallacy in the *Plessy* majority's claim that nothing in the Jim Crow law itself justified Plessy's claim that it marked blacks as inferior. The social and historical conditions into which blacks were born, both writers implied, gave them little choice but to interpret the statute that way. The question of the psychological effects of segregation was crucial to the decision reached in *Brown*, although it no longer used metaphors of badges or brands to detect them.

V

In order to declare school segregation unconstitutional the *Brown* Court faced a major dilemma: *Plessy* had declared that "separate but equal" laws, at least concerning intrastate transportation, violated neither the Thirteenth nor the Fourteenth Amendment. One way that the Court could have overcome precedent while claiming to adhere to it, would have been to use an extended historical essay to claim the authority of original intent. As Kelly points out, the Court seemed poised to adopt that strategy when after an initial hearing it ordered both sides to reargue the case in terms of the intent of the Fourteenth Amendment. But rather than appeal to history, a unanimous Court ruled that it was impossible to determine the intent of the amendment in terms of public education. Nonetheless, it still ruled that, despite the *Plessy* precedent, separate but equal educational facilities violated the equal protection clause of the Fourteenth Amendment.

To prove that equal facilities were not equal was no easy task. The Court did so by using social-science evidence to measure "intangible" factors caused by educational segregation. Even when a state provided equal facilities, the Court concluded, social-science evidence demonstrated that the mere fact of segregation "generates [in black children] a feeling of inferiority as to their status in the community and may affect their hearts and minds in a way unlikely ever to be undone. . . . Whatever may have been the extent of psychological knowledge at the time of *Plessy v. Ferguson*, this finding is amply supported by modern authority. Any language in *Plessy v. Ferguson* contrary to this finding is rejected."[45]

The focus on intangible effects invited the use of metaphor since one function of metaphor is to make visible that which is invisible. Tourgée, for instance, tried precisely this through his metaphor of a soul branded by a mark of infamy. No one can actually see a branded soul, but Tourgée's metaphor called attention to invisible, if important, psychological effects. Nonetheless, nowhere did the Court in *Brown* use metaphors of stigmas, badges, or brands. And for good reason. As we have seen, these metaphors were associated with the Thirteenth Amendment, which played no role in the Court's decision. Instead, it relied solely on the Fourteenth Amendment, the Thirteenth having been rendered ineffectual in civil rights cases by previous decisions.

To be sure, metaphors of marking are not inherently inappropriate for the Fourteenth Amendment. On the contrary, if a law stamps a group with a badge of inferiority, it would seem to violate the equal protection clause. Nonetheless, the most influential law review essay on the equal protection clause before *Brown* did not associate metaphors of marking with it. According to Joseph Tussman and Jacobus tenBroek, the Court could appeal to the clause to invalidate laws as discriminatory if they were "expressions of hostility or antagonism to certain groups."[46] In *Korematsu v. United States,* for instance, the Court had declared that "racial antagonism" can never be a reason for curtailing "the civil rights of a single racial group."[47] Thus, in his concurring opinion in *Oyama v. California* (1948) Justice Murphy called a law restricting aliens' rights to own property an expression of racism as "spawned of the great anti-Oriental virus."[48] If the Court were willing to follow Murphy's lead, Tussman and tenBroek asserted, "it could, no doubt, find that segregation laws aim at white supremacy or are

---

45. *Brown v. Board of Education,* 347 U.S. 483, 494 and 494–95 (1954).
46. Joseph Tussman and Jacobus tenBroek, "The Equal Protection of the Laws," *California Law Review* 37 (1949): 358.
47. 323 U.S. 214 at 216 (1944).
48. 332 U.S. 633 at 651 (1948).

spawned of the great anti-Negro virus and thus make belated amends for the shameful history of the 'separate but equal' evasion."[49] The Court could have followed Murphy's lead, but, as Tussman and tenBroek noted, it was reluctant to do so. Hostility, antagonism, and prejudice raise thorny questions of legislative intent and motive that the Court would just as soon avoid. Instead, it had tended to invalidate discriminatory legislation by "developing a doctrine according to which the equal protection clause is held to prohibit the achievement of certain purposes or ends."[50] True to form, the *Brown* Court avoided speculation about the intent of Jim Crow laws. Instead, it simply stated that segregated schools "generated" in black children a feeling of inferiority. This strategic avoidance would have been impossible if the Court had relied on metaphors of marking.

In his *Plessy* dissent Justice Harlan had claimed to read behind the thin disguise of the guarantee of equality to see the real intent of Jim Crow laws, which, he argued, was to maintain white supremacy. But the *Brown* Court did not follow Harlan's path. One reason why it did not is clearly stated by Judge Richard Posner. "It would have been awkward," Posner notes, "for a court, especially a federal court dominated

---

49. Tussman and tenBroek, "Equal Protection," 359. To call racism a "virus" introduces a cluster of metaphors of contagion associated with race that could and should be examined. Indeed, Murphy's metaphor plays off of a history of anti-Oriental thought that feared contact with Chinese and others because of a perceived danger of catching diseases or even a tendency toward moral degeneracy, such as a propensity to smoke opium. In *Plessy* Tourgée mocks similar beliefs about blacks. Addressing the question of whether the enforced separation of the races could be justified as a health measure, he asks: "What is the prohibited act in the statute in question in this case? The sitting of a white man or woman in the car in which a colored man or woman sits or the sitting of a colored man or woman in the car in which white men and women are sitting,—is this dangerous to the public health? Does this contaminate public morals? If it does from whence comes the contamination? Why does it contaminate any more than in the house or on the street? Is it the white who spreads the contagion or the black? And if color breeds contagion in a railway coach, why exempt nurses from the operation of the Act?" Quoted in *The Thin Disguise*, ed. Otto H. Olsen (New York: Humanities Press, 1965), 89. Historically metaphors of marking and contagion are linked. In ancient Greece the word for defilement was associated with that for pollution. For the Greeks, then, the lack of purity resulting from defilement was thought to be contagious. See Robert Parker, *Miasma: Pollution and Purification in Early Greek Religion* (Oxford: Oxford University Press, 1983). Attempts by proponents of affirmative action to call some racial classifications "benign" draw on this cluster of metaphors of contagion. For another use of the virus metaphor, see note 2 above.

50. Tussman and tenBroek, "Equal Protection," 361.

by northerners, to say to the southern legislators, 'We see through the reasons you give for segregation to your real motivations, which are evil.'"[51] Despite his shrewd analysis of the Court's political dilemma, Posner still argues that an implicit premise of the Court's decision was that segregation stigmatized blacks "by stamping them with a badge of inferiority."[52] What he does not explore is how the Court solved its political dilemma through a metaphor other than that of stigmatization.

The metaphor is one of "generation." It allowed the Court to avoid ruling on the motive behind Jim Crow laws just as it refused to rule on the original intention of the Fourteenth Amendment. To be sure, the Court unequivocally stated that segregated schools played a role in "generating" feelings of inferiority in black children. But its metaphor allowed it to avoid declaring whether those feelings were caused primarily by laws marking blacks as inferior from without, by an interior psychological mechanism within, or by a combination of the two. Thus the *Brown* Court had no need to challenge the *Plessy* Court's claim that blacks' interpretation of segregation laws, not the laws themselves, marked them with a badge of inferiority. For the *Brown* Court whether the sense of inferiority was a product of the law itself or blacks' interpretation of it was irrelevant. All that mattered was that the law, well-intentioned or not, played a role in generating it.

That point established, the Court then appealed to evidence that the *Plessy* Court, so it claimed, could not have known. Citing a lower court, it argued that the children's feelings of inferiority affected their motivation to learn and thus deprived them of "some of the benefits they would receive in a racial[ly] integrated school system."[53] Contributing to that deprivation, laws mandating separate but equal schools violated the equal protection clause of the Fourteenth Amendment.

Employing a strategic metaphor, the *Brown* Court used history in a much more subtle and, arguably, politically more effective way than the extended historical essay. Rather than appeal to history to establish an original intention in order to overrule existing precedent, the Court used metaphor to adhere to precedent while altering the course of history. Making no claim to overturn *Plessy*, the *Brown* Court metaphorically turned the history of racial discrimination on its head.

---

51. Posner, *Overcoming Law*, 62.
52. Posner, *Overcoming Law*, 61.
53. *Brown*, 494.

Or so we are frequently told. In fact, although the Court provided a new and needed turn to the country's history of race relations in the law, it did not bring about the radical reversal that the metaphor of turning something on its head implies. Indeed, it was not until twelve years later in the antimiscegenation case of *Loving v. Virginia* (1966) that the Court explicitly declared the intention of a Jim Crow law to be the perpetuation of white supremacy. In calling attention to *Brown*'s limits, I do not mean to minimize its importance. If *Loving* finally did what *Brown* did not, it is very likely that *Loving* would have been impossible without the turn made by the Court in *Brown*. Nonetheless, we do need to understand how *Brown* accomplished what it did. Important was its theory of constitutional interpretation.

By suggesting that it simply updated *Plessy* to bring it into line with present conditions, the *Brown* Court opened itself to charges of disregarding history. A historical approach, critics claimed, adheres to the original intention of a law. The *Brown* Court's approach was not, however, ahistorical; it was simply based on a different view of history. Opposing a static unchanging view of history, the *Brown* Court assumed what has been termed a modern view of history; that is, a belief that temporality is a component part of reality. If reality changes with time, a truly historical approach to the law has to update itself continually. This view of reality presents no theoretical problem for legislators, who can always pass new laws, but it does pose a problem for judges interpreting a Constitution written in the past. The *Brown* Court attempted to solve it by thinking of the Constitution as an organic document capable of continual growth. Given the Court's metaphor of generation in *Brown*, an organic view is an appropriate one, although "historians" attacked it for ignoring the fixed meaning of original intention, just as in the realm of literature New Critics were faulted by literary historians for holding a similar organic view of literary documents. Not explicitly stated in *Brown*, the Court's organicism was articulated in *Loving*.

In *Loving* the state of Virginia appealed to statements made during debates over the Freedmen's Bureau Bill to argue that the framers of the Fourteenth Amendment did not intend to make unconstitutional state antimiscegenation laws. But the Court rejected this appeal to historical evidence. "While these statements have some relevance to the intention of Congress in submitting the Fourteenth Amendment," Chief Justice Warren wrote, "it must be understood that they pertained to the passage of specific statutes and not to the broader, organic purpose of a constitutional amendment."[54] Armed with this distinction between specific statutes and a constitutional amendment, Warren declared that the "clear and central purpose of the Fourteenth Amendment was to eliminate all official state sources of invidious racial discrimination in the States."[55] An example of invidious state discrimination, the Virginia act was unconstitutional.

So in *Loving*, as in *Brown*, Warren used an organic theory of the Constitution rather than an explicit appeal to historical evidence to overcome precedent and declare a Jim Crow law unconstitutional. But if it is important to stress that *Brown* did not officially overturn the precedent of *Plessy*, it is also important to note that Warren's association of state antimiscegenation laws with white supremacy already had a constitutional precedent, even if a discredited one. Taney, after all, made the same association in *Dred Scott*. There is, of course, an important difference between Warren's attack on a history of legally sanctioned white supremacy and Taney's contribution to that history. But that difference does not negate the fact that both are at odds with Justice Gray's contention as a young lawyer that state antimiscegenation laws did not imply the superiority of one race over the other. Thus once again we are confronted with the paradox that those championing black rights assented to this important aspect of Taney's view of history while legitimators of segregation shared Gray's opposing view.

Even so, there is a crucial difference between the Court's argument in *Loving* and those made by Swayne and Harlan in the nineteenth century: *Loving*, like *Brown*, made no reference to stigmatization or marks of inferiority. And once again for good reason: *Loving*, like *Brown*, is a Fourteenth Amendment case. The story of how those metaphors got associated with the Fourteenth Amendment returns us to the question of how history is used in today's legal battles over affirmative action.

VI

As we have seen, the metaphor of stigmatization plays an important role in affirmative action debates. On the one hand, some believe that it is possible to have "benign" classifications that do not stigmatize. On

54. *Loving v. Virginia*, 388 U.S. 1 at 9 (1966).
55. *Loving*, 10.

the other, some agree with Justice Thomas that benign classifications are just as "noxious" as hostile ones because they continue to "stamp minorities with a badge of inferiority."[56]

But this disagreement obscures general agreement that *Brown* is based on a recognition that racial classifications have historically been used to stigmatize. The *Hopwood* court, for instance, writes, "The Court also has recognized that government's use of racial classifications serves to stigmatize. *See, e.g., Brown v. Board of Educ.*, 347 U.S. 483, 494 (1954) (observing that classification on the basis of race 'generates a feeling of inferiority')."[57] Similarly, in one of the strongest defenses of affirmative action by a member of the Court, Justice Brennan, writing for White, Marshall, and Blackmun in *Bakke*, cited *Brown* to support his historical claim that "After enactment of the Fourteenth Amendment the States continued to deny Negroes equal educational opportunity, enforcing a strict policy of segregation that itself stamped Negroes as inferior, *Brown I*, 347 U.S. 483 (1954)."[58]

This agreement is, I have tried to demonstrate, based on misreading of *Brown*, which never explicitly claims that legislation in and of itself stamped or stigmatized. In *Brown* legislation is simply part of a process in which feelings of inferiority were generated. Before going into possible consequences of that misreading, I want to ask why people are so prone to reading metaphors of marking in *Brown* when they are not on the page in front of them. The most obvious reason is that people read *Brown* in conjunction with *Plessy*. Because *Plessy* denied that Jim Crow laws in and of themselves stamped blacks with a badge of inferiority and because, in effect, *Brown* overruled *Plessy*, people have assumed that *Brown* must have declared what *Plessy* did not. But there is also a more interesting, if speculative, explanation.

As we have seen, metaphors of marking were originally associated with the Thirteenth Amendment, which was stripped of its force as a weapon in civil rights cases in *Hodges v. the United States*. In 1968, however, in *Jones v. Mayer Co.* the Court restored some of the amendment's

---

56. *Adarand Constructors, Inc. v. Pena*, 115 S.Ct. 2097 at 2119 (1995). See also Justice Stevens's claim that much affirmative action legislation indulges in racial stereotypes while disadvantaging those who do not benefit from it. "Although it stigmatizes the disadvantaged class with the unproven charge of past racial discrimination, it actually imposes greater stigma on its supposed beneficiaries" (*Richmond v. J. A. Croson Co.*, 488 U.S. 469 at 516–17 [1988]).

57. *Hopwood*, 32.

58. *Bakke*, 371.

power when it declared, "Insofar as *Hodges* is inconsistent with our holding today, it is hereby overruled."[59] In doing so it resurrected Congress's power under the Thirteenth Amendment "to determine what are the badges and the incidents of slavery, and the authority to translate that determination into effective legislation."[60] In a concurring opinion Justice Douglas made the remark that I quoted at the beginning of the essay about the Court witnessing a series of cases testifying to the spectacle of slavery unwilling to die. Linking these cases to badges of slavery lingering in the present, Douglas goes on to list mostly Fourteenth, not Thirteenth, Amendment cases, including *Brown*.

Douglas's list might be a sign of sloppiness. But it might also have been a shrewd attempt to suggest a Thirteenth as well as a Fourteenth Amendment precedent for the Court as it tried to forbid various discriminatory acts. The advantage of doing so would have been, as we have seen, that the Fourteenth Amendment, since the *Civil Rights Cases*, had been confined to state action, while the Thirteenth could apply to the discriminatory acts of one private citizen against another. Indeed, four years earlier Douglas, along with Chief Justice Warren, had joined Justice Goldberg in his concurring opinion in a sit-in case that used an extended historical essay to suggest that by limiting the Fourteenth Amendment to state action the majority in the *Civil Rights Cases* had violated the original meaning of the amendment.[61] Nonetheless, other members of the Court never rallied behind Goldberg's use of historical evidence to argue, as Harlan had in his *Civil Rights Cases* dissent, that the citizenship clause of the Fourteenth Amendment gave Congress the power to protect implied rights of equality for all citizens no matter who attempted to deny them. Recognizing Goldberg's failure to use history to overturn precedent and extend the power of the federal government to protect civil rights against the actions of private citizens, Douglas might well have tried for the same effect through a shrewd use of metaphoric slippage. But whether Douglas's metaphoric slippage was shrewdly calculated or the result of sloppy thinking, the Court started to evoke stigmatization in various Fourteenth Amendment cases. The result is the importance those metaphors have in today's affirmative action debates.

The first time that stigma is mentioned in an affirmative action case is in another opinion of Douglas's. Disagreeing with the majority's

---

59. *Jones v. Mayer*, 443 n. 78.
60. *Jones v. Mayer*, 440.
61. *Bell v. Maryland*, 378 U.S. 226 (1964).

refusal to rule on the affirmative action admission's policy of the University of Washington Law School in *De Funis v. Odegaard* (1974), Douglas dissented. "A segregated admissions process," he declared, "creates suggestions of stigma and caste no less than a segregated classroom, and in the end it may produce that result despite its contrary intentions. One other assumption must be clearly disapproved, that blacks or browns cannot make it on their individual merit. That is a stamp of inferiority that a state is not permitted to place on any lawyer."[62] A few years later in *Bakke* Brennan, White, Marshall, and Blackmun evoked the cardinal principle of stigmatization, causing others on the Court to adopt Douglas's argument that affirmative action programs themselves stigmatize and thus make it impossible to establish truly benign classifications.

That both sides of the debate could rely on Douglas's use of the metaphor is not surprising since Douglas's own stand on affirmative action was conflicted. On the one hand, he would seem to oppose all racial classifications for their power to stigmatize. Indeed, in *De Funis* he frequently stressed the need to consider applications in a racially neutral way. On the other, his notion of neutrality was not necessarily a color-blind standard. Pointing to the possible bias of LSAT scores against certain racial groups, he held out the possibility that neutrality meant that consideration must be given to members of those groups to compensate for that bias.

I do not want to overemphasize Douglas's role. The metaphor of stigmatization clearly did not originate with him. On the contrary, his use of it has interest because of prior uses by the Court.[63] Furthermore, there were other influences on members of the Court who used it in affirmative action cases. Brennan's argument, for instance, was strongly indebted to a 1969 *Harvard Law Review* essay on equal protection. That essay admitted, "Experience in America teaches that a racial classification will usually be perceived as a stigma of inferiority and a badge of opprobrium,"[64] but went on to argue that when the purpose of a classification is benign, it should be measured by a standard of rea-

---

62. 416 U.S. 312 at 343 (1974).

63. An interesting use occurs in *Korematsu v. United States* when Justice Frankfurter defends an action under war power: "That action is not to be stigmatized as lawless because like action in times of peace would be lawless" (323 U.S. 214 at 224 [1944]). It is impossible to know whether or not Frankfurter used the metaphor self-consciously in this case that upheld the use of racial classifications.

64. "Developments in the Law: Equal Protection," *Harvard Law Review* 82 (1969): 1127.

sonableness rather than the more rigorous standard of strict scrutiny. In turn, this essay cited a 1960 *Yale Law Journal* article to support its claim that "the social meaning of segregation is inequality, a stamping of one race with the mark of inferiority."[65]

The analysis of how law review essays help to fashion the Court's perception of history is beyond the scope of this essay. What interests me instead is what Douglas's examples tell us about possible uses of metaphor in the law. If metaphor allows innovative judges to give a new turn to legal history while remaining true to precedent, it also makes it impossible to control precisely how those in the future will use it. Metaphors, like that of stigmatization, may constitute a sort of memory within the law; what they memorialize, however, is open to change.

Open, but not infinitely so. Metaphors can suggest different meanings, but not all. Thus some metaphors are more appropriate than others for particular tasks. Having sketched out a brief history of the Court's use of metaphors of stigma, I now want to end by suggesting that judicial proponents of affirmative action made a strategic error in relying so much on them. Indeed, the notion of stigma seems to have served their political purposes little better than it served those of Taney in *Dred Scott*. If they hoped to evoke moral authority from the history of discrimination that it evokes, the weight of that history turned it into a tool for their political opponents on and off the Court. Progressives, after all, are not the only ones who can appropriate metaphors. As J. G. A. Pocock notes, it is one thing to explore the ways in which metaphor operates in language or discourse; it is another to explore the "politics of language." All metaphors have boundaries to their authority. "The politics really begins once we attempt to establish what those boundaries are, and who has the authority to determine them."[66]

VII

The strongest advocates of affirmative action feel that it should counter the effects of societal discrimination that continues to disadvantage people of color. But the notion of societal discrimination poses prob-

---

65. Charles Black, "The Lawfulness of the Segregation Decisions," *Yale Law Journal* 69 (1960): 424.

66. J. G. A. Pocock, "Tangata Whenua and Enlightenment Anthropology," *New Zealand Journal of History* 26 (1992): 29.

lems for the legal system. For instance, even Justice Powell, a moderate supporter of affirmative action in *Bakke*, called it "an amorphous concept that may be ageless in its reach into the past."[67] If the legal system seeks specific agents to blame when considering remedial action, societal discrimination blames the system, not individual agents. Many affirmative action programs try to sidestep this dilemma by benefiting those injured rather than identifying individual agents to blame. Trying to help in that effort, Brennan et al. turn to stigmatization to distinguish between those injured and those not. But the effort has failed for two reasons. First, those who did not benefit from these programs claimed to be injured by them. Second, stigma proved both too hard and too easy to detect.

It is too hard because in a post-*Brown* world it is very difficult to translate disadvantages caused by societal discrimination into signs of stigma. Even in *Brown* the Court had to evoke the category of the intangible when dealing with the obvious case of segregation, and the *Brown* Court did not have the burden of proving stigmatization. It is too easy because even those supposed to benefit from affirmative action programs can be shown to be stigmatized by them. Precisely because the history of legally sanctioned racial classifications has been so unjust, it has been almost impossible to make a compelling case for benign classifications that do not stigmatize. As a result, opponents are able to point to the very history of injustice that affirmative action tries to remedy to argue against its means.

Indeed, the question on the Court today is no longer whether stigmatization can be avoided. It is whether, given the risks of stigmatization, a program based on racial classifications can withstand "strict scrutiny."[68] To withstand strict scrutiny as defined by the Court a program has to demonstrate a "compelling governmental interest" and be "narrowly tailored to further that interest."[69] Thus the major battle is over how to define what Brennan in *Bakke* called "that inexact term, 'strict scrutiny.'"[70]

---

67. *Bakke*, 307.
68. "Strict scrutiny" can be traced to yet another Douglas opinion: *Skinner v. Oklahoma*. In the same opinion Douglas coins the phrase "invidious discrimination" (316 U.S. 535 at 541).
69. *Adarand Constructors*, 2117.
70. *Bakke*, 357.

For defenders of affirmative action the task is how to avoid a definition that is "'strict' in theory and fatal in fact."[71] But the more precision with which "strict scrutiny" has been defined the more fatal it has become for affirmative action programs. For instance, the court in *Hopwood* applies what it calls such a "steep" standard of strict scrutiny that hardly any program can withstand the test.[72] Rejecting Justice Powell's claim in *Bakke* that academic freedom gives schools a right to secure a diverse student body that enhances students' educational experience, it quotes the plurality in *Croson* to argue that remedying past discrimination is the only compelling governmental interest: "Classifications based on race carry the risk of stigmatic harm. Unless they are reserved for remedial settings, they may in fact promote notions of racial inferiority and lead to the politics of racial hostility."[73] They then define "remedial settings" so narrowly that very few would be able to pass strict scrutiny.

There is, to be sure, a certain irony when judges, who enthusiastically cite *Brown*, which relied so heavily on the notion of intangible effects, demand such concrete evidence of specific harm done by specific institutions to specific groups. There is also an irony when the same judges rely on the metaphor of "strict scrutiny," since it could be argued that "really" strict scrutiny might uncover lingering effects of racism. Nonetheless, they have so successfully appropriated the metaphor of stigmatization that appeals to it have little force against their arguments.

The failure of stigmatization to accomplish what Brennan et al. hoped it would points to a larger failure of strategy by advocates of affirmative action. They have continually evoked history as justification for their point of view, but in fact the history of racial discrimination offers the disconcerting lesson that it provides no clear lesson for present debates. Some believe that it necessitates a color-blind standard forbidding all racial classification; some that it necessitates benign classifications to wipe out societal discrimination so as to create a world in which a color-blind standard could be used without blinding courts to the historically disadvantaged condition of people of color; and others

---

71. *Bakke*, 362. The phrase is Gerald Gunther's in "The Supreme Court 1971 Term: Forward: In Search of Evolving Doctrine on a Changing Court: A Model for a Newer Equal Protection," *Harvard Law Review* 86 (1972): 8.

72. *Hopwood*, 34.

73. *Croson*, 493.

that it proves that racial classifications are allowable only in narrowly defined cases when a program is designed to remedy a particular governmental entity's discrimination against a particular group.

It might seem that history's failure to provide a clear lesson results from conflicting interpretation about the past. In fact, there is surprising agreement. For instance, most agree that *Brown* outlawed legally mandated segregation because it marked blacks with the stigma of inferiority. Why that shared agreement, flawed as it might be, does not provide a guide for present policies can be explained in part by comparing the Court's dilemmas in *Brown* and *Bakke*. In both the Court confronted a paradox. In *Brown* it faced the possibility that "separate but equal" might in fact not be equal. In *Bakke* it faced the possibility that, in Justice Blackmun's words, "In order to get beyond racism, we must first take account of race."[74] But if both cases involved a paradox, their paradoxes have different temporal dimensions. *Brown* confronted the dilemma of how to forbid a practice that the Court had already declared just. Affirmative action confronts the dilemma of how to remedy the effects of legal support of practices that most agree were unjust. *Brown*'s dilemma could be solved by pointing to empirical evidence in the past to convince people of the truth of its paradox. Thus although the Court did not rely on history to decide the original meaning of the Fourteenth Amendment, it did draw heavily on social-science evidence produced by history to demonstrate the harmful effects of segregated schools. In contrast, the paradox in *Bakke* is future-oriented. Since the future, unlike the past, is incapable of generating empirical evidence, no appeal to history can prove its truth. Instead, those believing in the *Bakke* paradox must ask citizens to trust them that affirmative action really is the best policy to end a racism that all justices on the Court agree should end.

Agreement that a history of legally sanctioned racial classifications had harmful effects may not provide a clear lesson on how best to remedy those effects; nonetheless, the role that stigma has played in forging the Court's agreement has proved detrimental to the cause of affirmative action. Indeed, the most revealing attack on the use of stigma comes from one of affirmative action's defenders: Justice Powell. In his *Bakke* opinion—now under attack for stressing affirmative action's positive stress on diversity—Justice Powell took Brennan et al. to task for

---

74. *Bakke,* 407.

their "pliable notion of 'stigma.'" "The Equal Protection Clause," he argued, "is not framed in terms of 'stigma.' Certainly the word has no clearly defined constitutional meaning. It reflects a subjective judgment that is standardless."[75]

Powell's criticism is telling, but not quite historically accurate. Stigma and the accompanying metaphors of badges and brands did have a fairly clear constitutional meaning, but that meaning was linked to the Thirteenth Amendment and the legacy of slavery. In that connection it served the important function of making visible slavery's continued effects in the present, a function resurrected in 1968 when the Court used the metaphor of a badge of inferiority to respond to the spectacle of an institution unwilling to die. But stigmatization became muddled when it was linked to the Fourteenth Amendment and lost its historical specificity. That muddle has hurt the cause of affirmative action.

For instance, one reason that the Court invalidated Richmond's affirmative action program in *Croson* was that it benefited minorities other than blacks who could not have been historically harmed by the Richmond city government. Stigma, it seems, has the danger of weighing down the Fourteenth Amendment by tying it to a version of the past that does not fully respond to the needs of today's increasingly multicultural society.[76] We should remember, instead, the Court's proclamation in *Hernandez v. Texas* (1954), "The Fourteenth Amendment is not directed solely against discrimination due to a 'two-class theory'—that is, based upon differences between 'white' and Negro."[77]

My point is not that the history of slavery has no effect on our present racial situation. On the contrary, it can still affect the life of blacks. But when it does, the Thirteenth Amendment should be evoked, not the Fourteenth. Doing so would recognize the unique historical situation of blacks without jeopardizing affirmative action's goal of benefiting other racial minorities.

Nor is my point that only blacks should be protected by the Thir-

75. *Bakke,* 294 n. 34.

76. Ronald J. Fiscus's argument for affirmative action is, to my mind, seriously flawed for forgetting that multicultural reality. For instance, when he proposes a group of newborns "roughly representative of the population of the United States," he imagines 50 percent male, 50 percent female, 80 percent white, and 20 percent black. *The Constitutional Logic of Affirmative Action* (Durham, N.C.: Duke University Press, 1992), 15.

77. 347 U.S. 475 at 478 (1954).

teenth Amendment. For instance, until after World War II Mexican-American children were segregated in many parts of the Southwest. Often, as was the case in Santa Ana, California, Mexican-American schools had a curriculum based on manual training with the assumption that the children would eventually be employed as agricultural laborers or domestic servants.[78] In retrospect, it seems clear that such an imposed curriculum could have been said to have stamped Mexican-Americans with a badge of servitude.

Another example is provided by the notorious *Hodges v. United States*. In the process of destroying the power of the Thirteenth Amendment, Justice Brewer noted that in "slave times in the slave States not infrequently every free Negro was required to carry with him a copy of a judicial decree or other evidence of his right to freedom or be subject to arrest. That was one of the incidents of slavery. By the act of May 5, 1892, Congress required all Chinese laborers within the limits of the United States to apply for a certificate, and anyone who after one year from the passage of the act should be found within the jurisdiction of the United States without such a certificate, might be arrested and deported."[79] But no one, he added, challenged the act under the Thirteenth Amendment. Once again, in retrospect, we might conclude that such a challenge should have been mounted.

The United States has a history in which racial groups have been marked as inferior because it was assumed that their appropriate place in society was tantamount to servitude. When such stigmatization occurs and when past effects of it linger to mark people in the present, the Thirteenth Amendment should without a doubt be evoked. Stigmatization of that sort, it is important to note, is clearly not relevant to affirmative action programs that encourage previously underrepresented groups to occupy more prestigious positions in society, not to return to a condition tantamount to servitude. Metaphors of stigmatization, we might say, have no historical place in Fourteenth Amendment jurisprudence. Nonetheless, the confusion of Thirteenth and

---

78. Gilbert G. Gonzalez, "Segregation of Mexican Children in a Southern California City: The Legacy of Expansionism and the American Southwest, *Western Historical Quarterly* (1985): 55–76. On the legal challenge to this segregation, which did not rely on a Thirteenth Amendment appeal, see Charles Wollenberg, *All Deliberate Speed* (Berkeley and Los Angeles: University of California Press, 1976), 123–32.

79. *Hodges*, 19.

Fourteenth Amendment issues continues to reign, as illustrated by the title of a recent collection of essays, *Removing a Badge of Slavery: The Record of "Brown v. Board of Education."*[80]

My "strict scrutiny" of the history of the Court's use of metaphors of marking makes possible the subtle, but important, discrimination needed to distinguish between Thirteenth and Fourteenth Amendment issues. To claim that such discrimination could resolve the debate over affirmative action would, to be sure, violate my lesson that history provides us with no clear lesson. Nonetheless, it is no violation to suggest that challenging the Court's present construction of the history of racial discrimination opens up new ways of framing the debate.

Most important, to confine metaphors of stigmatization to Thirteenth Amendment situations would help clarify the rationale for affirmative action's racial categories. Affirmative action has two basic goals. One is oriented toward the past and tries to remedy past wrongs. The other is oriented toward the future and tries to enhance the creation of a society in which people with economic and professional power are more representative of the diversity of the country at large. If my reading of history is correct, affirmative action's remedial aspects should have a basis in the Thirteenth Amendment and not be confused by evocations of the Fourteenth, especially the equal protection clause.

Indeed, whereas some opponents of affirmative action are fond of pointing to Harlan's *Plessy* dissent and his call for a "color-blind" Constitution, what they fail to remember is that he was equally intent on exposing the "thin disguise" of the Jim Crow law's guarantee of equality. The *Plessy* majority failed to see through that disguise because it confused Thirteenth and Fourteenth Amendment arguments when it implied that the law's guarantee of equal treatment ruled out the possibility that it stamped blacks with a "badge of inferiority." There is no more subtle perpetuation of the logic of the *Plessy* Court than when guarantees of equality in conjunction with metaphors of racial marking serve as a "thin disguise" to deny those historically disadvantaged a more secure place in United States society.

My point is not that the Fourteenth Amendment has no role in affirmative action appeals. But the proper place to evoke it is, however, for affirmative action's future-oriented goals, that is, its affirmative, not remedial, aspirations that are under attack. But if proponents are going to do so effectively, they have some work to do. One possibility would

80. Mark Whitman, ed., *Removing a Badge of Slavery: The Record of "Brown v. Board of Education,"* (Princeton, N.J.: Markus Wiener, 1993).

be to expand on arguments made a century ago by Harlan and Tourgée about affirmative guarantees in the Fourteenth Amendment's citizenship clause and to argue for diversity as part of a definition of citizenship. Another would be to follow the *Brown* Court, which saw the need to redefine the notion of equal protection in light of what the *Plessy* Court's definition had led to. Metaphoric itself, the notion of equal protection remains open to innovative redefinition.[81]

What the Fourteenth Amendment cannot do, however, is guarantee that actions in the present will "erase" unjust acts in the past. Remediation is often just, but it can never perfectly balance wrongs done in the past to the extent that they will be forgotten. We can no more erase past wrongs than we can erase from the body of United States law the ways that it has been marked by metaphors of racial marking. We can, however, use both the past and those metaphors innovatively to create a more equitable society in the future. This, it seems to me, is the real challenge to advocates of *affirmative* action.

That much said, I cannot help but end an essay so occupied with paradoxes by noting the paradox of my own method. From the start I have argued that frequently strategic uses of metaphor have allowed the Court to make history more effectively than explicit uses of history itself. Almost at cross-purposes to that claim, my essay has used a historical examination of metaphor to challenge existing precedent through an appeal to the original intention of various Court decisions, such as *Plessy* and *Brown*. In defense let me simply suggest that this methodological paradox might help to reinforce my related claim that the Court's uses of metaphor and history, while not identical, are intricately related.

---

81. The *Brown* court was well served by Tussman and tenBroek's 1949 essay on "Equal Protection." Proponents of affirmative action, by my reading, were less well served by the 1969 *Harvard Law Review* essay "Equal Protection," which evoked metaphors of stigmatization and benign classifications. What is needed perhaps is more innovative, certainly more effective, metaphors.

My argument for redefining the notion of equal protection to support affirmative action's positive goal of diversity is at odds with those proponents of "critical race theory" who propose abandoning the equal protection clause altogether. What these critics fail to recognize is both the power that the notion of equality has in our society *and* the possibility of redefining what equality entails. My stress on diversity also sharply distinguishes me from Fiscus, who claims that associating diversity with affirmative action has led to "rhetorical confusion" (*Constitutional Logic*, 113). My argument is much closer in spirit to that of Robert Post, especially his notion of affirmative action's role in creating possibilities for "an educated and critical citizenry that spans existing racial and ethnic differences." "Introduction: After *Bakke*," *Representations* 55 (1996): 9.

Analogical Reasoning and Historical Change in Law: The Regulation of Film and Radio Speech

G. Edward White

I

Two recurrent questions have surfaced in the efforts of scholars to arrive at a more precise formulation of the relationship of law to its social context. Are legal doctrines and legal institutions the equivalent of cultural artifacts, embodying and reflecting the context in which they are situated, or do they possess some intrinsic professional features that endow them with a degree of autonomy and insulation from that context? And, if one concludes that law retains a dimension of autonomy and insularity from the larger culture, where are the sources of that autonomy located?

An adequate understanding of the above two questions has been obscured by a persistent tendency among lawyers, in writing about their own profession, to give a celebratory spin to the autonomy of law, and an equally persistent tendency among social historians to react against that spin. On the one hand we have Roscoe Pound emphasizing "the tenacity of a taught legal tradition" in order to argue that judges from different class and regional backgrounds nonetheless cohered around a set of doctrinal principles in tort law. Pound's message was not simply that legal decisions could not be made fodder for crude "economic interpretations" of American history; it was also that the "taught legal tradition" signified fidelity to a higher set of established precepts and principles that made law more than simply a mirror of current social attitudes.[1]

On the other hand we have Lawrence Friedman announcing, in his *History of American Law,* "This book treats American law . . . not as a kingdom unto itself, not as a set of rules and concepts, not as the province of lawyers alone, but as a mirror of society. It takes nothing . . . as autonomous, everything as relative and molded by economy and society."[2] Friedman's refusal to treat law as "a kingdom unto itself" and as "the province of lawyers alone" suggests that he has been provoked by the implication, in commentators such as Pound, that only those versed in "the taught legal tradition" can understand its significance, and thus the history of law can only properly be written by lawyers.

Friedman also refuses to characterize law "as a set of rules and concepts." Presumably he is rejecting the notion that there is a "taught legal tradition" possessing the causative power assigned to it by Pound. Pound's "taught tradition" assumes that legal decisions are expressed in a distinctive professional discourse containing its own concepts, vocabulary, patterns of reasoning, and codes of implementation, and that the subjects of the decisions, although based on the raw materials of society at any point in time, are given legal significance by the discourse.

Recent work on the relationship of law to its social context appears to have largely abandoned the idea that law can be viewed entirely as a "mirror of society," containing no autonomous elements. Robert Gordon, for example, has argued that "legal forms and practices" do not simply "shift with every realignment of the balance of political forces," but rather "tend to become embedded in 'relatively autonomous' structures that transcend and, to some extent, help to shape the content" of social issues. Gordon recommends "study elaborating [the] peculiar internal structures" of legal discourse. Similarly Duncan Kennedy has sought to identify "legal consciousness as an entity with a measure of autonomy." Kennedy defines legal consciousness as "the body of ideas

1. Roscoe Pound, "The Economic Interpretation and the Law of Torts," *Harvard Law Review* 53 (1940): 365, and *The Formative Era of American Law* (Boston: Little, Brown, 1938), 82.

2. Lawrence M. Friedman, *A History of American Law* (New York: Simon and Schuster, 1973), 10.

through which lawyers experience legal issues," a "set of concepts and operations that evolves according to a pattern of its own."[3]

Let us assume the validity of this conception of law as "relatively autonomous," situated in a cultural context but at the same time possessed of an internal professional consciousness and discourse, as a working hypothesis. Then let us see if we may derive from that hypothesis a more precise sketch of the relationship of the social meanings of events—the process by which events in a culture are translated into social issues—to the legal meanings of those events.

II. The Role of Analogical Reasoning in Legal Discourse

Some recent work, intended to introduce the Anglo-American legal system and its patterns of legal reasoning to nonlawyers, has sought to identify the peculiar discursive practices of that system.[4] Two propositions advanced in that work are germane to my inquiry. One is that law is distinguished from other fields and disciplines in being essentially concerned with developing guidelines for human conduct, authoritative rules that citizens are expected to follow. The other is that the Anglo-American legal system is dominated by judge-made rules, decisions handed down in particular legal disputes that are justified by invocations of authoritative general principles.

Two distinctive features of law follow from these propositions. First, legal rules, in all cultures, must be sufficiently general so as to apply to a variety of prospective situations, not merely the precise legal dispute in which they are invoked. Otherwise their function of providing guidance for the future is inadequately served. Second, despite this requirement of generality, legal rules in the Anglo-American system are inevitably affected by the decisional context in which they have been invoked, so that no rule can be said to be so general as to cover all future cases. Indeed the relevance of existing rules to future cases is one

---

3. Robert Gordon, "Critical Legal Histories," *Stanford Law Review* 36 (1984): 101; Duncan Kennedy, "Toward an Historical Understanding of Legal Consciousness," *Research in Law and Sociology* 3 (1980): 4–5.

4. See George P. Fletcher, *Basic Concepts of Legal Thought* (New York: Oxford University Press, 1996); Kenneth J. Vandervelde, *Thinking Like a Lawyer* (Boulder: Westview Press, 1996).

of the abiding uncertainties of the system. The system contains a built-in tension between generality and particularity, between authoritative propositions designed to have widespread applicability and specific disputes, in which those propositions may be invoked, whose factual context may render the propositions more or less relevant.

Were the Anglo-American legal system similar to civilian systems, which locate their authoritative rules of law in a code, the question in every case would more approximate whether a particular set of conduct came within a particular code provision. The court's answer, in a civilian system, would be "yes," in which case the legal consequences of the conduct were already specified in the code, or "no," in which case either no consequences followed from the conduct or another provision of the code was applicable. In the Anglo-American system, where rules are judge-made, a third option exists. A judge might decide that although the rule declared in past cases did not precisely cover the facts of the case before the court, the consequences of not invoking the rule were worse than having a perfect fit, so the rule could be applied to the case by analogical reasoning.

Analogical reasoning is in fact the standard technique of reasoning in the Anglo-American legal system. It consists of establishing previously decided cases as authoritative because they embody certain rules that the system has internalized, and then giving legal weight to those cases as "precedents" that presumptively should be followed in subsequent disputes. New cases are then analogized to precedents, with one side attempting to show that the precedents are apposite and dispositive of the case at hand, and the other side attempting to show that they are inapposite, and an alternative legal rule is necessary for the decision.

The critical step in analogical reasoning is, of course, the determination of appositeness: the demonstration that a precedent is "like" a case under consideration or that it is "unlike" that case. As many commentators have noted,[5] appositeness is not simply a function of logic, but of policy choices, since the decision to treat a new case as "like" or "unlike" an existing one is a decision to follow or to avoid the rule governing the existing case. Indeed it is common, under the Anglo-Ameri-

---

5. A recent analysis of analogical reasoning in the Anglo-American legal system is Cass Sunstein, "On Analogical Reasoning," *Harvard Law Review* 106 (1993): 741. See also Vandervelde, *Thinking Like a Lawyer*, 86–98.

can system, for arguments making use of analogical reasoning to have an explicit policy component: "The case before us *should* be treated as governed by the rule in case A because the same policy considerations present in case A are present here."

To the nonlawyer analogical reasoning may appear to be subject to very few constraints, since courts always have the option to refuse to apply an existing rule to a new dispute on the ground that the rule is inapposite. But in practice the Anglo-American legal system, for reasons of stability and predictability, places a high value on following precedent and thus treats most previous decisions whose rules appear arguably apposite as being so. Moreover, even when courts reject one rule on the grounds that it is inapposite, they do not necessarily formulate a new rule on which to ground the particular decision in the case at hand. Rather, since the system does not encourage a proliferation of rules, most analogical reasoning turns out to be an exercise in choosing between alternative existing rules, both of which are arguably apposite.

Seen in this fashion, analogical reasoning appears as a significant constraint on legal decision-makers. Very rarely is the choice of creating an entirely new rule open to them: this rarity is conventionally called "a case of first impression." In most cases their choice is between following one line of cases, after deeming that line apposite and thus analogous, or following an alternative line. What is typically termed policy reasoning in legal disputes is perhaps better described as a version of analogical reasoning, where both sides are arguing that a particular set of precedents should be treated as analogous and governing because the same policy outcomes produced in those decisions should be produced here.

Thus the opportunities for creativity among lawyers and judges in the Anglo-American legal system do not come primarily from the opportunity to fashion new rules or to formulate new policies. They come rather from the opportunity to marshal rich and persuasive analogies. Since those analogies invariably summon up existing cases, rules, and principles, the discourse of American law is inherently time-bound and conservative. Almost invariably the rule that is propounded as a justification for deciding a current case is a rule already embedded in the system, though perhaps it is now being applied in a new form of dispute.

III.   Analogical Reasoning in Early
Mass-Media Cases

I now want to consider the following refinement on my earlier hypothesis about the relationship of law to its social context. Let us now assume that the "relative autonomy" of law, the factor that tends to produce a relative insulation of the legal profession from its social context, can fruitfully be glimpsed in the process of analogical reasoning. Let us assume further that analogical reasoning is itself a product of the special professional concern of law with situating legal decisions in an established corpus of rules and doctrines so as to promote stability and predictability. Finally, let us assume that legal decisions are a response to social and political concerns generated by the larger culture, and are to that extent products of historical time and circumstance.

If all these assumptions are granted, one would not expect the relationship between legal decisions and their social context to be fully linear. One would not expect that each time a pressing social issue is brought to the legal system, that system's response would be to treat the issue as historically unique, a case of first impression. On the contrary, one would expect that the response would be to situate the concern within professional discourse. If that discourse is dominated by analogical reasoning, one would expect efforts to identify the issue with established lines of cases, rules, or doctrines; to treat the issue as "like" previous issues that the law has resolved by recourse to some authoritative proposition. One would expect a newly pressing social issue to be recast in the familiar language of the law.

Motion Pictures, Radio, and the First Amendment

I now want to take up two examples of the process I have just characterized.[6] In both examples factors in early twentieth-century American culture contributed to the emergence of activities that were novel forms of communication. The potential impact of the activities was vast, and their presence raised issues that were arguably different from the sets of issues that had been associated with earlier communications media. The activi-

---

6. Both examples are discussed, for different purposes, in Reuel E. Schiller's "Policy Ideals and Judicial Action: Expertise, Group Pluralism, and Participatory Democracy in Intellectual Thought and Legal Decisionmaking, 1932–1970," Ph.D. diss., University of Virginia, 1997. Thanks to Professor Schiller for calling my attention to them.

ties were motion pictures and radio, mediums that relied on electronic means to communicate their messages and that were directed toward a mass audience. Prior to the advent of motion pictures and radio the experience of Americans with communication had been limited to the print media or to oral communications, such as lectures or addresses. Motion pictures and radio were clearly media of a different sort.

Motion pictures and radio both emerged in the first two decades of the twentieth century. The two media had come into existence in the late 1890s, with Edison's discovery of the "kinetoscope," a machine that displayed a moving image within a booth, and Marconi's discovery that signals could be transmitted through the earth's atmosphere by use of an electrical spark, an antenna, and "cohering" devices that attracted radio waves. By 1910 moving pictures had begun to be exhibited commercially and amateurs had begun to experiment with the transmission of wireless signals. By 1920 the first commercial radio station, KDKA in Pittsburgh, had gone on the air and the commercial distribution of silent films had become a common phenomenon.[7]

From their outset motion pictures and the radio possessed common elements that appeared to distinguish them from conventional forms of expression. First, their electronic character arguably invested them with an immediacy and an intrusiveness not found in ordinary speech or in the print media. The technical sophistication required to create movies or to put on radio programs also limited the number of speakers and placed visual or aural "effects," many of them illusory, at the center of the communication process. There was arguably an emotional impact from being exposed to dramatic scenes in movies or on the radio that transcended any comparable impact from books or speeches. Thus from the outset of moving pictures and the radio their critics were worried about the capacity of those media to be used as "propaganda," by which they meant the generation of emotionally affecting but artificial images that were created electronically.

Motion pictures and radio also emerged as mass media at a period in time when the Progressive movement had developed as a political force in American life. Historians have characterized Progressivism in a variety of ways, but most would agree that its core cultural mission was to come to terms with the perceived complexity and diversity of

7. See Erik Barnouw, *A Tower in Babel: A History of Broadcasting in the United States,* vol. 1 (New York: Oxford University Press, 1966), 9–38; Richard S. Randall, *Censorship of the Movies* (Madison, University of Wisconsin Press, 1968), 10–21.

early twentieth-century American life.[8] The momentum of urbaniza-
tion and industrialization, coupled with increased immigration,
notably of immigrants from cultures whose ethnic, religious, and ideological orientation appeared "foreign" to old-stock Americans, stimulated a renewed concern with traditional American values, morals, and
practices. Progressivism combined this urgency to reaffirm traditional
elements in American culture with a confidence that established elites
could facilitate the assimilation of newer groups by educating them in
old-stock codes of conduct.

Both motion pictures and radio broadcasts were symptomatic of
the challenges Progressives felt posed by modern American life. They
were symbols of the increasing power and ubiquity of technology.
They were also symbols of the increasingly mass character of communication. They could speak, through artificially created visual and aural
aids, to Americans who could not read English sufficiently well to
appreciate printed media. They also appeared to be determinedly
"lowbrow" in their orientation, pitching their messages at an adoles-
cent level and thereby being accessible to viewers or listeners with a
poor command of the language. They were thus media that appeared to
cry out for governmental regulation.[9]

Governmental regulation itself was something about which Progressives were in the main enthusiastic. The belief in "progress" that
animated members of the Progressive movement was founded, in part,
on a confidence in the capacity of properly educated and trained
humans—"experts"—to manage the complexities of modern life and
thereby make the future better than the past. The nonpartisan commission, and the state or federal administrative agency, symbolized this
Progressive faith in expertise. These bodies were to be divorced from
partisan politics, staffed by persons with sufficient scientific training to
make sense of their environment, and dedicated to educating the public through enlightened policymaking. Since both the movies and radio
were susceptible of generating influential but socially deleterious mes-

8. See Daniel T. Rodgers, "In Search of Progressivism," *Reviews in American History*
10 (1982): 113.

9. For a discussion of Progressive attitudes toward moving pictures, see Lary May,
Screening Out the Past: The Birth of Mass Culture and the Motion Picture Industry (New York:
Oxford University Press, 1980); and Edward deGrazia and Roger K. Newman, *Banned
Films* (New York: Bowker, 1982), 7–24. For evidence of the concern of early radio execu-
tives with "lewd" or politically controversial material, see Barnouw, *A Tower in Babel*,
86–87.

sages, their regulation seemed essential. No sooner had movies begun to be distributed on a widespread basis than city councils and state officials began to take an interest in their content, and to establish some form of administrative preclearance.[10] A similar development occurred when radio stations began to proliferate in the 1920s: a Federal Radio Commission was created to grant licenses, based on the "public interest, convenience, and necessity."[11]

Why both moving pictures and radio broadcasts continue to be treated as both distinct from other forms of oral and written communication, and subject to much greater regulation, has been a recurrent question for commentators.[12] My focus here is on the relationship between their treatment and the historical origins of legal regulation of the movies and radio broadcasts. I include in the phrase "historical origins" the time-bound body of legal discourse, including the available arguments and analogies, that existed for policymakers considering the treatment of moving pictures and radio in their early twentieth century.

We have already seen that the mass character, the immediacy, and the "artificial" quality of motion picture and radio broadcasts, coupled with the Progressive Era's tendency to approve of governmental regulation by experts, stimulated an interest in subjecting the motion picture and radio industries to some form of regulatory apparatus. But, from a contemporary perspective, an obvious roadblock would seem to exist for regulation of the content of films and radio programs. That roadblock is the First Amendment, incorporated against the states through the Fourteenth Amendment's due process clause. Under modern First Amendment doctrine governmental efforts to regulate the content of speech are presumptively suspect, requiring the government

10. DeGrazia and Newman, *Banned Films*, 8–15; Garth Jowett, "'A Significant Medium for the Communication of Ideas,'" in *Movie Censorship and American Culture*, ed. Francis Couvares (Washington, Smithsonian Institution Press, 1996), 258–59.

11. Barnouw, *A Tower in Babel*, 211–15. Regulation of radio differed from that of moving pictures from the outset in that the only content review exercised by administrators was through the process of granting or renewing licenses. But although the Federal Radio Commission, created in 1927, was expressly prohibited from censoring program content (id., 197–98), it was nonetheless taken into account in the licensing process. See [Mark DeWolfe Howe], "The Freedom of Radio Speech," *Harvard Law Review* 46 (1933): 989.

12. Two good overviews are Thomas G. Krattenmaker and Lucas A. Powe Jr., *Regulating Broadcast Programming* (Cambridge: MIT Press, 1994); and Couvares, *Movie Censorship*.

to show a "compelling" interest in the regulation. But the early history of film and radio broadcast regulation was dominated by cases in which courts not only permitted federal and state agencies to engage in content regulation of both films and broadcasts, but also failed to treat such regulation as raising any serious First Amendment difficulties. How could this have come about?

To answer that question requires attention to a set of multiple factors affecting the conceptualization of motion pictures as forms of expression in the early twentieth century. Some of those factors have already been mentioned. Motion pictures were in their infancy and were overwhelmingly perceived of as an "entertainment" medium, appealing to a mass, and largely "lowbrow," audience through their novelty. Because of their mass appeal, which included an appeal to children, because of the assumption that those producing and distributing motion pictures would seek to emphasize their sensationalist features, and, finally, because of the Progressive Era's enthusiasm for administrative regulation, the motion picture industry was considered eminently regulable even though it dealt in communication.

In addition to these previously discussed factors, there was another that had a significant effect on the legal treatment of motion pictures. This was the state of First Amendment theory and doctrine in the early twentieth century. Expansive interpretations of the First Amendment have become so commonplace since the close of World War II that one might be inclined to surmise that protection for free speech has always been a cherished American principle. But the First Amendment was not incorporated in the Fourteenth and enforced against the states until 1925;[13] not a single "subversive" speech conviction was invalidated on First Amendment grounds by the Supreme Court until 1931;[14] and between 1897 and 1927 speakers were convicted for making an address on the Boston Common without a permit,[15] advocating public nudity,[16] criticizing the judges of the Colorado Supreme Court,[17] and attending a convention of the California branch

---

13. The first case "incorporating" the First Amendment against the states through the due process clause of the Fourteenth Amendment was *Gitlow v. New York*, 268 U.S. 652 (1925).

14. The first Supreme Court cases invalidating criminal convictions on First Amendment grounds were *Stromberg v. California*, 293 U.S. 359 (1931); and *Near v. Minnesota*, 283 U.S. 697 (1931).

15. *Davis v. Massachusetts*, 167 U.S. 43 (1897).

16. *Fox v. Washington*, 236 U.S. 273 (1915).

17. *Patterson v. Colorado*, 205 U.S. 454 (1907).

of the Communist Labor Party.[18] Moreover, a whole host of expressions were implicitly treated as not amounting to "speech" for First Amendment purposes, including "the lewd and obscene, the profane, the libelous, . . . the insulting or 'fighting' words,"[19] and commercial expressions.[20]

Motion Pictures as "Expression": The Mutual Film *Case*
In 1915 the Supreme Court of the United States decided the case of *Mutual Film Corp. v. Ohio Industrial Commission.*[21] The decision, which was unanimous, was to set the terms of free speech for the moving-picture industry for the next thirty-seven years. Under the principles of *Mutual Film* moving pictures were not considered "speech" for First Amendment purposes and could therefore be regulated or censored with impunity. But despite its great significance, the *Mutual Film* case had some unusual features. First of all, it did not arise because a particular film had been "banned" because of its content, but because a Michigan commercial films distributor objected to the process by which its films entered the state of Ohio.

All films scheduled to be distributed in the state of Ohio were first reviewed by a board of censors operating under the authority of the state Industrial Commission. The board had been established by a 1913 statute and given discretion to determine the "moral and educational character" of incoming films and to approve only those appropriately "moral" or "educational," or those that were "amusing and harmless." The film's distributors were charged a fee for the process. The Mutual Film Company objected to the fee and to the time delays imposed by the board's review. It alleged that its films "depicted dramatizations of standard novels, exhibiting many subjects of scientific interest, the properties of matter, the growth of the various forms of animal and plant life, . . . explorations and travels, [and] events of historical and current interest." It claimed that nothing in its films was "of a harmful

---

18. *Whitney v. California,* 274 U.S. 357 (1927).

19. These categories of expressions remained unprotected through World War II, and some continue to receive no protection or a "lower level" of protection. See *Chaplinsky v. New Hampshire,* 315 U.S. 568 (1942).

20. *Valentine v. Chrestensen,* 316 U.S. 52 (1942). For a general discussion of the comparatively late emergence of libertarian theories of the First Amendment in American history, see G. Edward White, "The First Amendment Comes of Age," *Michigan Law Review* 95 (1996): 1.

21. 236 U.S. 230 (1915).

or immoral character."[22] The Ohio board of censors contradicted this characterization of Mutual Film's products.[23]

A second feature of the case that appears unusual, in retrospect, was that neither side argued that the First Amendment was relevant to it. The reason for that was a technical one. Since the case involved a process of censoring the content of motion pictures that was instituted by a state rather than the federal government, and the First Amendment had not yet been applied against the states, there was, strictly speaking, no "First Amendment" issue in the case. There was, however, the issue of whether motion pictures were "speech," because the Ohio Constitution had a provision stating that "no law shall be passed to restrain or abridge the liberty of speech."[24] Because the Supreme Court of the United States eventually addressed and resolved that issue, the case was taken as providing guidance not only on the speech clause in the Ohio Constitution but on the status of moving pictures in free-speech jurisprudence generally.

The issue of whether motion pictures were "speech" was thus central to Justice McKenna's opinion for the Court in *Mutual Film*. In addressing that issue McKenna resorted to the conventional legal discourse, containing conventional analogies, of his time. He sought to place the legislative-administrative scheme challenged in *Mutual Film* into one of two jurisprudential categories. Either it was a "law restraining or abridging speech," in which case it was invalid under the Ohio Constitution, or it was a law restraining or abridging some other "liberty," in which case the Court needed to decide whether it was an appropriate exercise of state police powers.

In McKenna's professional discourse, the statute in *Mutual Film* was "like" one or another type of statute with which that discourse was familiar. It was either analogous to a law that repressed "the freedom of opinion and expression,"[25] or it was analogous to a law restricting rights of property, contract, or other Fourteenth Amendment "liberties." If it were analogous to the former type of law, films

---

22. Id., 232.
23. In "The Good Censor: Race, Sex, and Censorship in the Early Cinema," *Yale Journal of Criticism* 7 (1994): 234–37, Francis G. Couvares notes that among the films to be distributed by the Mutual Film Company was D. W. Griffith's *Birth of a Nation*.
24. 236 U.S. at 237, citing Section 11, Article 1 of the Ohio Constitution.
25. Id., 243.

could not be censored prior to being exhibited. If, on the other hand, it were analogous to the latter, the police power to protect the morals of the public could be invoked as a justification for prior administrative screening of films.

McKenna's opinion seemed somewhat unsure as to how to proceed with the requisite analogical exercise. He began by suggesting that motion pictures "may be used for evil, and against that possibility the statute was enacted." He added that they had a "power of amusement" and could reach children as well as adults, and these features made them "the more insidious in corruption by a pretense of worthy purpose or if they should degenerate from worthy purpose." Moreover, moving pictures might "excite . . . and appeal . . . to . . . a prurient interest," and "there are some things that should not have pictorial representation in public places and to all audiences." All of these statements suggested that McKenna was finding the mass appeal of movies, and their emotive dimensions, as making them fit subjects for police power regulation.

But the problem with that line of reasoning was that nearly all of the characteristics McKenna attributed to films could have been attributed to novels or to political pamphlets. These might appeal to mass audiences, reach children, address "prurient" subjects, or arouse emotions. So either McKenna was suggesting that when novels or political pamphlets exhibited those tendencies they could be censored, in which case the Ohio free-speech clause was rendered a nullity, or he was suggesting that there was something particularly dangerous about "pictorial representation," as distinguished from verbal representation of subjects.

It turns out that he intended to make the latter suggestion. Indeed he intended to reject altogether the analogy that motion pictures were like novels or pamphlets, which were expressions of opinion. They were instead like theater productions, regarded as eminently regulable by municipal authorities through a licensing process. When a theater production was screened as part of that process, McKenna argued, "[i]t seems not to have occurred to anybody . . . that freedom of opinion was repressed in the exercise of the power. . . . The rights of property only were considered as involved."[26] Similarly, the exhibition of motion pictures, for McKenna, was

---

26. Id., 244.

a business, pure and simple, originated and conducted for profit, like other spectacles, not to be regarded . . . as part of the press of the country or as organs of public opinion. They are mere representations of events, of ideas and sentiments published and known, vivid, useful, and entertaining no doubt, but . . . capable of evil, having power for it, the greater because of their attractiveness and manner of exhibition.[27]

One wonders how, if the exhibition of moving pictures was merely a "business" with no element of "opinion," movies were especially "capable of evil" because of the "power" and "attractiveness" of their "manner of exhibition." McKenna was not the last film critic to have difficulty separating medium from message.

The theater analogy was a particularly charged one for McKenna to invoke, given the status of theater productions in late nineteenth- and twentieth-century America. Theaters had been subjected to a municipal licensing process in states such as New York as early as the 1830s, and in 1862 the New York legislature passed a statute regulating "places of public amusement." The purpose of the legislation was to separate theater productions from liquor and prostitution, and in compliance with the act some theater establishments erected partitions separating their barrooms from their stage areas. Nonetheless critics of the theaters periodically revealed that traffic between the barrooms and stage areas was common; that there was a coded regime of interactions between waitresses in the barrooms and customers designed to raise the possibility of sexual encounters in other parts of the establishment; and that the proprietors of the theaters were making payments to the local police to prevent prostitution raids.[28]

Theaters were thus regularly associated, throughout the late nineteenth and early twentieth centuries, with "unwholesome" activities. In addition theaters required a relatively large public space, making them subject, as were vaudeville shows or concerts, to a host of public-safety regulations. The licensing process and its requirements provided a easy wedge for content regulation, and in the early twentieth century theater

---

27. Id.
28. See Daniel Citzrom, "The Politics of Performance: Theater Licensing and the Origins of Movie Censorship in New York," in Couvares, *Movie Censorship*, 17–20.

operators periodically had their licenses revoked for operating on Sundays, for failing to maintain appropriate space between their stages and their barrooms, or for exhibiting risqué productions.[29]

Thus the theater analogy presented a form of expression that was treated as eminently regulable because of its associations with public space and because of its further associations with unwholesomeness. As theaters were establishing themselves and being conceptualized in this fashion, the infant motion picture industry grew up in their midst. Initially conceived of as visual novelty acts within the rubric of vaudeville shows, motion pictures, with the emergence of the kinetoscope and the ability to transmit a series of rapidly moving visual images, entered their nickelodeon phase in the first decade of the twentieth century. Soon they evolved from one among many vaudeville acts to an independent form of public amusement. In the conventional regulatory structure of public amusements, they had some advantages over theaters, vaudeville shows, and concerts: they did not require much space and they could offer short productions to relatively small, constantly changing audiences. Hence the nickelodeons were able to obtain "common-show" licenses, were significantly cheaper than concert or theater licenses, which were issued routinely by the mayor rather than on a discretionary basis by the police department, and did not subject licensees to the safety regulations associated with larger structures and audiences.[30]

As the movie industry emerged from its nickelodeon phase to the exhibition of longer films with more detailed story lines, it became clear that motion pictures were becoming less like visual novelties and more like theater productions. At the same time some sociological features of the motion picture industry became apparent to critical observers. One feature was a tendency in the industry to cater to immigrant groups in urban centers and to be operated by recent immigrants, mainly Italians and Jews. A second was a tendency to cater to children. A third was a tendency to exhibit "sensationalist" pictures, such as narratives of dance halls, observers leering at women as the wind blew their skirts, visits of tourists to Chinese opium dens, or the exploits of urban crimi-

---

29. See Citzrom, "The Politics of Performance," 18–27.

30. See id., 20–22, for a discussion of the treatment of nickelodeon shows in New York City in the first decade of the twentieth century.

nals.[31] It was apparent that a principal attraction of motion pictures was their ability to communicate to nonliterate audiences or audiences whose first language was not English. It was also clear that entrepreneurs in the movie industry needed to hold their audience's attention in a genre where words were not yet spoken. Hence an orientation toward "sensational" subjects seemed natural, if potentially disturbing.

Thus as movies evolved the theater analogy loomed increasingly larger. Both media catered to a popular, "lowbrow" audience, both relied strongly on emotive visual images, and both were tinged with an air of salaciousness. To make the parallel complete—at least in the eyes of apprehensive early-twentieth-century observers—the nickelodeons, like the theaters, operated on Sundays. In 1908 the reformist mayor of New York City, George B. McClellan, responding to pressure from mainly Protestant religious groups, revoked the licenses of all the motion picture operators in the city, about 550 persons. His revocation order stated that any renewal of a moving-picture show's license would be predicated on that establishment's written agreement not to operate on Sunday. He added that he reserved the right to revoke licenses "on evidence that pictures have been exhibited by the licensees which tend to degrade or injure the morals of the community."[32]

It may have been the apparent attractiveness of movies to immigrant groups, symbolized by their Sunday performances—ostensibly to audiences who did not regard that day as holy—that invested the medium with elements of unwholesomeness. It may have been their focus on "sensationalist" themes to which children and illiterates could relate. It may have been the emotive quality of movie messages, or it may have been a combination of all of these elements. In any event, it became clear to those Progressives concerned with the purification of American life and increasingly fearful of mass culture that motion pictures contained all the sinister potential of theaters. As the theater analogy sunk in, the conclusion that the content of movies could be regulated followed.

McKenna's opinion in *Mutual Film* embraced the theater analogy as well: motion pictures, like theaters, were exhibitions for profit,

---

31. Id., 29–30.

32. McClellan's statement accompanying his revocation order was quoted in the *New York Times*, December 25, 1908. See also Citzrom, "The Politics of Performance," 33–34.

"mere representations of events" that the state could regulate pursuant to an interest in preserving the safety and morals of the public. It is hard to say whether McKenna's disinclination to analogize movies to protected expressions of communication, such as novels or pamphlets, demonstrated that he had embraced all of the overtones of the theater analogy, so that he believed there was something peculiarly threatening in the "lowbrow" appeal of the movies. But whatever his motivation, the legal discourse in which he was operating, by encouraging the characterization of motion pictures as "like" theaters, directed him toward his conclusion. That discourse also enabled him, when asked to choose whether to treat expressions in motion pictures under the rubrics of "speech" or "police power liberty," to make use of the latter rubric's permissive treatment of governmental regulations whose purpose was to protect the morals of the public. Thus administrative censorship of the morals became unproblematic.

There was another dimension of the *Mutual Film* case that guided McKenna toward the result he reached. This was the fact that the censorship at issue was being performed by an administrative agency. As noted, Progressives were enthusiastic about such agencies as units of government. Agencies combined, in their view, a freedom from partisanship, an expertise, and a capacity to respond to social problems in an efficient fashion. Progressives were not particularly sanguine about the conventional legislative process as a response to social ills because they believed that "special interests" tended to influence and even to corrupt legislatures. Administrators, on the other hand, were not elected officials and thus less susceptible to lobbying. They qualified for their positions by virtue of their expert training.

The statute challenged in *Mutual Film* was a typical Progressive scheme: a delegation of power from a legislature to an administrative agency to perform specialized regulatory functions. The delegation was often broad, either containing no standards at all or reciting open-ended standards such as "the public interest, convenience, and necessity." The theory of open-ended delegations was that administrators were in a particularly good position to solve specialized problems because they were trained, nonpartisan experts. The *Mutual Film* statute, for example, assumed that the members of the board of movie censors of the Ohio Industrial Commission would be able to determine "what is educational, moral, amusing or harmless" in evaluating films.[33]

The lawyers for the Mutual Film Company had argued that Ohio's delegation of the task of regulating the content of movies to a board of censors, unaccompanied by any evaluative standards, "[left] decision to arbitrary judgment, whim and caprice."[34] McKenna responded to that argument by declaring that the "general terms" of the delegation "get precision from the sense and experience of men." He meant the sense and experience of administrators, a class of men who combined specialized knowledge with the absence of partisanship and who could thus be trusted to make decisions that would "become certain and useful guides in reasoning and conduct."[35] The theory of administrative delegation, McKenna noted, was grounded on those assumptions of administrator nonpartisanship and expertise: "If this were not so, the many administrative agencies created by the state and National governments would be denuded of their utility."[36]

In sum, McKenna's conceptualization of *Mutual Film* made the case into a property case, with films being treated as businesses rather than communications; a police power case, in which the state could invoke its powers to protect the morals of the public to regulate property rights; and an administrative law case, in which a group of experts had been delegated power to regulate a specialized area on behalf of the public generally. This conceptualization invoked familiar analogies, such as the theater analogy, and prevented *Mutual Film* from being seen as a free speech case.

To an important extent, therefore, the Supreme Court's early-twentieth-century treatment of film censorship can be understood by unraveling the professional discourse, with its allegedly relevant analogies and assumptions, in which cases such as *Mutual Film* were set. Had a more libertarian corpus of free-speech doctrine existed at the time, arguments that films were "like" novels or political tracts might have been more persuasive, and the Court might have grasped that the discernible emotive impact of motion pictures was itself a form of communication, analogous to vivid speaking or writing.

Nonetheless it would be hazardous to conclude that the Court's

---

33. Citzrom, "The Politics of Performance," 245.
34. Id.
35. Id., 246.
36. Id.

conclusion in *Mutual Film*—that administrative censorship of motion pictures raised no serious First Amendment problems—was entirely a consequence of the "relative autonomy" of legal discourse. The Court's decision in *Mutual Film* was also undoubtedly affected by the embryonic state of films themselves. In 1915 "motion pictures" still consisted of silent, nickelodeon-type productions, consisting of "a series of instantaneous photographs or positive prints of action . . . projected upon a screen with great rapidity." For the most part they resembled "short subjects" rather than sustained dramas; they contained no dialogue; they had little plotting or character development. They were, in short, distinguished mainly for the novelty of their visual images, pictures set in rapid motion on a screen. Under the circumstances one could imagine their being analogized more to a kaleidoscope, and especially more to a theater production, than to a novel. That analogy did not so much come from legal discourse as from the experience of the average citizen in 1915.

The relatively narrow conception of "free speech" in movies that prevailed at the time of the *Mutual Film* decision was thus not simply a product of the tenor of late-nineteenth- and early-twentieth-century First Amendment jurisprudence. It was also a product of the difficulty contemporaries had in analogizing motion pictures to the conventional forms of speech—lectures, essays, novels, and other books—and the ease with which they could analogize motion pictures to theater productions, whose content had implicitly and explicitly regulated since their infancy. In both instances the analogizing process had its roots in the larger culture as well as in legal discourse.

Radio and the First Amendment
If one turns from regulation of motion pictures to regulation of radio, one finds some striking parallels. Again an administrative regime was developed to supervise what was taken to be a specialized, technical area; again that regime freely censored the content of the regulated medium; again such censorship was not found to raise First Amendment problems. In addition, similar assumptions about administrative expertise affected the courts' treatment of radio censorship cases, and the difficulty courts and commentators had in analogizing radio broadcasting to conventionally protected speech was accentuated by the novelty of radio communication.

From the origins of radio its status was affected by what most

Americans perceived as the mysterious, highly technical nature of the medium. Radio waves were transmitted through some bizarre electronic process involving sparks and towers, moved into what was originally called the "ether," a region of the earth's atmosphere that was particularly receptive to the waves, and were received through another bizarre electronic process, one that decoded the messages in the ether and translated them back into their original form.[37] Once Marconi's "wireless" transmission process was grasped, a number of early-twentieth-century amateur electronics buffs were able to build sets that received signals from distant regions. By 1912 the United States government had realized two things about radio communication: messages could be sent long distances, making radio a valuable medium for ships sending distress signals, and if more than one signal was communicated on a particular wavelength, interference would result, producing static and rendering the signal useless.

With ship distress signals in mind, the government, in the Radio Act of 1912, began the process of licensing radio stations and assigning frequencies on "the spectrum," a term employed to represent the range of available frequencies on which radio signals could be sent at the time. The first signals were sent along what are now called low or medium wave frequencies, the equivalent of "AM" radio. They could travel long distances, especially at night, but they tended to be susceptible to interference from stations within ten kilocycles of their assigned frequency. In the 1912 Radio Act Congress was primarily concerned with the military and safety implications of spectrum interference, so the act mainly sought to separate frequencies used by the armed forces from those used by commercial stations and amateurs. For a time the number of stations was sufficiently small that once amateurs were moved out of the range of commercial and military frequencies spectrum interference was reduced.

---

37. In the late 1920s Senator Clarence C. Dill, author of the Radio Act of 1927, which created the Federal Radio Commission, forerunner of the Federal Communications Commission, had a private conversation with Chief Justice William Howard Taft. Dill was concerned that the constitutionality of the Radio Act might be challenged, and the Supreme Court might have trouble understanding whether radio was "commerce" for the purposes of permitting it to be regulated by the federal government. Dill reported Taft as responding that "if I'm to write a decision on this thing called radio, I'm afraid I'll have to get in touch with the occult." Taft told Dill that he would do his best to avoiding taking jurisdiction over any case involving the regulation of the radio industry. Clarence Dill, unpublished interview with Ed Craney, 1964, quoted in Barnouw, *A Tower in Babel*, 257–58.

By the 1920s, however, commercial stations had begun to come into the market in large numbers, and between 1923 and 1926 the regulatory powers of the secretary of commerce, who had been licensing stations and assigning frequencies since 1912, were curtailed in two cases.[38] The result of those cases was that the secretary of commerce was required to issue licenses for new stations, but had no power to assign stations to particular frequencies or to limit either the transmission wattage of stations or the hours they broadcast.[39] This produced chaos in the radio industry. Nearly two hundred stations entered the market in 1926 and stations began experimenting with various frequencies, levels of wattage power, and broadcasting hours, seeking to maximize their audience.[40]

Congress responded to this situation by passing the Radio Act of 1927. That act, for the first time, unequivocally declared that the government of the United States owned the airwaves. It established a Federal Radio Commission to license stations, assign frequencies, determine the hours of broadcasts, and regulate the transmission power of stations. The FRC was composed of seven commissioners, who were given discretion to regulate broadcasting in accordance with the "public interest, convenience, or necessity."[41] It was originally anticipated that the FRC would be in existence for only one year, in order to restore structure to the radio industry, and would then delegate radio licensing to the secretary of commerce. But by 1929 this delegation had not occurred, and Congress gave the FRC an indefinite regulatory mandate.[42]

After coming into existence the FRC considered whether its mandate to license stations in accordance with the "public interest, convenience, or necessity" extended to content-based evaluations of radio programming. The Radio Act of 1927 had prohibited the FRC from employing its licensing process to exercise "the power of censorship over the radio communications or signals transmitted by any radio sta-

38. *Hoover v. Inter-city Radio*, 286 F. 1003 (D.C. Cir. 1923); *United States v. Zenith Radio Corp.*, 12 F.2d 616 (N.D.Ill. 1926).

39. See Barnouw, *A Tower in Babel*, 189–90. Prior to 1926 the secretary of commerce had assigned stations to designated frequencies and also controlled the hours a given station could broadcast so as to minimize interference.

40. See Jora R. Minasian, "The Political Economy of Broadcasting in the 1920s," *Journal of Law and Economics* 12 (1969): 399–401.

41. 44 Stat. 1162 (1927). For additional detail on the FRC and its early efforts to regulate the content of radio broadcasts, see Schiller, "Policy Ideals and Judicial Action," 605–14.

42. 46 Stat. 50 (1929).

tion," or to "interfere with the right of free speech by means of radio communications," although at the same time the FRC was permitted to exclude "obscene, indecent, or profane language" from the airwaves.[43] The two provisions were not necessarily inconsistent, however, since there was no indication that "obscene, indecent or profane language" had any constitutional protection at the time.

In two annual reports, issued in 1928 and 1929, the FRC claimed authority to consider the content of station programming under the "public interest, convenience, and necessity" standard, and to refuse to renew a station's license if it found that station's programming "uninteresting" or "distasteful."[44] The content of radio programs, the FRC concluded, should conform to "the tastes, needs, and desires of all substantial groups of the listening public."[45] It instituted a practice of renewing licenses every three months (a process later extended to six months)[46] in order to create incentives on the part of stations to offer programs with acceptable content. By 1930 a commentator applauded the fact that under the "public interest, convenience, or necessity" standard the FRC "has had to give its opinion on . . . the excessive use of ordinary commercial phonograph records, on the use of obscene or indecent language, . . . [or] whether a station giving a service of general interest is to be preferred to a station which acts as the mouthpiece for a particular school of political, religious, or economic thought."[47]

In 1930 the FRC declined to renew the license of station KFKB, operating out of Milford, Kansas, on the grounds that the public interest, convenience, or necessity would not be served by the station's continuing to broadcast. The station had been established by Dr. J. R. Brinkley, who also operated the Brinkley Hospital and the Brinkley Pharmaceutical Association in Milford. Dr. Brinkley's principal source of income came from "prescriptions" that he offered to radio listeners on the show "Medical Question Box," which aired three times a day on KFKB. Listeners would write in to Dr. Brinkley at the station with medical complaints. He would read their letters over the air and in the great

---

43. See 44 Stat. 1172 (1927).

44. Federal Radio Commission, *Second Annual Report* (1928), 169.

45. Federal Radio Commission, *Third Annual Report* (1929), 34

46. Federal Radio Commission, *Sixth Annual Report* (1932), 7.

47. Louis G. Caldwell, "Radio and the Law," in *Radio and Its Future*, ed. Martin Codel (London: Harper and Brothers, 1930), 234–35. Caldwell was the first general counsel to the Federal Radio Commission.

bulk of cases he would designate one of his prescriptions, referred to only by number, as a remedy for the complaint. He had no additional contact with the "patients." The prescriptions were dispensed through the Brinkley Pharmaceutical Association, whose members paid a fee to the radio station each time they sold a prescription. Evidence submitted at the license renewal hearing indicated that in the period between February and April, 1930, the Brinkley Pharmaceutical Association had earned $27,856.40 through the sale of "Medical Question Box" prescriptions.[48]

In the renewal hearing the FRC found that much of the programming on KFKB was "entertaining and unobjectionable in character." It concluded, however, that the "Medical Question Box" program was "inimical to the public health and safety, and for that reason . . . not in the public interest." It cited the fact that Dr. Brinkley had never seen any of the patients for which he prescribed treatment and that he had based his diagnoses only on symptoms described by patients in letters. It reproduced one excerpt from the "Medical Question Box" as "typical":

> Sunflower State, from Dresden, Kans. Probably he has gall stones. No, I don't mean that, I mean kidney stones. My advice to you is to put him on Prescription No. 80 and 50 for men, also 64. I think that he will be a whole lot better. Also drink a lot of water.[49]

Dr. Brinkley challenged the FRC's denial of KFKB's license on the ground that it amounted to "censorship," citing the language in the Radio Act of 1927. The U.S. Court of Appeals for the District of Columbia Circuit[50] concluded that because the radio business was "impressed with a public interest and because the number of available broadcast-

---

48. *KFKB Broadcasting Ass'n v. Federal Radio Commission*, 47 F.2d 670, 671 (D.C. Cir. 1931).

49. Id., 671–72.

50. The Radio Act of 1927 originally provided that appeals from FRC decisions would be to the Court of Appeals for the D.C. Circuit, and that the court could "take additional evidence, alter or revise the decision appealed from, and enter judgment as it saw fit" (44 Stat. 1169 [1927]). In *Federal Radio Comm. v. General Electric Co.*, 281 U.S. 464 (1930), the Supreme Court held that the FRC was an administrative agency and hence its decisions could not be subjected to de novo review by a court. Congress responded by amending the Radio Act of 1927 to limit judicial review of the FRC's decisions to questions of law (46 Stat. 844 [1930]).

ing facilities is limited, the [FRC] is necessarily called upon to consider the character and quality of service to be rendered." It pointed out that "[t]here has been no attempt on the part of the commission to subject any part of [KFKB]'s broadcasting matter to scrutiny prior to its release." A determination of whether a station was operating in the public interest, convenience or necessity involved "tak[ing] note of [that station]'s past conduct, which is not censorship."[51] The D.C. Circuit declined to substitute its "judgment and discretion" for that of the FRC on the case.

A similar approach was adopted in *Trinity Methodist Church v. Federal Radio Commission*,[52] a 1932 decision. In that case radio station KGEF, owned by the Reverend Dr. Robert ("Fighting Bob") Shuler, leased its facilities to the Trinity Methodist Church, which put on "programs furnished by religious, philanthropic, educational, and musical organizations."[53] Three of the twenty-three hours a week devoted to broadcasting featured Dr. Shuler, who delivered a series of attacks on various persons and groups. The FRC found that Shuler

> attacked the bar association for its activities in recommending judges, charging it with ulterior and sinister purposes. . . . [H]e charged particular judges with sundry immoral acts. He made defamatory statements against the board of health. He charged that the labor temple in Los Angeles was a bootlegging and gambling joint. . . . He freely spoke of "pimps" and prostitutes. He alluded slightingly to the Jews as a race, and made frequent and bitter attacks on the Roman Catholic religion and its relations to government.[54]

When KGEF's license came up for renewal in September 1930, the FRC denied its application, citing Shuler's inflammatory remarks. Trinity Methodist Church appealed on the ground that the decision had violated the First Amendment.

The D.C. Circuit's analysis of the First Amendment issue came per-

---

51. *KFKB Broadcasting*, 672.

52. 62 F.2d 850 (1932).

53. See *Trinity Methodist Church v. Federal Radio Comm.*, 53 Sup. Ct. 317 (1933) (brief for petitioner in petition for certiorari).

54. 62 F.2d at 852.

ilously close to suggesting that free speech did not exist on the radio. It first intimated that the First Amendment might be confined to previous restraints on publication, with speakers being amenable to subsequent punishment.[55] It next claimed that Congress, in the exercise of its legislative power, could "refuse a renewal of license to one who has abused it to broadcast defamatory and untrue matter." The problem with this claim was that Shuler had not been convicted of defamation, and much of his commentary had amounted to extravagant opinions.

The heart of the D.C. Circuit's opinion, however, came in a paragraph in which it argued that the extensive potential impact of the radio medium made it a particularly dangerous forum for the communication of offensive speech and therefore one susceptible to administrative regulation. "If it be considered," the court said,

> that one in possession of a permit to broadcast in interstate commerce may, without let or hindrance from any source, use these facilities, reaching out, as they do, from one corner of the country to the other, to . . . offend the religious susceptibilities of thousands, inspire political distrust and civic discord, or offend youth and innocence by the free use of words suggestive of sexual immorality, and be answerable for slander only at the instance of the one offended, then this great science, instead of a boon, will become a scourge, and the nation a theater for the display of individual passions and the collision of personal interests.[56]

The court added that the loss of a radio license for the transmission of inflammatory broadcasts was "neither censorship no previous restraint, nor . . . a whittling away of the rights guaranteed by the First Amendment" because broadcasters were free to communicate their views in other ways, "subject, of course, to be required to answer for the abuse thereof."[57] It suggested that the particular evil in *Trinity*

---

55. "It may . . . be laid down as a fundamental principle that . . . the citizen has in the first instance the right to utter or to publish his sentiments, though, of course, upon condition that he is responsible for any abuse of that right." The court cited Blackstone's *Commentaries*, which confined protection for free speech to immunity from prior restraints (id., 851).

56. Id., 852–53.

57. Id., 853.

Methodist Church was the "continued use of an instrumentality of commerce" to subject others to personal abuse.

The above language suggested that the same reasons why radio was a regulated medium provided a justification for limitations on radio speech. Radio's potential to reach vast audiences meant that radio speakers' comments might have wide impact and thus wide potential for harm. Moreover, the scarcity of radio frequencies caused by the problem of spectrum interference—the primary rationale for governmental regulation of radio broadcasts—meant that administrative control of the radio industry was a necessity. Administrative control meant administrative discretion, and discretionary judgments by expert administrators could take into account the special features of an industry, including a communications industry. *Trinity Methodist Church* suggested that the impact of the First Amendment on FRC licensing proceedings might be negligible.

In a 1933 commentary entitled "The Freedom of Radio Speech," Mark DeWolfe Howe reviewed the *KFKB* and *Trinity Methodist* cases and concluded that "[w]here the limitation of discussion has promoted the interest of all, it has frequently been sustained," and that radio speech might prove an apt example of this proposition. Howe's analysis conceded that the FRC's licensing process amounted to an "indirect previous restraint" on applicants because of the constant threat of a license forfeiture should the FRC conclude that "a station ha[d] broadcast speeches . . . inimical to the public interest." This amounted to regulation of the content of broadcasts, which lead Howe to surmise that "either radio communication must be found to be outside the protection of the First Amendment, or consideration of program content in the exercise of the licensing power must be justified on grounds of social necessity."[58]

Howe believed that although analogies might suggest that radio speech was outside the protection of the First Amendment altogether, they were not persuasive. He pointed to motion pictures, citing the *Mutual Film* decision, as "not part of the press within the meaning of the First Amendment." But, apparently retaining the assumptions about the orientation of motion picture shows that controlled McKenna's opinion in *Mutual Film*, Howe asserted that "to a far greater extent than the cinema, radio is an organ for the expression of opinion

---

58. Howe, "Freedom of Radio Speech," 991. Howe was identified as the contributor of this anonymous note in the masthead of the *Harvard Law Review* issue.

on matters of public concern."[59] The fact that the electronic character of radio transmissions had made possible a "wider publication" of radio speech did not alter the nature of that speech.[60]

Howe also rejected the argument that since the federal government owned the airwaves, it could exclude stations entirely from the air, and that greater power included a lesser power to regulate the program content of stations that were licensed. He felt that this argument had not prevailed in the case of government power to withhold second-class mail privileges: the postal power was still subject to the First Amendment. So Howe believed that radio speech enjoyed some First Amendment protection. At the same time he believed that "social interests" favored content regulation of radio speech.

One of those interests was the government's interest in "the preservation of intelligible communication" over the airwaves, which had stimulated the administrative scheme embodied in the Radio Act of 1927. Since an interest in keeping the airwaves from being distorted by interference required some regime for allocating frequencies, and some limitation on the number of broadcasting stations was necessary, one could argue that "the social desirability of attaining the best use of the available facilities" became "proportionately great." Further, radio had "a quality of instrusiveness into the home" that might make the medium "offensive to adults and dangerous to children" if some control over the content of programs were not exercised. Finally, radio had achieved a "tremendous following," which Howe associated with "popular approval of . . . educational and informational programs." He believed that regulation of program content was necessary to keep broadcasting "at a high level." To the extent that each of these social interests was furthered by "the commission's examination of programs," Howe concluded, "a clear justification" for the abridgement of radio speech was provided.

In examining the variables affecting the early treatment of radio speech, one can see how the time frame of the radio cases produced subtle differences from the *Mutual Film* case. By the early 1930s the First

---

59. By "public concern" Howe seems to have meant that radio broadcasts tended to be on less trivial subjects than moving-picture shows. In a sense the experience of the *KFKB* and *Trinity Methodist* cases confirmed this assumption, because the bulk of the stations' programming was devoted toward classical music broadcasts, and even the objectionable portions were oriented toward the "public" issues of health and ideological exchange.

60. Howe, "Freedom of Radio Speech," 991.

Amendment implications of cases had come to be taken more seriously than at the time of World War I. The Court had concluded that protection against governmental restrictions on speech was not limited to prior restraints, and Howe was sensitive to the fact that a licensing scheme for radio stations that took program content into account might create a "chilling effect" on opinions expressed over the air. He was also aware that expressions communicated over the radio were not precisely analogous to the *Mutual Film* description of expressions communicated in film: they more resembled the opinions communicated in books or speeches. The medium of radio may have been a novelty, but it was not simply aural "entertainment." The content of its programs was an important part of its appeal.

When Howe engaged in analogical reasoning to clarify the First Amendment status of radio speech, he found the *Mutual Film* treatment of films as comparable to theater productions inapposite. At the same time he found another of the analogies bequeathed to him by McKenna in *Mutual Film* apposite. Radio communications employed a particular kind of specialized technology, and that technology required a limitation on the number of radio frequencies in order to ensure intelligibility of radio signals. The market could not be trusted to produce an optimum level of radio transmission on its own, as the experience of the 1920s had shown. Since radio signals crossed state lines with impunity, the ideal candidate to regulate the radio market was the federal government, and the ideal regulatory forum was a federal administrative agency, since frequency allocation should be nonpartisan and required expertise.

Radio speech was thus "like" speech in a motion picture in one important respect: it required attention by some administrative regulatory agency. And since radio speech was also "like" film speech in being intrusive, pervasive, and accessible to children, its content was a relevant concern of the regulatory body. Thus radio speech, although not seen as identical to film speech, was also not seen as identical to speech in a novel, a pamphlet, or a political address. It was seen as in a category of expressions whose content was eminently regulable because of a variety of social interests in their regulation. Some of those interests were associated with the unique characteristics of the medium of radio; others followed from the presence of a regulatory scheme itself. The dominant analogies in the professional discourse in which early radio speech cases were considered served to force radio broadcasts into a class of expressions whose content was eminently regulable.

The Current Status of Film and Radio Speech
Given the origins of regulation of motion pictures and radio broadcasts, one might have expected that censorship of the former medium might currently be more entrenched than that of the latter. The source of that expectation would lie in the fact that commentators and courts were quick to recognize that the content of radio speech was very similar to other oral speech, the differences resting mainly in the medium of communication. Film, on the other hand, was initially thought of as less of an ordinary means of communicating substantive messages than as a novel form of displaying images, more resembling a camera than a book. *Mutual Film* treated film speech as not even raising First Amendment issues, and that position remained authoritative until 1948.[61]

Radio speech, however, is currently restricted far more significantly than film speech. Radio speech, in fact, has never enjoyed anything like the First Amendment protection extended to print media, whereas film speech, since the 1960s, has. Newspapers do not have to grant access to their space to their political opponents, or any persons they criticize in print,[62] but radio and television stations are required to give equal access to opposing points of view when they either endorse or afford space to speakers in political campaigns.[63] Nonobscene but "indecent" material can appear in books or other print media with impunity, but the Federal Communications Commission can revoke the license of any radio or television station that broadcasts material the commission deems offensive or indecent.[64] In contrast, since 1965 administrative preclearance of the content of films without indepen-

61. Even then the theory of *Mutual Film* was not openly discarded. In *United States v. Paramount Pictures* Justice William O. Douglas, for a majority of the Court, stated that "we have no doubt that motion pictures, like newspapers and radio, are included in the press whose freedom is guaranteed by the First Amendment" (334 U.S. 131, 166 [1948]). But Douglas's statement was unnecessary to the decision in *Paramount Pictures*, and *Mutual Film* was not overruled until *Joseph Burstyn Inc. v. Wilson*, 343 U.S. 495, 502 (1952).

62. *Miami Herald v. Tornillo*, 418 U.S. 241 (1974).

63. *Red Lion Broadcasting v. FCC*, 395 U.S. 367 (1969).

64. *FCC v. Pacifica Foundation*, 438 U.S. 726 (1978). In that case the satirist George Carlin delivered a twelve-minute monologue before a live theater audience that was broadcast over a New York radio station at two in the afternoon. The monologue, entitled "Filthy Words," poked fun at the taboos imposed on certain words by repeating them in humorous combinations. A listener, who heard the broadcast with his young son, issued a complaint to the FCC, who granted the complaint, including it in Pacifica Foundation's file for relicensing purposes. The Supreme Court, in upholding the FCC, held that the FCC had the power to regulate offensive but nonobscene speech on radio and television. It cited the "uniquely pervasive" character of broadcast media and their unique accessibility to children (id., 748).

dent judicial review has been unconstitutional,[65] and since 1971 obscenity has been treated as the only constitutionally permissible basis for movie censorship.[66]

In searching for the explanation for the different treatment of radio speech and film speech, one encounters again the role of analogical reasoning in law and the associated question of law's relative autonomy from its social context. Let us consider the details of the comparative history of radio and film regulation with those themes in mind.

As we have seen, regulation of films took place through state-created boards of censors, whose discretion, under the *Mutual Film* precedent, was virtually unreviewable and extended to content-based determinations. But administrative regulation of films was tied to a theory of films as, on the one hand, a novel form of entertainment, essentially consisting of a stringing together of visual images, and on the other hand, a potentially salacious form of public amusement, akin to theater productions. Such a theory might have appeared to be grounded in experience when films were silent "short shorts" packaged together in a reel and when they typically featured "sensationalist" topics. It came to appear less so as films introduced sound and began to portray a variety of sustained types of dramatic stories, with plotting and characterizations, akin to novels. By 1952 the Supreme Court had concluded that "motion pictures are a significant medium for the communication of ideas," capable of "direct espousal of a political or social doctrine" or "the subtle shaping of thought which characterizes all artistic expression."[67]

With this shift in the conception of film speech, the analogy to print media speech became apparent, and it was not surprising that as early as 1957 the Court was intimating that the only basis on which state or local administrative boards could censor movies was on the grounds of their being obscene.[68] The movie industry seized upon that situation by proposing its own regulatory code. The industry had developed its own production code as early as 1934, and enforced it, until the 1950s,

65. *Freedman v. Maryland*, 380 U.S. 51 (1965).

66. *Grove Press v. Maryland Board of Censors*, 401 U.S. 480 (1971).

67. *Burstyn v. Wilson*, 501.

68. *Roth v. United States*, 354 U.S. 476 (1957). See the discussion in deGrazia and Newman, *Banned Films*, 95–96.

quite severely.[69] But in 1968, taking advantage of the Supreme Court's stringent test for obscenity and fearful of a public reaction against pornography, the Motion Picture Association of America implemented an age-classification system, in which an industry-sponsored private agency, the Code and Rating Administration, assigns G, PG (now subdivided to PG13), R, and X ratings to movies before their distribution. The ratings are largely concerned with sexuality, profanity, and violence in a given film.

Thus governmental censorship of the movies now occupies approximately the same status as censorship of print media: municipalities can only regulate the content of obscene publications. Whether this situation is affected by the moving-picture industry's self-regulation is uncertain, but the industry obviously has believed for many years that self-regulation is in its interest. The fact that the industry's ratings are age-oriented also suggests why self-regulation has emerged: the industry fears that movies may be thought of as pervasive and uniquely accessible to children, in the manner of radio or television, and thus unlike books or magazines.[70]

In contrast, radio and television have from their outset been seen as necessarily regulable because of the technical qualities of the broad-

---

69. DeGrazia and Newman, *Banned Films,* 43–72. Self-censorship as a response to the threat of regulation had in fact been a feature of the movie industry almost from its origins. In response to McClellan's temporary closing of the moving-picture houses in New York City in 1908, for example, the Moving Picture Exhibitors Association requested, in March 1909, that the People's Institute, which had had success establishing voluntary censorship criteria for the live theatre industry, create a Board of Censorship to review the contents of all films shown in New York City. Subsequently, in June 1909, the People's Institute created a National Board of Censorship of Motion Pictures (the NBC), to be funded by movie exhibitors and manufacturers. The NBC remained influential until the 1920s, opposing efforts on the part of states and localities to establish their own censorship boards. By the 1920s it had come to be perceived as a captive of the movie industry, and was eventually supplanted by the Motion Picture Producers and Distributors Association, based in Hollywood, which was a powerful influence on the content of movies, and by the screenwriting process in the movie industry, for the next three decades. For the history of self-censorship in the movie industry in the 1920s and thirties, see Richard Maltby, "'To Prevent the Prevalent Type of Book,'" in Couvares, *Movie Censorship,* 97–128. Maltby argues that the Motion Picture Producers and Distributors Association self-consciously exerted a form of censorship on novels and plays that were adapted for the screen, eliminating their "highbrow" and often their more risqué, controversial, or potentially shocking features.

70. It is interesting in this respect that the Telecommunications Act of 1996 anticipates an analogous rating system for television (and presumably radio) shows.

cast medium. The regulatory apparatus that was created by the Radio
Act of 1927, with licensing mechanisms, a "public interest, convenience, or necessity" standard, content-based administrative determinations, and deferential court review, still exists. Remarkably, the principal justification for that regulatory apparatus—the assumption that
the airwaves were "scarce" because of the phenomenon of spectrum
interference—has been recently acknowledged by the Supreme Court
to no longer be valid.[71] Nonetheless the Court has declined to modify
its broadcast jurisprudence, and the FCC remains a ubiquitous regulatory force, resulting in radio and television speech being significantly
less "free" than communications in other media.

Now let us place the above details in the thematic framework of
this essay. If one looks at the apparently paradoxical status of film and
radio speech in contemporary America—a onetime novelty medium,
initially thought of as not communicating opinions at all, now being
treated as analogous to books and magazines, and a medium whose
communicative content is widely recognized as greatly resembling that
of the print media remaining under a regime of significant content regulation—one is struck by two features of the history of film and radio
speech cases. The first feature is that radio speech was, virtually from
its origins, regulated by a federal administrative agency, and federal
administrative regulation was thought—because of the "scarcity"
premise—as absolutely necessary to the development of the medium.
In contrast the content of films, although initially thought of as eminently regulable, was thought of as more akin to the contents of other
goods, such as fruits or vegetables, than to the contents of books or
magazines. Films were not scarce; films did not inevitably cross state
lines; films were, in short, recognizable products. Regulation thus took
the conventional form, for the early twentieth century, of state or local
boards of review.

---

71. See *Turner Broadcasting v. FCC,* 114 S. Ct. 2445, 2457 (1994). Two features of the
broadcast market have contributed to the decline of "scarcity." First, the technology now
exists to send waves through the atmosphere at very high frequencies, so that the
"bands" originally conceived as limiting signals have now significantly expanded. Second, alternative methods for sending radio and television signals, such as cable and
direct satellite systems, have enabled many more stations to enter the market. It seems
fair to say, in fact, that the only current limits on the number of stations in the cable television market come from the capacity of producers to create diverse programming and
the capacity of viewers to embrace multiple channels. There are, of course, many more
radio and television stations currently operating in the United States than there are newspapers, so it is hard to know what "scarcity" in the broadcast industry means these days.

The second feature of the early history of film and radio speech cases is that film was not initially seen as "speech" at all, but radio was. Film was not initially analogizable to anything that qualified as "speech" in the early twentieth century: cameras were not speech, photographs were not speech, kaleidoscope instruments were not speech, even theater productions were not speech. Radio was clearly an instrument for communicating ideas, analogizable to a book or to an oral address. What made radio different from conventional speech was the way opinions were communicated, not the substance of the communications. What made film different was that it merely represented events; it did not "communicate" ideas at all.

So one might have anticipated that the discourse of professional reasoning would have had a far more difficult time discovering "speech" implications in early film cases than in early radio cases. As *Mutual Film* illustrated, this is precisely what happened. But then the collective legal perception of film as a communicative medium began to change. It did not change, however, in a linear fashion, mirroring changes in the film industry or in the public's reaction to films. Talking pictures originated in the 1920s; by the 1930s classic novels were being adapted to the screen; by the 1940s the movie industry was regarded as a more prominent communications medium, at least for young persons, than the book industry. Yet as late as 1948 the Supreme Court of the United States had declined to see any First Amendment implications in the censorship of films.

The analogy of film to kaleidoscopes or other "entertainments" that did not principally communicate ideas, or were in any event eminently regulable, had become entrenched in legal discourse. Thus it was not until 1952 that the Supreme Court concluded that *Mutual Film*'s conception of the communicative impact of films had misunderstood the nature of the film medium. For more than twenty-five years most American moviegoers had understood perfectly well that movies could communicate opinions as well as books. But the legal system had not yet developed a discourse that was receptive to that analogy.

The situation with respect to radio speech had a different emphasis, but was no different in kind. Students of the radio medium understood initially that it was essentially about the communication of opinions. But because it was regarded as a "special" medium, a "scarce" medium, a medium requiring government "ownership" to be effective, it was treated as a medium whose activities could be modified by gov-

ernmental administrators in accordance with "public interest, convenience, or necessity." The analogies in the radio speech cases were different analogies. Radio was like banking or utilities or railroading: its
activities needed to be regulated in the public interest. The activities in
the radio industry were obviously activities that had to do with communication. But that made no difference. Since the quality of radio
broadcasts was as important as the quality of railroads or public utilities, the content of broadcasts could be regulated. As Howe put it, radio
broadcasts were speech, but there were strong social interests driving
the regulation of that form of speech.

In the case of film a long period existed in which public perceptions about the nature of the medium were not reflected in analogies in
legal discourse. In the case of radio an even longer period has existed.
Radio regulation started with the assumption that radio was scarce.
Radio is not scarce now, and the listening public is well aware of that
fact. Indeed radio has not been scarce at least since FM stations
expanded the spectrum of the airwaves after World War II, and the
"scarcity" of the television market, in the period in which television
channels were limited to three network stations per local market, was
as much a function of FCC regulatory policies as it was of technological
imperatives. When ultrahigh frequency channels became feasible, they
did not immediately flood the market, again because of FCC policies. It
has taken FCC deregulation as well as cable technology to produce the
current multichanneled market.[72]

So the governing premise permitting significant content regulation
of radio speech—that radio speech, like all aspects of radio, can be regulated because of the scarce nature of the medium—is probably not one
that most members of the public would understand, let alone agree
with. Yet it is that premise that continues to allow radio broadcasts to
be analogized to the price structure of railroads or public utilities in
legal discourse.

IV. Conclusion: Toward a More Precise
Understanding of Law and Its Social Context

It thus appears that it is not enough to explain legal decisions by seeing
them simply as "mirrors of society" at a given point in time. Nor is it

---

72. See Krattenmaker and Powe, *Regulating Broadcast Programming,* 277–96.

enough, of course, to see legal decisions as entirely insulated from their social context. *Mutual Film*'s understanding of the nature of the film medium eventually became so inconsistent with most Americans' sense of what that medium was like that *Mutual Film* was overruled. But when *Mutual Film* was decided, most Americans, whether they were lawyers or not, thought of moving-picture shows as being essentially like theater productions, with all of the overtones that analogy contained.

I believe that to arrive at a more precise understanding of the relationship between law and its social context one needs to ask two sets of questions. First, what concerns are especially vital for the larger culture in which legal decisions are set at a given time? Second, what analogies exist in legal discourse to respond to those concerns? Asking one set of questions without the other will invariably result in a clumsy and misguided impression of how law relates to its context in America. Addressing both sets of questions allows one to explain some of the surface dissonances and peculiarities of the law, which may tempt observers to label legal institutions as inherently conservative or isolated from society at large. If those dissonances and peculiarities are seen, instead, as manifestations of the process by which cultural issues are situated in a distinctive professional discourse dominated by analogical reasoning, they can help us grasp the essence of how the legal profession receives and attempts to resolve the concerns that are addressed to it.

Contributors

Joan Dayan is Professor of English at the University of Arizona.

Soshana Felman is Thomas E. Donnelley Professor of French and Comparative Literature at Yale University.

Thomas R. Kearns is the William H. Hastie Professor of Philosophy and Professor of Law, Jurisprudence and Social Thought at Amherst College.

Dominick LaCapra is Bryce and Edith Bowmar Professor of Humanistic Studies at Cornell University.

Austin Sarat is the William Nelson Cromwell Professor of Jurisprudence and Political Science and Professor of Law, Jurisprudence and Social Thought at Amherst College. He is past president of the Law and Society Association.

Reva B. Siegel is Professor of Law at Yale University.

Brook Thomas is Professor of English at the University of California, Irvine.

G. Edward White is University Professor, John B. Minor Professor of Law and History, and E. James Kelly Research Professor at the University of Virginia.

Index

Abolitionism, 255. *See also* Slavery
Abortion rights, 6–9, 164–65, 175
Abuse: and the abyss of trauma, 75–79; civilized, 38–42; Felman on, 38–42, 75–79
Abyss, 69–80; between law and literature, 81–84; of estrangement, 48
Acknowledgment, of reality, 86
ACLU (American Civil Liberties Union), 172, 217
Acquittals, 55–56
Adams, John, 144
Addictions, 47–48
Adkins v. Children's Hospital, 7, 155–59
Aesthetics: and formalism, 121, 124; symbolic, 101; and the trials of Flaubert and Baudelaire, 96, 101, 103, 115, 121, 124
Affirmative action, 131–32; and *Bakke (Regents of the University of California v. Bakke)*, 136–37, 251, 271, 273, 275, 277; objections to, 136–39; and stigmatization, 251–52, 273–81; two basic goals of, 280
Alcatraz Island, 192–93
Alstyne, William Van, 252
Althusser, Louis, 62–63
American Notes for General Circulation (Dickens), 193
Analogical reasoning, 22–24, 283–317; in early mass-media cases, 288–316; role of, in legal discourse, 285–87
Ancient Law (Maine), 254
Anderson v. Salant, 231

Antelbellum period, 259
Antihumanism, 123
Antimiscegenation law, 260, 269
Antiterrorism and Effective Death Penalty Act, 229
Appelate court decisions, 17–18
Archimedes, 109
Arendt, Hannah, 42
Arizona Correctional Industries, 190
Arizona Department of Corrections, 183–224
Arpaio, Joe, 185, 186
Atiyeh v. Capps, 203
Autonomy, 119, 120
Autotelic language, 120–21

Bad faith, 122
Badges, 249–81
Bailey, William, 209, 211, 212
Bakke (Regents of the University of California v. Bakke), 131, 136–37, 251, 271, 273, 275, 277
Barbie, Klaus, 96
Barfield, Owen, 253–54
Baudelaire, Charles, 16, 95–130
Beckett, Samuel, 127–28
Bell, Derrick A., Jr., 250
Bendheim, Alice, 192, 222
Benjamin, Walter, 64, 115
Bersani, Leo, 120–21
Billaut, Adolphe, 102
Bill of Rights, 226
Bishop, Stephen, 218
"Black holes," narrative, 73, 74–75
Blackstone, William, 162

Blindness, judicial, 25–93
Bliss, Janet, 238
Bolling v. Sharpe, 166–67
Booth v. Maryland, 8–9
Bork, Robert, 131, 138–39
Boston Globe, 33
Bounds v. Smith, 223, 241–44, 246
Bradley, Joseph, 258–59
Brandeis, Louis, 8
Brands, 249–81
Brennan, William, 169–73, 228, 230, 251–52, 275–76
Brewer, David, 279
Brinkley, J. R., 304–5
Brinkley Pharmaceutical Association, 304–5
Brown, Henry Billings, 261
Brown, Nicole, 22, 32–33, 52–55, 61, 70, 87–89
Brown v. Board of Education, 7, 21, 166, 168, 182, 250, 264–77, 281
Bushnell, Horace, 149

Cable Act, 160–61
Camp, Maxime du, 104
Camus, Albert, 87, 92
Canonization, 120
"Carnivaliesque" phenomena, 125–27
Cases, legal. *See* Decisions, judicial
Casey v. Lewis, 8–9, 192, 216–21, 225, 233–41, 246–47
"Cathected" objects, 97
Causality, 80
Cautionnement, system of, 103–4
Celan, Paul, 84
Censorship, 103–4, 301–2, 313–14
Chain gangs, 184–92, 229
Cherry Hill (Eastern State) Penitentiary, 193
Christ, 125
Christian, David, 225–26, 228, 230
Christianity, 99, 102, 109–10, 119. *See also* Religion
Citizenship: clause of the Fourteenth

Amendment, 281; and marriage to foreign nationals, 160–61; and sex discrimination, 132, 134, 143, 160–61
Civil rights, 147, 228, 256–60, 262–63, 272
Civil Rights Act, 256, 258
Civil Rights Cases, 258–60, 262–63, 272
Civil War, 135–36, 146–47, 165, 169, 255, 260, 263–64
Cliché, 118–19
Clines, Francis X., 75, 92
Closure, sense of, 58
Cochran, Johnny, 56–57, 59
Code and Rating Administration, 313
Code Noir, 183
Color-blindness, metaphor of, 263–64, 276, 280
Comic spirit, 126–28
Commercialism, 124
Commodification, 104
Communist Labor Party, 293
Complex Detention Unit (Arizona State Prison, Tucson), 187–88
Confederacy, 227
Confession, 70, 85–88, 92–93
Confinement, solitary, 192–98, 205, 229
Cornell, Drucilla, 12
Courage, 110
Cover, Robert, 184
Craig v. Boren, 171–72, 173
Creativity, 22
Croson, 276, 278
Cross-legal nature, of trials, 39–41
Culler, Jonathan, 121
Curtis, Benjamin, 255

Daniel, Peter, 255
Davis, J. M., 231
Death, 30, 122–23; civil, 224–47; penalty, 214, 220, 224–25
Death Row Chain Gang, 188
Decisions, judicial: *Adkins v. Chil-*

dren's Hospital, 7, 155–59; *Anderson v. Salant*, 231; *Atiyeh v. Capps*, 203; *Bolling v. Sharpe*, 166–67; *Booth v. Maryland*, 8–9; *Bounds v. Smith*, 223, 241–44, 246; *Brown v. Board of Education*, 7, 21, 166, 168, 182, 250, 264–77, 281; *Casey v. Lewis*, 8–9, 192, 216–21, 225, 233–41, 246–47; *Craig v. Boren*, 171–72, 173; *Croson*, 276, 278; *De Funis v. Odegaard*, 273; *Dred Scott v. Sandford*, 21, 41, 135, 250–60, 270, 274; *Frontiero v. Richardson*, 169–74; *Gluth v. Kangas*, 215, 237–38, 244; *Hans v. Louisiana*, 153; *Hernandez v. Texas*, 278; *Hewitt*, 205–6, 211–12; *Hodges v. the United States*, 263, 271, 279; *Hook v. State of Arizona*, 234; *Hopwood*, 252, 271, 276; *Jones v. Mayer Co.*, 271–72; *Kenyon v. Saunders*, 231; *Knauff v. Shaugnessy*, 214; *Korematsu v. United States*, 266; *Lewis v. Casey*, 183; *Lochner v. New York*, 155; *Loving v. Virginia*, 269–70; *Madrid v. Gomez*, 208; *Maryland Trooper's Association v. Evans*, 252; *Meachum*, 203–5; *Monaco v. Mississippi*, 153; *Morrisey v. Brewer*, 204; *Muller v. Oregon*, 155–58, 160; *Mutual Film Corp. v. Ohio Industrial Commission*, 293–301, 308–12, 315–17; *Oyama v. California*, 266; *Payne v. Tennessee*, 8, 23; *Planned Parenthood v. Casey*, 6–9; *Plessy v. Ferguson*, 7, 21, 259, 261–68, 270–71, 280–81; *Roe v. Wade*, 6–7; *Ruffin v. Commonwealth*, 225–28, 230, 237, 241–42; *Sandin v. Connor*, 202, 206–8; *Superintendent v. State of Arizona Improvement Company*, 231; *Trinity Methodist Church v. Federal Radio Commission*, 306–8; *Turner v. Safley*, 220, 223–24; *United States v. Rhodes*, 256; *University of California v. Bakke*, 131, 136–37, 251, 271, 273, 275, 277; *Westbrook v. The State*, 231, 233; *Wolff v. McDonnell*, 199–200

Declaration of Indendendence, 146–47
Declaration of Sentiments, 146–47
De Funis v. Odegaard, 273
Denial, legal, 59–60
Department Order 902, 245–46
Dickens, Charles, 193
Difference, abyss of, 72–73
Dignity, 20, 42
Directions newsletter, 244
Domestic violence: Felman on, 38–42, 46–47, 52–53, 55, 58–64; and the image of a battered face, 52–53, 58, 61; invisibility of, 58–64; and suffragists, 151
Donahue, 185
Douglas, William, 251, 272–74
Dreams, "cultural," 32–33
Dred Scott v. Sandford, 21, 41, 135, 250–60, 270, 274
Dualities, 40, 67
Du Bois, W. E. B., 265
Due-process doctrine, 155, 205, 207, 291
Dunne, John Gregory, 52
Durkheim, Emile, 126

Eastern State Penitentiary, 193, 198–99
Economist, The, 78
Edison, Thomas, 289
Edwards, Bryan, 202
Eichmann, Adolf, 42–43, 96
Eighth Amendment, 8
Eleventh Amendment, 153
Epic memory, 14, 18
Epistemology, 26–28, 30, 80–81
Equal Rights Amendment (ERA), 165–66, 169–70
Evil, 23, 118; and the regulation of film and radio speech, 295, 307; and stigmatization, 257
Existentialism, 122

Experimentation, 17, 128
Eyewitnesses, 60–61

Face, battered, images of, 52–53, 58, 61
Falco, M., 95, 101–3, 114–15
Family values, 99, 101
Fantasy, 32–33
FCC (Federal Communications Commission), 311, 314, 316
Fehrenbacher, Don E., 255
Feminism, 124, 160, 163–65
Fifteenth Amendment, 147
Fifth Amendment, 166, 169
Film, 23, 283–317
First Amendment, 23, 214, 288–317
Flaubert, Gustav, 16, 95–130
Fleurs du mal, Les (Baudelaire), 95–130
Forgetfulness, of law, 20
Formalism, 120–21, 123, 203
Founding Fathers, 134
Fourteenth Amendment, 6, 21; due process clause, 291; equal protection clause, 166–77, 277–78; and prison systems, 206, 230, 237; and the regulation of film and radio speech, 291, 294–95; and sex discrimination, 17–18, 132, 141–42, 147, 158, 164–77, 182; and stigmatization, 255–61, 265–81
FRC (Federal Radio Commission), 303–7
Freedman's Bureau Bill, 256, 269
French islands, 183
Freud, Sigmund: historical duality in, 67; the repetition of historical events in, 40; the "return of the repressed" in, 30; and Sartre, 123
Friedman, Lawrence, 284
Frontiero v. Richardson, 169–74
Fugitive Slave Law, 256
Fuhrman, Mark, 39
Fundamentalism, religious, 128–29

Georgia Penal Code, 232

Ginsburg, Ruth, 18, 177–79
Gluth v. Kangas, 215, 237–38, 244
Goldman, Ronald, 33, 93
Gordon, Robert, 284
Gray, Horace, 260–61, 270
Guilt: of collectivities, 98–99; Felman on, 26, 39, 46, 51, 56, 86; and speech, 86. See also Confession
Guizot, François, 103

Hacking, Ian, 210
Haiti, 226
Hans v. Louisiana, 153
Hard Copy, 185
Harlan, John Marshall, 259–64, 267, 270, 272, 280–81
Harvard Law Review, 273
Hermeneutics, 2, 24, 123
Hernandez v. Texas, 278
Hewitt, 205–6, 211–12
Historiography, 16, 97–100
History of American Law (Friedman), 284
Hodges v. the United States, 263, 271, 279
Holmes, Oliver Wendell, 157
Hook v. State of Arizona, 234
Hopwood, 252, 271, 276
Horwitz, Morton, 7–8
Howe, Mark DeWolfe, 308–10
Hughes, Charles Evans, 250, 260
Humane Restraint Company, 190

Imagination, 27
Indictments, 55–56
Inferiority, sense of, 21
Integrity, 75, 78
Intertextuality, 15, 120
Invisibility, 58–62
"Ironic" consciousness, 118
I Want To Tell You (Simpson), 91

Jackson, Robert, 214
Jacobi, Mary Putnam, 150
James, Steven C., 222

Jaspers, Karl, 42
Jim Crow laws, 21, 181, 265, 267–68, 270–71, 280
Jones v. Mayer Co., 271–72
Jordan, Robert A., 74
Juries, 13, 59–60

Kafka, Franz, 87, 93
Kalman, Laura, 3
Kelly, Alfred H., 252–53, 254–55, 265
Kennedy, Anthony, 6–7
Kennedy, Duncan, 284–85
Kenyon v. Saunders, 231
King, Martin Luther, Jr., 136
King, Rodney, 15, 39–41, 61–64, 68–69
Knauff v. Shaugnessy, 214
Korematsu v. United States, 266
Kreutzer Sonata, The (Tolstoy), 15, 25–93
Kundera, Milan, 1

Laughter, 126–28
Legal cases. *See* Decisions, judicial
Legal events, concept of, 32
Legitimacy, 5–6, 9, 14, 100; and prison systems, 183–84; and the trials of Flaubert and Baudelaire, 110, 115, 128
Lewis, Samuel, 220–22, 233–36, 239
Lewis v. Casey, 183
Liability, 99
Lincoln, Abraham, 226
Literature: authority of, 84–85; and law, abyss between, 81–84; and law, separate jurisdictions of, 26–28
Lochner v. New York, 155
Los Angeles Times, 33
Loving v. Virgina, 269–70
Lynch Manufacturing Company, 190

Madame Bovary (Flaubert), 95–130
Madrid v. Gomez, 208
Maier, Charles, 1
Maine, Henry, 254
Maistre, Joseph de, 126

Maricopa County Jail, 185–86
Marriage: and the common-law doctrine of marital service, 137–38, 145–47, 150–51, 155, 158, 160, 164, 175; to foreign nationals, 160–61; in *The Kreuzer Sonana*, 46–47; and the trials of Flaubert and Baudelaire, 112–13, 116; and violence, 15, 26–93
Marshall, Thurgood, 9, 23, 228, 249
Marxism, 122, 123
Maryland Trooper's Association v. Evans, 252
Mass media, 22–23, 283–317
Materialism, 109
McClellan, George B., 298
McFadden, James, 196–98, 200, 207–8, 212–14
Meachum, 203–5
Mercy, 91–94
Metaphor, 21–22, 249–81
Mexican-Americans, 279
Michelman, Frank, 153
Minimum-wage law, 155–56
Monaco v. Mississippi, 153
Morality: Felman on, 47–48; and formalism, 121; and imprisonment, 201, 204; and the regulation of film and radio speech, 293; and sexual addictions, 47–48; and the trials of Flaubert and Baudelaire, 102, 106–7, 108–12, 119, 121, 128–29
Moran, Brenda, 58–59
Morrisey v. Brewer, 204
Motion Picture Association of America, 313
Mots, Les (Sartre), 122
Muecke, Carl, 212–14, 222–25, 233–37, 240, 243–44
Muller v. Oregon, 155–58, 160
Muni, Paul, 191
Murphy, Frank, 266–67
Mutual Film Corp. v. Ohio Industrial Commission, 293–301, 308–12, 315–17

National Women's Party, 156
Nazi Party, 98
New Yorker, The, 42
New York Review of Books, The, 52–53
Nietzsche, Friedrich, 1
Nihilism, 123, 124
Nineteenth Amendment: and abortion, 164–65, 175; interpreting, 152–66; and sex discrimination, 17–18, 132–33, 141–43, 152–72, 181
Nominalism, 210
Nora, Pierre, 10–11, 12, 15, 67
Nuremberg trials, 96, 98

Obsession, 28–29, 50
O'Connor, Sandra Day, 6–7
Ohio Industrial Commission, 293–301, 308–12, 315–17
Opinions, judicial. *See* Decisions, judicial
Order to Show Cause, 239
Osiel, Mark, 11
Otherness, 122
Oyama v. California, 266

Patterson, Orlando, 185
Paul, Alice, 156
Payne v. Tennessee, 8, 23
Pelican Bay State Prison (SMU I), 183, 194–98, 200–201, 208, 211–14
Pinard, Ernest, 102, 104–11, 113, 116, 120
Planned Parenthood v. Casey, 6–9
Plato, 106
Plessy v. Ferguson, 7, 21, 259, 261–68, 270–71, 280–81
Plot summaries, 107
Pochoda, Dan, 237–39
Pocock, J. G. A., 274
Police powers, 23, 299
Posner, Richard, 267–68
Pound, Ezra, 126
Pound, Roscoe, 283
Powell, Lewis, 131, 136–37, 180, 275, 277–78

Prisons, 13, 19–20, 183–247; and chain gangs, 184–92, 229; and civil death, 224–47; solitary confinement in, 192–98, 205, 229
Progressive Era, 22–23, 155, 289–92, 298–99
Property rights, 23, 138, 231, 297

Racism: and the abyss between races, 74–75; and the O. J. Simpson trial, 15, 26, 30–41, 56–57, 74–75; and prison systems, 225–27; and sex discrimination, 131–32, 135–36, 146, 166–74, 178–79, 181; and stigmatization, 21–22, 249–81. *See also* Jim Crow laws; Slavery
Radio, 23, 283–317
Radio Act, 23, 302–5
Realism, 16, 102, 108, 114, 118, 123
Reason, 9, 124; analogical, 22–24, 283–317; and prison systems, 222–23; and sex discrimination, 175
Recapitulations, 90–91
Reconstruction Era, 132, 136, 147
Rehnquist, William, 8–9. *See also* Rehnquist Court
Rehnquist Court, 202–3, 205–6, 211. *See also* Rehnquist, William
Reid, John Philip, 3
Religion: and "carnivaliesque" phenomena, 125–26; and fundamentalism, 128–29; and the trials of Flaubert and Baudelaire, 106–7, 113, 116, 119, 124–29. *See also* Christianity
Removing a Badge of Slavery: The Record of "Brown v. Board of Education" (Whitman), 280
Repressed, return of the, 30
Republican Party, 147, 152, 169
Revue de Paris, 104
Roe v. Wade, 6–7
Roquentin, Antoine, 122
Rousseau, Jean-Jacques, 114